Nuzi Texts and Their Uses as Historical Evidence

Society of Biblical Literature

Writings from the Ancient World

Theodore J. Lewis, General Editor

Associate Editors

Number 18
Nuzi Texts and Their Uses as Historical Evidence
by Maynard Paul Maidman
Edited by Ann K. Guinan

NUZI TEXTS AND THEIR USES AS HISTORICAL EVIDENCE

by

Maynard Paul Maidman

Edited by

Ann K. Guinan

Society of Biblical Literature
Atlanta

NUZI TEXTS AND THEIR USES AS HISTORICAL EVIDENCE

Library of Congress Cataloging-in-Publication Data

Maidman, M. P.
Nuzi texts and their uses as historical evidence / by Maynard Paul Maidman ; edited by Ann Guinan.
p. cm. — (Writings from the ancient world / Society of Biblical Literature ; no. 18)
Includes bibliographical references and index.
ISBN 978-1-58983-213-8 (pbk. : alk. paper)
1. Nuzi (Extinct city)—Economic conditions—Sources. 2. Akkadian language—Texts. 3. Hurrians—Social life and customs—Sources. 4. Land titles—Registration and transfer—Iraq—Nuzi (Extinct city) I. Guinan, Ann. II. Title.
PJ3721.N8M347 2010b
492'.1—dc22

2010008664

Printed in the United States of America on acid-free, recycled paper conforming to ANSI/NISO Z39.48-1992 (R1997) and ISO 9706:1994 standards for paper permanence.

FOR JANICE

Contents

Series Editor's Foreword

Writings from the Ancient World is designed to provide up-to-date, readable English translations of writings recovered from the ancient Near East.

The series is intended to serve the interests of general readers, students, and educators who wish to explore the ancient Near Eastern roots of Western civilization or to compare these earliest written expressions of human thought and activity with writings from other parts of the world. It should also be useful to scholars in the humanities or social sciences who need clear, reliable translations of ancient Near Eastern materials for comparative purposes. Specialists in particular areas of the ancient Near East who need access to texts in the scripts and languages of other areas will also find these translations helpful. Given the wide range of materials translated in the series, different volumes will appeal to different interests. However, these translations make available to all readers of English the world's earliest traditions as well as valuable sources of information on daily life, history, religion, and the like in the preclassical world.

The translators of the various volumes in this series are specialists in the particular languages and have based their work on the original sources and the most recent research. In their translations they attempt to convey as much as possible of the original texts in fluent, current English. In the introductions, notes, glossaries, maps, and chronological tables, they aim to provide the essential information for an appreciation of these ancient documents.

The ancient Near East reached from Egypt to Iran and, for the purposes of our volumes, ranged in time from the invention of writing (by 3000 B.C.E.) to the conquests of Alexander the Great (ca. 330 B.C.E.). The cultures represented within these limits include especially Egyptian, Sumerian, Babylonian, Assyrian, Hittite, Ugaritic, Aramean, Phoenician, and Israelite. It is hoped that Writings from the Ancient World will eventually produce translations from most of the many different genres attested in these cultures: letters (official and private), myths, diplomatic documents, hymns, law collections, monumental inscriptions, tales, and administrative records, to mention but a few.

Significant funding was made available by the Society of Biblical Literature for the preparation of this volume. In addition, those involved in preparing this volume have received financial and clerical assistance from their respective institutions. Were it not for these expressions of confidence in our work, the arduous tasks of preparation, translation, editing, and publication could not have been accomplished or even undertaken. It is the hope of all who have worked with the Writings from the Ancient World series that our translations will open up new horizons and deepen the humanity of all who read these volumes.

Theodore J. Lewis
The Johns Hopkins University

Acknowledgments

This volume owes a good deal to the wisdom, knowledge, and labor of a number of individuals. The comments, criticisms, and comments of colleagues have resulted in a better work than it would have been otherwise. So my thanks go to Giovanna Biga, Israel Eph'al, Jeanette Fincke, Brigitte Lion, Lucio Milano, David I. Owen, Gernot Wilhelm, and Carlo Zaccagnini. For help with matters of style, structure, and writing in general, I am grateful to Daniel Y. Maidman, Madeline Noveck, and my mother, Lena Strauss. My student, Richard Aronson, typed many of the transliterations, a task accomplished with cheerfulness and intelligence. I also thank Theodore Lewis, general editor of Writings from the Ancient World, for his constant moral support and seemingly endless patience. Only in these ways did he ever pressure me. Billie Jean Collins bore the brunt of daily confrontation with a technically recalcitrant manuscript. I thank her heartily. Ann K. Guinan, my editor, contributed in all the above areas, save the typing. Her sagacity, humor, and friendship are dear to me. For the errors remaining in the volume I claim credit for myself.

I dedicate this book to Janice P. Warren, my helpmate, whose love and encouragement have, in a myriad ways, made the writing of this book, and much else besides, a true joy.

Abbreviations

AASOR	The Annual of the American Schools of Oriental Research
AJSL	*American Journal of Semitic Languages and Literatures*
Akk.	Akkadian
AnOr	Analecta Orientalia
AOAT	Alter Orient und Altes Testament
AoF	*Altorientalische Forschungen*
AOS	American Oriental Series
br.	brother of
BAR	British Archaeological Reports
BASOR	*Bulletin of the American Schools of Oriental Research*
BSMS	*The Bulletin of the Society for Mesopotamian Studies*
CAD	Oppenheim, et al. *The Assyrian Dictionary of the Oriental Institute of the University of Chicago.* Chicago: The Oriental Institute of the University of Chicago, 1956–.
CH	Code of Hammurabi
CHANE	Culture and History of the Ancient Near East
CRRAI	Compte rendu, Rencontre assyriologique internationale
d.	daughter of
EN 9/1	Tablet published in Ernest R. Lacheman, D. I. Owen, and M. A. Morrison. "Excavations at Nuzi 9/1." Pages 355–702 in *General Studies and Excavations at Nuzi 9/1*. Edited by D. I. Owen and M. A. Morrison. SCCNH 2. Winona Lake, Ind.: Eisenbrauns, 1987.
EN 9/3	Tablet published in Ernest R. Lacheman and D. I. Owen. "Excavations at Nuzi 9/3." Pages 85–357 in *General Studies and Excavations at Nuzi 9/3*. Edited by Ernest R. Lacheman and D. I. Owen. SCCNH 5. Winona Lake, Ind.: Eisenbrauns, 1995.
EN 10/1	Tablet published in Jeanette Fincke, "Excavations at Nuzi 10/1, 1–65." Pages 379–468 in *Richard F.S. Starr Memorial Volume*. SCCNH 8. Edited by David I. Owen and Gernot Wilhelm. Bethesda, Md.: CDL, 1996.

EN 10/2 Tablet published in Jeanette Fincke, "Excavations at Nuzi 10/2, 66–174." Pages 219–373 in *General Studies an Excavations at Nuzi* 10/2. SCCNH 9. Edited by David I. Owen and Gernot Wilhelm. Bethesda, Md.: CDL, 1998.

EN 10/3 Tablet published in Jeanette Fincke, "Excavations at Nuzi 10/3, 175–300." Pages 169–304 in *General Studies and Excavations at Nuzi* 10/3. SCCNH 12. Edited by David I. Owen and Gernot Wilhelm. Bethesda, Md.: CDL, 2002.

ERL Tablet or tablet fragment once in the collection of E. R. Lacheman

f the PN following this sign is that of a female

f. father of

g.d. granddaughter of

g.f. grandfather of

g.s. grandson of

GN geographical name

h. husband of

HSAO Heidelberger Studien zum Alten Orient

HSS Harvard Semitic Series

HSS V Tablet published in Edward Chiera, *Texts of Varied Contents*. Cambridge, Mass.: Harvard University Press, 1929.

HSS IX Tablet published in Robert H. Pfeiffer, *The Archives of Shilwateshub Son of the King.* Vol. 2 of *Excavations at Nuzi*. Cambridge, Mass.: Harvard University Press, 1932.

HSS XIII Tablet published in Robert H. Pfeiffer and Ernest R. Lacheman, *Miscellaneous Texts from Nuzi, Part I.* Vol. 4 of *Excavations at Nuzi.* Cambridge, Mass.: Harvard University Press, 1942.

HSS XIV Tablet published in Ernest R. Lacheman, *Miscellaneous Texts from Nuzi,* Part II. Vol. 5 of *Excavations at Nuzi.* Cambridge, Mass.: Harvard University Press, 1950.

HSS XV Tablet published in Ernest R. Lacheman, *The Administrative Archives*. Vol. 6 of *Excavations at Nuzi.* Cambridge, Mass.: Harvard University Press, 1955.

HSS XVI Tablet published in Ernest R. Lacheman, *Economic and Social Documents.* Vol. 7 of *Excavations at Nuzi*. Cambridge, Mass.: Harvard University Press, 1958.

HSS XIX Tablet published in Ernest R. Lacheman, *Family Laws*. Vol. 8 of *Excavations at Nuzi*. Cambridge, Mass.: Harvard University Press, 1962.

JAOS *Journal of the American Oriental Society*

JCS *Journal of Cuneiform Studies*

JEN	Joint Expedition with the Iraq Museum at Nuzi
JEN I	Tablet published in Edward Chiera, *Inheritance Texts*. Vol. 1 of *Joint Expedition [of the American School of Oriental Research in Baghdad] with the Iraq Museum at Nuzi*. Paris: Geuthner, 1927.
JEN II	Tablet published in Edward Chiera, *Declarations in Court*. Vol. 2 of *Joint Expedition [of the American School of Oriental Research in Baghdad] with the Iraq Museum at Nuzi*. Paris: Geuthner, 1930.
JEN III	Tablet published in Edward Chiera, *Exchange and Security Documents*. Vol. 3 of *Joint Expedition [of the American School of Oriental Research in Baghdad] with the Iraq Museum at Nuzi*. Paris: Geuthner, 1931.
JEN IV	Tablet published in Edward Chiera, *Proceedings in Court*. Vol. 4 of *Joint Expedition [of the American School of Oriental Research in Baghdad] with the Iraq Museum at Nuzi*. Philadelphia: American Schools of Oriental Research, 1934.
JEN V	Tablet published in Edward Chiera, *Mixed Texts*. Vol. 5 of *Joint Expedition [of the American School of Oriental Research in Baghdad] with the Iraq Museum at Nuzi*. Philadelphia: American Schools of Oriental Research, 1934.
JEN VI	Tablet published in Ernest R. Lacheman. *Miscellaneous Texts*. Vol. 6 of *Joint Expedition [of the American School of Oriental Research in Baghdad] with the Iraq Museum at Nuzi*. New Haven: American Schools of Oriental Research, 1939.
JEN VII	Tablet published in Lacheman, Ernest R. and Maynard P. Maidman, *Joint Expedition with the Iraq Museum at Nuzi 7: Miscellaneous Texts*. SCCNH 3. Winona Lake, Ind.: Eisenbrauns, 1989.
JEN VIII	Tablet published in Maynard P. Maidman, *Joint Expedition with the Iraq Museum at Nuzi 8: The Remaining Major Texts in the Oriental Institute of the University of Chicago*. SCCNH 14. Bethesda, Md.: CDL, 2003.
JENu	Joint Expedition with the Iraq Museum at Nuzi, unpublished tablet (= Oriental Institute catalogue number)
JESHO	*Journal of the Economic and Social History of the Orient*
JNES	*Journal of Near Eastern Studies*
N.A.B.U.	*Nouvelles Assyriologiques Brèves et Utilitaires*
NPN	Gelb, Ignace J., Pierre M Purves, and Allan A. MacRae, *Nuzi Personal Names*. OIP 57. Chicago: University of Chicago Press, 1943.

NTF	Nuzi text fragment from the Harvard Semitic Museum, recently catalogued
OIP	Oriental Institute Publications
OA	*Oriens Antiquus*
PIHANS	Publications de l'Institut historique-archéologique néerlandais de Stamboul
PN	personal name
P-S	Tablet published in Pfeiffer and Speiser 1936
QGS	Quaderni di geografia storica
RA	*Revue d'Assyriologie et d'Archéologie Orientale*
RGTC	Répertoire Géographique des Textes Cunéiformes
RHA	*Révue Hittite et Asianique*
RIMA	The Royal Inscriptions of Mesopotamia, Assyrian Periods
RlA	*Reallexikon der Assyriologie und voderasiatische Archäologie*
s.	son of
SAA	State Archives of Assyria
SAA 1	Tablet published in Simo Parpola, *Letters from Assyria and the West*. Part 1 of *The Correspondence of Sargon II*. Helsinki: Helsinki University Press, 1987.
SAA 6	Tablet published in Theodore Kwasman and Simo Parpola, *Tiglath-Pileser III through Esarhaddon*. Part 1 of *Legal Transactions of the Royal Court of Nineveh*. Helsinki: Helsinki University Press, 1991.
SAA 7	Tablet published in F. M. Fales and J. N. Postgate, *Palace and Temple Administration*. Part 1 of *Imperial Administrative Records*. Helsinki: Helsinki University Press, 1992.
SAA 8	Tablet published in Hermann Hunger, *Astrological Reports to Assyrian Kings*. Helsinki: Helsinki University Press, 1992.
SAA 10	Tablet published in Simo Parpola *Letters from Assyrian and Babylonian Scholars*. Helsinki: Helsinki University Press, 1993.
SAA 11	Tablet published in F. M. Fales and J. N. Postgate, *Provincial and Military Administration.* Part 2 of *Imperial Administrative Records.* Helsinki: Helsinki University Press, 1995.
SAA 12	Tablet published in L. Kataja and R. Whiting, *Grants, Decrees and Gifts of the Neo-Assyrian Period.* Helsinki: Helsinki University Press, 1995.
SAA 13	Tablet published in Steven W. Cole and Peter Machinist, *Letters from Priests to the Kings Esarhaddon and Assurbanipal*. Helsinki: Helsinki University Press, 1998.
SAA 15	Tablet published in Andreas Fuchs and Simo Parpola, *Letters from*

	Babylonia and the Eastern Provinces. Part 3 of *The Correspondence of Sargon II.* Helsinki: Helsinki University Press, 2001.
SCCNH	Studies on the Civilization and Culture of Nuzi and the Hurrians
S.I.	cylinder seal impression
SMN	[Harvard] Semitic Museum, Nuzi [catalogued artifact]
Sum.	Sumerian
TSO	Texte und Studien zur Orientalistik
UF	*Ugarit-Forschungen*
w.	wife of
WAW	Writings from the Ancient World
YNER	Yale Near Eastern Researches
ZA	*Zeitschrift für Assyriologie und Vorderasiatische Archäologie*

Symbols

[ ]	restored text
< >	scribal omission
« »	scribal plus
...	three or fewer words/signs missing
....	four or more words/signs missing

Notes

Personal names are rendered, for the most part, according to *NPN.*

Geographical names are rendered, for the most part, according to Fincke 1993.

Personal names of females are usually rendered in the text translations without the feminine marker, e.g., “Mary,” not “^{f}Mary.” The feminine marker is appended where gender ambiguity would otherwise result. The marker also appears, regularly, in the index of personal names.

Ancient Near Eastern Royal Chronologies

Assyria

Aššur-rabi I	
Aššur-nadin-aḫḫe I	
Enlil-naṣir II	1430–1425
Aššur-nirari II	1424–1418
Aššur-bel-nišešu	1417–1409
Aššur-rim-nišešu	1408–1401
Aššur-nadin-aḫḫe II	1400–1391
Eriba-Adad I	1390–1364
Aššur-uballiṭ I	1363–1328
Enlil-nirari	1327–1318
Arik-den-ili	1317–1306
Adad-nirari I	1305–1274

Babylonia

Kadašman-harbe I	
Karaindaš	
Kurigalzu I	
Kadašman-Enlil I	
Burnaburiaš II	1359–1333
Karahardaš	1333
Nazibugaš	1333
Kurigalzu II	1332–1308
Nazimaruttaš	1307–1282

The dates for Babylonia and Assyria are based on Brinkman, apud Oppenheim 1977: 338, 345 resp.

MITTANNI

Parattarna I	ca. 1500–1480
Šauštatar I	ca. 1480–1460
Paršatatar	ca. 1460–1440
Šauštatar II	ca. 1440–1410
Parattarna II	ca. 1410–1400
Artatama I	ca. 1400–1375
Šutarna II	ca. 1375–1355
Artašumara	ca. 1355–1350
Tušratta	ca. 1350–1335

COMPOSITE ROYAL CHRONOLOGIES CALIBRATED TO NUZI GENERATIONS

<table>
<tr><th></th><th>Nuzi</th><th>Assyria</th><th>Mittanni</th><th>Babylonia</th></tr>
<tr><td>ca. 1460</td><td>1</td><td></td><td>Paršatatar</td><td></td></tr>
<tr><td>ca. 1435</td><td>2</td><td></td><td>Šauštatar II</td><td></td></tr>
<tr><td>ca. 1410</td><td>3</td><td rowspan="2">Enlil-naṣir
Aššur-nirari II
Aššur-bel-nišešu
Aššur-rim-nišešu
Eriba-Adad</td><td rowspan="2">Parattarna II
Artatama I
Šutarna II
Artašumara</td><td></td></tr>
<tr><td>ca. 1385</td><td>4</td><td>Kadašman-Enlil I</td></tr>
<tr><td>ca. 1350</td><td>5</td><td>Aššur-uballiṭ I</td><td>Tušratta</td><td>Burnaburiaš II</td></tr>
</table>

Maps and Genealogical Charts

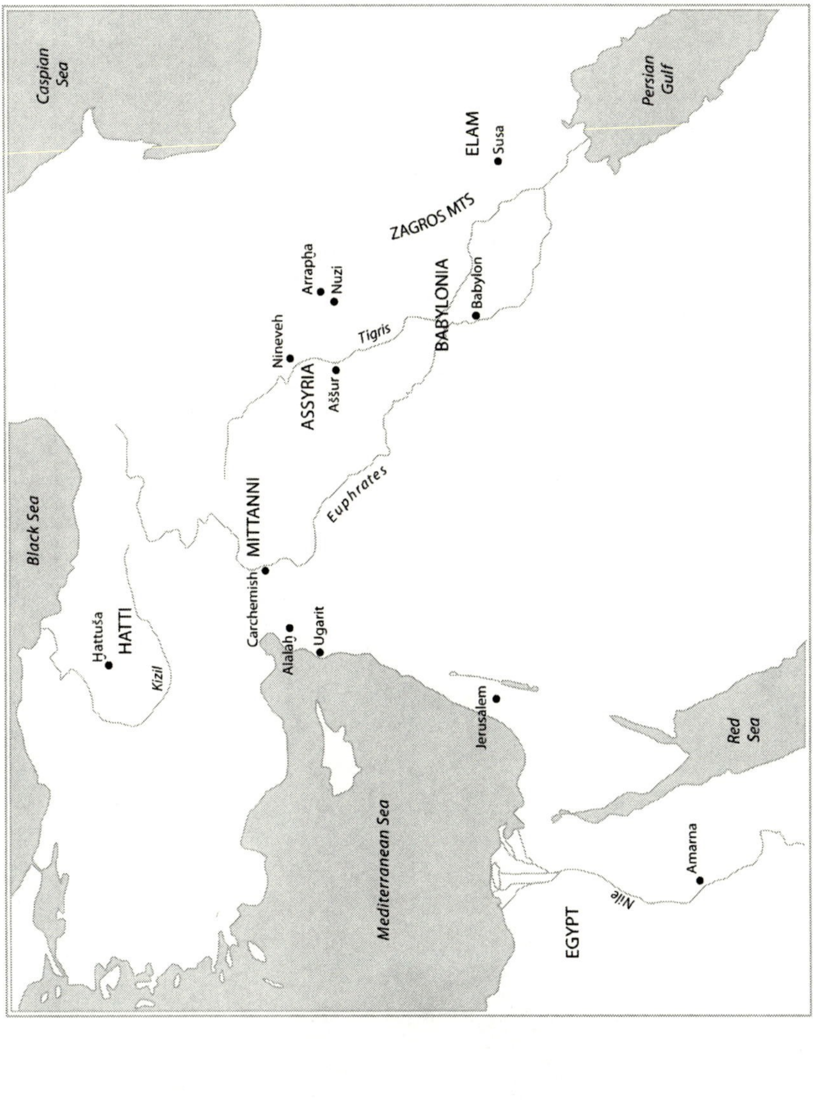

Map of the Ancient Near East

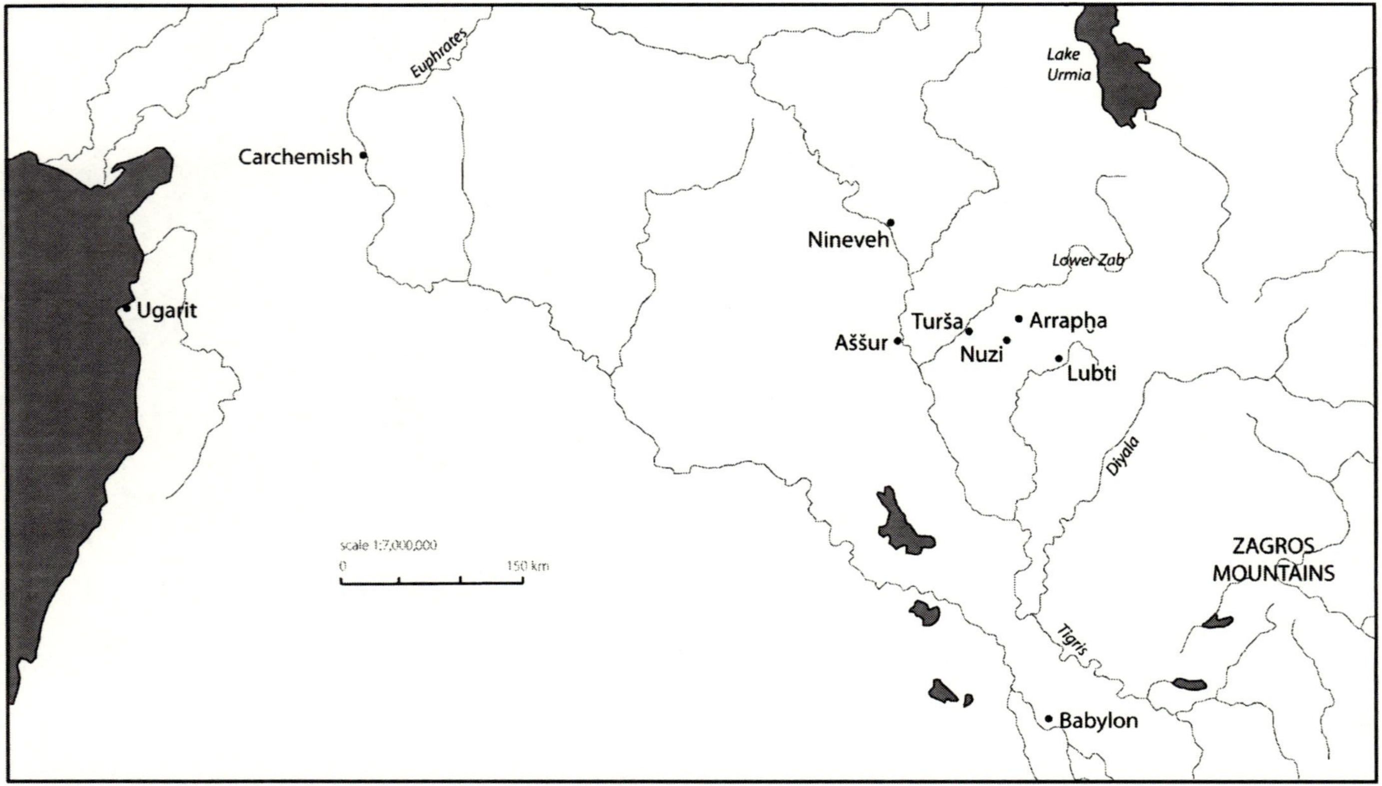

Map of Northern Syria and Iraq

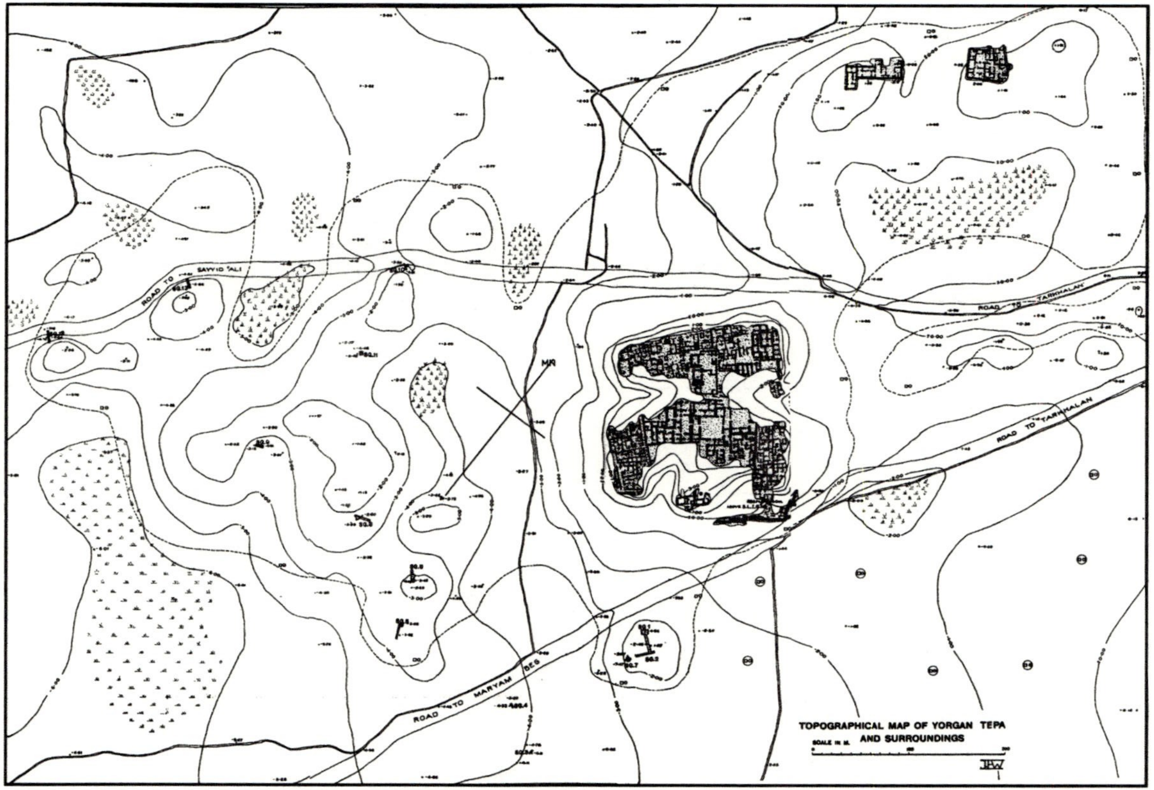

Map of Nuzi and Its Vicinity (Starr 1937: plan 2)

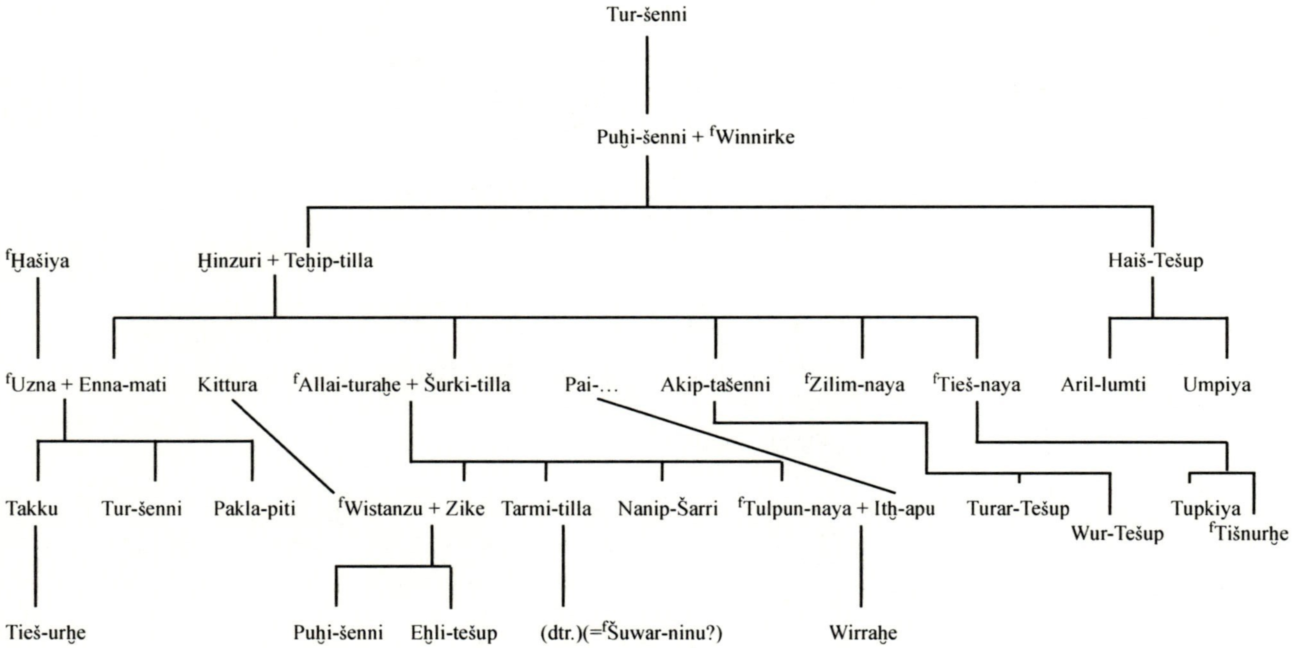

The Teḫip-tilla Family Tree

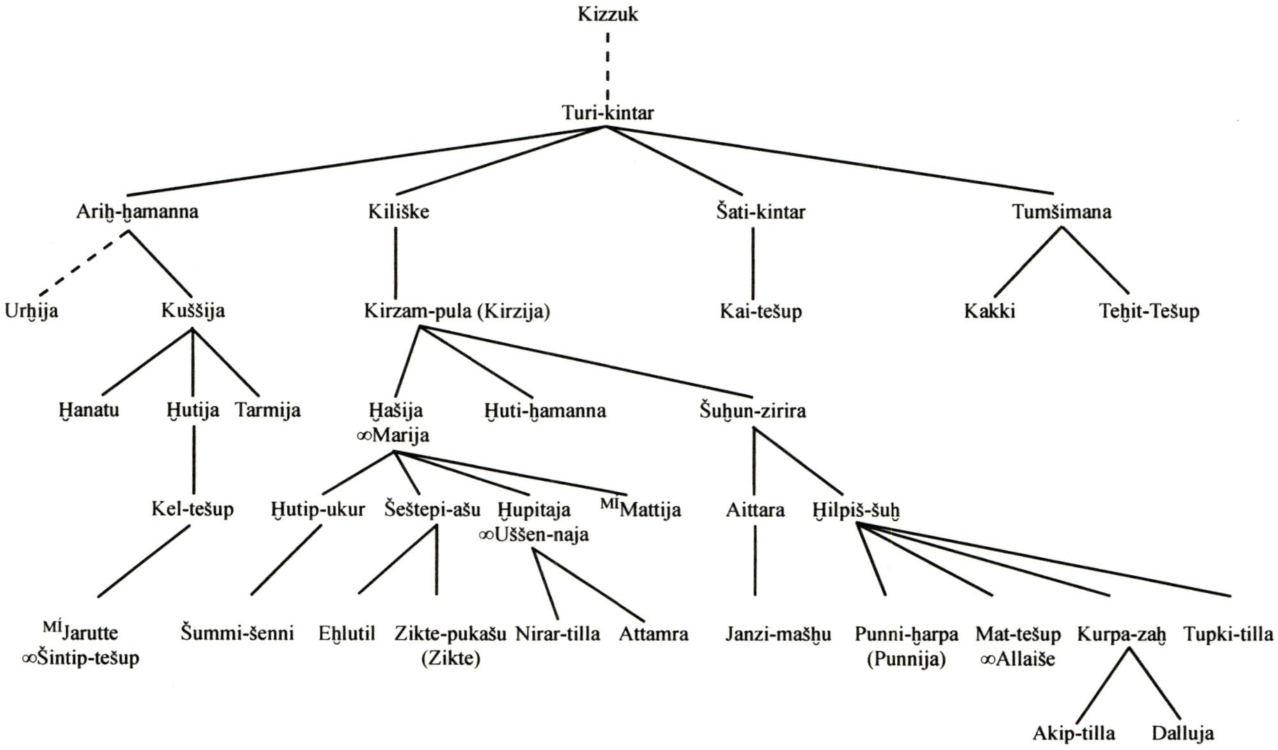

The Kizzuk Family Tree. After Dosch and Deller 1981: 97.

<table>
<tr><th>Genera-
tion</th><th>Arrapḫa Royal
Family</th><th>Family of
Tehip-tilla</th><th colspan="3">Family of Kizzuk</th><th>An Important
“Family” of
Scribes</th><th>Dates*/Events</th></tr>
<tr><td></td><td></td><td>(Tur-šenni)</td><td colspan="3">(Kizzuk)</td><td></td><td>ca. 1500/1475</td></tr>
<tr><td>1</td><td>(Kip-tešup)</td><td>Puḫi-šenni</td><td colspan="3">Turi-kintar</td><td>Apil-sin</td><td></td></tr>
<tr><td>2</td><td>Itḫi-tešup</td><td>Teḫip-tilla</td><td colspan="3">Kiliške</td><td>Taya</td><td></td></tr>
<tr><td>3</td><td>Ḫišmi-tešup</td><td>Enna-mati</td><td colspan="2">Kirzam-pula</td><td>Ariḫ-
ḫamanna</td><td>Itḫ-apiḫe</td><td></td></tr>
<tr><td>4</td><td>Silwa-tešup</td><td>Takku</td><td rowspan="2">Ḫašiya
Ḫutip-uku
Šummi-
šenni</td><td rowspan="2">Šuḫun-zirira
Ḫilpiš-šuḫ
Kurpa-zaḫ
Akip-tilla</td><td rowspan="2">Kuššiya
Ḫutiya
Kel-tešup
^{f}Yarutte</td><td>Turar-tešup</td><td>Assyrian attack on Turša</td></tr>
<tr><td>5</td><td>Tatip-tilla</td><td>Tieš-urḫe</td><td>Šamaš-rêṣuya</td><td>ca. 1355–1351: Nuzi is destroyed and Aššur-uballiṭ of Assyria and Tušratta of Mit-tanni are alive.</td></tr>
</table>

*The dates in this column are based on the assumption of Aššur-uballiṭ regnal years of 1365–1330 B.C.E.

Nuzi Relative Chronologies: Partial Family Trees of a Few Important Families

INTRODUCTION

Nuzi Texts and Their Uses as Historical Evidence is both the title of this volume and its program. The book, in accordance with the design of Writings from the Ancient World, "provide[s] up-to-date, readable [I trust], English translations of writings recovered from the ancient Near East."[1] In the present instance, ninety-six texts from Nuzi are presented in transliteration, translation, and contextual commentary. Thus this volume of translations illustrates the range of documents contained in the Nuzi corpus. That is what the book is.

What the book is *about* is history. These texts, purposefully chosen and ordered, are not mere antiquarian curiosities. They contribute to our knowledge and understanding of the past, both the past of the community that generated these documents and that of the state and region of which Nuzi was part. As we shall see below ("More on the Aims of the Present Volume"), the texts from Nuzi are peculiarly apposite to perform this function. Indeed, in one area, the relations between Nuzi's parent state, Arrapḫa, and Assyria, that relationship cannot at all be understood without the Nuzi texts.

This contribution to Writings from the Ancient World, then, is the presentation of Nuzi texts and the elucidation of their significance as important sources for history. It starts with texts and returns to texts. The text, therefore, is the first thing we must consider.

THE TEXT

Archaeology may generally be defined as the discipline whereby physical remnants of past human activity are exhumed, defined, and classified within a series of larger contexts (for example, artifact typology or regional dynamics or chronological correlation). The role of archaeology in the investigation of humanity's past is most crucial in those periods when non-verbal artifacts are all that remain of human activity, that is, in periods before the invention of writing or before writing was committed to imperishable media. In such periods, archaeology's artifacts and the study of their contexts are central to the elucidation of the human past. The stories these objects tell may be elicited only by depending on the methods and ingenuity of archaeology and its sister discipline, prehistory. And the result *is* "prehistory," the study of humanity before the survival of written records.

Once records appear, the rules of the game change. Unlike the non-verbal artifacts, writing enables us to enter, however haltingly, the minds of the writers through their thoughts made explicit, thoughts preserved in words that transcend the life of the writer and the locale in which he lived. Those verbal remnants of past reality make possible—and for the first time—the construction and writing of history. In other words, no text, no history.[2] My friends who contend that there is qualitative continuity between so-called prehistory, before preserved writing, and "history," when we read texts created by the people we study, miss the essential point, that writing, as potentially the most direct articulation of thought, allows, even forces, us to investigate humanity on a subtler, more nuanced and precise level than is possible in human prehistory. Different rules, different epistemological problems and issues separate the archaeologist and prehistory from the historian and history.[3] And so writing is a prerequisite to human history and ancient writings are a prerequisite for the writing of ancient history.

I asserted that the text is where we start. To the text we ultimately return. This is true, not only for this work, but for the study of ancient history itself. The ancient historian seeking to determine data from the past and attempting to make sense of those data starts by looking at the documents the archaeologist digs up. And if the historian filters the documents through the lenses of cultural bias or historiographic theory or post-modern impulse, nevertheless the return is always to the text; back and forth, but always returning in order to touch base or to test or to discover.

Not all writings are created equal. Original, archival documents are those with which this series mainly deals. They are defined as primary sources because they are part of the reality they describe,[4] a segment of the processes and events whose nature historians seek to trace. They are treaties and contracts, memoranda and tax lists and much more. Overwhelmingly, the written survivals of the ancient Near East are primary sources.

By contrast, much of what we know of non-Near Eastern antiquity stems from secondary sources, looking back on what they describe. When we turn to the history of Greece, Rome, or Israel, great swathes of the past—the Israelite United Kingdom, the Persian wars, the entire Roman Republic—come down to us mostly through the writings of historians in antiquity who themselves chose, selected, and edited documents accessible to them, rumors they heard, or thoughts they learned or conceived. They undertook the very task that the ancient Near Eastern primary sources allow and compel us to achieve for ourselves. Those ancient historians, via a long (and sometimes problematic) history of transmission of their manuscripts, leave us with literary, so-called historical, secondary sources. They are seductive and, at the same time, comforting. Right or wrong, sophisticated or crude, and in whatever way biased (but always biased), Herodotus or Livy or the historical books of the Hebrew Bible bequeath to us a coherent picture, a structure of meaning that appeals to our own need and desire to make order out of informational chaos. There is hardly a modern volume of Israelite, Greek, or Roman history that does not, in part and at some level, feel like the biblical book of Kings or *The Persian Wars* or the *History of Rome*. This perceived coherence and dynamic process is what renders the Greco-Roman past so immediately accessible and apprehensible to us, so comfortable, so instructive. Those ancient historians were good.

We have no comparable ancient historiography from the ancient Near East, except for Israel. And that virtual absence of secondary literary sources renders the history of, for example, Mesopotamia relatively opaque, the object of well-meaning pity on the part of our Greco-Roman scholarly brethren. We are seen rummaging around our "washing bill[s] in Babylonic cuneiform,"[5] inventories, ration lists, assorted letters, and so on, doomed to bump from tree to tree with no hope of discerning the forest. And indeed we should very much like to have a Babylonian Herodotus to describe *his* perception of the forest. But ultimately, if we have to choose between someone else's forest and the trees by means of which we can come up with our own forests, we easily choose the latter. That is one reason that primary sources most usually trump secondary sources.[6] *The Persian Wars* is great literature[7] and an entrée into the ancient world,[8] and Herodotus's drama of Greek versus Persian is one of the artistic glories of Western civilization. But a Herodotus largely removes the construction of history from our hands. We can only deal with, even seek to undo, what he has intellectually digested, creatively transformed, and artfully fashioned.[9]

For the historian, then, the text, that is, the primary, epigraphic, source, is a unique source in attempting to construct and to reconstruct the past. Historical theory, overarching structure, and archaeological data are all necessary where available. But primary texts, when present, are the most attractive single means of historical reconstruction. They supersede secondary sources, they are to be preferred to synthetic treatments, ancient or modern, and they stand above theoretical constructs abstractly considered, and built in not-so-splendid isolation. The primary text, in short, occupies a privileged position.

Therefore, when primary sources abound and reflect a given phenomenon from several angles and in depth,[10] it is the historian who should feel privileged. Mesopotamian historians are in this happy position. And, as we shall presently see, students of Nuzi are an especially fortunate lot. So we turn from considering texts *qua* texts to the Nuzi texts in particular.

Nuzi[11]

Ancient Nuzi, buried beneath modern Yorghan Tepe, lies 13 kilometers (8 miles) southwest of Kirkuk, in northern Iraq. The Late Bronze Age town yielding the documents upon which this volume focuses[12] existed from around 1500 to 1350 B.C.E. when, as we shall see below (ch. 1), it was destroyed by the Assyrians, led almost certainly by King Aššur-uballiṭ I.

The plain on which Nuzi is located ends about 16 kilometers (10 miles) to the east at the foothills of the Zagros Mountains. In the Nuzi period, these hills were inhabited by tribes, notably Kassite and the Lullubian tribes. To the west, across the Lesser Zab River lay the city of Aššur, capital of the state of Assyria. To the southeast lay Babylonia. During this period, Nuzi was part of the kingdom of Arrapḫa with its capital at Arrapḫa, modern Kirkuk. This petty kingdom was itself under the political sway of the kingdom of Mittanni whose heartland lay between the upper Tigris and the upper Euphrates. Assyria, to the east of Mittanni, and Arrapḫa, to the east of Assyria, were both vassal states of Mittanni until Assyria broke free of Mittanni. Assyria's conquest of Arrapḫa (of which the destruction of Nuzi was a manifestation) was an expression of that new independence.

Nuzi's economy was chiefly agricultural, although animal husbandry, long-distance commerce, and some small-scale manufacture are well attested. Dry-farming was practiced. Developed artificial irrigation (canals, ditches) is also present, no doubt as a hedge against years of insufficient rainfall. One gets the overall impression that Nuzi was a significant regional center within the kingdom of Arrapḫa.

The site of Nuzi consists of a walled town, roughly square-shaped about the size of eight American-football fields (i.e., about 200 × 200 meters), as well as several suburban building complexes, only two of which have been even partially excavated. The walled town contained at its center a cultic quarter containing a complex of temples and a large government house (called "palace," literally, "big house," in the texts) from which the local administration operated. Administrative quarters and a series of private dwellings covering several neighborhoods occupied the rest of the main mound. Clusters of villas occupied two excavated suburban complexes.

What makes Nuzi unusual, if not actually unique, however, are the clay tablets, the documents, that seemingly gushed from the ground as archaeologists unearthed this town. Between 6,500 and 7,000 tablets came from this site, all within the Late Bronze Age period of some 150 years only. And almost all of them come from known archaeological contexts. They came from everywhere at Nuzi, from the government administrative complexes, from houses in all the urban neighborhoods, from each of the suburban villas, and even a few dozen from the temple complex.[13] The density of documentation in space and time[14] and their distribution amongst private homes and public institutions alike (over three dozen archives may be isolated) from all over the main mound and the suburbs allow us to view local phenomena from different perspectives offering different kinds of data. These documents in their thousands include contracts for labor, deeds of sale, testamentary wills, slave sales, ration lists, inter-office memoranda, trial records, even scholastic texts. And much more.

This documentary treasure trove, in its quality as well as its numbers, is, I think, unique in the ancient world. It allows historians to be better informed about the social, economic, even the political and military life of Nuzi over time and from different points of view than is possible for any other urban community anywhere in the ancient world.

This is why Nuzi merits, among other things, a volume of its own in Writings from the Ancient World.

More on the Aims of the Present Volume

With so many documents at hand representing so many categories of communication, composing a chrestomathy, a sampler of different text genres found in the Nuzi corpus, becomes an easy task. Indeed the only difficulty is that we are presented with so many riches. There are too many texts and genres for a single book. The present effort does not solve that dilemma. Notwithstanding the difficulty of too many texts, organization of the volume according to text type would seem the natural way to proceed. However, that course would ignore an important characteristic stressed above. The Nuzi corpus is distinguished by its great quantity of material, by its distribution over dozens of well-contextualized archives—archives both public and private—and by its extension over five generations.[15] All these factors invite close reading of the texts even by beginners at a level other than that of sampler. The situation is ideal for organizing documents historically, that is, organizing them in such a manner that historical features and problems may be identified and examined. The present volume undertakes this organization.

Therefore, this work has two primary aims. It presents a variety of texts and text types from Late Bronze Age Nuzi. Many kinds of documents are represented: private real estate deeds of sale, trial records, inventories, records of expenditure, and so on. Therefore, it serves as a chrestomathy.[16] For a full catalog of genres, see the Index of Text Genres (p. 296). But these texts are not presented according to type or genre or even findspot.[17] And this brings us to the second primary purpose of this volume. Texts are presented as evidentiary material, elucidating certain events, issues, and problems the historian confronts in studying Nuzi. Specifically, the ninety-six texts presented below are divided into five groups dealing with five topics:

1. Nuzi and the political force responsible for its demise;
2. the crimes and trials of a mayor of Nuzi;
3. a multi-generational legal struggle over title to a substantial amount of land;
4. the progressive enrichment of one family at the expense of another through a series of real estate transactions;
5. the nature of the *ilku*, a real estate tax whose dynamic is a crux in defining the economic and social structure of Nuzi as a whole.

In three cases (2, 3, 4), where particular and narrow events are the focus, all texts dealing with the topic are presented. They have been taken from particular archives.[18] The nature of institutional enterprise (individual/private, family, governmental[19]) is thereby illuminated. In the other two cases (1, 5), issues are the focus of investigation. The presentation of texts is not exhaustive, since no substantial benefit would result from comprehensive treatment.[20] The relevant texts have been culled from all available material, that is, from any Nuzi archive able to contribute to the elucidation of the issue.

It should be noted a propos cases 1 and 5 that excavated tablets from places other than Nuzi, but which exhibit features close to or identical to Nuzi tablets, are not employed. Specifically the tablets from Tel el-Faḫḫar (possibly ancient Kurruḫanni) have been omitted from the present volume. Nor are tablets used which, while potentially useful, arise from clandestine rather than "scientific" excavations, that is, the Kirkuk tablets.[21] In the latter case, this is not because of any sense that unprovenienced tablets do not deserve publication. It is because the use of any such tablet weakens (not destroys) any argument being mounted. Fortunately, the provenienced Nuzi corpus is so vast and comprehensive that the resulting loss of data is minimal.[22] In other projects and research, I would happily exploit this valuable unprovenienced documentation, where appropriate.

The Five Case Studies

Each of the five case studies is assigned a chapter. What follow are brief sketches of these chapters and remarks pertaining to the significance of the topic treated. More detailed discussion of these issues appears at the outset of each chapter.

CHAPTER ONE: ASSYRIA AND ARRAPḪA IN PEACE AND WAR

The largest single segment of this volume in terms of texts presented, thirty in all, deals with Nuzi's relations with Assyria and Assyrians. Although Nuzi, as part of the kingdom of Arrapḫa, was an element of the empire of Mittanni, it lay on the eastern border, not of Mittanni itself, but of Assyria, the once and future super-power of the upper Tigris region. Indeed, throughout much of Assyrian history, the city of Arrapḫa (the capital to which Nuzi directly answered) was considered a key, venerable, and prestigious city of the Assyrian heartland. For Nuzi, therefore, Assyria was a neighbor of great importance and rightly so: Assyria eventually replaced Mittanni as ruler of Arrapḫa, destroying the kingdom and, as our texts all but prove, Nuzi itself.

What fascinates us in the present context is that the political and military processes surrounding these developments are known to us, not from Assyrian sources, but from the Nuzi texts. It was not the winners who chronicled the story of their triumphs.[23] It was the losers who wrote the story of their own demise.[24] Not only that, these political and military events are to be perceived, not from so-called (and erroneously labeled) historical texts.[25] Rather, we can piece together what happened from administrative and economic texts. Such documents, usually intended to serve other purposes, establish nonetheless the course of Arrapḫa-Assyria relations leading to Nuzi's destruction. This section of the volume and the introductory comments to the body of documentation presented there, detail the latter stages of Nuzi's political history, the stages in which Assyria looms ever larger until the overwhelming end.

CHAPTER TWO: CORRUPTION IN CITY HALL

Of the many dossiers which can be reconstructed from among the Nuzi texts, surely the most interesting, even compelling, are the twenty-four documents making up the records of the misdeeds of Nuzi's one-time mayor, Kušši-ḫarpe, and of his lackeys. Misappropriation of public funds, acceptance of bribes, aggravated acceptance of bribes ("aggravated" because the *quid pro quo* was never tendered), extortion, theft, aggravated theft (i.e., breaking and entering), kidnapping, abduction to rape, rape—all the usual crimes we associate with political corruption—are attested in these texts. If these mundane crimes of relatively small-town politicos lack the dazzle and international significance of the Neo-Assyrian plot to assassinate an emperor (Parpola 1980), or if they lack the magisterial hauteur and narrative potential of Gilgamesh of Uruk's habitual harassment of Uruk's citizens and their appeal to the goddess for relief (Gilgamesh, Standard Version, I:67–78; cf. Exod 2:23–24), for sheer detail and sustained development, these two dozen texts and the multiple offences alleged therein are without parallel in ancient primary records of any period or place.

And yet, perhaps of greater significance than this detailed documentation of ongoing corruption is the incidental light shed by these records on aspects of municipal administration in northern Iraq in the middle of the second pre-Christian millennium. Through this misbehavior, the characters populating these depositions inform us as to correct behavior and appropriate governance. The nature of offices, governmental pecking order, mayoral responsibility,[26] all these are indirectly communicated by these descriptions of the perversion of norms.[27] What is proper is revealed by impropriety. There are many nuggets from this rich vein, including one in particular.[28] The Nuzi É.GAL, lit. "big house," usually translated "palace," is the building (and institution) of government and administration. It has no royal dimension in these texts. No king resides there or is said to control that precinct (see text #45, especially). Rather, it may be the site of strictly local administration.[29] (If "palace" continues to be used in these translations, it is because "government house" can become unwieldy, a cumbersome locution. "Palace sheep" is much to be preferred to "sheep belonging to government house.")

Chapter Three: A Legal Dispute over Land: Two Generations of Legal Paperwork

The Kizzuk dossier commands interest for several reasons. It is, first of all, another vivid example of coverage in depth of a single phenomenon, in this case a dispute over legal title to lands and to real property contained therein. Seven documents yield a dynamic account of charge, countercharge, and the not quite unambiguous testimony of the hamlets located within the disputed territory. In addition, it transpires that the dispute involves opposing families from the same clan. This is the stuff of nuanced micro-history.

Second, the dossier informs us about different aspects of the legal system itself as they apply to a single case. The establishment of a class-action suit, trials, an appeal to a higher legal authority, the return of the case to the lower court, and affidavits—all these are involved in this case.

Furthermore, we are exposed to legal tactics—if I understand the course of events correctly. The ultimately successful party wins, not by refuting the evidence brought against it, but by undermining the legal grounds upon which the evidence is offered.

Add to these points of interest the fact that the family of the victorious plaintiff is ethnically Kassite (most Nuzians were Hurrian) and that the issue is a very large tract of land, and one understands how this dossier of litigation can contribute much to our perception of legal, economic, and social life at Nuzi.

Chapter Four: The Decline and Fall of a Nuzi Family

As noted earlier in this introduction, the fact that Nuzi has yielded such a plethora of archives—public and private, urban and suburban, bureaucratic and family—and the fact that these archives come from a confined area and cover a closely defined yet lengthy span of about five generations—perhaps 125 years—mean that we need not be satisfied with a mere skeletal or impressionistic sketch of a few activities by several individuals. Rather we may examine in depth the activities and the machinations of the powerful families and rulers of the community. We may trace their tactics over the generations. We see their activities changing, both in response to changing conditions at large and to changing domestic circumstances. On the domestic scene, we observe the bifurcation of nuclear families and the re-formation of family alliances. Furthermore, we learn about, not only the chief families of the community, but the middling households as well. These groups are elsewhere in Mesopotamia often ill-attested, if at all. Their character is but meagerly understood or exemplified. At Nuzi, documents from the chief families reveal the fates of those families whom they exploit. The stronger families at times exploit certain other families repeatedly, systematically, and extensively. Thus, we gain insight into the progressive pauperization of some of Nuzi's propertied families, not only through records of repeated activities by the predators but by the multiple recorded appearances of those upon whom they preyed.[30]

A fine example of this phenomenon appears in this dossier. The family of Ḫišmeya son of Itḫišta is attested in ten documents, all probably (the last nine certainly) attesting to progressive ill fortune and exploitation by Enna-mati son of the famous Teḫip-tilla and by Enna-mati's wife, Uzna. Thus, we witness in detail the continuing prosperity of the Teḫip-tilla family through the industry of their first-born sons. And we witness the inexorable decline of a landowning peasant family, represented by a widow and her three grown sons.

Chapter Five: The Nature of the *ilku* at Nuzi

This chapter scans the entire corpus of Nuzi texts to hone in on the nature and execution of one of Nuzi's several taxes, the ubiquitous *ilku*. As the casual reader's eyes become heavy-lidded and glaze over, I should emphasize that the problem of the *ilku* is not merely technical and of no great consequence (though such problems are appropriately of great ongoing interest to scholars of the past).

It is a crux in understanding the entire society and economy of Nuzi. The *ilku* is a type of real estate tax, and for many decades scholars have variously considered this tax to attach either to the "original" owners of land and to their heirs or to the land itself, that is, to the current legal owners of the land regardless of whether or not the land remained with the original family (i.e., retained or sold). This is important because, if the former were the case, then it indicates that land assigned to an individual *was meant to tie that individual and his family to the land*. That, in turn, means that, at Nuzi, land was *de jure* inalienable and hence was not truly privately owned property. If the *ilku* stayed with its original payers, so did the land. At least it was supposed to. The advocates of the definition of *ilku* as a tax attaching to original owners perforce advocated the position that (a) land in the kingdom of Arrapḫa was palace land and that the owners were, in effect, feoff holders; or (b) Arrapḫa land was somehow communally owned.

This position was seemingly buttressed by a peculiarity of the Nuzi texts. Much, perhaps most, of the real estate which did change hands, did so employing a contractual formula that expressed adoption. The seller of the land adopted the buyer as a son and ceded the land to him as an "inheritance share." The buyer, in turn, tendered to his new father a "gift," often corresponding to the going rate of the value of the land. This deal was interpreted as a circumvention of the inalienability of land by the device of bringing the buyer into the family circle by means of this adoption.

We will see below that, whatever the function of such adoptions was, circumvention was not the motive. Real estate was bought and sold and exchanged openly and by several means and explicitly uses the language of alienation and sale, all this alongside the more allusive, otiose language of family adoption. Some of this persistent and unambiguous textual evidence is presented in chapter five. Land *was* transferred and the *ilku* was transferred along with the title to that land. Neither was inalienable. In other words, private ownership existed, existed openly, and was seemingly widespread in the world of the Nuzi texts. Whatever economic regime characterized Nuzi and Arrapḫa at large, it was not feudal, and not solely (or even predominantly) communal (if it was communal at all); rather it was essentially private. Landlords consisted of individuals, families, royal retainers, even the palace itself. But private landlords they were and they remained. This is why establishing the nature of the *ilku* is important. It is a crux for understanding what sort of society we are dealing with when we read these documents. That alone justifies devoting a chapter to the *ilku* as part of this volume.

But we study the *ilku*, not only because it is fundamental to our understanding of the economic structure of Nuzi, but as an object lesson. The twin mistaken notions that land is formally inalienable and that the *ilku*-tax is likewise inalienable were articulated over seven decades ago and have taken hold and been repeated since, largely as "received knowledge." Some scholars long ago recognized and demonstrated the falsity of this claim. Yet the old truths do indeed die hard.[31] Tradition, inertia, even ideology, as well as the notion that "everybody knows that *x* is the case," conspire to mislead even careful scholars.[32] Two very recent (depressingly recent) examples involve, unfortunately, a history of Mesopotamia (van de Mieroop 2007: 154, claiming that Nuzi land is inalienable[33]) and a history of ancient Israel written by a giant of ancient Near Eastern studies (Liverani 2005: 26, claiming that the transfer of Nuzi land by adoption means that such land was not transferred until the death of the "father"). No one is immune from this sort of error. We all rely on authorities for knowledge outside our own areas of expertise. This chapter's cautionary tale is therefore of general relevance.

Nuzi in the Ancient World

Ultimately, Nuzi's distinction for the historian of antiquity lies in its large volume of documents. These tablets span five generations but also cluster to the last years of the town's existence. They are mostly well contextualized. Their archaeological findspots and their documentary congeners are mostly clearly defined. Discrete archives stem from assorted government offices and from private families. They come from the main mound and several extramural dwellings. The sheer breadth and depth of coverage elevate an appreciation of Nuzi to the level enjoyed by the Ur III state or Neo-Babylonian Uruk.

What seems to separate Nuzi from Ur or Uruk or Mari for the historian is, not so much the volume of material (though even Nuzi is dwarfed by Mari or Ur or Kaniš in this regard), as the seeming isolation in which Nuzi finds itself. It is a well-documented community, but the community appears consigned to a regional island. Its contacts with better known cities and lands of the Near East are sporadic and laconic. Like Gudea's Lagaš of the late-third millennium, Nuzi lacks extensive international context though, in both cases, we know that such context existed. Thus Nuzi is understandable locally but cannot effectively be compared to its geographical or chronological neighbors. Compounding this difficulty, Nuzi was initially compared in its socio-legal characteristics to the society of the patriarchs from the biblical book of Genesis. This project of comparison was flawed both methodologically and in terms of the positive results claimed.[34] Worse yet in the present context, it compared an isolated Nuzi to a patriarchal world also isolated, detached from lands, personalities, and events recognizable as part of a larger, well-attested world. One result of this quixotic adventure was that the value of Nuzi to the historian was denigrated, as linked to the discredited attempt to locate the world of Abraham, Isaac, and Jacob. And, at the same time, Nuzi was unconsciously tarred with the patriarchal brush: as the stories of Israel's ancestors were depicted on a lonely, literary canvas with little or no background, so too was Nuzi somehow tangible, but not quite real, not quite part of this world.

This geo-political isolation of Nuzi was compounded and aggravated by several other factors. The documents lack a precise and widespread dating system, forcing Nuzi's events to float in a world of "circa"s and "around"s and "approximately"s. Also, Nuzi legal formulary seems all but divorced from those of its Babylonian, Assyrian, and Hittite neighbors. Thus it was not only isolated but different, seemingly radically so.

But the very volume of the textual material that Nuzi places at our disposal supplies to the historian the means by which Nuzi can escape its isolation, its perceived exoticism, and its very unfairly perceived irrelevance. The present volume points to several such escape routes. First, and of greatest immediate moment, ch. 1 exploits Nuzi's government administrative archives and a few private texts to trace the relations between Arrapḫa, the state of which Nuzi was part, and Assyria. The documents establish that Arrapḫa's existence and destruction can be integrated into the larger world of Late Bronze Age international power politics. Indeed, Assyria's attacks on Nuzi and its neighbors probably mark the first stage of Assyria's emergence from the thrall of its imperial master, Mittanni.[35] Records from Assyria, Babylon, Hatti, and Egypt can be shown to be relevant to this military exercise.[36] In turn, Nuzi and its texts are now to be considered anchored to the larger Near Eastern world in which it was located and embedded.

Chapter 5 deals with the nature of a local real estate tax and its workings through assorted contractual vehicles. One important outcome of this investigation is the demystification of real estate transfer in Nuzi society. Allegedly idiosyncratic relations between landownership and land taxes are revealed not to be idiosyncratic at all. Although the mechanics of Nuzi legal form may be somewhat unusual (that is what makes any local practice local), the dynamic of real estate alienation appears the same as elsewhere in the ancient Near East.

Thus, on the local, socio-legal level (ch. 5) as on the international political level (ch. 1), Nuzi is demonstrably part and parcel of the surrounding world, not an isolate, a dreamlike society of disembodied practices and exotic structures. And that realization redounds to the benefit of Late Bronze Age history at large. For Nuzi, with its thousands of documents, its dozens of archives, and its fairly well-recorded archaeological record, now emerges as an important source through which its neighbors can better be understood.

That is why the Nuzi texts are important Writings from the Ancient World.

Appendix 1: Findspots

Among the data given for each text presented herein is the findspot, that is, the location in Nuzi from which the tablet was excavated. The following is a list of the findspots, where known,[37] of these ninety-six tablets.[38] These constitute vital data in the historical analysis of the corpus. Scholarly disregard of this information has led, in the past, to badly skewed historical conclusions.

A 23	Eastern suburb. Archive of Šilwa-tešup "son of the king."
A 26	Eastern suburb. Archive of Šilwa-tešup "son of the king."
A 34	Eastern suburb. Archive of the family of Akkuya son of Katiri and of Ilānu son of Tayuki.
A 41	Eastern suburb. Archive of Šilwa-tešup "son of the king."
C 19	Main mound; north of temple area. Archive of the family of Zike son of Ar-tirwi.
C 28	Main mound; north of temple area. Archive of the family of Zike son of Ar-tirwi.
D 3	Main mound; north of temple area. Arsenal or treasury. Mostly royal grain receipts.
D 6	Main mound; north of temple area. Arsenal or treasury. Mostly royal grain receipts.
F 24	Main mound; southwest of temple area. Archive of the families of Ṣill-apiḫe and Teḫip-šarri. Mostly contracts.
G 29	Main mound; temple area. Mostly private contracts.
K 32	Main mound; palace area. Contracts of (local) Queen Tarmen-naya.
K 465[39]	Main mound; southwest section. Tablet store room (Starr 1939: 282).
L 2 or M 2[40]	Main mound; palace area. Records of the trial of Kušši-ḫarpe and other texts written by the same scribe.
N 120	Main mound; palace area. Archive of the family of ^{f}Tulpun-naya and of others. Many tablets regarding military matters.
R 76	Main mound; palace area. Administrative and other records of the royal family, especially of the local queen.
T 10	Western suburb. Archive of the family of Ḫilpiš-šuḫ son of Šuḫun-zirira.
T12	Western suburb. Archive of the family of Ḫutiya son of Kuššiya.
T13	Western suburb. Archive of the family of Tarmi-tilla son of Šurki-tilla.
T15	Western suburb. Archive of the family of Teḫip-tilla son of Puḫi-šenni.[41]

T16 Western suburb. Archive of the family of Teḫip-tilla son of Puḫi-šenni.

T19 Western suburb. Archive of the family of Teḫip-tilla son of Puḫi-šenni.

Appendix 2: Texts with Seal Impressions

Assorted texts have been published in hand copies that fail to render seal impressions or to indicate their presence (e.g., by including "S.I." at the appropriate place). Other texts are published in transliteration only and similarly fail to note any seal impressions. These texts are:

Texts ## **1**, **6**, **7**, 11, **13**, 14, 15, 17 (text damaged), 18, 30 32 (text damaged), **35**, **37**, 38 (text damaged), **39**, 41, 42, **43**, **45**, 47?, **48**, **49**, **50**, 52, **53**, **56**, **57**, **58**, **59**, **60**, **61**, **62**, 63, **64**, **67**, 69 (text damaged), **70**, **71**, **73**, **74**, **82**, **83**, 84, **85**, **86**, 94, **95**, **96**.

Some of these documents explicitly note, in the wording of the texts themselves, the presence of seal impressions. Such texts are indicated here in boldface. The reader should be aware that, on the odd occasion, a text will note the presence of a seal impression where it is not, in fact, present. (These are probably draft texts.) This means that texts marked in boldface probably, but not necessarily, indicate that seal impressions are present. Texts not marked in boldface, that is, documents not mentioning seal impressions, probably lack such impressions at all. All other texts note, where appropriate, the presence of seal impressions.

Chapter One
Assyria and Arrapḫa in Peace and War

Arrapḫa at Peace with Assyria

The relations between Assyria and the bordering kingdom of Arrapḫa (of which Nuzi was an important center) were dominated by hostility, apparently at first sporadic (text #13), ultimately regular and inexorable.[1] It ended in Nuzi's destruction, attested by the archaeological record of devastation[2] rather than by reportage. But it must not be imagined that confrontation alone marked the relations between Assyria and this small outpost of the empire[3] of Mittanni (almost always called Ḫanigalbat in the Nuzi texts). Earlier,[4] peaceful relations are attested, and not rarely. For two generations, at least, before Nuzi's downfall, there existed normal diplomatic, commercial, and other relations between Assyria and Arrapḫa. Assyrians are described as engaged in peaceful pursuits in Arrapḫan territory in texts from the Nuzi horizon.[5] Chariots from the Nuzi region may have been exported to Assyria (text #1). Assyrians are present in Arrapḫan territory as diplomats (texts ##2, 3, 4), and, once, an Assyrian is identified as a scribe (text #5). Assyrians as legally unattached aliens even appear as slaves for Nuzians (texts ##5, 6, 7).[6] These men all sell themselves into slavery, no doubt because of economic distress. These include at least one skilled laborer, a scribe. The status of one (see text #7) is *ḫapiru*, a lower-class resident alien. The status of the other two is implicitly the same.[7] Thus our texts recognize Assyrians in Nuzi. Texts from Assyria, if such were recoverable, would likely attest to Nuzians and other Arrapḫans in Assyria.[8]

Arrapḫa's Military Preparations

During Nuzi's last generation, there is clear evidence that the political climate turned ominous and ultimately catastrophic. This was not a sudden turn of events, however. The Arrapḫan military infrastructure and planning seem to have developed in an orderly fashion to judge from the administrative texts that abound in the government archives.[9] The presence and apparently orderly integration of Ḫanigalbatian (i.e., Mittannian) military contingents into the Arrapḫan army also imply sustained and gradual planning. And even the Assyrian attack on the Turša region, described at length in text #13 and its associated texts, texts ## 14–17, cannot have taken place in the last days of Nuzi, since normal economic activity continued elsewhere in the Arrapḫa state perhaps for several years after the clash.[10]

But decisive hostilities were looming indeed. A directive issued from the main administrative center in the capital city, Arrapḫa, is crucial as a pivotal piece of evidence for this historical reconstruction (text #8). It orders those mayors in the border areas of the kingdom (i.e., the Assyrian border, the only one from which danger could have emanated, as we shall see) to quell disquiet in those areas, emphasizing mayoral culpability for failure to do so. Since a copy of the document was found at Nuzi, clearly this town was deemed responsible for part of the Arrapḫa–Assyria border.[11] Text #9 is a muster of archers, clearly a preparation for armed conflict.[12] Whether or not this particular text derives from this period of preparation or from a time after hostilities broke out, such musters must have taken place toward the start of these battles.[13] Also to be discerned, probably at this stage, is the involvement of the Mittannian army. Text #10, an inventory of bronze scales taken for fashioning armor, notes the different types or styles of armor used by Arrapḫans and by their Mittannian overlords.[14] Such records frequently show that actual hostilities had taken place. For example, text #11 describes military equipment some of which was lost and some used in battle. Text #12 describes chariotry of the left and right wings which did not return from battle.[15]

Arrapḫa at War with Assyria

The Northwestern Front: The Battle of Turša

Text #13, another pivotal text in the schema, is a very lengthy catalog of the losses in men, real property, and mobilia inflicted on the region of Turša, on this western frontier of Arrapḫa. Captured property is described by its geographical origin and by its destination as war booty. The attackers are identified as Assyrians. Four further texts derive from this attack, each cataloging property taken or, in one case, the leadership of the places to which property was delivered. Text #14 which, like text #13, derives from a private Nuzi archive belonging to a family with Turša interests, describes part of the same battle and some of the places to which spoils were brought. Text #15, from a government archive on the main mound of Nuzi, lists, like parts of text #13, slaves captured from Arrapḫan towns and sent to Assyrian locations. The Assyrian capital, Aššur, is explicitly mentioned twice as a place where slaves from Arrapḫa now live. Text #16, from the same room as text #15, details oxen captured from Arrapḫa and delivered to places at least two of which are mentioned in other texts. Assyrians are mentioned no fewer than four times as responsible for this predation. Finally, text #17, from a mixed private and public archive names the leadership of towns and *dimtu*s linked to the target locations of spoil mentioned in earlier texts. Some of the names of these leaders are conspicuously Assyrian.

The term *dimtu* denotes a rural tower and, secondarily, a rural district in which such a tower is located. *dimtu* appears in the Nuzi texts with both meanings, but especially the latter. In this volume, I will indicate which meaning I think applies in a given case by "translating" "*dimtu*-tower" and "*dimtu*-district" as appropriate.

Five texts, therefore, deal directly with a successful attack on Turša. And of these, three (texts ##13, 15, 16) mention Assyrians or Aššur explicitly, while the other two implicitly implicate the Assyrians as the aggressors.

And so, the war for which Nuzi was preparing was actually fought. In beginning this chapter, it was asserted that Assyria was Arrapḫa's (and Mittanni's) military enemy. It was in that context that, earlier, pacific relations between Nuzi and Assyria were described. And here it has been demonstrated and now must be repeated: Assyria, and no other power, appears as Arrapḫa's enemy and, therefore, ultimately its destroyer. No texts *at all* link Arrapḫa hostilities to any power other than Assyria. This point deserves emphasis because it has commonly been asserted in the past[16] (though such assertions have been challenged[17]) that Babylon, "the land of Akkad" in the Nuzi texts, was the destroyer of Nuzi, not Assyria. But this is most unlikely because there are so many mentions of Assyria in this context, and because perusal of the war documents reveals only one possible text, text #18, in which Babylon even appears. Assyria appears in the same text, and the context is too laconic and obscure to bear the burden of such a far-reaching conclusion as that Babylon was a serious enemy of Arrapḫa's.[18] But however one depicts Babylon in text #18, that is also how one must depict Assyria. Their appearances exactly parallel each other.[19] And this is one of the strengths of this volume of Nuzi texts—this is one of the strengths of the series, Writings from the Ancient World. The reader is instructed (if not forced) to describe and analyze the past after actually having read the primary source material. Here, actual examination of the relevant corpus of writings reveals the virtual nonexistence of evidence regarding Babylonian aggression against Arrapḫa.[20] If Babylon was involved at all, it was probably in a skirmish with Assyria as Assyria marched

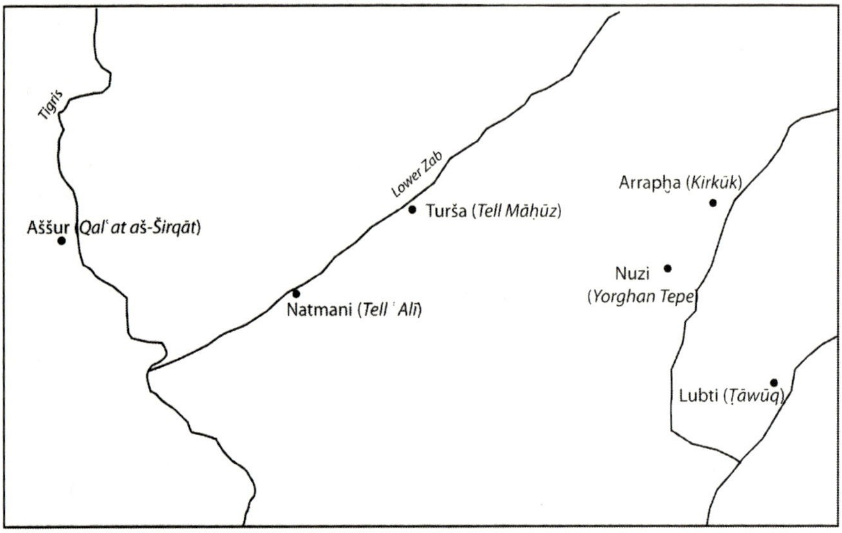

The Theater of the Arrapḫa-Assyria War

through Arrapḫa on its way to the Babylonian border.[21] Recognizing this situation, we may now attempt to order other records of the Assyrian conquest.

Assyrian War Strategy

The Battle of Turša took place at or near the start of hostilities with Arrapḫa. As noted above, its outcome did not signal Nuzi's (or Arrapḫa's) end. That only took place months later or even longer.[22] Furthermore, the Turša region is located close to Assyrian territory (see the map above)[23] And so it would have been attacked first. Other towns mentioned in Nuzi texts in connection with military activity are Apena, Arn-apu, Arwa, Lubti, Ṣilliya, and Zizza. Of these, only the location of Lubti is known with probability. It is southeast of both Assyria and Turša, indeed it is at the eastern limit of the Arrapḫan state and close to Babylonia. If Assyrian activity has been perceived correctly, then the following description is a logical interpretation. Assyria attacked and captured the area of Turša in western Arrapḫa, on the Assyrian border. Eventually, from that base, Assyrian forces advanced southeast, attacking Zizza and Apena, and probably Arn-apu and Arwa, somewhere in south central Arrapḫa, south of the city of Arrapḫa and more immediately south of Nuzi.[24] By heading southeast, the Assyrian army would have bypassed Nuzi and the capital city itself, prizes to be collected once the rest of Arrapḫa was captured (cf. Sennacherib's strategy in Judah). From Zizza and Apena, the army would have moved to Lubti (and Ṣilliya, mentioned together with Lubti). Thus the military progress of Assyrian forces would be complete, from Turša in the northwest to Lubti in the southeast. One recalls here the words of a great Assyrian conqueror of some two and a half centuries later, Tiglath-Pileser I: "I marched to Karduniaš [i.e., to Babylonia]. I conquered from the city Turšan on the other [i.e., eastern] side of the Lower Zab [River], the city of Arman[25] of Ugarsallu, as far as the city Lubdu. I crossed over the river…."[26] Thus both logic and analogy (itself a very powerful tool in the hands of careful historians of this time and place) combine to make reasonable sense of the inchoate data at our disposal.

One presumes that then, Nuzi (which yields these data up to this stage) would have been mopped up and finally Arrapḫa captured.[27] Unfortunately, it is only by an argument from silence (and archaeological inference in the case of Nuzi) that one can deduce this last stage.

The Central Front: Zizza, Apena, and Neighbors[28]

Apena and Zizza, in any case, were the loci of Arrapḫan forces. Zizza especially seems to have been the site of considerable activity. Three records describe men (texts ##19 and 20), horses (text #19), and equipment (text #21) which did not return from battle there. A dolorous account (text #22) informs that thirty-eight soldiers (from Nuzi?) were captured in Zizza, when the enemy occupied that town, as were an additional ten or more from the neighboring town of Apena. That Zizza was lost may also be suggested by a date formula (text #23).[29]

Apena was also defended, at least in part, by soldiers from Mittanni (text #24).[30] One text (text #25) describes Mittannian chariotry[31] stationed in the towns of Arn-apu and Arwa. Arwa, at least, has been identified as being in the neighborhoods of Zizza and, indirectly, of Apena as well.[32]

The Southeastern Front: Lubti and Ṣilliya[33]

Finally, in the southeast, battles appear to have been fought at Lubti and Ṣilliya.[34] Text #26 links the two towns as sites of chariot confrontations.[35] Text #27 repeats the datum that chariotry was sent to Lubti.[36] A further document (text #28) describes the dispatch from Nuzi of charioteers to Temtena in the vicinity of Lubti. The charioteers actually arrive in the towns of Irḫaḫḫe and Teliperra. These places, therefore, must be near Temtena—near Lubti. Text #29 again refers to the town of Teliperra. The enemy, it is implied, controls that settlement and may be threatening to inflict (additional) damage unless persuaded to abstain from further action. A man (a prisoner of war, probably) from Lubti surfaces in the Assyrian capital of Aššur (text #30). This last text is telling. Part of the rationale for assigning the responsibility for Nuzi's destruction to the Babylonians is the site of this battle: the southeastern location of the battle allegedly demanded a Babylonian foe rather than an Assyrian enemy. Here, it is made explicit that a man of Lubti (probably more than one) was sent to the Assyrian capital of Aššur before disappearing altogether.[37]

1. *P-S* 84 (SMN 2056)

Findspot: Room N120[38]
Publication: Pfeiffer and Speiser 1936: 50[39]
Edition: None[40]

This is a simple inventory. A chariot is transferred from stores to an individual. He takes it to Assyria.

Obverse
1 1 ^{GIŠ}GIGIR *a-šar*
2 ^{m}*A-ki-pa-pu*
3 DUMU *Ḫa-ši-pa-pu*
4 *le-qú-ú-ma*
5 *a-na* ^{m}*Ar-ru-um-ti* DUMU (*sic*)
6 *na-din ù*
7 ^{m}*Ar-ru-um-ti*
8 *i-na* KUR *Aš-šur*
9 *ú-bi-la*
Reverse
10 NA$_4$ ^{m}*Ḫa-ši-ip-til-la*
11 DUMU *Ḫu-ti-ya*

P-S 84

(1–9) 1 chariot was taken from Akip-apu son of Ḫašip-apu and was given to Aril-lumti son of. (*sic*) And Aril-lumti took it to the land of Assyria.

(10–11) Seal of Ḫašip-tilla son of Ḫutiya.

2. HSS XIV, 48 (SMN 3268)

Findspot: Room D3
Publication: Lacheman 1950: pl. 23
Edition: None[41]

This text is an account of some barley expenditures taken from government stores during a single month[42] and is closely related to other such ration lists.[43] The order of the entries appears to reflect, at least in part, a governmental hierarchy, Thus, barley for a queen appears early on (line 3), while that for an upper- to mid-level bureaucrat is listed later (line 11). Late still appear rations for young male slaves (lines 35–36[44]). That entry is followed shortly thereafter by rations for twenty foreign females (lines 38–41).[45] The final entry appears to be for bird feed (line 45).

If this impression of administrative hierarchy is correct (the pecking order is *not* transparent or explicit throughout), then one may deduce that certain other offices or individuals appear where they do because of their status. A case in point is represented by lines 1–2, specifying a six-day supply of feed for the horses of what should be the head of this hierarchical list. The cuneiform wedges identifying this party are, unfortunately, ambiguous. They could represent "10 sons" of the king[46] or "royal foot (soldiers)."[47] But neither possibility is beyond question. In favor of the interpretation "10 sons" (and, therefore, against "royal foot") are the following considerations. It *is* the first entry, and princes—even horses of princes—would fit well as the first entry. Furthermore, there are objections to the alternative. The wedges, easily read as 10 DUMU, that is, "10 sons," are not really read well as GÌR, that is, as "foot."[48] And it would be peculiar for a military contingent to appear in such a list of individuals and, latterly, lower-class slave groups. Finally, it is unclear why or how foot soldiers have horses.

On the other hand, none of these points is insuperable or decisive. And, if these were princes, why always 10?[49] The presence of the initial "10"-wedge *is* the required first element in the sign for "foot." And why is this group mentioned so often if it does not represent a military unit? And so, finally, the issue is not totally resolved.

Clearer, however, is the matter of the Assyrian envoys who appear, and appropriately so, toward the start of this list (lines 12–13).[50]

Perhaps of as much significance as are any of these observations for us, as students of the past, is the following. Documents whose *raison d'être* lies in one sphere (in this case, bureaucratic accounting of comestibles for government officials and animals) can yield important information in other areas that are of no direct interest to the writer or his intended audience. In this case, a dry account tells us of the regularized presence of Assyrians in Nuzi and of their inclusion in the local officialdom. It is a pacific presence, at least on the surface.

Obverse

1 7 ANŠE 2 BÁN ŠE.MEŠ *a-na* 6 UD^{-mi}

2 *a-*[*n*]*a* ANŠE.KUR.RA.MEŠ *ša* 10$^{?}$ DUMU$^{?}$.MEŠ LUGAL

3 1 (PI) 3 BÁN ŠE *a-na* SAL.LUGAL^{-ti}

4 2 A⸢N⸣ŠE ŠE *a-na* ^{m}*Ḫé-el-ti-ip-te-*<*šup*>[51]

5 1 (PI) 2 BÁN ŠE *a-na* ^{m}*Ku-ul-pè-na-tal*

6 4 BÁN 4 SILA$_3$ ŠE *a-na ša* A.MEŠ

7 4 BÁN 4 SILA$_3$ ŠE ^{m}*Pa-i-til-la*

8 4 BÁN 4 SILA$_3$ ŠE ^{m}*Wi-ir-ra-aḫ-ḫé*

9 1 (PI) ŠE ^{m}*Til-ta-aš-šu-ra*

10 1 (PI) ŠE ^{m}*Ú-i*$^{!}$(=BI)*-r*[*a*]*-at-ti*

11 1 ⸢ANŠE⸣$^{?}$ 1[+1$^{?}$] BÁN ŠE ^{m}*A-ki-ya* SUKKAL

12 ⸢2$^{??}$ A⸣[NŠE$^{?}$] ⸢5 BÁN⸣$^{?}$ ŠE.MEŠ *a-na* 5 UD^{-mi}

13 *a-na* $^{\text{LÚ.ME[Š}}$*ú*]*-bá-ru-ti ša* KUR *Aš-šur*

14 5 BÁN ŠE.[MEŠ *a*$^{?}$*-na*$^{?}$ ^{m}AM[52]]-^{d}XXX

15 [n] ANŠE [n BÁN] ⸢ŠE.M⸣EŠ ⸢*a*⸣*-na ša ú-*[ ] ⸢x x⸣

16 1 AN⸢Š⸣E 1 BÁN 4 SILA$_3$ ŠE.MEŠ *a-na* A[NŠE].KUR.RA

17 [*ša*] ŠU ^{m}*Ša-at-t*⸢*a*⸣*-ú-az-*[*za*]

18 [n] ANŠE 4 BÁN 4 [SIL]A$_3$ ŠE *a-na* A[NŠE$^{?}$.KUR$^{?}$.RA$^{?}$]

19 *ša* ŠU ^{m}*Ša-*⸢*te*⸣*-en-*⸢*šu*⸣*-*[*uḫ*]

20 1 ANŠE 1 (PI) 2 BÁN ŠE.MEŠ *a-*[*na*]

Lower Edge

21 5 BÁN ŠE.M[EŠ] ⸢*a-n*⸣*a* [ ]

22 1 (PI) ŠE.M[EŠ *a-na*]

23 1 (PI) ŠE.M[EŠ *a-na*]

24 1 ANŠE 1 (PI) [ŠE.MEŠ] ⸢*a*⸣*-n*[*a*]

25 [^{m}]*Ḫu-ti-pu-*⸢*ra*⸣*-aš-š*[*e*]

26 1 ANŠE 2 BÁN 4 SIL⸢A$_3$⸣ ŠE.MEŠ

27 *a-na* ^{m}*T*[*a-t*]*i-ip-te-šup*

28 2 ANŠ[E n$^{?}$+] 1 SILA$_3$ ŠE.MEŠ

29 *a-n*[*a* ANŠE$^{?}$.KUR$^{?}$].R⸢A⸣$^{?}$ *ša* ^{m}*Te-ḫi-ip-t*[*il-la*]

30 ⸢2$^{?}$ A⸣[NŠE$^{?}$] Š[E$^{?}$ *ša*$^{?}$ *ḫ*]*a*$^{!?}$*-za-an-nu*

31 *a-na* ^{m}*A-kip-t*[*a-še-e*]*n-ni*

32 1 ANŠE 5 BÁN [ŠE].MEŠ *a-na* [ ] ⸢*x*⸣

33 *i-na* ITI *Ḫi-a-ri* [ ] ⸢x x⸣ [($^{?}$)]

34 5 BÁN ŠE ^{m}*Ti-ir-wi-*[*na-ta*]*l*

35 2 ANŠE 4 BÁN ŠE.MEŠ [*a-na*] 6 *ṣú-ḫa-ru*

36 *a-na* 2 ITI-^{ḫi}

37 4 BÁN ŠE ^{m}*Al-wi-šu-*⸢*uḫ*⸣
38 8 ANŠE ŠE.MEŠ *a-na* 17 SAL.MEŠ
39 *ša* KUR *Ku-uš-šu-uḫ-ḫi ù* ⸢*a*⸣*-na*
40 3 SAL.MEŠ *ša* KUR *Nu-ul-lu-a-i-*⸢*ú*⸣
41 *a-na* ⸢2 ITI-^{ḫi}⸣

42 1 (PI) 3 BÁN ŠE *ki-ma pu-ḫi-šu-nu*
43 *ša* $^{LÚ.MEŠ}$*ši-na-ḫi-lu-uḫ-li*
Upper Edge
44 6 ANŠE ŠE.MEŠ *a-n*⸢*a*⸣ ZÍD.DA
a-na ^{m}*Ut-ḫap-ta-e*
45 2 ANŠE ŠE *a-na* MUŠEN.MEŠ *a-na* ^{m}*Te-ḫi-pa-pu*
Left Edge
46 [ŠU.N]IGIN$_2$ 5⸢9⸣ ANŠE 3 BÁN Š⸢E⸣.MEŠ *eš-šu-tù*
47 [*š*]*a*$^{?}$ ITI-^{ḫi} *Ḫi-*[*a*]*-ri š*⸢*a*⸣ *na-áš-rù*

HSS XIV, 48

(1–36) 7 homers, 2 seahs of barley for 6 days for the horses of 10(?) sons(?) of the king; 9 seahs of barley for the queen; 2 homers of barley for Ḫeltip-te<šup>; 8 seahs of barley for Kulpen-atal; 4 seahs, 4 *qa*s of barley for "those of the water";[53] 4 seahs, 4 *qa*s of barley, Pai-tilla; 4 seahs, 4 *qa*s of barley, Wirraḫḫe; 6 seahs of barley, Tiltaš-šura; 6 seahs of barley, Ụir-atti; 1 homer(?), 1 (+1?) seah(s) of barley, Akiya, the *sukkallu*[54]; 2(??) homers(?), 5 seahs(?) of barley for 5 days for the envoys of the land of Assyria; 5 seahs of barley [for?] Rîm-sin; … homer(s) … [seah(s)] of barley for those who …; 1 homer, 1 seah, 4 *qa*s of barley for the horses [under] the authority of Šatta-ụazza; … homer(s), 4 seahs, 4 *qa*s of barley for the horses(?) under the authority of Šaten-šuḫ; 1 homer 8 seahs of barley for …; 5 seahs of barley for …; 6 seahs of barley [for] …; 6 seahs of barley [for] …; 1 homer, 6 seahs [of barley] for Ḫutip-urašše; 1 homer, 2 seahs, 4 *qa*s of barley for Tatip-tešup; 2 homers …(?) 1+…(?) *qa*s of barley for the horse(s)(?) of Teḫip-tilla; 2(?) homers(?) …(?) [of barley] of the mayor(?) for Akip-tašenni; 1 homer, 5 seahs [of barley] for … in the month of Ḫiari …; 5 seahs of barley, Tirwin-atal; 2 homers, 4 seahs of barley [for] 6 youths for 2 months.

(37–41) 4 seahs of barley, Alwišuḫ; 8 homers of barley for 17 women of Kassite-Land (and) for 3 women of the land of the Lullubians for 2 months.

(42–45) 9 seahs of barley as replacement (grain) of the assistants to the second-in-command; 6 homers of barley for flour for Utḫap-tae; 2 homers of barley for the birds, for Teḫip-apu.

(46–47) Total: 59 homers, 3 seahs of fresh barley which were taken out (from the stores) for(?) the month of Ḫiari.

3. HSS XIV, 50 (SMN 3272)

Findspot: Room D3
Publication: Lacheman 1950: pl. 25
Edition: None[55]

This text is related to text #2. See the introductory remarks to that document.

Obverse

1 1 ⸢ANŠE⸣ 1(PI) 3 BÁN ŠE.MEŠ [*a-n*]*a*!
2 ANŠE.KUR. ⸢RA⸣.MEŠ [*ša*]10? DUMU?.MEŠ LUGAL
3 *a-na* 2 UD-^{mi} *a-na* UR[U] ⸢*T*⸣*a-še-ni-we*
4 1 BÁN 4 SÌLA ŠE *a-na* SAL.[LUGAL]-$^{⸢ti⸣}$
5 2 BÁN ŠE *a-na* ^{m}*Ḫu-t*[*i*]-*pu*-[*ra*?-*aš*?-*še*?[56]]
6 1 BÁN 4 SÌLA ŠE ^{m}*Ḫu-t*[*i*?-]
7 1 BÁN 4 SÌLA ŠE ^{m}*Eḫ-l*[*i*?-]
8 1 BÁN ŠE *ša* A.MEŠ
9 1 BÁN ŠE *a-na* 1 ANŠE.KUR.[RA]
10 *a-šar* ^{m}*In-zi-ya*
11 1 ANŠE ŠE *a-*[*n*]*a*
12 *ú-bá-ru-*⸢*ti*⸣ *ša* KUR [*Aš-š*]*ur*
13 2 BÁN Š[E] ^{m}*Til-*⸢*ta*⸣*-aš š*⸢*u*⸣*-ra*
14 2 BÁN Š[E ^{m}]*Ú-i-ra-*[*a*]*t-t*[*i*]
15 1 BÁN 4 SÌLA ŠE ^{m}⸢*Ta*⸣*-ti-*⸢*ip*⸣*-til-la*

Reverse

16 2 A[NŠE ŠE n BÁN Š]E *a-na* ZÍD.DA
17 *a-na* [URU -*n*]*i-we*
18 Š[U.NIGIN$_2$ n A]NŠE 3[(+1? or 2?) BÁN ŠE]
19 *i*+*na* [ ] *ni* [ ]
20 *š*[*a*]

HSS XIV, 50

(1–17) 1 homer, 9 seahs of barley for the horses [of] 10(?) sons(?) of the king for 2 days for the town of Tašenni; 1 seah, 4 *qa*s of barley for the queen; 2 seahs of barley for Ḫutip-u[rašše?]; 1 seah, 4 *qa*s of barley for Ḫu-ti(?)-…; 1 seah, 4 *qa*s of barley, Eḫ-li(?)-…; 1 seah of barley, "those of the water"; 1 seah of barley for 1 horse (boarded) at Inziya's; 1 homer of barley for the envoys of the land of Assyria; 2 seahs of barley, Tiltaš-šura; 2 seahs of barley, Ụir-atti; 1 seah, 4 *qa*s of barley, Tatip-tilla[57]; 2 homers [n seah(s)] of barley for flour, for/to … [the town of] …-ni.

(18–20) Total: … homers, 3 (or 4 or 5) [seahs of barley] in … of/for … .

4. *EN* 9/3, 284 (SMN 3505)[58]

Findspot: Room F24[59]

Publications: Lacheman 1958: 93 (transliteration); Lacheman and Owen 1995: 270 (copy)

Editions: Deller and Fadhil 1972: 200; Lion 2005: 200

This is a simple inventory of animals distributed. In the case of the Assyrian the animals are given. In the other case, they are sold.

Obverse

1 2 UDU.SAL.MEŠ

2 *a-na* $^{\text{LÚ.MEŠ}}$

3 *ú-ba*[60]*-ru-ti*

4 *ša* KUR *Aš-šur*

5 1 MÁŠ 4 UDU.SAL[61]

6 *a-na* KÙ.BABBAR

Lower Edge

7 *a-na* NIN.DINGIR.RA

Reverse

8 *ša* URU

9 *A-pè-na-aš*

10 *na-ad-nu*

EN 9/3, 284

(1–4) 2 ewes for the envoys of the land of Assyria.

(5–10) 1 billy goat (and) 4 ewes were given for silver (i.e., were sold) to the high priestess of the town of Apena.

5. *JEN* VI, 613 (JENu 919)

Findspot: Room T16
Publication: Lacheman 1939a: pl. 560
Edition: None[62]

Text #5 is a contract of self-enslavement in which an Assyrian enters the household of the pre-eminent Nuzi real estate magnate of his generation. The great-grandson of this same magnate would eventually be an officer of Arrapḫan forces fighting against the Assyrians.

Obverse
1 ^{m}*At-ti-la-am-mu* DUMU *A*-[ ]
2 *Aš-šu-ra-a-a-ú i*+*na* ⸢É⸣ [*ša*]
3 ^{m}*Te-ḫi-ip-til-la* DUMU *Pu-ḫi*-[*še-en-ni*]
4 *a-na* ÌR-*ti i-ru-ub* [*a-di*]
5 ^{m}*Te-ḫi-ip-til-la bal*-[*tú*]
6 *ù* <^{m}>⸢*A*⸣*t-ti-la-am-m*[*u i-pal-la-aḫ-šu*]
7 *ù e-nu-ú-*«*nu-*»*ma* [^{m}*Te-ḫi-ip-til-la*]
8 *im-tù-ú-tù ù* [^{m}*At-ti-la-am-mu*]
9 *a-na* DUMU ^{m}*Te-ḫi-i*[*p-til-la*]
10 *pu-uḫ-šu* ^{LÚ}DUB.[SAR[63]]
11 *i-na-an-dì-in* [*ù* (*i*-)*il-la-a*]⸢*k*⸣
12 *ù* [^{m}]*Te-ḫi-ip-til-la a-n*[*a*]
13 ^{m}⸢*At*⸣*-ti-la*-⸢*a*⸣*m-mu* ŠE.B[A]
14 ⸢*ù*⸣ *lu-b*[*u*]*-ul-ta i-na-an-*[*din*]
15 *šum-ma* ^{m}*At-ti*-⸢*l*⸣*a-am-mu*
16 *i*-[*n*]*a-an-na-ma i-re-eq*
Lower Edge
17 10 [MA].NA KÙ.BABBAR [*ù*] 10 MA.NA KÙ.SIG$_{17}$
18 ⸢Ì⸣.LÁ.E
Reverse
19 IG[I $^{(m)}$]*Š*[*úk*]*-ri-ya* DUMU *Ku-ri-iš-ni*
20 IGI ^{m}*Pa*-⸢*i*⸣*-til-la* DUMU ⸢*K*⸣*e-li-ya*
21 IGI ^{m}*Ša-ka$_4$*-⸢*ra-a*⸣*k-ti*
22 DUMU ⸢*Ar-ti*⸣*-i*[*r*]*-wi*

23 IGI *A-ki-ti-ir-wi* DUMU *Ki-pí-*[ ]
24 IGI *Ta-i-še-en-*[*ni*] ⸢D⸣UMU *A-ḫ*[*u-ši-na*[64]]
25 IGI *It-ḫi-iš-ta* ⸢DUMU *A-ar*⸣-[*ta-e*]
26 IGI *Mu-šu-ya* DUMU *A-ša-*[*tu*$_4$*-ni*[65]]
27 IGI *Mi-il-ka*$_4$*-a-pu* DUMU *A-*[ ]
28 IGI *Te-eḫ-pí-ru* DUB.S[AR]

S.I.

29 ^{NA_4}⸢K⸣IŠIB ^{m}*Ša-kà-ra-*[*ak-ti*]

S.I.

30 ^{NA_4}KIŠIB ^{m}*Šúk-ri-y*⸢*a*⸣

Upper Edge

S.I.

Left Edge

31 ^{NA_4}KIŠIB *Pa-i-til-la*

JEN VI, 613

(1–4) Attilammu son of A-…, an Assyrian, entered the household [of] Teḫip-tilla son of Puḫi-šenni, (and) into slavery.

(4–11) As long as Teḫip-tilla lives, Attilammu [shall serve him], and when Teḫip-tilla dies, then [Attilammu] shall supply to the son of Teḫip-tilla a substitute scribe in his stead [and (then)] go (on his way).

(12–14) And Teḫip-tilla shall supply to Attilammu food and clothing.

(15–18) Should Attilammu leave now, he shall weigh out 10 minas[66] of silver [and] 10 minas of gold.

(19–28) Before Šukriya son of Kurišni; before Pai-tilla son of Keliya; before Šakarakti son of Ar-tirwi;[67] before Akit-tirwi son of Kipi-…; before Tai-šenni son of Aḫušina; before Ithišta son of Ar-tae; before Mušuya son of Aša-[tuni]; before Milk-apu son of A-…; before Teḫpiru, the scribe.

(29–31) (*seal impression*) Seal impression of Šakarakti; (*seal impression*) seal impression of Šukriya; (*seal impression*) seal impression of Pai-tilla.

6. *JEN* V, 446 (JENu 942)

Findspot: Room T16
Publication: Chiera 1934b: pl. 178
Editions: None[68]

Text #6, like text #5, is a self-sale into slavery by an Assyrian. These texts demonstrate, both the "open borders" obtaining during this period, and the economic strength of Arrapḫans vis-à-vis at least some Assyrians, possibly escapees or refugees from the Assyrian state.

Obverse

1 ^{m}*Wa-aš-ka*$_4$*-bi-ya*

2 *ša* KUR *Aš-šu-ur ù*

3 [*r*]*a-ma-an-šu-ma a-na* ÌR.MEŠ-*ti*

4 [*a-n*]*a* ^{m}*Te-ḫi-ip-til-la* DUMU *Pu-ḫi-še-en-ni*

5 [*uš-te-r*]*i-ib-šu šum-ma*

6 [^{m}*Wa-aš-ka*$_4$]-⸢*bi-y*⸣*a ma-am-ma*

7 [KI.BAL^{-a}]*t*[69] *ù i-qa-ab-bi*

8 [*a-na-ku la* Ì]R ^{m}*Te-ḫi-ip-til-la*

9 [*i-na*]-*an-din*

10 [10 MA.NA KÙ.BABBAR *ù* 10] MA.NA KÙ.SIG$_{17}$

11 [*a-na* ^{m}*Te-ḫi-ip-til*]-*la u-ma-al-la*

.

.

.

Reverse

.

.

.

12 [IGI $^{(m)}$*Šú*]*k-ri-ya* DUMU *Ku-ri-iš-ni*

13 ^{NA_4}KIŠIB ^{m}*Ša-te-en-šu-uḫ* AB.BA

14 ^{NA_4}KIŠIB ^{m}DINGIR-*ta-ni ši-*⸢*b*⸣*i*

JEN V, 446

(1–5) Waškapiya of the land of Assyria, of his own accord, enslaved himself for (the benefit of) Teḫip-tilla son of Puḫi-šenni.

(5–11) Should Waškapiya, anyone (*sic*),[70] [abrogate (this agreement)] by announcing: "[I am not] a slave," he shall supply … .[71] He shall pay [to] Teḫip-tilla [10 minas of silver and 10] minas of gold.

…

(12) [Before] Šukriya son of Kurišni.

(13–14) Seal impression of Šaten-šuḫ, witness; seal impression of Ilu-dannu, witness.

7. *JEN* V, 458 (JENu 157a + 157c)

Findspot: Room T15
Publication: Chiera 1934b: pl. 187
Edition: None[72]

Like texts ##5 and 6, text #7 is a self-sale of an Assyrian, here dubbed a "*ḫapiru*," a class of deracinated person in a state of seemingly perpetual economic inferiority and dependence. He is a class of person who is (a) usually foreign to the community in which he finds himself; and (b) of no fixed legal status in that community (unlike, for example, an *ubāru*, a foreign envoy with status in, and support from, the local government to which he is accredited). The *ḫapiru* is thus a marginal person, supports himself accordingly, often by brigandage, mercenary activity, or, as in the case of this text, by selling himself into slavery.[73]

Obverse
1 $^{\ulcorner\text{m}\urcorner}$[74][ÌR]-*ku-bi* ^{LÚ}*ḫa-pí-r*[*u*]
2 *ša* KUR *Aš-šu-ur*
3 *ù* ⸢*ra*⸣-*ma-an-šu-ma a-na*
4 ÌR-*t*[*i*] *a-na* ^{m}*Te-ḫi-ip-til-la*
5 DUMU *Pu-ḫi-še-en-ni uš*-[*te-ri-ib-šu*]
6 *ù šum-ma* ^{m}ÌR-*ku-bi*
7 KI.BAL-^{at}-*ma ù uš-t*[*u*]
8 É ^{m}*Te-ḫi-ip-til-la ú-u*[*ṣ-ṣí*]
9 *ù* 1 LÚ *eṭ-la pu-u*[*ḫ-šu*]
10 *a-na* ^{m}*Te-ḫi-ip-til-la i+n*[*a-an-din*]

---

11 IGI *Mu-uš-te-šup* DUMU *Ḫa*-[*ši-ya*[75]]
12 IGI *Pí-ru* DUMU *Na-iš-k*[*é-el-pè*]
13 IGI *Šu-pa-a-a* DUMU *Ar*-[*ta-tal*]
14 IGI *Ḫa-na-ak-ka*$_4$ DUMU *Še*-[*ka*$_4$-*ru*]
15 IGI *Še-ka*$_4$-*ru* DUMU *Eḫ*-[*li*?-*ya*?]
16 IGI *Ḫa-ma-an-na* DUMU *M*[*a-re*?-*eš*?-*ri*?]
17 IGI *Ni-iḫ-ri-ya* DU[MU *En*?-*na*?-*a*?-*a*?]
18 IGI *Ké-eš-ḫa-a-a* D[UMU]
Lower Edge
19 IGI *Ta-ú-ka*$_4$ DUMU *A*-[ ]
Reverse
20 IGI *Tù-ra-ri* DUMU *Aš*?-[ ]
21 IGI *Ar-te-ya* DUMU SILIM-*pa-li-iḫ*-$^{\ulcorner\text{d}}$IM⸣[76]

22 IGI *Ta-a-a* DUMU *A-pil*-XXX DUB.SAR
23 ^{NA_4}KIŠIB ^{m}*Mu-uš-te-šup* DUMU *Ḫa-*[*ši-ya*]
24 ^{NA_4}KIŠIB ^{m}*Šu-pa-a-a* DUMU *Ar-ta-*[*tal*]
25 ^{NA_4}KIŠIB ^{m}*Pí-*[*ru* DUMU *Na-iš-ké-el-pè*]
26 ^{NA_4}KIŠIB ^{m} [*Ta-a-a*] DUB.SAR [(?)]

JEN V, 458

(1–6) Warad-kûbi, a *ḫapiru* from the land of Assyria, of his own accord, enslaved himself for (the benefit of) Teḫip-tilla son of Puḫi-šenni.

(7–10) Should Warad-kûbi abrogate (this agreement) by leaving the household of Teḫip-tilla, he shall supply to Teḫip-tilla 1 male, a young man, (as) [his] substitute.

(11–22) Before Muš-tešup son of Ḫašiya; before Piru son of Naiš-kelpe; before Šupaya son of Arta-atal; before Ḫanakka son of Šekaru; before Šekaru son of Eḫ-[liya?]; before Ḫamanna son of M[âr?-ešrī?]; before Niḫriya son of [Ennaya?]; before Kešḫaya son of …; before Tauka son of A-…; before Turari son of Aš?-…; before Ar-teya son of Šalim-pāliḫ-adad; before Taya son of Apil-sin, the scribe.

(23–26) Seal impression of Muš-tešup son of Ḫašiya; seal impression of Šupaya son of Arta-atal; seal impression of Piru [son of Naiš-kelpe]; seal impression of [Taya], the scribe.

8. HSS XV, 1 (SMN 3126)

Findspot: Room C28
Publications: Lacheman 1939b: 115; 1955: pl. 1[77]
Editions: Jankowska 1969: 273–75; Zaccagnini 1979c: 17–19; Cassin 1982: 114–17

This document is an exemplar of a general order to mayors (it affects mayors and owners of *dimtu*-settlements), here given to a single mayor of an otherwise unattested town.[78] It appears specially targeted to the authorities of border towns—not just of any territory.[79] No special order, especially from the Arrapḫan crown, would be needed for strictly local police matters, and Muš-teya, sealer of this document, is a king of Arrapḫa. The matters dealt with here are "national," even "international," not local, and seem but a few steps removed from placing these districts on a war footing.

Obverse

1 [*ki-na-an-na a-n*]*a*[80] ^{LÚ}*ḫa-za-an-nu ša* URU *Ta-šu-uḫ-ḫé-*⌜*we*⌝

2 [LUGAL[81] *ṭe*$_4$]-⌜*e*⌝-*ma* ⌜*iš*⌝-*ta-ka*$_4$-*an-šu-nu-*[*ti*]

3 [*at-t*]*a*$^{!?}$-⌜*ma*⌝-*an-nu* ^{LÚ}*ḫa-za-an-nu*

4 [*š*]*a* URU-*šu pa-ṭì-šu i+* ⌜*na*⌝ *li-mì-ti-šu-ma*

5 *i+na*$^{!}$(= ŠA)-*aṣ-ṣa-ar i-ba-aš-ši-i* AN.ZA.KÀR

6 *ù i+na* EDIN.NA *ša* URU-*šu ša na-du*$_4$-*ú*

7 *ù* ^{LÚ}*ḫa-za-an-nu i+na-aṣ-ṣa-ar*

8 *ù i+na pa-ṭì-šu ša* URU-*šu ḫu-ub-tù ša iḫ-bu-*[*t*]*ù*

9 *lu-ú la* ⌜*ya*⌝-*nu* KÚR.MEŠ *ša i-du-ku*

10 ⌜*ù ša*⌝ *i-leq-qú-ú lu-ú la ya-nu ù*

11 ⌜*šum*⌝-*ma i+na* ZAG-*šu ša* URU-*šu ḫu-*⌜*ub*⌝-*tù*

12 *ša iḫ-bu-tù ša* KÚR.MEŠ *ša i-leq-qú-ú*

13 *ù ša i-du-ku i-ba-aš-ši-i*

14 *ù* ^{LÚ}*ḫa-za-*[*a*]*n-nu-ú pì-ḫa-as-sú na-ši*

15 *šum-ma mu-un-*[*n*]*a-ab-tù ša* $^{<\text{KUR?}>}$*Ar-ra-ap-ḫé*

16 *ša iš-tu* [Z]AG-*šu ša* URU [*š*]*á-a-šu*

17 *ša it-ta-bi-tu*$_4$ *ù i+na* KUR *ša-ni-ti*

18 *ša i-ru-bu i-ba-aš-ši*

19 *ù* ^{LÚ}*ḫa-za-an-nu-um-ma pì-ḫa-as-sú na-ši*

20 *i-ba-aš-ši-ma* AN.ZA.KÀR *ša i+na*

Lower Edge

21 *pa-ṭì-šu ša* URU *šá-a-šu*

22 *ša na-du-ú*

23 *ù* ^{LÚ}*ḫa-za-an-nu*

Reverse

24 ⌜*pì*⌝-*ḫa-as-sú na-ši*

25 *ù* ^{LÚ}GAR.KUR $^{\text{LÚ.MEŠ}}$⌜EN.MEŠ⌝

26 AN.ZA.KÀR.MEŠ *ṭup-pá-t*[*i*$^{?}$]

27 *a-na a-ḫi-in-nu-ú*

28 *i+na-an-dì*<*-na*>*-aš-šu-nu-ti*

29 *ù ki-na-an-na-ma ṭe*$_4$-*e-ma*

30 *i-ša-ka-an-aš-šu-nu-ti*

31 *šum-ma iš-t*⌜*u*⌝ A[N].ZA.KÀR-*ma*

32 *ša-a-šu ša*$^{!}$(= KI) ⌜*i*⌝+*na*$^{!}$(= LA)[82] *ḫ*[*u-u*]*b-ti-šu*

33 *š*[*a*] *ú-uṣ-ṣú-ú ša i-ba-aš-ši*

34 *š*[*a*] ⌜KÚR⌝.MEŠ ⌜*i*⌝-*du-ku ù š*[*a*]

35 ⌜*i*⌝-*le*⌜*q-qú-ú*⌝ *i-ba-aš-ši-*⌜*i*⌝

36 *ù* ^{LÚ}EN.MEŠ AN.ZA.KÀR *šá-a-šu*

37 *i+na ar*$^{!}$(= Ù)-*ni ka*$_4$-*ši-id ù*

38 AN.ZA.KÀR *e-leq-qè*
39 [*t*]*e-qè-er-re-ba-ma ù at-tù-nu*
40 [*t*]*a-qà-ab-ba-ma*
41 [*iš-t*]*u šu-du-ti* LÚ *šá-a-šu*
42 [*la it-ti-i*]*q ù* KÚR.MEŠ
43 [ ] ⸢KÚR⸣.MEŠ-*ma*
44 [ ]-*qè* ⸢*ù*⸣ *šum-ma iš-tu*
Upper Edge
45 [*šu-du-ti ša i*]*t-ti-qú i-ba-aš-ši*
46 [*at-ta ṣa*]-*bat-sú-ma*
Left Edge
47 *ù i*+[*n*]*a* É.<GAL> *li-li-ka*$_4$
48 NA$_4$ ^{m}*Mu-uš-te*[*ya* (LUGAL)]
S.I.

HSS XV, 1

(1–2) [The king] issued a directive [as follows] for the mayor of the town of Tašuḫḫe.[83]

(3–5) Each and every mayor shall guard any borderland of his town('s jurisdiction) up to its (furthest) limit.

(5–7) The mayor must guard (any) abandoned *dimtu*,[84] being in the hinterland of his town.

(8–9) No robbery may be committed within the borderland of his town.

(9–10) No enemy may kill or plunder.

(10–14) And if in its (i.e., the town's) borderland any robbery should be committed or any enemy plunder or kill, then the mayor bears the responsibility.

(15–19) If any Arrapḫan fugitive (i.e., from the kingdom of Arrapḫa) flees from the borderland of that town and reaches another land, then the mayor bears any and all responsibility.

(20–24) The mayor bears responsibility for (any) abandoned *dimtu* in the borderland of that town.[85]

(25–30) And the governor shall give tablets individually to each of the *dimtu* owners and he shall issue the directive as follows:

(31–38) "If anyone leaves that *dimtu* for purposes(?) of robbery (or) if any enemy kills or plunders, then the *dimtu* owner (involved) has committed an offense, and I shall take the *dimtu* (from him).

(39–44) You[86] shall approach me and tell me. And that man [shall not] evade (this) proclamation. And … enemies, and … enemies … .[87]

(45–47) And if anyone evades [the proclamation], [you], seize him and have him come to <government> house."[88]

(48) Seal of [King?] Muš-teya. (*seal impression*)

9. HSS XV, 22 (SMN 1136)

Findspot: Room A41
Publication: Lacheman 1955: pl. 23
Edition: None

Text #9 is a list of archers including, where applicable, the officers under whom they serve.

Obverse
1 [^{m}]*A-ka*$_4$*-a-a* ^{m}*Ki-*[*p*]*u*$^{?}$*-uk*<*-kà*$^{?}$> ^{m}*Ši-*[ ]
2 3 LÚ.MEŠ *ša* ^{GIŠ}P⸢A⸣N *ša* ^{m}*Še-*[ ]
3 [^{m}]*Ḫa-ši-ip-til-la* ^{m}*A-kap-še*[(*-en-ni*)]
4 ^{m}*Ni-nu-a-tal* 3 ⸢LÚ⸣.MEŠ *ša* $^{GI[Š}$PAN]
5 *ša* ^{m}*Ši-mi-ka*$_4$*-t*[*al*] ^{m}*Ta-a-ni*
6 ^{m}*Šur-ki-til-l*⸢*a*⸣ [^{m}]*Ú-na-a-a*
7 ^{m}*Ḫa-na-ak-k*[*a*$_4$ 2+] 2 LÚ.MEŠ *ša* ^{GIŠ}P⸢A⸣N
8 *ša* ^{m}*Be-la-a*[*m*]*-ni-ra-ri*
9 ^{m}*En-na-ma-*[*t*]*i* ^{m}*Sí-ka*$_4$*-ar-ri* [(?)]
10 ^{m}*Ki-in-k*[*i-y*]*a* 3 LÚ.MEŠ *ša* [^{GIŠ}PAN]
11 *ša* ^{m}*Ta-*⸢*ú*⸣*-ka* ^{m}ÌR-^{d}<*aš*$^{?}$>*-šur*
12 ^{m}*Še-ḫa-al-*⸢*t*⸣*e* ^{m}*Na-ḫi-iš-šal-mu*
13 ^{m}*En-na-ma-ti* 4 LÚ.MEŠ *ša* ^{GIŠ}PAN
14 ^{m}*Nu-mi-ku-tù ša* ^{GIŠ}PAN
15 ^{m}*Ḫé-es-sú ša* ^{GIŠ}PAN
16 ^{m}*Ut-ḫap-ta-e ša* ^{GIŠ}PAN
(space)
17 10+⸢10⸣ LÚ.MEŠ *ša* ^{GIŠ}PAN *ša*
18 [Š]U$^{?}$ ^{m}*Ḫa-ši-ik-ku* WA-*na* [(?)]
Reverse
19 ^{m}*Ḫu*$^{?}$*-*[*r*]*e-en-ni e-de*$_4$*-nu*
20 ^{m}UD$^{?}$-[x] *e-de*$_4$*-nu*
21 ^{m}*A-*⸢*x-x*⸣*-e e-de*$_4$*-nu*
22 3 LÚ.MEŠ [ ] ⸢*e-de*$_4$⸣-[*nu*$^{?}$]
S.I.

HSS XV, 22

(1–16) Akaya, Kipukka(?), Ši-…; 3 archers (lit. "men of the bow") of Še-… . Ḫašip-tilla, Akap-še[nni?], Ninu-atal; 3 archers of Šimika-atal. Tanu, Šurki-tilla, Unaya, Ḫanakka; [2+] 2 archers of Bêlam-nirari. Enna-mati, Sikarri(?), Kikkiya; 3 [arch]ers of Tauka. Warad-aššur(?), Šeḫal-te, Naḫiš-šalmu, Enna-mati; 4 archers. Numi-kutu, archer. Ḫessu, archer. Utḫap-tae, archer.

(17–18) 20 archers under the command(?) of Ḫašikku … .

(19–22) Ḫu(?)-renni, unattached; UD(?)-…, unattached; A-…-e, unattached. 3 … men, unattached.

10. HSS XV, 5 (SMN 3156)

Findspot: Room C28
Publications: Lacheman 1939b:173; 1955: pl. 5[89]
Edition: Zaccagnini 1979b: 4

This text is a work assignment.[90] The first part has four sections. In each, an individual receives a number of bronze scales. From these scales, it appears that these named men are to fashion three items of armor: body, sleeves, and helmet. These items constitute a (full) set of armor.[91] The second part of the text specifies the overall purpose of the activity: four sets of armor for use by a particular ten-man platoon or squad. Two sets of armor are described as Ḫanigalbatian and two as Arrapḫan. If these types of armor (distinguished in this text by different numbers of scales utilized in each type) reflect differences in Ḫanigalbatian and Arrapḫan equipment standards,[92] then this text is significant, for the text would then imply that the two armies, the imperial (Ḫanigalbatian) and the local (Arrapḫan) are integrated at the level of the ten-man unit,[93] probably a chariot unit.[94]

Obverse

1 5 *ma-ti kùr-ṣí-i[m-t]ù ša* IM-*šu*

2 5 *ma-ti [kùr-ṣí-i]m-tù ša* ⸢*a*⸣-*ḫi-šu*

3 2 *ma-t[i* KI.MI]N *ša*[!] *gur-pí-sú* 1 *li-im* 2 *ma-ti kùr-ṣí-im-tù ša* ZABAR

4 ^{m}*Ni-in-ki-te-šup il-qè*

---

5 5 *ma-ti* KI.MIN [*š*]*a* IM-*šu*

6 3+[2 *m*]*a-ti* KI.MIN [*ša*] *a-ḫi-šu*

7 2 *ma-*⸢*t*⸣*i* ⸢KI⸣.MIN [*ša*] *gur-pí-sú* (erasure)

8 1 [*l*]*i*-[*i*]*m* 2 *ma-ti* [KI.MI]N *ša* ZABAR
9 ^{m}[ ]- ⸢x x⸣ [*il*]-*qè*

---

10 5 *ma*-⸢*ti*⸣ 1 *šu-ši* KI.MIN *ša* IM-*šu*
11 1 [+n *ma-t*]*i* 1 *šu-ši* KI.MIN *ša a-ḫi-šu*
12 [1$^{?}$] *ma-ti* [10+] 30 KI.MIN *ša gur-pí-sú-ma* (erasure)
Lower Edge
13 [n] *ma-ti* 1 *šu-ši* KI.MIN *ša* ZABAR
14 [^{m}*X*]- ⸢*li*⸣-*ya il*-<*qè*>

---

15 [5$^{?}$ *ma*]- ⸢*ti*⸣$^{?}$ KI.MIN *ša* IM-*šu*
Reverse
16 [n] ⸢*ma-ti*⸣ [n$^{?}$+] 20 ⸢K⸣I.MIN *ša a-ḫi-šu*
17 1 *ma-ti* [n$^{?}$+10+] 10 KI.MIN *ša gur-pí-sú*
18 7 *ma-ti* 20 KI.MIN *ša* ZABAR
19 ^{m}*Ḫa-na-a-a il-qè*
20 2 *ta-pa-lu sà*-⸢*r*⸣*i-am ša* ^{KUR}*Ḫa-ni-in-gal-bat*
21 2 *ta-pa-lu* KI.MIN *ša* ^{KUR}*Ar-ra-ap-ḫe*
22 *ša e-ma-an-ti ša* ^{m}*Kur-m*⸢*i*⸣*-še-en-ni*

HSS XV, 5

(1–4) 5 hundred scales for its body (armor), 5 hundred scales for its sleeves, 2 hundred ditto (i.e., scales) for the helmet. 1 thousand 2 hundred bronze scales, Ninki-tešup took.

(5–9) 5 hundred ditto for its body (armor), 4 [+1] hundred ditto for its sleeves, 2 hundred ditto [for] the helmet. 1 thousand 2 hundred bronze ditto, … took.

(10–14) 5 hundred sixty ditto for its body (armor), 1 [+n] hundred sixty ditto for its sleeves, and [1?] hundred 30 [+10] ditto for the helmet …. hundred sixty bronze ditto, …-liya took.

(15–19) … hundred 20 [+n?] ditto for its body (armor), … hundred 20 [+n?] for its sleeves, 1 hundred 10 [+10+n?] ditto for the helmet. 7 hundred 20 bronze ditto, Ḫanaya took.[95]

(20–22) 2 sets of Ḫanigalbat armor, 2 sets of Arrapḫa armor for the 10-man unit of Kurmi-šenni.[96]

11. HSS XIII, 195 (SMN 195)

Findspot: Room A26
Publication: Pfeiffer and Lacheman 1942: 31[97]
Edition: None

Text #11 is a list of military equipment of various sorts. The equipment was, variously, lost, taken from stores, accounted for, and expended in battle.

Obverse

1 [n] ^{GIŠ}PAN.MEŠ *it-ti*
2 [^{m}*Ḫa*]-*ši-ip-a-pu ḫal-qa-at*
3 5 ^{KUŠ}*iš-pa-tu*$_4$
4 30 TA.ÀM GI.MEŠ-*nu*
5 *i-na* ŠÀ-*šu-nu ša na-du-ú*
6 5 *pu-ra-ku*
7 1 ^{GIŠ}PA *ša* KÙ.BABBAR *uḫ-ḫu-zu*
8 1 *né-en-sé-tu*$_4$
9 1 *ṣí-mi-it-tu*$_4$ ^{KUŠ}*a-ša-tu*$_4$ AŠ ŠÀ-*šu*-[*nu* x x]
10 *an-nu-tu*$_4$ *ú*-[*nu-tu*$_4$]
11 *ša* ^{m}*Ḫa-ši-ip-a-pu*
12 *iš-tu*$_4$ *ša-lu-ul-ti* MU$^{\text{-ti}}$
13 *ša uš-te-ṣú-ú*

Reverse

14 3 *ta-pa-lu sà-ri-am ša* IM.MEŠ *ša* ZABAR
15 1-*nu-tu*$_4$ *sà-ri-am ša* IM
16 *ša* GAB 1 MA.[NA *š*]*a* ZABAR
17 1-*nu-tu*$_4$ *sà-ri-am* [*ša*] IM *ša* KUŠ.MEŠ
18 *ša a-ḫi-šu*[-*nu*$^?$ *ša* ZA]BAR
19 5 *gur-pí*-[*sú ša* ZABAR$^?$]
20 3 GÍR.MEŠ [*ša* x x]-*na*
21 ⸢3⸣ GÍR.MEŠ [x x]
22 (destroyed)
23 [x x x]-*šu-ti*
24 *ša aš-bu*
25 [x] GI.MEŠ 6 GI.MEŠ
26 [^{m}*A-ka*]*p-ur-ḫé a-na* KÚR.MEŠ
27 [*it*]-*ta-sú-uk*

HSS XIII, 195

(1–2) [n] bows, (that were) with Ḫašip-apu, are lost.[98]

(3–13) 5 quivers (with) 30 arrows placed in each (quiver); 5 *purāku*-garments;[99] 1 staff, decorated in silver; 1 washbowl; 1 yoke (with) reins.[100] This is the equipment that Ḫašip-apu took out the year before last.

(14–24) 3 sets of bronze body armor; 1 suit of body armor for the chest (weighing) 1 mina of bronze; 1 suit of leather body armor for the arms (i.e., sleeves) … bronze; 5 helmets of [bronze?]; 3 daggers [of] …; 3 daggers … which are present.

(25–27) … arrows, Akap-urḫe shot 6 arrows at the enemy.

12. HSS XV, 99 (SMN 3125)

Findspot: Room C28
Publication: Lacheman 1939b: 173; 1955: pl. 65[101]
Edition: Dosch 2009: 158–59 (text #60)

This text is an inventory of chariots of the two wings of Nuzi's army (better: of the Nuzi contingent of the Arrapḫan army). This and other texts demonstrate that the army was thus divided into two and, furthermore, that this division was not solely used as components of a battle array, but was in force in various administrative contexts such as arms and food distribution. Zaccagnini (1979b: 21–22) observes this and notes actual functional differences between the two wings.[102]

The verb pertaining to some of these chariots and some men (see lines, 1–5 and 17–19) is Akkadian *alāku*. This can mean "to go" but also "to come (back)." Obviously, it makes a difference whether chariots fail to go to battle or fail to come back. Both are possible in this and similar contexts, but, on balance, the latter seems a likelier translation. The nature of battlefield losses seems more important to record because more immediately useful for future planning. Documents such as text #21, below, also point in the direction of this translation. That lengthy list, a "tablet of equipment that is not going/coming back" (line 1), connects the items specified with the (losing) battle at Zizza. Losses from this battle (i.e., items not "coming back") seem to follow logically from the event itself.

In the present text, we do not learn the location of the battle, but we can deduce that, for the Arrapḫan forces, the outcome was devastating. Of fifty-eight chariots of the left wing (line 9), only twenty-four seem to have returned (lines 6–8). The other thirty-four (by subtraction; cf. lines 1–4) appear to have been lost in battle (line 5).[103]

Obverse
1 [ ]-*ti* ^{GIŠ}⸢GIGIR⸣
2 [*ša*] ⸢ŠU ^{m}*Wa-ḫ*⸣*a-*⸢*a*⸣*r-ta-e*
3 [n$^?$+1+] 3 KI.MIN *ša* ŠU ^{m}⸢*Ša*⸣*-ar-te-šup*
4 [n$^?$+1+] 3 KI.MIN *ša* ŠU ^{m}⸢*Ḫa*⸣*-ip-*⸢LUGAL⸣
5 *ù š*[*u-n*]*u la i-il-la-ku*
6 5 KI.MIN *ša* ŠU ^{m}*Še-kàr-til-la*
7 10 KI.MIN *ša* ŠU ^{m}*Kél-te-šup*
8 9 KI.MIN *ša* ŠU ^{m}*Tar-mi-ip-ta-še-ni*
9 ŠU.NIGIN$_2$ 58 ^{GIŠ}GIGIR *ša šu-me-li*
(space)
Reverse
10 [n$^?$+] 6 KI.MIN *ša* ŠU ^{m}*En-na-mu-ša*
11 [n$^?$+] 4 KI.MIN *ša* ŠU ^{m}*Tar-mi-ya*
12 [n$^?$+] 6 KI.MIN *ša* ŠU ^{m}*Ka*$_4$*-i-til-la*
13 [n$^?$+] 5 KI.MIN *ša* ŠU ^{m}*Ni-ḫé-er-te-šup*
14 [n$^?$+] 4 KI.MIN *ša* ŠU ^{m}*Tup-ki-til-la*
15 [n$^?$+2$^?$+] 7 KI.MIN *ša* ŠU ^{m}*Ḫu-ta-a-na-pu-e*
(space)
16 ŠU.NIGIN$_2$ 36 ^{GIŠ}GIGIR *ša* ZAG
17 [^{m}]*Ur-ḫi-til-la* ^{m}*Tar-mi-til-la*
18 [^{m}]*Al-ki-te-šup*
19 [ ] ⸢*ša*⸣ la DU-*ku-ni*

HSS XV, 99

(1–5) … chariot(s) under the command of Waḫri-tae; 4 [+n?] ditto under the command of Šar-tešup; 4 [+n?] ditto under the command of Ḫaip-šarri. *They* are not coming back.

(6–8) 5 ditto under the command of Šekar-tilla; 10 ditto under the command of Kel-tešup; 9 ditto under the command of Tarmip-tašenni.

(9) Total: 58 chariots of the left (wing).

(10–15) 6 [+n?] ditto under the command of Enna-muša; 4 [+n?] ditto under the command of Tarmiya; 6 [+n?] ditto under the command of Kai-tilla; 5 [+n?] ditto under the command of Niḫri-tešup; 4 [+n?] ditto under the command of Tupki-tilla; 7 [+2?] ditto under the command of Ḫutanni-apu.

(16) Total: 26 chariots of the right (wing).

(17–19) Urḫi-tilla, Tarmi-tilla, …, Alki-tešup; … who are not coming back.

13. *JEN* V, 525 (JENu 696)

Findspot: Room T16
Publication: Chiera 1934b: pl. 486
Edition: Chiera and Speiser 1927: 56–60

Text #13 has a simple pattern. It is a narrative, consisting of a series of parallel sections. Each section names one or more individuals, once a *dimtu*-tower, and once the palace, and enumerates his or their or its losses. The predators who take the items are the Assyrians, and the items, except those destroyed, are brought to an individual and/or to a place, which must also be Assyrian. Specifically, the items captured are taken from towns, mostly from Turša, from *dimtu*s (probably meaning both towers and districts), and from and near wooded areas, and from the plain abutting a river. These items are brought *to* other towns and *dimtu*s and once to the house of Aššur-dayyān. The tablet ends with "seal impression of Takku," though no such impression appears on the tablet. Text #13 is lined. Sometimes the lines divide sections, sometimes not.

The individuals victimized are named by place, by patronymic, by status or occupation, or by name alone. The losses include sheep, cattle, barley (burned), and men (both captured and killed). These men, when identified by other than "LÚ," that is, "a man," or a PN, are named as shepherds, palace slaves, a palace shepherd, and a slave. Some men are named by PN and patronymic (i.e., prior to capture they were independent), sometimes with a son or, generally, offspring. In addition to these losses, *dimtu*-towers are destroyed.

Text #13 ("A" in remarks below) and *JEN* VI, 670 ("B") are virtual duplicate texts, extending, at times, to containing the same spelling errors. However, there *are* differences of note. Where the documents overlap directly (i.e., where both tablets are preserved at the same points in the text), "B" contains a slightly fuller text. Significantly, whereas both assert that Takku sealed the tablet ("A" at line 73; "B" at line 61'), only "B" actually bears a seal impression.[104] Therefore, it appears that "A" was a (faulty?) draft, expanded (and thereby corrected?) by "B," which was therefore sealed. Why these texts were retained—especially "B," which one would have expected to be sent on to the palace—remains unclear.[105] "A" is here used as the basic exemplar of the text because it is far better preserved than is "B." Important information preserved in "B" and absent in "A" is noted at the appropriate points in the translation of "A."

Obverse

1 2 *ma-ti* UDU.ḪÁ.MEŠ 2 $^{\text{LÚ.MEŠ}}$SIPA *ša* ^{m}*Wi-ir-zi-ya-e*

2 *iš-tu* URU *Túr-šá a-na* $^{\text{LÚ.MEŠ}}$*Aš-šu-ra-a-ú*

3 *il-te-qú-ú i+na* URU *Ḫa-bu-ú*$^{!}$ (=TAP)-*bá ul-te-ri-bu*

---

4 5 LÚ.MEŠ *ša* ^{m}*Wa-aq-ri-ya* DUMU *Ú-a-az-zi*
5 *iš-tu* AN.ZA.KÀR *Pí-i-e il-te-qú-ma*
6 *i+na* URU *Ta-az-zu-e ul-te-ri-bu*
7 2 LÚ.MEŠ *ša* ^{m}*A-pu-uš-ka*$_4$ DUMU *It-ḫi-ip*-LUGAL
8 *iš-tu* AN.ZA.KÀR *ša Be-e-lu-*⌜*e*⌝$^{!!}$[106]
9 *il-te-qú-ma i+na* AN.ZA.KÀR *ša* ^{m}⌜*P*⌝*ur-na-m*[*i-*(*iz*)*-za*]*-aḫ ul-te-ri-bu*
10 4 LÚ.MEŠ *ša* ^{m}*Ú-na-ap-ta-e* DUMU *Al-ki-te-šup*
11 ^{m}*Pu-ḫi-še-en-ni* DUMU *Wa-an-ti-ya*
12 *ù Pu-ḫi-še-en-ni-ma* DUMU *Ta-a-a it-ti* DUMU-*šu-ma*
13 *iš-tu* AN.ZA.KÀR *ša* ^{m}*Ḫa-iš-te-šup il-te-qú-ma*
14 *i+na* URU *Pár-pa-ra ul-te-ri-bu*

---

15 ^{m}*Ku-tùk-ka*$_4$ DUMU *Ú-ṣú-ur-me-šu ù* ^{m}*A-ki-ya*
DUMU *Gi*$_5$*-mil-li-ya*
16 *iš-tu* URU *Túr-šá il-qú-ma i+na* URU *Pár-pa-ra*
ul-te-ri-bu
17 ^{m}*Ni-im-ki-ya* ^{LÚ}ÈR É.GAL *iš-tu* URU *Túr-šá* <*il*$^{?}$-(*te*$^{?}$-)*qú*$^{?}$(-*ma*$^{?}$)>
18 *i+na* URU *Pár-pa-ra ul-te-ri-bu-ma*

---

19 50 UDU.ḪÁ.MEŠ 2 $^{LÚ.MEŠ}$SIPA *ša* ^{m}*Pa-ak-la-pí-ti*
20 DUMU *En-na-ma-ti iš-tu* AN.ZA.KÀR AN.TA
21 *ša* ^{m}*Te-ḫi-ip-til-la il-te-qú-ú*$^{!?}$ (=NI) *i+na* URU *Ta-az-zu* KI.MIN

---

22 AN.ZA.KÀR *ša* ^{m}*Tar-mi-ya* DUMU *Ú-na-ap-še-en-ni ḫé-pí*
23 1 LÚ-*šu i-du-ku-uš ù ša-nu-ú*
24 LÚ *il-te-qu-ú i+na* AN.ZA.KÀR *ša* ^{m}*Pur-na-*<*mi*>*-za-aḫ*
ul-te-ri-bu
25 3 LÚ.MEŠ *ša* ^{m}*Ḫu-lu-uk-ka*$_4$ DUMU *Zi-in-na-a-*<*a*$^{?}$>
26 *ù i-na* ŠÀ$^{-bi}$*-šu-nu* 1^{-en} *i-du-ku*

Lower Edge

27 *ù* 2 LÚ.MEŠ *i+na* URU *Ki-pár-ra-ap-ḫe* KI.MIN
28 ^{m}*Ḫé-ek-ru ša*[107] ^{m}*En-šúk-rù*

---

29 *iš-tu* URU *Túr-šá il-te-qú-ma*

Reverse

30 *i+na* URU *Ki-pár-ra-ap-ḫe ul-te-ri-bu*
31 1 ÈR$^{-dì}$ *ša* ^{m}*Tar-mi-ya*
32 DUMU *Ú-na-ap-še-en-ni iš-tu* URU *Túr-šá*

33 *il-te-qú i+na* URU *Ki-pár-ra-ap-ḫe* KI.MIN
34 ^{m}*Ḫu*$^{!}$*-zi-ri* ^{LÚ}SIPA *ša* É.GAL$^{-lì}$
35 *i-du-ku-uš*

---

36 ^{m}*A-ni-na-pí ù* ^{m}*Bal-ṭù-ka*$_{4}$*-ši-*<*id*>[108] 2 LÚ.MEŠ
37 *ša* ^{m}*Ta-ak-ku iš-tu* URU *Túr-šá il-te-qú*
38 *i+na* É *ša* ^{m}*Aš-šur*-DI.KU$_{5}$ *aš-bu*

---

39 DUMU-*šu ša* ^{m}*Šur-ki-til-la iš-tu* GIŠ.TIR *il-qu-ma*
40 <*i-na*> URU *Pár-pa-ra ul-te-ri-bu*

---

41 ^{m}*Ta+ a-nu ša* ^{m}*Ú-na-ap-ta+ e i+na* URU *Ki-pár-ra-ap-ḫe* KI.MIN
42 ^{m}*Er-wi-ḫu-ta ša* ^{m}*It-ḫi-til-la* DUMU *Šúk-ri-ya*$^{!}$
43 *iš-tu* URU *Túr-šá* TI *i+na* URU *Ta-az-zu* KI.MIN

---

44 ^{m}*Pu-ḫi-še-en-ni ù*
45 ^{m}*A-ni-na-pí iš-tu* URU *Túr-šá*
46 *il-te-qú-ma i-na* <AN.ZA.KÀR>[109] *Mu-ul-ḫa-a-ni aš-bu*
47 ^{m}*Ar-ši-mi-ka*$_{4}$ ^{LÚ}ÈR É.GAL *iš-tu*
48 URU *Túr-šá il-qú-ma i+na* URU *Ḫa-bu-bá* KI.MIN
49 ^{m}*Še-el-la-pa-*<*i*> DUMU *Šúk-ri-ya*
50 *iš-tu* URU *ša* ^{m}*Ta-a-ku il-te-qú-ma*
51 *i+na* AN.ZA.KÀR *Mu-ul-ḫa-ni* KI.MIN
52 AN.ZA.KÀR *ša* ^{m}*Na-nu-pé-er-ra ḫé-pí*
53 ^{m}*Ḫa-na-tù it-tì* [*š*]*e-er-ri-šu il-te-qú-ma*
54 *i+na* AN.ZA.KÀR *ša* ^{m}⸢*Pur*⸣*na-mi*$^{!}$*-iz-za-aḫ* KI.MIN
55 DUMU-*šu ša* ^{m}*Šúk-ri-te-šup* DUMU *Ša-ma-ḫul*
56 *i+na ú-sal-li il-te-qú i+na* URU *Ki-pár-ra-ap-ḫe* <*ul-te-ri-bu*>

---

57 ^{m}*Ta-a-a ù* ^{m}*Šúk-ri-pa-*<*pu*$^{?}$> *iš-tu*
58 AN.ZA.KÀR *ša* É.GAL *ša a-aḫ* GIŠ.TIR
59 *il-qu-ú i+na* AN.ZA.KÀR
60 *ša* ^{m}*Pur-na-mi-iz-za-aḫ ul-te-ri-bu*
61 ^{m}*Ḫa-ši-pa-pu* AŠ *ú-sal-li* TI$^{-qí}$

Upper Edge

62 *i-na* URU *Ki-pár-ra-ap-ḫe*
63 *ul-te-ri-bu*
64 DUMU-*šu* ^{m}*Ḫa-lu*$^{!}$(=KU)*-še-en-ni iš-tu* URU *Túr-šá il-te-qú-ma*
65 *i+na* URU *Ki-pár-ra-ap-ḫe ul-te-ri-bu*
66 ^{m}*Qí-pu* ^{LÚ}ÈR É.GAL *iš-tu*

67 URU *Túr-šá il-te-qú* NA? ḪA?

Left Edge

68 2 *ma-ti* ANŠE ŠE *ša* ^{m}*Ta-ak-ku i+na* URU *Túr-šá*

69 *ša šar-pu* ^{m}*A-ḫu-ku-ya ka-dú* < >

70 <AN.ZA.KÀR>[110] *ša* É.GAL *ša pí-i* GIŠ.TIR AŠ URU *T*[*úr*?-*šá*?]

⸢i⸣l-te-qú

71 AN.ZA.KÀR *ša I-ri-mu ḫ⸢é⸣-pí*

72 2 LÚ 6 GUD *il-qú-ú*

73 ^{NA_4}KIŠIB ^{m}*Ta-ak-ku*

JEN V, 525

(1–3) They took 2 hundred sheep and 2 shepherds of Wirziyae from the town of Turša to the Assyrians, having brought (them [i.e., sheep and shepherds]) into the town of Ḫabūba.

(4–6) They took 5 men of Waqriya son of Ụazzi from the *dimtu* of Pie and brought (them) into the town of Tazzu.

(7–9) They took 2 men of Apuška son of Itḫip-šarri from the *dimtu* of Belu(e) and brought (them) into the *dimtu* of Purnamiz-zaḫ.[111]

(10–14) They took 4 men of Unap-tae son of Alki-tešup (and) Puḫi-šenni son of Wantiya and Puḫi-šenni son of Taya with his son, from the *dimtu* of Ḫaiš-tešup[112] and brought (them) into the town of Parpara.

(15–16) They took Kutukka son of Uṣur-mêšu and Akiya son of Gimilliya from the town of Turša and brought (them) into the town of Parpara.

(17–18) <They? took?>[113] Nimkiya, a palace slave, from the town of Turša, and they brought (him) into the town of Parpara.

(19–21) They took 50 sheep (and) 2 shepherds of Pakla-piti son of Enna-mati from the eastern *dimtu* of Teḫip-tilla[114] (and) ditto (i.e., "brought [them]") into the town of Tazzu.

(22–24) The *dimtu*(-tower) of Tarmiya son of Unap-šenni[115] was destroyed. They killed one of his men and they took away a second man, bringing (him) into the *dimtu* of Purnamiz-zaḫ.

(25–27) From amongst 3 men of Ḫulukka son of Zinnaya, they killed 1 and ditto (i.e., "brought") 2 men into the town of Kip-arrapḫe.

(28–30) Ḫekru of (i.e., belonging to) En-šukru

---

they took from the town of Turša and brought into the town of Kip-arrapḫe.

(31–33) They took 1 slave of Tarmiya son of Unap-šenni[116] from the town of Turša; ditto (i.e., "they brought [him]") into the town of Kip-arrapḫe.

(34–35) They killed Ḫuziri, a palace shepherd.

(36–38) They took Anin-api and Balṭu-kašid, 2 men of Takku, from the town of Turša, (and) they are presently in the house of Aššur-dayyān.[117]

(39–40) They took the son of Šurki-tilla from the forest and brought (him) <into> the town of Parpara.

---

(41) Ditto (i.e., "They brought") Tanu of (i.e., belonging to) Unap-tae[118] into the town of Kip-arrapḫe.

(42–43) They took Erwi-ḫuta of (i.e., belonging to) Itḫip-tilla son of Šukriya from the town of Turša; ditto (i.e., "they brought [him]") into the town of Tazzu.

(44–46) They took Puḫi-šenni[119] and Anin-api from the town of Turša, and they are presently in <the *dimtu* of> Mulḫani.

(47–48) They took Ar-šimika, a palace slave, from the town of Turša and ditto (i.e., "brought [him]") into the town of Ḫabūba.

(49–51) They took Šellapai son of Šukriya from the town of Taku and ditto (i.e., "brought [him]") into the *dimtu* of Mulḫani.

(52) The *dimtu*(-tower) of Nanuperra was destroyed.

(53–54) They took Ḫanatu together with his offspring and ditto (i.e., "brought [them]") into the *dimtu* of Purnamiz-zaḫ.

(55–56) They took the son of Šukri-tešup son of Šamaḫul by the river side; <they brought (him)> into the town of Kip-arrapḫe.

(57–60) They took Taya and Šukrip-apu from the palace *dimtu* at the edge of the forest; they brought (them) into the *dimtu* of Purnamiz-zaḫ.

(61–63) They took Ḫašip-apu by the riverside; they brought (him) into the town of Kip-arrapḫe.

(64–65) They took the son of Ḫalu-šenni from the town of Turša and brought (him) into the town of Kip-arrapḫe.

(66–67) They took Qîpu, a palace slave, from the town of Turša … .

(68–69) 2 hundred homers of barley of (i.e., belonging to) Takku, in the town of Turša, which were burned.[120]

(69–70) They took Aḫu-kuya together with (*sic*) <   > the palace <*dimtu*> at the entrance to the forest in the town of Turša(?).

(71) The *dimtu*(-tower) of Iripu was destroyed.

(72) They took 2 men (and) 6 oxen.

(73) Seal impression of Takku.[121]

14. HSS XIII, 383 (SMN 383)

Findspot: Room T19
Publication: Pfeiffer and Lacheman 1942: 72[122]
Edition: None[123]

This text is linked to text #13 by at least one common toponym and by context. Captured items are brought to Kip-arrapḫe. Chariots (and other forces?) based in Tazzu (probably) raid into the countryside, capturing livestock, killing people, and setting forest land on fire. That the attackers are Assyrian follows from the GN(s), which are associated with Assyria in text #13. That the victims are Arrapḫans follows from the findspot of this tablet. Like text #13, this document comes from the Nuzi archives of the family of Teḫip-tilla son of Puḫi-šenni. Thus the connections of the actions here described to the events noted in text #13 are beyond doubt.

Obverse
1 1 [x x x]
2 URU [x x x]
3 *ḫa-ab-*tu_4 ⸢*ù*⸣
4 KI-IB-ZU *i-na* [x]
5 URU *Ki-pá-ar-ra-ap-ḫe*
6 *šu-ru-ub ù*
7 KI-IB-ZU [*a*$^{?}$]-*na*$^{?}$
8 ^{LÚ}*ḫa-za-*[*an-nu*]
9 *ša* URU *Ki-*[*pá-ar-ra-ap-ḫe*]
Reverse
10 *na-din*
11 ^{GIŠ}GIGIR.MEŠ *ù* [x x]
12 *iš-tu* URU *Ta-*[*az*$^{?}$*-zu*$^{?}$(*-e*$^{?}$)]
13 *i-na* EDIN *uk-te-eš-*[*ši-id*]
14 GUD.MEŠ UDU.MEŠ *iḫ-ta-ab-tù*
15 LÚ.MEŠ *id-du-ku*
16 *ù* ^{GIŠ}TIR$^{!}$.TIR$^{!}$.MEŠ[124]
17 *iš-ta-ra-ap*
Upper Edge Destroyed

HSS XIII, 383

(1–10) 1 … the town of … were taken away, and KIBZU[125] was/were brought into the town of Kip-arrapḫe and … KIBZU was/were given to(?) the mayor of Kip-arrapḫe.

(11–17) Chariots and … from the town of Ta[zzu?] raided the open country. They took away oxen (and) sheep. They killed people and set fire to the forest(!) land.

15. HSS XVI, 393 (SMN 3255)

Findspot: Room D3
Publication: Lacheman 1958: 115[126]
Edition: None[127]

This tablet, from the main mound, was part of the local government's records. Texts ## 13 and 14, similar in content, were presumably meant for the same destination. The government, it appears, was meant to make good the losses enumerated in these texts, in the aftermath of the Assyrian military success. That the city of Aššur is mentioned here as the place where some of the lost goods ended up further demonstrates that the Assyrians were the hostile force alluded to in these tablets. Other GNs from texts ## 13 and 14 further link this text with the events earlier described. The disposition of some of the slaves as well as their PNs suggest that at least some of the erstwhile slaves were Assyrians. That Assyrians did become slaves in Arrapḫa is already known through such documents as texts ##5–7.

Obverse

.
.
.
1 *i-na* ⸢x⸣ GAL *a-*[*ši-ib*]
2 ^{m}*Ar-*[*ru*]*-um-pa* ÌR *ša* [x x x x]
3 *iš-tu* URU *Túr-šá it-*[*ta-bi-it*]
4 *i-na* URU *Ki-pár-ra-ap-ḫe*
5 *i-te-ru-ub*
6 *um-ma* ^{m}*Ḫa-a-pur-ḫé-ma*
7 ^{m}*Zi-iz-za* ÌR*-ya ni-*[x x x]
8 *iš-tu* URU *Túr-šá it-ta-bi-*[*it*]
9 *i-na* URU *Ki-pár-ra-ap-ḫe-we*
10 *i-te-ru-ub*
11 *um-ma* ^{m}*Tù-ra-ar-te-šup-*<*ma*>

Lower Edge
12 ^{m}*Ṣí-il-la-ku-bi* ÌR-*ya*
13 *iš-tu* URU *Ka-*<*ra*>[128]*-na it-ta-bi-it*
14 *i-na* URU *Aš-š*[*ur*] *a-ši-ib*
Reverse
15 ^{m}*Ip-ša-ḫa-lu* ÌR *ša*
16 ^{m}*Te-ḫi-ip*-LUGAL *ša* URU *Na-at-ma-né iš-tu* ⸢IM ar⸣-*ka*$_4$-*aš-še il-te-qu-ú*
17 *i-na* É ^{md}IM-[x x x]-*na*-[x] ⸢*i-na* URU *Aš-šur a-ši-ib*⸣
18 *um-ma* ^{m}*Ip-ša-ḫa-lu-*<*ma*> 1 ÌR-*ya*
19 ^{md}[X]-*ri*-[x] *ša* URU DINGIR-*áb*$^{!}$-*ra*$^{!}$-*še-mi-we*[129]
20 *iš-tu* [URU *Ka-ti*[130]]-*ri-we il-*[*te-qú-ú*]
21 *ù i-na-a*[*n-n*]*a i-na* É-*šu a-ši-ib*
22 *um-ma* ^{m}[*En*$^{?}$-*na*$^{?}$]-*pa-li-ma ša* [x x x]
23 ^{m}*Pá-i-til*-[*la*] ÌR-*ya* BA-*li*-[x x]
24 *i-na* URU *Na-at-ma-né* ⸢x⸣ [x x x]
25 *ù* ^{m}*Aš*-[…]-*šá-a-ni* É.MEŠ ⸢x⸣ [x x x]
26 [x x x x] *ù i-na-an-na* [x x x]

.
.
.

HSS XVI, 393

(1) … dwells.

(2–5) Arrumpa, slave of …, has fled from the town of Turša (and) has entered into the town of Kip-arrapḫe.

(6–10) Thus Ḫap-urhe: "Zizza, my …(?) slave, has fled from the town of Turša (and) has entered into the town of Kip-arrapḫe."

(11–14) Thus Turar-tešup: "Ṣilli-kûbi, my slave, has fled from the town of Karāna (and now) resides in the city of Aššur."

(15–17) They took Ipša-ḫalu, slave of Teḫip-šarri, of the town of Natmane, from …; he resides in the house of Adad-…-na-… in the city of Aššur.

(18–21) Thus Ipša-ḫalu: "They took 1 of my slaves, …-ri-… of the town of Ilabra(t)-šemī, from the town of Katiri, and now he resides in his (own) house."[131]

(22–26) Thus [Enna?]-pali: "… Pai-tilla, my slave, … in the town of Natmane … and Aš-…-šāni, … houses … and now …

16. *EN* 9/3, 472 (SMN 3266)

Findspot: Room D3
Publication: Lacheman and Owen 1995: 312
Edition: None

Like other texts in this group, this document lists items "taken" and "brought." In this case, the spoil consists of oxen[132] taken from Arrapḫan to Assyrian towns. Several GNs are familiar elsewhere in the group. It is repeatedly noted that Assyrians do the taking. This text comes from the same archive as text #15.

Obverse

1 *um-ma* ^{m}*Um-pí-ya-ma* 4 GUD.[MEŠ *iš-tu*]
2 URU GEŠTIN-*na* $^{\text{LÚ.[ME]Š}}$*Aš-šu-ra-i*$^{!}$(=BI)-⸢*ú*⸣ [*il-te-qú-ú*]
3 *i+na* URU *Tar-mi-ya-we uš-te-*[*r*]*i-*[*bu*]

---

4 *um-ma* ^{m}[*U*]*m-pí-ya-ma* 1 ⸢GUD⸣ [*i*]*š-tu*
5 URU GEŠTIN-*na* $^{\text{LÚ.MEŠ}}$*Aš-šu-ra-*⸢*i*⸣*-ú il-*[*te-qú-ú*]
6 *i+na* ⸢U⸣RU *In-ta-rù*/*aš-we uš-te-ri-b*[*u*]

---

7 [*um-ma* ^{m}]⸢*A*$^{?}$*-k*⸣$a_4$$^{?}$*-a-a-ma* 6 GUD.MEŠ
8 [*iš-tu*] URU *Ka-r*[*a-(an-)na*]*-we* $^{\text{LÚ.M[EŠ]}}$*Aš-*[*šu-ra-i-ú*]
9 [*il*]*-te-qú-ú ù* ⸢x x⸣ [ ]
10 [$^{\text{L]Ú?.MEŠ}}$SA-TAB-B[A$^{?}$] UŠ ⸢*ù*⸣$^{?}$ [ ]
11 [ ] ⸢x⸣ [ ]

———————————————— ?

12 [*um*$^{?}$]- ⸢*ma*$^{?}$ ^{m}*Ḫa-ši*⸣$^{?}$-[*ip*$^{?}$*-ti*]*l*$^{?}$*-la-ma* ⸢x x⸣*-a*
13 2 GUD.MEŠ-*ya* $^{\text{⸢LÚ⸣.MEŠ}}$ *Aš-šu-ra-*⸢*i*⸣*-ú*
14 *i+na* URU *I-la-ab-*[*ra*]*-aš-še-*[*mi uš-te-ri-bu*]
15 *um-ma* LÚ.MEŠ *ša* U[RU$^{?}$] *a*$^{?}$ [ ]
16 IN.NU.MEŠ *a-*[*na*$^{?}$ GU]D$^{?}$.MEŠ [ ]
17 *ù* GUD.MEŠ ⸢x⸣ ^{m}*Ak-*[ ]
18 [($^{?}$)] GUD.MEŠ$^{!}$(=ME) NI ⸢x⸣ [ ] ⸢x x⸣ [ ]

---

19 [*um-m*]*a* ^{m}*Ḫu*$^{?}$-⸢*ti*⸣$^{?}$-[*ya*$^{?}$]*-ma* PA$^{?}$ [ ]
20 [ ] ⸢x x⸣ [ ]
.
.
.

rest of obverse, lower edge, start of reverse destroyed

Reverse

.

.

.

21 2 ⸢GUD$^{?}$ *ù*⸣$^{?}$ 1$^{?}$ [ ]

22 ⸢*ù*⸣$^{?}$/UDU *i+na* URU ⸢x⸣ [ ]

23 [n$^{?}$ U]DU$^{?}$.MEŠ 1 GUD [ ]

24 ^{m}*Ni-ik*-AN(-)[ ] ⸢x x⸣[ ] ⸢x x⸣ [ ]

25 *um-ma* ^{m}*Pil-maš-še-m*[*a*] ⸢x⸣ [ ]

26 2 GUD.MEŠ-*ya* [ ]

27 *ù i+na* URU [ ] ⸢x⸣ [ ]

rest of reverse not inscribed

EN 9/3, 472

(1–3) Thus Umpiya: "Assyrians [took] 4 oxen [from] the town of Karāna, bringing (them) to the town of Tarmiya."

(4–6) Thus Umpiya: "Assyrians took 1 ox [from] the town of Karāna, bringing (it) to the town of Intaru (or: Intaš)."

(7–11) Thus Akaya(?): "Assyrians took 6 oxen [from] the town of Karāna, and ....

--- (?)

(12–18) Thus Ḫašip-tilla(?): ... "Assyrians [brought?] 2 of my oxen to the town of Ilabra(t)-šemī. Thus the men of the town(?) (of) ...: "Straw for(?) the oxen(?) .... And Ak-... ... oxen .... Oxen ....

(19–20) Thus Ḫutiya(?): "...."

....

(21–27) .... 2 oxen(?) and(?) 1(?) ... and(?)/sheep(?) (brought??) to the town of ... . n sheep(?), 1 ox, Nik-AN-... (brought??).

Thus Pilmašše: "... 2 of my oxen ... and into the town of ... ."

17. HSS XVI, 328 + *EN* 10/2, 136 (SMN 656+SMN 1760B [=1695?])

Findspots: Room A23 + A23

Publications: Lacheman 1958: 94 (HSS XVI, 328 only)[133]; Fincke 1998a: 330; (*EN* 10/2, 136 only)

Editions: Lewy 1959: 24–25 (HSS XVI, 328 only)[134]; Fincke 1998b: 376–77

The pieces of this tablet were found in the suburban Nuzi house of Šilwa-tešup "son of the king." Both private and government texts were stored in this official's private compound. This text may fit into the latter category. It appears to list the notables of precisely those towns and *dimtu*s to which the Assyrians took items according to text #13. The PNs are conspicuously Akkadian for the most part (not Hurrian as is most common in Arrapḫa[135]). Aššur-dayyān (line 12) is probably the very individual mentioned in text #13 as having received two men of Arrapḫa (lines 36–38). The reason the men in this text are singled out is unknown. It is perhaps they who must be dealt with in the recovery of the "lost" goods.[136] The recently recovered last eight lines of this text suggest as much. The surviving isolated words might suggest disposition or return of Arrapḫan prisoners of war.

Obverse

1 ^{m}*Tul-pí*-LUGAL

2 ^{m}*Ku*$^{!}$(= ŠU)-*ul-pè-en*-DI.KU$_5$[137]

3 *ša* URU *Ḫa-bu-ba*

4 ^{m}MI.NI-^{d}MAR.TU *ša* URU *Ta-az-zu-e*

5 ^{m}*Pur-na-mi-za-aḫ ù*

6 ^{m}*Pu-un-né-e-a ša*

7 AN.ZA.KÀR *Pur-na-mi-iz-za-aḫ*

8 ^{m}*Ša-aš-šur*$^{!}$(= ŠÚK)-SIG$_5$.GA ^{LÚ}*ḫa-za-an-nu*

9 *ša* URU *Pár-pá-ra*

10 ^{m}*Be-lu-qar-ra-ad*

11 ^{LÚ}*ḫa-za-an-nu ša* URU *Ki-pár-ra-ap-ḫe*

12 ^{m}*Aš-šur*$^{!}$(= ŠÚK)-DI.KU$_5$ *ša* URU DINGIR-*ab-ra-aš-še-mi*

13 ^{m}DINGIR-KAM *ša* AN.ZA.KÀR *Mu-ul-ḫa-ni* [x x]

Lower Edge

14 [*an-nu-t*]*u*$_4$ LÚ.MEŠ

Reverse

.

.

.

15 [ ] ⸢x x x⸣ [ ]

16 [ ] ⸢$^{LÚ?.MEŠ}$⸣$^{!?}$ *Ar-ra-ap-ḫa-* ⸢*ú*⸣- [(?)]

17 [U]RU.DIDLI

18 [ ] *ka*$_4$*-an-na-ti*

19 [ ] ⸢x⸣ x *x-ni*

20 [*a*]-*i-ka*$_4$-*am-me-e*
21 [ ] ⌜x⌝ LÚ? AZ ZU RI/UŠ
22 [ ] ⌜*ù*⌝ *li-il-li-kà*

HSS XVI, 328 + *EN* 10/2, 136

(1–13) Tulpi-šarri (and) Kulpen-dayyān of the town of Ḫabūba; Ṣilli-amurri of the town of Tazzu; Purnamiz-zaḫ and Punniya of the *dimtu* of Purnamiz-zaḫ;[138] Ša-aššur-damqa, mayor of the town of Parpara; Bêlu-qarrād, mayor of the town of Kip-arrapḫe; Aššur-dayyān of the town of Ilabra(t)-šemī; Ilu-êriš of the *dimtu* of Mulḫani ...

(14) These are the men ...[139]

(15–22) .... Arrapḫans .... towns .... fetters(?) .... somewhere .... and let him go (or: "he should go").

18. HSS XIII, 63 (SMN 63)

Findspot: R76[140]
Publication: Pfeiffer and Lacheman 1942: 11[141]
Edition: None

This short document is, at one level, simple to understand. It is a note listing two sets of equipment removed from a storehouse in a given month. Each outfit was distributed to different parties at different places on different occasions. The occasions involve, respectively, Babylonians and Assyrians. And killing takes place. Simple.

But this text abounds in obscurities. Are the Babylonians, and, later in the text, Assyrians, killing or being killed? Who are their opponents? Ḫanigalbatians? Arrapḫans? Each other? Unnamed others? Are the opponents even the same in each case? (We do not know friend from foe.) Why are they mentioned together, having precisely analogous positions in the text? And, especially, why are they mentioned together, since the events take place in two different places, perhaps even at opposite ends of the Arrapḫan geographical horizon, rendering a common logistical connection unlikely? Some key geographical names are obscure. Where is NašBAT (and is "Našbat" the correct spelling of this name?)? Where is Taribatue? Questions, questions. In sum, we do not have any clear idea regarding the actors, the actions, the stage, or the circumstances of this text. In the group of texts comprising this chapter, "Akkad" is isolated to this document.

Therefore, we can reach no firm (or even shaky) conclusion regarding Babylonian involvement in the Arrapḫa-Assyria struggle marking the end of Nuzi.

The issue of logistics, mentioned above, is tied up with the direct function of the text. Both the military events *and* the stores removed from the storehouse occur in the Arrapḫan month of Impurtannu, probably March-April.[142] The events upon which we focus serve, at least, as a date formula: "Expenditures were made at the same time that events X and Y transpired."[143] But there is probably more to it than that. In the case of the Babylonians, there seems to be little other than date to join the events. It is different with the Assyrians. The Assyrians are involved in Taribatu and the items taken are meant for Taribatu. Thus it looks like the first item, if linked with the Babylonians, has an unclear relationship to the event.[144] By contrast, the second item is given to a town involved in an Assyrian military action.

What *is* clear (if only partially) is that, if Nuzi is reacting to news contained in this text, it is to Assyrian activity. Babylonia, as before, seems not to have played a role against Arrapḫa, at least not an obvious one.

Obverse

1 1-*nu-tu*$_4$ TÚG.MEŠ

2 *te-er-de*$_4$*-en-nu a-dì-i*

3 *ša ḫul-la-an-nu*

4 *a-na* ^{m}*Um-pí-ya* DUMU *Ta-wa-re-en-til-la*

5 *šum-ma* LÚ.MEŠ *ša* KUR *Ak-ka*$_4$*-dì*

6 *i-na* ITI-^{hi} *Im-pur-tan-nu*

7 *i-na* KUR *Na-áš*-BAT

8 *i-duk-ku-uš-šu-nu-ti*

9 1-*nu-tu*$_4$ TÚG.MEŠ

10 *te-er-de*$_4$*-en-nu*

11 *a-na* LÚ.MEŠ *ta-al-mi*

Reverse

12 *ša* URU *Ta-ri-ba-tú-e*[145]

13 *šum-ma* LÚ.MEŠ

14 *ša* KUR *A-šur*

15 *i-na* URU *Ta-ri-ba-tú-e*$^{!}$

16 *i-na* ITI-^{hi} *Im-pur-tan-nu*

17 *i-duk-ku-uš-šu-nu-*<*ti*>

18 *an-nu-tu*$_4$

19 *i-na* ITI-^{hi}

20 *Im-pur-tan-nu*

21 ⌜*iš*⌝*-tu* É *na-kam-ti*

22 ^{m}*Ti-ir-wi-na-tal*
23 *na-áš-ru*

HSS XIII, 63

(1–8) 1 second-rank outfit, including blanket/wrap, to Umpiya son of Tawaren-tilla (at the time) when men of the land of Akkad were killed[146] (or: killed them) in the month of Impurtannu in the land of NašBAT.

(9–17) 1 second-rank outfit for the *talmu*[147]-men of the town of Taribatu(e), (at the time) when men of the land of Assyria were killed (or: killed them) in the town of Taribatu(e) in the month of Impurtannu.

(18–23) These (items) were removed in the month of Impurtannu from the storehouse by Tirwin-atal.

19. HSS XV, 29[148] (SMN 2039+2238)

Findspot: Room N120[149]
Publications: Lacheman 1939b: 195; Lacheman 1955: pl. 28
Edition: Dosch 2009: 152–54 (text: #58)

Texts ##19, 20, and 21 are lists of men, horses, and equipment that failed to return from (battle) in the town of Zizza.[150] Each list is subdivided according to the military officer in charge of the lost items. Totals are then given. To the extent that the names of the officers survive, each list deals with the same officers, all belonging to the left (wing) of the army. Note that another text, HSS XV, 114, enumerates horses under the command of these same individuals, again designated as belonging to the left (wing).[151] In addition, the left (wing) is there identified as "of the land of Ḫa-… ." Traces of the rest of this toponym survive and seem to preclude the restoration "Ḫanigalbat," that is, Mittanni.[152] This conclusion is consistent with the PNs linked with the left (wing) in various texts. They are "local" names, that is, names consistent with the general Nuzi onomasticon. They are charioteers, platoon leaders.[153] That Ḫanigalbatian soldiers bear a different sort of name seems borne out by the examples in text #24. Since HSS XV, 114 fails to mention either the purpose of the list or any particular battlefield, that and similar documents are not treated here, despite the presence there of these same officers.

Text #19 describes the loss ("[they] did not come back") of men and horses at the battle at the town of Zizza. The first segment (lines 1–8) is self-contained. It lists (six or more) horses belonging to specific individuals, (all) under the command of a specific officer. Because of the content of the rest of the document, I assume this list consists of lost animals.

The rest of the text is not totally clear, but the following interpretation seems least strained. Human losses are listed by commanders under whose authority the dead soldiers (and a horse) served. These losses are then summarized (lines 38–42) in a clear fashion: thirteen men whose horses are "full"[154] and ten or more men dubbed *šukituḫlu*[155] That summary is followed by a total of the human losses and that of a single horse from the army's left wing that fought at Zizza.[156]

Since the losses are clearly defined in this summary, designations of "*malû*-men" in the body of the text (lines 10, 11, etc.) do not mean "full-men," but, elliptically, "men with full horses." This is made explicit in line 32. The partially effaced final totals accord reasonably well with the individual numbers surviving in this partially destroyed text. Unaccountably, three people are referred to by their horses in one section (lines 22–24) and probably in two other sections as well (lines 27–28, 32–33). The one equine fatality listed in the summary (line 40) likely refers to the detail in line 18.[157]

Obverse

1 1 ŠU ⸢x⸣ [ ] ANŠE.KUR.RA-*šú ša* $^{<m>}$*Ip-š[á-ḫ]a-lu*
2 ANŠE.KUR.[R]A [*š*]*a* ^{m}*El-ḫi-ip-til-la*
3 ANŠE.[KUR].RA *ša* ^{m}*Ta-mar-ta-e*
4 ANŠE.[K]UR.RA [*š*]*a* ^{m}*Še-*⸢*en*⸣*-na-ta-a-ti*
5 2 + [2 L]Ú.MEŠ *an-nu-tu*$_4$ ANŠE.KUR.RA-*šú-*[*nu*]
6 1 [AN]ŠE.KUR.R[A] *ša* ^{m}*Šúk-ra-a-pu*
7 [1$^{?}$ ANŠ]⸢E.KUR.RA⸣ *ša* ^{m}*Ḫa-ši-ya* [ ]
8 *ša* ŠU ^{m}⸢*A*⸣*-ru-pa-ša-aḫ*

---

9 ^{m}*Mu-ut-t*[*a*]-⸢*ki*$^{?}$*-il*$^{??}$⸣ ^{m}(erasure) [^{m}]
10 3 LÚ *an-nu-*⸢*ti*⸣ *ma-lu-ú* [*š*]*a* ŠU ^{m}*Wa-aḫ-*⸢*ri-ta*⸣*-e*

---

11 ^{m}*Tar-mi-ya* [^{m}*Z*]*i-k*⸢*é*⸣ [2 L]Ú *ma-lu-ú*
12 ^{m}*Šúk-*[*r*]*i-te-*⸢*šup*⸣ $^{<m?>}$⸢x x⸣*-te-šup* 2 LÚ *šu-k*[*i*]*-tuḫ-lu*
13 *ša* Š[U] ^{m}*Ka*$_4$*-w*[*i-in-n*]*i*

---

14 ^{m}*Pa-i-til-la m*[*a-lu*]-⸢*ú*⸣ ^{m}*Ki-pa-li šu-ki-tuḫ-lu*
15 *ša* ŠU ^{m}*A-kip-š*[*e-en*]*-ni*

---

16 ^{m}*Ḫa-na-ka*$_4$ ^{m}*Ka*$^{!}$-⸢*i*⸣*-te-šup* DUMU *A-ka*$_4$*-wa-ti-il*
17 ^{m}*A-ka*$_4$*-wa-ti-il* D⸢UM⸣U *Pa-at-ti-ya* 3 ⸢LÚ⸣ *ma-lu-ú*
18 1 ANŠE.KUR.RA *ša*$^{!}$ ^{m}*Tar-mi-til-la* DUMU *Tù-ra-ri*

19 *ša* ŠU ^{m}*Ti-e-eš-ur-ḫe*

---

20 ^{m}*Šu-mu*$^{!}$*-ul-lì-ya* ^{m}⸢*Ḫu*⸣*-ti-ip*-LUGAL-*ri* 2 LÚ *šu-k*[*i-tuḫ-l*]*u*
21 *ša* ŠU ^{m}(erasure = ⸢*Tù*⸣)*-ra-*⸢*ar*⸣*-te-šup*[158]

---

22 1 ANŠE.KUR.RA *ša* ^{m}*Ḫu-*[*u*]*t-te-šup* 1 ANŠE.KUR.RA ^{m}*Ḫu-ti-ḫa-ma-an-na*
23 1 ANŠE.KUR.RA *ša* ^{m}*E-*[*ḫ*]*e-el-te-šup* 3 ⸢LÚ.M⸣EŠ *an-nu-t*[*i*$^{?}$]
24 *ša* ŠU ^{m}*Šá-ar-*⸢*te*⸣*-šup*

---

25 ^{m}*Pur-ni-ḫu* ^{m}*E-ḫ*[*e*]*-el-te-šup* ^{m}*Ur-ḫi-*⸢*t*⸣*e-š*[*up*]
26 3 L[Ú] *an-nu-ti šu-ki-tuḫ-lu ša* ŠU ^{m}*I-ri-*⸢*ri*⸣*-til-la*

---

27 [ ] ⸢x x⸣ [*šu-k*]*i-tuḫ-lu* 1 ANŠE.KUR.RA ^{m}*Ḫ*[*a*]-⸢*ši*⸣*-pa-a-pu*
28 [*š*]*a* ŠU ^{m}*Pa-i-til-*[*la*]

---

29 [ ]-RI

.
.
.

Reverse

.
.
.

30 [^{m}]-⸢x⸣-*ri*-⸢*ya*⸣
31 [*ša* Š]⸢U ^{m}*Te*⸣-[*ḫi*]-⸢*i*⸣*p-til-la*

---

32 ^{m}*Te-eš-šu-y*[*a* A]NŠE.KUR.RA *ma-lu-*⸢*ú*⸣
33 *ša* ŠU ^{m}*A-kip-ta-še-en-ni*

---

34 ^{m}*Ḫu-ti-pa-a-pu* ^{m}*Tuk-ki-til-la* 2 LÚ *an-nu-ti*
35 *ma-lu-ú ša* ŠU ^{m}*Tar-mi-til-la*

---

36 ^{m}*Ni-ir-pí-te-šup šu-ki-tuḫ-lu*
37 *ša* ŠU ^{m}*Ur-ḫi-til-la*

(blank)
38 13 LÚ.MEŠ *an-*[*nu*]*-tu*$_4$ ANŠE.KUR.RA-*šu-nu*
39 *ma-lu-ú* 10[+n$^{?}$ L]Ú.MEŠ *an-nu-tu*$_4$ *šu-ki-t*[*uḫ-l*]*u*
40 ŠU.NIGIN$_2$ 21+[2+n$^{?}$ LÚ.MEŠ] *ù* 1 ANŠE.KUR.RA

41 *ša i+na* ⸢URU Z⸣[*i-z-z*]*a la* DU-*ku*.MEŠ-*n*[*i*]
42 *ša šu-mé-li*

HSS XV, 29

(1–5) 1 … . A horse of Ipša-ḫalu; a horse of Elḫip-tilla; a horse of Tamar-tae; a horse of Šenna-tati. The horses of these 2+[2] men … .

(6–8) 1 horse of Šukr-apu; [1?] horse of Ḫašiya. … who were under the command of Aru-pašah.

(9–10) Mutta-kil(?) … . These 3 *malû*-men were under the command of Waḫri-tae.[159]

(11–13) Tarmiya; Zike. 2 *malû*-men. Šukri-tešup; …-tešup. 2 *šukituḫlu*-men who were under the command of Kawinni.

(14–15) Pai-tilla, a *malû*; Kipali, a *šukituḫlu* who were under the command of Akip-šenni.

(16–19) Ḫanakka; Kai-tešup son of Akawatil; Akawatil son of Pattiya. 3 *malû*-men. 1 horse of Tarmi-tilla son of Turari; (all of) whom were under the command of Tieš-urḫe.

(20–21) Šumulliya; Ḫutip-šarri. 2 *šukituḫlu*-men who were under the command of Turar-tešup.

(22–24) 1 horse of Ḫut-tešup; 1 horse, Ḫuti-hamanna; 1 horse of Eḫli-tešup. These 3 men are under the command of Šar-tešup.

(25–26) Purniḫu; Eḫli-tešup; Urḫi-tešup. These 3 *šukituḫlu*-men were under the command of Iriri-tilla.

(27–28) … *šukituḫlu*. 1 horse, Ḫašip-apu. … who was/were under the command of Pai-tilla.

(29–31) … … … …-riya, [who was/were] under the command of Teḫip-tilla.

(32–33) Teššuya, a (i.e., "his") *malû*-horse, under the command of Akip-tašenni.

(34–35) Ḫutip-apu; Tupki-tilla. These 2 *malû*-men were under the command of Tarmi-tilla.

(36–37) Nirpi-tešup, a *šukituḫlu*, who was under the command of Urḫi-tilla.

(38–42) These 13 men, their horses (being) *malû*; these (other) 10 [+?] men, *šukituḫlu*. Total: 21 [+2+? men] and 1 horse of the left (wing) who did not come back from the town of Zizza.

20. HSS XV, 40 (SMN 2230)

Findspot: Room N120
Publication: Lacheman 1939b: 190–91; Lacheman 1955: pls. 36–37[160]
Edition: Dosch 2009: 149–51 (text #57)

This text enumerates, in its summary, very large losses of horseless men (lit. "men who do not have horses"), probably a locution for "infantry," at a battle in the town of Zizza.[161] The victims are first grouped according to the names of their commanding officers. Subtotals are given for each grouping. Sometimes the figures given for each group do not correspond to the number of names listed. See lines 18–20, 32–34,[162] 43–46 (probably), 47–49, at least. Furthermore, the final total seems to be somewhat larger than the sum of the groups.

Some of the PNs encountered in text #20 are rare or unique. Analysis of frequency of PNs according to occupation or other kinds of contexts (e.g., infantrymen) might well be worth studying. Patterns of ethnicity and/or social class and/or economic status in such contexts might result.

On the place of text #20 among others of approximately the same genre, see above, comments to text #19.

Obverse

1 *ṭup-p*[*u*] *ša* LÚ.MEŠ *š*[*a*]
2 [*it*?]-*ti* [ ] *X*-⸢*x*-*x*⸣ [ ][163]

---

3 ^{m}⸢x x x ⸣ DUMU *Ḫa-šu*-⸢*ar*⸣?
4 ^{m}*Ḫa-ši*-⸢*ip*⸣-*til-la* ⸢DU⸣MU *Šúk*-⸢*ri*⸣-*ya*
5 2 LÚ.MEŠ *š*[*a* Š]U ^{m}*Wa-ḫa*-[*a*]*r-ta*-[*e*]

---

6 ^{m}*Ḫu-ti*-⸢*ip*⸣-LUGAL ^{m}⸢*I*⸣*r-šu-u*[*ḫ-ḫe*$_{1/2}$]
7 ^{m}*Kàr-ra-t*[*e*] ^{m}*Ka*$_{4}$-⸢*ni*⸣?-*a* ^{m}*Ta-i*-[ ]

8 ^{m}*A-ki-ya* [n L]Ú.MEŠ *ša* ŠU ^{m}*Ka$_4$-w*[*i-in-ni*]

---

9 ^{m}*Ḫu-ti-y*[*a* ^{m}*Z*]*i-li-*⸢*pa*⸣*-pu* ⸢x⸣-[ ]
10 ^{m}*Še-eḫ-li-*[n?]+1 LÚ.MEŠ ⸢*š*⸣*a* Š[U ^{m}]

---

11 ^{m}*Ḫa-i-*⸢*iš-te*⸣-[*šup* ^{m}]*Un-*⸢x⸣-[ ]
12 ^{m}*Ḫu-ut-ti-ir-wi* ^{m}⸢*X*⸣*-pu-*[ ]
13 ^{m}*Ar-ti-wa-aḫ-ri* ^{m}⸢*Pa-a-a* ^{m}*X*⸣-[ ]
14 ^{m}*A-ri-ik-kur-we-e* 9 LÚ.MEŠ
15 *ša* (erasure) ŠU ^{m}*Ti-e-eš-ur-ḫé*

---

16 ^{m}*Zi-li-ya* ^{m}*Ta-pu-ya* ^{m}*Tar-mi-til-la*
17 ^{m}*Pa-i-ik-ku* 4 LÚ.MEŠ *ša* ŠU ^{m}*Tù-ra-ar-te-šup*

---

18 ^{m}*Kùr-ri* ^{m}*Ḫé-er-ru* ^{m}*Er-wi-*LUGAL
19 ^{m}*Ḫa-a-ú-ar-pí* ^{m}*Pa-i-til-la*
20 4 (*sic*) LÚ.MEŠ *ša* ŠU ^{m}*Ša-ar-te-šup*

---

21 ^{m}*A-ri-im-ma-ak-ka$_4$* ^{m}*Šúk-ri-ya*
22 ^{m}*Ḫu-ti-ip-til-la* 3 LÚ.MEŠ *ša* <ŠU ^{m}>[164] *I-ri-ri-til-la*

---

23 ^{m}*Ku-šu-ya* ^{m}*Ik-ka$_4$-ak-ka$_4$* ^{m}*Ú-*⸢*ki*⸣?-[ ]
24 ^{m}*Na-an-te-e-a* ^{m}*Te-ḫi-pa-a-pu*
25 ^{m}*Zi-il-te-e-a*
Lower Edge
26 6 LÚ.MEŠ *ša* ŠU ^{m}*Tù-li-pa-a-pu*

---

27 ^{m}*Te-eš-šu-*[*y*]*a* ^{m}*Pa-*⸢*i*⸣*-til-la*
28 ^{m}*Ur-pí-*⸢*te*⸣ ^{m}*A-wi-iš-ta-e*
Reverse
29 ^{m}*Ta-a-pu* ^{m}*Tar-m*[*i*]*-til-la*
30 ^{m}*Ḫa-ši-ip-til-l*[*a* ^{m}*Š*]*u-ur-te-e-a*
31 8 LÚ.MEŠ *ša* ŠU ^{m}*Tar-mi-ip-ta-š*[*e*]*-ni*

---

32 (erasure) ^{m}*I*[*n*]*-ti-ya*
33 ^{m}*Ta-e* ^{m}*Eḫ-li-*⸢*te*⸣*-šup*
34 4 (*sic*) LÚ.MEŠ *ša* ŠU ^{m}*I-ri-ri-te-šup*

---

35 ^{m}*Al-ki-ya* ^{m}*Ur-*[*ḫ*]*i-ya* ^{m}*Ip-šá-ḫa-lu*
36 ^{m}*Tup-ki-til-la* ^{m}*Ḫ*[*u-t*]*i-ya* ^{m}*Zi-líp-til-la*

37 ^{m}*Pa-a-zi* 7 LÚ.[MEŠ *š*]*a* ŠU ^{m}*Te-ḫi-ip-til-la*

38 ^{m}*Ta-ú-la* ^{m}*Ḫa-n*[*a*$^{?}$-*a*$^{?}$]-*a* (erasure)
39 ^{m}*Ka*$_{4}$*-na-ka*$_{4}$ ^{m}*Ur-*⸢*ḫi*⸣*-te-šup*
40 ^{m}*Ḫu-ti-ya* ^{m}*Še-ka*$_{4}$*-a-a* ^{m}*Šúk-ri-te-šup*
41 ^{m}*A-pè-na-tal* ^{m}*Ur-ḫi-til-*⸢*la*⸣ [^{m} -*i*]*p*$^{?}$*-ta-e*[165]
42 10 LÚ.MEŠ *ša* ⸢ŠU⸣ [^{m}*A*$^{?}$*-ki*$^{?}$*-i*]*p*$^{?}$*-ta-še-e*[*n-ni*]

43 ^{m}*Ki-pa*-RI [^{m}*A-ki*]*p-ta-še-en-n*[*i*]
44 ^{m}*Ḫa-na-a-a* [^{m}*Zi*]*-ké* ^{m}*Ni-in-*[ ]
45 ^{m}*Pu-ú-y*[*a* ^{m}*A-k*]*ip-til-la* 8 (*sic*) LÚ.[MEŠ]
46 *ša* ŠU ^{m}*K*[*é-e*]*l-te-šup*

47 ^{m}*Šu-ra-pí* [^{m}]*Zi-líp-še-en-ni*
48 ^{m}*Ur-ḫi*-LUGAL ^{m}*Ma-at-te-e-a* ^{m}*A*[*r*$^{?}$-]
49 ^{m}*Ar-ta-ḫu-me* 7 (*sic*) LÚ.MEŠ *ša* ŠU ^{m}*Ur-ḫi-til-l*[*a*]

50 ^{m}*Ki-pí-y*⸢*a*⸣ ^{m}⸢*A-kip-t*⸣[*e*$^{?}$*-šup*$^{?}$] ^{m}*Zi-ké*
51 ^{m}*Še-kà*[*r-ti*]*l-la* [n LÚ.MEŠ]
52 *š*[*a*] ŠU ⸢^{m}⸣[ ] ⸢x⸣ [ ] ⸢x⸣

53 ^{m}⸢X-x DU⸣MU$^{?}$ *Eḫ-li-te-šup*
Upper Edge
54 [^{m}]⸢x-x-x⸣ ^{m}*Tù-r*⸢*a*⸣-[ ]
55 [ ]-⸢GI$^{?}$⸣ 2 [+n$^{?}$ LÚ].MEŠ
56 [*ša*] Š[U ^{m}]*Na-an-t*⸢*e*⸣*-šup*
Left Edge
57 [ŠU.N]IGIN$_{2}$ 1 *ma-at* 1 LÚ.MEŠ *ša* ANŠE.KUR.RA.MEŠ *la i-šu-ú a-na*
58 [ ] *i+na* URU *Zi-iz-za ša la* DU-*ku*.MEŠ-*ni ša šu-me-li*

HSS XV, 40

(1–2) A tablet of men who … with(?). … .[166]

(3–5) … son of Ḫašu-ar(?), Ḫašip-tilla son of Šukriya. 2 men under the command of Waḫri-tae.

(6–8) Ḫutip-šarri, Ir-šuḫḫe, Karrate, Ka-ni(?)-ya, Tai-…, Akiya. … men under the command of Kawinni.

(9–10) Ḫutiya, Zilip-apu …, Šeḫli-… . n+1 men under the command of … .

(11–15) Ḫaiš-tešup, Un-…, Ḫut-tirwi, …-pu-…, Arti-waḫri, Paya, …, Arik-kuruwe. 9 men under the command of Tieš-urḫe.

(16–17) Ziliya, Tapuya, Tarmi-tilla, Paikku. 4 men under the command of Turar-tešup.

(18–20) Kurri, Ḫerri, Erwi-šarri, Ḫau(-)arpi, Pai-tilla. 4 (*sic*) men under the command of Šar-tešup.

(21–22) Arim-matka, Šukriya, Ḫutip-tilla. 3 men under <the command of> Iriri-tilla.

(23–26) Kušuya, Ikkakka, U-ki(?)-…, Nan-teya, Teḫip-apu, Zil-teya. 6 men under the command of Tulip-apu.

(27–31) Teššuya, Pai-tilla, Urpite, Awiš-tae, Tapu, Tarmi-tilla, Ḫašip-tilla, Šur-teya. 8 men under the command of Tarmip-tašenni.

(32–34) (erasure) Intiya, Tae, Eḫli-tešup. 4 (*sic*) men under the command of Iriri-tešup.

(35–37) Alkiya, Urḫiya, Ipša-ḫalu, Tupki-tilla, Ḫutiya, Zilip-tilla, Pazi. 7 men under the command of Teḫip-tilla.

(38–42) Taula, Ḫanaya(?), Kanakka, Urḫi-tešup, Ḫutiya, Šekaya, Šukri-tešup, Apen-atal, Urḫi-tilla, …-ip(?)-tae. 10 men under the command of Akip(?)-tašenni.

(43–46) KipaRI, Akip-tašenni, Ḫanaya, Zike, Nin-…, Puya, Akip-tilla. 8 (*sic*) men under the command of Kel-tešup.

(47–49) Šûr-abi, Zilip-šenni, Urḫi-šarri, Mat-teya, Ar(?)-…, Artaḫume. 7 (*sic*) men under the command of Urḫi-tilla.

(50–52) Kipiya, Akip-tešup(?), Zike, Šekar-tilla … [men] under the command of … .

(53–56) … son(?) of(?) Eḫli-tešup, …, Tura-…, …-GI?. 2+n? men under the command of Nan-tešup.

(57–59) Total : 1 hundred 1 horseless men[167] of the left (wing) to … (and) who did not come (back) from the town of Zizza.

21. HSS XV, 14 + *EN* 10/3, 194 (SMN 2214+2698+2271.5)

Findspots: Room N120 + Room N120? + findspot unknown
Publications: Lacheman 1939b: 184 (SMN 2214); 1955: pls. 11–12 (SMN 2214+2698); Fincke 2002a: 227 (SMN 2271.5)
Editions: Dosch 2009: 155–57 (text #59; SMN 2214+2698 only); Fincke 2002b: 311–12 (SMN 2271.5 only)

Text #21, like texts ##19 and 20, lists losses of the Arrapḫan army's left wing incurred at Zizza. Like the other two texts, this document, before summarizing the losses, divides those losses according to the commanders who were responsible for the items lost. Unlike the other texts, this one bears a superscription identifying the subject matter: "tablet of equipment that did not come (back)." The equipment consists of three categories of item: leather body armor for men, leather body armor for horses, and the enigmatic *paraššannu*, apparently a specialized and relatively rare commodity.[168] *paraššannu* losses are measured in ones and twos—once three—whereas lost armor for men range in number from four to fourteen, while horse armor is lost in numbers ranging from one to five.[169]

Adding the respective individual numbers yields, for armor for men, 123+x sets. The total in this category reads "[1] hundred[170] 28." So it is plausible that the missing number at the start of line 49 is "5". The individual numbers for horse armor yields 29 plus four or five unknown quantities. The summary total has x+2, so x should equal "40–41." Based on the surviving numbers, "50–51" or higher is unlikely. The sum of the losses of *paraššannu* totals 19 to 21 plus one unknown number. x+1 is the summary total. The missing number should be "20". We cannot be far off if we number all the losses at: 128 sets of armor for men; 41 suits of armor for horses; 21 *paraššannu*.

We may assume that the loss in armor roughly corresponds to the loss of human and equine forces killed and captured. As with the human losses in text #20 (101 men), these losses are very sizeable. Zizza was a battle, not a skirmish.

Two general observations are in order. A listing of equipment that did not return from battle seems far more useful than an inventory of equipment not sent in the first place (although the latter *is* possible). It certainly represents fresher and, therefore, more crucial information. Therefore, the Akkadian verb rendered "go" or "come" is here to be translated "come (back)." See already briefly above, comment to text #12. Second, the proportion of human to equine armor losses makes sense: there would have been larger infantry (plus charioteer?) losses than losses of horses, corresponding to the relative size and vulnerability of the forces.

Finally, the names of the commanders reconstructed in this text, where damaged, are reconstructed from parallel texts, especially text #20.

Obverse

1 *ṭup-pu ú-nu-tu*$_4$ *ša la* DU-[*ku*]
2 10 *ta-pa-lu sà-ri-am ša* ⸢LÚ⸣
3 5 *ṣí-mi-it-ti sà-ri-am ša* AN[ŠE.KUR.RA]
4 *ša* ŠU ^{m}*A-ru-pa-ša-aḫ*

---

5 ⸢10? *ta-pa-lu*⸣ *sà-ri-am ša* LÚ
6 [n] *ṣí-m*[*i-i*]*t-ti sà-ri-am ša* AN[ŠE.KUR.RA]
7 *ša* ŠU ^{m}*Wa-*[*ḫ*]*a-ar-ta-e*

---

8 7 *ta-pa-l*[*u sà-r*]*i-am ša* LÚ 2 *ṣí-mi-*[*it-ti sà-ri-am*]
9 *ša* ANŠE.KUR.R[A 1-*nu*]-*tu*$_4$ *pa-ra-aš-ša-an-n*[*u*]
10 *ša* ŠU ^{m}*Ka*$_4$*-wi-*[*i*]*n-ni*

---

11 8 *ta-pa-lu sà-r*[*i*]*-am ša* LÚ
12 3 *ṣí-mi-it-ti* ⸢*s*⸣*à-ri-am ša* A[NŠE.KUR.RA]
13 *ša* ŠU ^{m}*A-kip-š*[*e-e*]*n-ni*

---

14 5 *ta-pa-lu sà-r*[*i-am*] *ša* LÚ 1 [+? *sà-ri-am ša* ANŠE.KUR.RA]
15 2 *ṣí-mi-it-*t[*i pa-r*]*a-aš-*[*ša-an-nu*]
16 *ša* ŠU ^{m}*Tù-ra-a*[*r-te-šup*][171]

---

17 14 *ta-pa-lu sà-ri-a*⸢*m*⸣ [*ša* LÚ]
18 2 *ṣí-mi-it-tu*$_4$ *sà-*[*ri-am ša* ANŠE.KUR.RA]
19 1-*nu-tu*$_4$ *pa-ra-aš-ša-*[*an-nu ša* ŠU ^{m}]

---

20 7 *ta-pa-lu sà-r*[*i-am ša* LÚ]
21 3 *ṣí-mi-it-*[*ti sà-ri-am ša* ANŠE.KUR.RA]
22 1-*nu-tu*$_4$ *pa-ra-aš-*[*ša-an-nu ša* ŠU ^{m}]

---

23 5 *ta-pa-lu sà-ri-a*[*m ša* LÚ]
24 1-*nu-tu*$_4$ *sà-ri-am ša* ANŠ[E.KUR.RA]
25 2 *ṣí-mi-it-*[*ti*] *pa-ra-*[*aš-ša-an-nu*]
Lower Edge
26 ⸢*ša*⸣ ŠU ^{m}*I-ri-*⸢*ri*⸣*-ti*[*l*]*-*⸢*la*⸣

---

27 6 *ta-pa-lu sà-ri-am ša* [LÚ]
28 [n] *ṣí-mi-it-ti sà-ri-*[*am ša* ANŠE.KUR.RA]
Reverse
29 [n+]1 *ṣí-mi-it-t*[*i*] *pa*[*ra-aš-ša-an-nu*]
30 [*š*]*a* ŠU ^{m}*Na-an-*[*te-šup*][172]

---

31 6+[2] *t*[*a-p*]*a-lu* [*s*]*à-ri-am š*[*a* LÚ]
32 4 *ṣi-mi-i*[*t*]*-ti sà-ri-a*[*m ša* ANŠE.KUR.RA]
33 1-*nu-tu*$_4$ *pa-ra-aš-*⸢*š*⸣*a-an-nu*
34 *ša* ŠU ^{m}*Tù-li-pa-*⸢*a-p*⸣[*u*]

---

35 8 *ta-pa-lu sà-r*⸢*i-a*⸣[*m ša* LÚ]
36 4 *ṣí-mi-it-ti* [*sà-ri-am ša* ANŠE.KUR.RA]
37 2 *ṣí-mi-it-ti* [*pa-ra-aš-ša-an-nu*]
38 *ša* ŠU ^{m}*Tar-mi-ip-*[*ta-še-en-ni*][173]

---

39 5 *ta-pa-lu sà-ri-*⸢*am*⸣ *š*[*a* LÚ]
40 1-*nu-tu*$_4$ *pa-ra-aš-ša-an-nu š*[*a* ŠU ^{m}]

---

41 4 *ta-pa-lu sà-ri-am ša* LÚ
42 1-*nu-tu*$_4$ *sà-ri-am ša* [A]NŠE.KUR.RA *š*[*a* ŠU ^{m}]

---

43 8 *ta-pa-lu s*[*à-r*]*i-am ša* LÚ
44 2 *ṣí-mi-i*[*t-t*]*i sà-ri-am ša* A[NŠE.KUR.RA]
45 2 *ṣí-mi-it-*[*t*]*i pa-ra-aš-ša-an-nu* [*ša* ŠU ^{m}*Ké-e*]*l-te-šup*[174]

---

46 [1+]4 *ta-pa-lu s*[*à-r*]*i-am ša* LÚ
47 [n] ⸢*ṣí*⸣*-mi-i*[*t*]*-ti sà-ri-a*⸢*m*⸣ *ša* AN[ŠE.KUR.RA]
48 [*pa-r*]*a-aš-ša-an-nu ša* ŠU ^{m}*A-k*[*ip-ta-še-en-ni*][175]

---

49 [n *ṣí*]*-mi-i*⸢*t*⸣*-ti š*⸢*à*⸣*-ri-am* [*ša* LÚ n *sà-ri*]*-am* <ša> ANŠE.KUR.RA
50 [*ša* Š]U ^{m}⸢*Tar*⸣*-mi-til-l*[*a*]

---

51 8 *ta-pa-*⸢*lu*⸣ *sà-ri-am ša* [LÚ]

52 3 *ṣí-mi-it-ti pa-ra-*[*aš-ša-an-nu*]
53 *ša* ŠU ^{m}*Ur-ḫi-til-la*

Upper Edge
54 5 *ta-pa-lu sà-ri-am ša* LÚ 1-*nu-t*[*u*$_4$ *sà-ri-am*]
55 *ša* ANŠE.KUR.RA 2 *ṣí-mi-it-ti* ⸢*p*⸣[*a-ra-aš-ša-an-nu*]
56 *ša* ŠU ^{m}*Kùr-mi-še-en-ni*
Left Edge
57 [ŠU.NIGIN$_2$ 1 *m*]*a-at* 28 *ta-pa-lu sà-ri-am* KUŠ *ša* [LÚ]
58 [n]+2 *ṣí-mi-it-ti sà-ri-am* KU[Š *ša* ANŠE.KUR.RA]
59 [n]+1 *ṣí-mi-it-ti pa-ra-aš-ša-a*[*n-nu* URU *Zi-i*]*z-za*
60 *ša la* DU-*ku*.MEŠ-*ni ša* GÙB

HSS XV, 14

(1) Tablet of equipment that did not come (back).

(2–4) 10 sets of body armor for a man (and) 5 suits (lit. "pairs") of body armor for a horse, (all) from the stores (lit. "belonging to," "under the command of") Aru-pašaḫ.

(5–7) 10(?) sets of body armor for a man (and) n suits of body armor for a horse, (all) from the stores of Waḫri-tae.

(8–10) 7 sets of body armor for a man, 2 suits of [body armor] for a horse, (and) a unit of *paraššannu*[176] (all) from the stores of Kawinni.

(11–13) 8 sets of body armor for a man (and) 3 suits of body armor for a horse, (all) from the stores of Akip-šenni.

(14–16) 5 sets of body armor for a man, 1 [+n? … body armor for a horse], (and) 2 suits of *paraššannu*, (all) from the stores of Tura[r-tešup].[177]

(17–19) 14 sets of body armor [for a man], 2 suits of body armor [for a horse], (and) a unit of *paraššannu*, [(all) from the stores of] … .

(20–22) 7 sets of body armor [for a man], 3 suits [of body armor for a horse], (and) a unit of *paraššannu*, [(all) from the stores of] … .

(23–26) 5 sets of body armor [for a man], a unit of body armor for a horse, (and) 2 suits of *paraššannu*, (all) from the stores of Iriri-tilla.

(27–30) 6 sets of body armor for [a man], n suits of body armor [for a horse], (and) n+1 suits of *paraššannu*, (all) from the stores of Nan-[te]šup.[178]

(31–34) 8 sets of body armor for [a man], 4 suits of body armor for [a horse], (and) a unit of *paraššannu*, (all) from the stores of Tulip-apu.[179]

(35–38) 8 sets of body armor [for a man], 4 suits of [body armor for a horse], (and) 2 suits of [*paraššannu*], (all) from the stores of Tarmip-[tašenni].[180]

(39–40) 5 sets of body armor for [a man] (and) a unit of *paraššannu*, (all) from [the stores of]… .

(41–42) 4 sets of body armor for a man (and) a unit of body armor for a horse , (all) from [the stores of]… .

(43–45) 8 sets of body armor for a man, 2 suits of body armor for a horse, (and) 2 suits of *paraššannu*, [(all) from] the stores of Kel-[tešup].[181]

(46–48) 5 sets of body armor for a man, n suits of body armor for a horse, (and) … *paraššannu*, (all) from the stores of Akip-[tašenni].[182]

(49–50) n suits (*sic*) of body armor [for a man (and) n … of] body armor <for> a horse, [(all) from] the stores of Tarmi-tilla.

(51–53) 8 sets of body armor for [a man] (and) 3 suits of *paraššannu*, (all) from the stores of Urḫi-tilla.

(54–56) 5 sets of body armor for a man, a unit [of body armor] for a horse, (and) 2 suits of *paraššannu*, (all) from the stores of Kurmi-šenni.

(57–60) [Total: 1] hundred 28 sets of leather body armor for [a man], n+2 suits of leather body armor [for a horse], (and) n+1 suits of *paraššannu* … of the left (wing) who did not come (back) [from the town of] Zizza.

22. HSS XV, 43 (SMN 3096)

Findspot: Room C28
Publications: Lacheman 1939b: 187; Lacheman 1955: pl. 41[183]
Edition: None[184]

Text #22 is a text of a type which has already appeared in this series. It is a catalog of losses. Here, 38 soldiers are listed as captured in Zizza (not merely as "who did not come [back]" from Zizza) by the enemy. Before the summary statement, their number (though their names are not given) is divided according to how many were lost to each of five commanders. Unusually, a statement is appended that ten men from the town of Apena were also captured in Zizza. Also unusually, the document is sealed (i.e., signed).

Obverse
1 [12$^{?}$ LÚ.MEŠ] *a-lik* EDIN.NA
2 *ša* ŠU ^{m}⸢*Ḫa*⸣-*ši-ip-til-la* ^{m}*Ki-il-ta-mu-li* ^{LÚ}*a*-ZU
3 6 LÚ.[MEŠ *a*]-*lik* EDIN.NA
4 *ša* ŠU [^{m}]-⸢*x*⸣-*a*-RI
5 3 ⸢LÚ⸣.MEŠ *a-li*]*k* EDIN.NA
6 *š*[*a*] ŠU ^{m}⸢*Ḫi*⸣$^{?}$-*iš-mé-ya*
7 16 LÚ.MEŠ *a*-⸢*li*⸣*k* EDIN.⸢NA⸣
8 *ša* Š[U] ^{m}⸢*Šur*⸣$^{?}$-*ki-til-la*
9 1 LÚ *a-l*[*ik*] EDIN.NA
Lower Edge
10 [*š*]*a* ŠU ^{m}[*E*]*ḫ-li-ya*
Reverse
11 ŠU.NIGIN$_2$ 38 [L]Ú.MEŠ
12 ⸢*a*⸣-*lik* EDIN.N⸢A⸣ *i+na*
13 [U]RU *Zi-iz-za*
14 [*e*]*s-ru*$^{!}$ *šum-ma* ^{LÚ}KÚR<.MEŠ$^{?}$>
15 [*i-na*] URU *Zi-iz-za*
16 ⸢*ú*⸣-*ši-bu*
17 [n$^{?}$+] 10 LÚ.MEŠ *ša* URU *A-pè-na-aš*
18 ⸢*i*⸣+*na* URU *Zi-iz-za es-ru* (erasure$^{?}$)
Upper Edge
S.I.
19 NA$_4$ [^{m}]-*en-ni*

HSS XV, 43

(1–10) [12?] *ālik ṣēri*[185] under the command of Ḫašip-tilla, Qîšt-amurri, the physician(?)[186]; 6 *ālik ṣēri* under the command of …-a-RI; 3 *ālik ṣēri* under the command of Ḫ(?)išmeya; 16 *ālik ṣēri* under the command of Šur(?)-ki-tilla; 1 *ālik ṣēri* under the command of Eḫliya.

(11–16) Total: 38 *ālik ṣēri* confined in the town of Zizza when(!) (lit. "if"[187]) the enemy occupied (i.e., "began to occupy," lit. "dwelled [in]") the town of Zizza.

(17–18) 10+x? men of the town of Apena were confined in the town of Zizza (erasure?).

(19) (*seal impression*) Seal of …-enni.

23. HSS XIV, 131 (SMN 898)

Findspot: No Room Number
Publication: Lacheman 1950: pl. 63
Edition: None

This brief and mostly straightforward list of disbursements is rendered significant in the present instance because of the date formula (lines 10–12). As rendered here, the formula refers to the occasion of Zizza's occupation by the enemy (i.e., the Assyrians).[188] N.B. The occasion is here considered the moment an ongoing occupation began, not the start of an occupation that has come and gone. The text can support the latter interpretation,[189] but my interpretation of the course of the Arrapḫa–Assyria war demands the former interpretation. In other words, this text *may* support the position espoused here but cannot be used as unambiguous evidence for it. Fortunately, the date formula does not have to bear such heavy weight.[190]

Obverse

.
.
.

1 [ ] ⌜x x x⌝ [ ]
2 ⌜*a-na*⌝ SAL.LUGAL-*ti*
3 *ša* URU DINGIR.MEŠ *na-a*⌜*d-nu*⌝

---

4 1 ANŠE ŠE *a-na bá-la-li*

5 1 (PI) 1 BÁN ŠE *a-na a-ka*$_4$*-li*
6 1 (PI) 2 BÁN GIG
7 *an-nu-tu*$_4$ *i+na* ITI-^{ḫi} *Ḫi-in-zu-ur-r*[*i*]$^?$*-we*
8 *a-na* SAL.LUGAL *ša* URU *Nu-zi*
9 *na-ad-nu*

---

10 *an-nu-tu*$_4$ *šu-un-du*$_4$
11 KÚR.MEŠ *i+na* URU *Zi-iz-za*
Lower Edge
12 *aš-bu ù*
13 *na-áš-ru*
Reverse
14 2 ANŠE ŠE *a-*⸢*n*⸣*a bá-la-li*
15 1 (PI) 2 BÁN ŠE *a-na* ⸢*a*⸣*-ka*$_4$*-li*
16 1 ANŠE 1 (PI) 2 BÁN GIG.MEŠ
17 2 A⸢N⸣ŠE 1 (PI) ŠE.MEŠ *a-na bá-ap-pí-ra*
18 4 [A]NŠE 2 BÁN ŠE *a-na* NUMUN.MEŠ
19 1*-nu-tu*$_4$ *i+na* ITI-^{ḫi} *Ḫi-*⸢*x*⸣*-ar-ri-we*
20 [*a-n*]*a* SAL.LUGAL *ša* URU *A*[*n*$^?$*-zu*$^?$*-kál*$^?$*-li*$_{1/3}$$^?$ *na-ad-nu*]

---

21 [n Š]E *a-na bá-l*[*a-li*]
.
.
.

HSS XIV, 131

(1–3) … given to the Āl-ilāni queen.[191]

(4–9) 1 homer of barley for brewing, 7 seahs of barley[192] for eating (and) 8 seahs of wheat. These (items) were given to the Nuzi queen[193] in the month of Ḫinzuri.[194]

(10–13) And these (items) were taken out (of stores) at the time when the enemy occupied (i.e., "began to occupy," probably) the town of Zizza.

(14–20) 2 homers of barley for brewing, 8 seahs of barley for eating, 1 homer 8 seahs of wheat, 2 homers 6 seahs of barley for "beer bread,"[195] 4 homers 2 seahs of barley for seed.

(The above) unit(?) (of grain)[196] [was given] to the Anzukalli(?) queen[197] in the month of Ḫiari[198](?).

(21) n ... [of] barley for brewing.... .

24. HSS XV, 32

Findspot: Room G29
Publication: Lacheman 1955: pl. 30
Edition: None

Text #24 lists Ḫanigalbatian soldiers[199] stationed in the Arrapḫan town of Apena. First, the names of the soldiers are given. These are followed by a summary total, followed by a definition of their status and homeland. There follow the name of the company commander[200] and the place the company is stationed.

The precise identity of this group of sixty is embedded in line 26. Unfortunately, apart from the datum that they hail from the country of Ḫanigalbat, the answer is obscured by a rare term and partially effaced signs. Four or five suggestions have been hazarded, most positing an otherwise unattested term for a kind of troop. The suggestion proposed here is almost (but not quite) as troubling, involving a term for "contribution" otherwise used for the donation of items by an inferior toward a superior party. But in the end, the conundrum of line 26 is not crucial. It is clear in any case that the sixty are foreigners from Ḫanigalbat stationed at Apena, certainly in aid of Arrapḫan forces.

This text is unique in that the Ḫanigalbatian force is made up of men whose personal names are radically different (as a group) from those usually found in the Nuzi texts. Of the thirty-one PNs sufficiently preserved to be compared to other names found at Nuzi, sixteen (possibly seventeen) occur once, that is, only here in text #24. A further four names appear twice—both times in the present document. Therefore, over two-thirds of the surviving names appearing in text #24 appear in this text only. Of the remaining PNs, two are similarly unique to the document but contain elements appearing elsewhere in the Nuzi onomasticon, one occurs once elsewhere, and seven appear two or more times elsewhere.[201] It is difficult to avoid the conclusion that the foreign nature of these names ties in with the foreign origin of this company, the country of Ḫanigalbat. That is, it seems clear that this cluster of unique and rare names represents a name-giving tradition that is linguistically Ḫanigalbatian, or, as it is more commonly known, Mittannian.[202] If the Mittannian capital city, Waššukanni, and its texts are ever discovered, a comparison of that onomasticon with that of text #24 would be illuminating. If they were substantially congruent, then this would mean that the Mittannian military (hailing from its metropolis?), or at least a discrete contingent of the army, was ethno-linguistically Mittannian, and not Hurrian. (The Hurrian language supplies the lion's share of personal names from Nuzi, names that are so unlike the majority of those found in text #24.) It would be illuminating regardless of whether or not there were substantial overlaps. Positive or negative ethno-linguistic connections would clarify the origins of this company of soldiers.[203]

Obverse

1 ^{m}*Pa-an-ka-a-at-ti* ^{m}*Pa-ra-ka-aš-šu-ša/ra*
2 ^{m}*Ta-ku-uḫ-li* ^{m}*Ut-ti-iz*$^{!}$*-za-na*
3 ^{m}*Pa-an-tu*$_4$ ^{m}*Ši-na-mu* ^{m}*Ḫa-ši-is-sí*
4 ^{m}*Ú*-UD-*ti* ^{m}*Pa-a-a* ^{m}*Eḫ-li*
5 ^{m}*Ké-ez-za* ^{m}*Zi-ki-il-ta*
6 ^{m}*A-pu-uš-ka*$_4$ ^{m}*Ú-ra-at-ta*
7 ^{m}*Ta-a-ku* ^{m}*A-ri-ip-šu-ri-ḫe*
8 ^{m}*A-as-sà* ^{m}*Ú*-UD-*ti*
9 ^{m}*Ku-ú-pí* ^{m}*A-ta-šu* ^{m}*Ú-ru*

---

10 (erased)

---

11 ^{m}*Ke*-⸢*ez*⸣-zi ^{m}⸢*Ú*⸣*-ra-at-t*⸢*a*⸣
12 ^{m}BE-*l*[*a*$^{?}$]-⸢GI⸣$^{?}$ ^{m}*T*[*a-k*]*u-uḫ-li*
13 ^{m}*Šu*-[-*t*]*a* ^{m}⸢*Pí*⸣*-ya*
14 ^{m}*Pí*-[ ]-AS-*n*[*a*][204] ^{m}*Na-i-pa*
15 [^{m}*Z*]*i*-⸢*x*⸣*-ta* ^{m}*Uš-šu*-UD-*ti*
16 [^{m}]-⸢x-x⸣-[x]-*te* ^{m}*Pu-ḫi-še-en-ni*
17 [^{m}]-⸢x-x⸣-[(?)] ^{m}*Tuḫ-mu-ka*$_4$-RI
18 [^{m} -*š*]*u*$^{?}$-⸢x⸣ [^{m}] ⸢*Ú*⸣*-a-at-ti*
19 [^{m}]-⸢x⸣ ^{m}*I*[*s*$^{?}$*-s*]*a*$^{?}$*-ar*$^{?}$
20 [^{m}]-*eš*$^{?}$ ^{m}*A-r*⸢*a*$^{?}$*-a*⸣$^{?}$
21 [^{m} ^{m}]-⸢*x*⸣*-ḫi-a*-RI
22 [^{m}]-*eš*$^{?}$ ^{m}*Ki*$^{?}$-[ ]- ⸢*x-ka*$_4$⸣$^{?}$-[*n*]*a*$^{?}$

Lower Edge Destroyed

Reverse

23 [^{m}] ⸢$^{m?}$ x-x⸣ [ ]
24 ^{m}*Tù-uk-ki* ^{m}*Áš-ra-at*-[ ]
25 ^{m}*A-ás-sú* ^{m}*Šá-an-ti-te-a*
26 ŠU.NIGIN$_2$ 1 *šu-ši* LÚ.MEŠ
27 *ta-mar-ti a*[*n-n*]*i ša* KUR ⸢*Ḫa-ni-g*⸣*al-bat*

28 *a-tuḫ-lu* ᵐ*Ú-*⌜*ru*⌝
29 *i+na* URU *A-pè-na ša aš-bu*

(rest of reverse uninscribed)

HSS XV, 32

(1–24) Pankātti (*sic*), Parakkaššu-ša/ra, Takuḫli, Uttaz-zina, Pantu, Šinamu, Ḫašissi, U-UD-ti,[205] Paya, Eḫli, Kezzi, Zikilta, Apuška, Uratta, Takku, Arip-šuriḫe, Āssa, U-UD-ti, Kupi, Atašu, Uru,

---

(one line erased)

Kezzi, Uratta, BE-la(?)-GI(?), Takuḫli, Šu-…-ta, Piya, Pi-…aSna, Naipa, Zi-…-ta, Uššu-UD-ti, …-te, Puḫi-šenni, …, TuḫmukaRI, …-šu(?)-…, Ụatti, …, Issar(?), …-eš(?), A-rā(?), …, …-ḫiaRI, …-eš(?), Ki(?)-…-ka(?)-na(?), …, …, Tukki, Ašrat-…(?), Āssu, Šantiteya.

(25–29) Total: 1 (unit of) sixty men. This is the contribution(??)[206] of the country of Ḫanigalbat—Uru (being the) *atuḫlu*-officer—which is/was stationed in the town of Apena.

25. HSS XIV, 171 (SMN 3362)

Findspot: Room D6
Publication: Lacheman 1950: pl. 78
Edition: None[207]

Text #25 is a memorandum of sorts relating to the distribution of barley for rations (though a kind of beer and an obscure other item are added as an afterthought seemingly). The date of the document and, given the context, the occasion of the distribution was the stationing of Ḫanigalbatian chariotry in the towns of Arn-apu and Arwa.[208] Arwa was close to Zizza and, indirectly, to Apena as well. Therefore, text #25 and text #24 seem to be related contexts.

The quantity of barley distributed demands that there were slightly more than two hundred charioteers involved here. This means that, at most, about one hundred chariots were stationed in these towns, if no reserve charioteers or support personnel were numbered among these two hundred-plus men.

Obverse
1 9 *ma-ti* 10 ANŠE ŠE.MEŠ
2 *ša* ^{GIŠ}GIGIR.MEŠ
3 *ša* KUR *Ḫa-lì-gal-bat*
4 *ša* 43 UD^{-mi} *ša* KÚ$^{!}$
5 1 BÁN T[A].ÀM
6 *it-ti bi-il-li-šu*
7 *ù it-ti*
Lower Edge
8 *ḫi*$^{?}$*-ši*$^{?}$-⌈*x*⌉-WA-*ri-šu*
Reverse
9 *šu-un-du*$_4$
10 ^{GIŠ}GIGIR.MEŠ <*ša* KUR> *Ḫa-lì-gal-bat*
11 [A]Š URU *Ar-na-a-pu-we*
12 ⌈*ù*⌉ *i+na* URU *Ar-wa*
13 *ú-ši-bu*

HSS XIV, 171

(1–8) 9 hundred 10 homers of barley for the chariots of the land of Ḫanigalbat for 43 days for eating (at) 1 seah (each, i.e., per charioteer per day) together with his (i.e., each charioteer's) *billu*-beer and with his … .

(9–13) When the chariots <of the land of > Ḫanigalbat were stationed in the town of Arn-apu and in the town of Arwa.

---

26. HSS XIV, 249 (SMN 523)

Findspot: Room R76
Publications: Lacheman 1939b: 206 (cuneiform copy); 1950: pl. 103 (cuneiform copy)[209]; 1950: 7–8 (HSS XIV, 523; same text – transliteration)
Edition: None

Text #26 is an inventory of garments distributed to assorted parties. The first three disbursements took place, it is noted, when chariots engaged in battle in the town of Ṣilliya. The disbursements are to be linked to this event.[210] After one further disbursement, another is made to an officer of the Ḫanigalbatian chariotry when the chariotry (i.e., the same Ḫanigalbatian chariotry) engaged in battle at

Lubti. The text concludes with the notation that all the disbursements were from Nuzi stores and took place in a single month.

Lubti is located in the southeast of the kingdom of Arrapḫa and so it is likely, though not certain, that Ṣilliya is similarly to be located.[211] It is, in any case, clear from this document that Ḫanigalbatian chariotry was deployed, not only in central Arrapḫa (text #25; cf. text #24), but in eastern Arrapḫa as well. Nuzi, it is to be emphasized, survived to this point and was able to supply even auxiliary armed forces relatively far afield. And, of course, these records were found stored at Nuzi, demonstrating that town's relative longevity in the struggle with Assyria. It survived Assyrian victories first in the west and then in the east. Nuzi and the city of Arrapḫa itself fell in the last stages of the Assyrian conquest.

This text contains a number of terms relating to realia. Differentiating context is lacking and so many of these words elude precise translation.[212]

Obverse

1 1 TÚG *nu-ḫé a-dì-i i+na ḫul-la-an-ni*

2 *a-na* ^{m}*Ḫu-ut-te-šup* DUMU LUGAL *na-ad-nu*

3 1 TÚG *ši-la-an-nu a-dì-i*

4 *i+na ḫul-la-an-ni a-na* ^{m}*Ḫu-ta-ur-ḫé*

5 DUMU *Ḫu-ti-pu-ra-aš-še na-ad-nu*

6 1 TÚG *lu-bu-ul-tù a-dì-i*

7 *i+na ku-sí-ti a-na* ^{m}*Ur-ḫi-til-la* DUB.SAR *na-ad-nu*

8 *an-nu-tu*$_4$ *šu-un-du*

9 ^{GIŠ}GIGIR.MEŠ *i+na* URU *Ṣíl-lí-ya-we*

10 *ta-ḫa-za i-pu-uš-šu-nu-ti* ^{m}*Ti-ir-wi-na-tal iš-tu* É *na-kam-ti*
:ná-aš-ru

11 1-*nu-tu*$_4$ GÚ.È$^{!}$.MEŠ <*ši*>*-na-ḫi-lu* 1-*nu-tu*$_4$ *né-be-ḫu ši-na-ḫi-lu*

12 *a-na* ^{m}*En-na-ma-ti* ^{LÚ}*la-sí-mu na-⸢a⸣d-nu*

13 ^{m}*Ku-ul-pè-na-tal iš-tu* É *na-kam-ti*

14 *na-áš-ru*

15 2 TÚG.MEŠ *ši-la-an-nu*

16 *a-dì-i i+na ḫul-la-an-ni*

Lower Edge

17 *a-na* $^{\text{LÚ.MEŠ}}$ *a-tuḫ-le-e*

18 *ša* ^{GIŠ}GIGIR.MEŠ

Reverse

19 *ša* KUR *Ḫa-lì-gal-bat*

20 *šu-un-du* ^{GIŠ}GIGIR.MEŠ

21 *i+na* URU *Lu-ub-ti*

22 *ta-ḫa-za i-ip-pu-šu*

23 *na-ad-nu ù*
24 ^{m}*Ḫé-el-ti-pá-pu*
25 *it-ta-šar*
(space[213])
26 *an-nu-*tu_4 TÚG.MEŠ *i+na* ITI-^{ḫi}
27 *Ḫu-ú-re*
28 *iš-tu* É *na-kam-ti*
29 *ša* URU *Nu-zi*
30 *ša na-áš-ru*

HSS XIV, 249

(1–10) 1 garment (made) of *nuḫu* together with a blanket/wrap were given to Ḫut-tešup son of the king. 1 *šilannu*-garment together with a blanket/wrap were given to Ḫuta-urḫe son of Ḫutip-urašše. 1 *lubuštu*-garment together with a *kusītu*(-garment) were given to Urḫi-tilla, the scribe.

Tirwin-atal withdrew these (items) from the storehouse when the chariots did battle in the town of Ṣilliya.[214]

(11–14) An outfit of second-quality cloaks (and) an outfit of second-quality *nēbeḫu*-belts were given to Enna-mati the runner.

Kulpen-atal withdrew (these items) from the storehouse.

(15–25) 2 *šilannu*-garments together with a blanket/wrap were given to the *atuḫlu*-officers of the chariots of the country of Ḫanigalbat when they did battle in the town of Lubti. And Ḫeltip-apu withdrew (these items).

(26–30) These are the garments that were withdrawn from the storehouse of the town of Nuzi in the month of Ḫure.[215]

27. HSS XIV, 174 (SMN 951)

Findspot: unknown
Publication: Lacheman 1950: pl. 79
Edition: Fadhil 1983: 111b

This document is straightforward. Does the fact that the barley destined for the chariotry comes from the (Nuzi) queen's allotment rather than from general stores indicate distress at Nuzi?

Obverse
1 50 ANŠE ŠE.MEŠ

2 *iš-tu* ŠE.MEŠ *ša* SAL.LUGAL
3 ^{m}*Ta-ti-ip-til-la*
4 *ù* ^{m}*Ti-ir-wi-na-tal*
5 *it-ta-áš-ru*
6 ^{m}*Ti-eš-ur-ḫé il-qè*
7 *šu-un-du* ^{GIŠ}GIGIR<.MEŠ?>
Lower Edge
8 *i+na* URU *Lu-um-t*[*i*]
9 *ú-ri-du*
Remainder blank

HSS XIV, 174

(1–9) Tatip-tilla and Tirwin-atal withdrew 50 homers of barley from the barley of the queen (and) Tieš-urḫe took it, on the occasion when the chariots went down to the town of Lubti.

28. HSS XIV, 238 (SMN 3064)

Findspot: Room C19
Publications: Lacheman 1939b: 177; 1950: pl. 96[216]
Edition: None

Text #28 resembles a disbursement list but is actually a kind of narrative in three parts. First, a truncated command (it lacks a verb) given by an official, Šar-tešup, seems to be quoted (lines 1–4). It orders that twenty-five men be given barley. Next, the occasion of this order is described: enemy presence in a town (lines 5–8; the section of most interest to this chapter). Finally, fulfillment of the order is reported: twenty-five charioteers went from Nuzi to two minor towns delivering (the barley, most probably; lines 9–15).

The dispatch of barley and charioteers is occasioned by an enemy attack on Temtena, and that fact is of interest here because Temtena is to be located in the neighborhood of Lubti,[217] where, according to texts ## 26 and 27, military action was taking place.

Obverse
1 [*um*?-*m*]*a*? ^{m}⸢*Ša*⸣-*ar-te-šup-ma*
2 [n ANŠE +n?] 2 SILA$_3$ ŠE *a-na qà-ti* «*ti*»
3 ⸢*a*⸣-*na* 25 LÚ.MEŠ *a-na* 2 ⸢U⸣D

4 ⌜*i*⌝-*na* ITI *Sa*$^!$-*bu-ut*
5 ⌜*š*⌝*u-un-du*$_4$ *iq-ta*$^!$(=ŠA)[218]-*bu-ú*
6 KÚR.MEŠ ⌜*a*⌝-*na ḫu-r*[*a*]-*dì-im-ma*
7 *i+na* UR[U] *T*⌜*e*⌝-*em-te-na*
8 *il-li-ka*$_4$-⌜*am*⌝-*mi*
Lower Edge
9 ⌜*ù*⌝ 25 LÚ.M[EŠ]
Reverse
10 *a-šar* ^{GIŠ}GIGIR.MEŠ
11 *iš-tu* URU *Nu-zi*
12 *il-li-ik-ki-i-ma*
13 AŠ URU *Ir-ḫa-aḫ-ḫé*
14 *ù* AŠ URU *Te-li-pè-er-ra*
15 *it-tab-lu-šu-nu-ti*

HSS XIV, 238

(1–4) Thus(?) Šar-tešup: "…[219] 2 *qa*s of barley to the authority of, for 25 men,[220] for 2 days in the month of Sabûtu(?)."[221]

(5–8) (This directive was issued) when it was said, "the enemy came into the town of Temtena on campaign."[222]

(9–15) Now, 25 men came out[223] of Nuzi from the chariot depot (and) they brought them (i.e., the barley, surely) to the town of Irḫaḫḫe and to the town of Teliperra.

---

29. HSS XIV, 248 (SMN 643)

Findspot: Room R76
Publications: Lacheman 1939b:208–9 (cuneiform copy); Lacheman 1950:pl. 102 (cuneiform copy)[224]; Lacheman 1950:45–46 (HSS XIV, 643; same text – transliteration)
Edition: None

Text #29 is a record of disbursements, mostly of garments, given to particular parties and taken from stores by persons entrusted with that responsibility. (The same PNs of such persons recur in other, similar texts.[225]) In three cases, the occasions of the disbursements are given. One of those (lines 23–24) reveals that the enemy was occupying the town of Teliperra, known to be near Lubti. The enemy was apparently threatening to do further harm or damage. The neighboring town of Irḫaḫḫe happens to be mentioned in the very next entry (lines 25–26). Text #28 pairs these two towns in a military context.[226]

The sense of the last five lines of this document is obscure.

Obverse

1 ⸢1 TÚG 1⸣-*nu-tu*$_4$ *na-aḫ-la-a*[*p-tu*$_{3/4}$]

2 1-*nu-tu*$_4$ *ḫul-la-an-nu*

3 *ši-na-ḫi-lu*.MEŠ *a-na te-ḫu-uš-ši*[227]

4 *a-na* ^{m}*A-kip-ta-še-en-ni ki-zi-iḫ-ḫu-ri*

5 *šu-un-dù* ^{d}X-*nu-zu-ḫé iz-qú-pu*

6 *na-ad-nu i+na* ITI-^{ḫi} *Še-eḫ-li*

7 ^{m}*Ti-ir-wi-na-tal iš-tu na-kam-ti*

8 *i*⸢*t*⸣-*ta-šar*

(one line completely destroyed)

9 ⸢x⸣ [ ]

---

10 1-*nu-tu*$_4$ *na-aḫ-la-ap-tu*$_4$

11 1-*nu-tu*$_4$ *ḫul-la-an-nu*

12 *a-na* DUMU.MEŠ ^{m}*E-ḫé-el-te-šup*

13 *ša* URU *Ti-la na-ad-nu*

14 ^{m}*Ḫé-el-ti-pa-pu it-ta-š*⸢*ar*⸣[*š*]-*u-un-du* ^{m} $^{«m»}$*Zi-ké ṣú-ḫa-ar*

15 1 TÚG 1-*nu-tu*$_4$ *ḫul-la-a*[*n-nu*[228]]

16 *1*-[*nu-tu*$_4$] *na-aḫ-la-a*[*p-tu*$_{3/4}$]

Lower Edge

17 ⸢*iš-tu*⸣ [*n*]*a-kam-ti* ⸢x⸣[229]

18 [^{m}]*Ḫu-ut-te-šup* DUMU LU⸢GAL⸣

Reverse

19 [*it*]-*ta-šar*

---

20 [1 TÚ]G 1-*nu-tu*$_4$ *na-aḫ-la-ap-t*[*ù*]

21 1-*nu-tu*$_4$ *ḫul-la-an-nu šina-ḫi-*⸢*lu*⸣

22 *a-na* LÚ *ša* URU *Te-li-pè-er-ra*

23 *šu-un-dù* KÚR.MEŠ *is-sé-eḫ-*⸢x⸣$^{?}$-*lu*

(space)

24 *ù šu-ú a-na šu-ul-ma-ni il-li-ka*$_4$ *na-ad-nu*

---

25 1 TÚG 1-*nu-tu*$_4$ *na-a*⸢*ḫ*⸣-*la-ap-tu*$_4$ *šina-ḫi-lu*

26 *a-na* LÚ *ša* UR[U *I*]*r-ḫa-aḫ-ḫé na-ad-nu*

---

27 2 *zi-a-na-tu*$_4$ 4 *al-lu-ur-ru*
28 ^{m}*Ku-ul-pè-na-tal iš-tu na-kam-ti it-ta-šar*

---

29 1-*nu-tu*$_4$ *na-aḫ-la-ap-tu*$_4$ *šina-ḫi-lu*
30 1 ^{DUG}*bu-ṣú ša* 2 SILA$_3$ Ì.DÙG.GA *el*$^{!}$*-li*
31 [*a-n*]*a* ^{m}*Ḫa-ši-ip*$^{?}$*-tù*$^{?}$[230] *na-ad-nu*
32 [^{m}*T*]*i-ir-wi-na-tal iš-tu*
33 [*n*]*a-kam-ti i-na* ITI-^{ḫi} *Ké-nu-ni*
Upper Edge
34[231] [*š*]*a* URU-DINGIR.MEŠ *it-*⌜*t*⌝*-a-šar*

---

35 [1] ⌜^{TÚG}⌝*tù-ut-tù-bu a-ši-an-nu*
36 [*ki*$^{?}$*-na*$^{?}$*-a*]*ḫ*$^{?}$*-ḫé*[232] *ši-la-an-nu*
Left Edge
37 [*i-n*]*a* ITI-^{ḫi} *Ké-nu-ni ša* URU-DINGIR.MEŠ *it*$^{!?}$(=IŠ)-[*ta*$^{?}$*-šar*$^{?}$]
38 [^{m}]*Ka*$_4$*-ar-mi-ša iš-šuk a-na* $^{<m>}$*Ku-ul-pè-*[*na-tal*]
39 *na-ad-nu*

HSS XIV, 248

(1–8) 1 garment (and) an outfit of cloaks (and) an outfit of second-quality blankets/wraps, for *teḫušši*,[233] were given to Akip-tašenni the *kiziḫḫuru*[234] on the occasion when they set up (the image of) Tešup-of-Nuzi. Tirwin-atal withdrew (these items) from the storehouse in the month of Šeḫli.[235]

---

(9) ....

(10–14) An outfit of cloaks (and) an outfit of blankets/wraps were given to the sons of Eḫli-tešup of the town of Tilla.[236] Ḫeltip-apu withdrew (these items) on the day of Zike the Youth.

(15–19) 1 garment, an outfit of blankets/wraps, (and) an outfit of cloaks. Ḫut-tešup son of the king withdrew (these items) from the storehouse.[237]

(20–24) [1] garment, an outfit of cloaks, (and) an outfit of second-quality wraps were given to a (or: the) man of the town of Teliperra when the enemy were aggravated, and he (i.e., the man from Teliperra) went in order to (tender a) present (for pacification [i.e., as a bribe]?).

(25–26) 1 garment (and) an outfit of second-quality cloaks were given to a/ the man of the town of Irḫaḫḫe.

(27–28) 2 *ziyanātu*[238]-blankets (and) 4 *allūru*-garments. Kulpen-atal withdrew (these items) from the storehouse.[239]

(29–34) An outfit of second-quality cloaks (and) 1 *buṣu*-container of (i.e., containing) 2 *qa*s of pure perfumed oil were given to Ḫašip(?)-tu(?). Tirwin-atal withdrew (these items) from the storehouse in the month of Kenūnu-of (the city of)-Āl-ilāni.[240]

(35–37) [1] *tuttubû*-cloak, (decorated with sewn) *aššiyannu*-decorations, (in) purple(?) and *šillannu*. Karmiše withdrew (??) (and) chose(?)[241] (these items) in the month of Kenūnu-of (the city of)-Āl-ilāni; they were given to Kulpen-atal.[242]

30. HSS XVI, 391 (SMN 3252)

Findspot: Room D3
Publication: Lacheman 1958: 114[243]
Edition: None

Text #30 is presented here although it is not directly related to the military campaigns described in this chapter.[244] It is a brief list of three entries and an addendum. The entries identify individuals gone missing from three towns. The summary identifies the individual in charge of the three men identified. Although only the second man is identified as a slave, all three, lacking patronymics (and hence freeborn status), are likely to have been slaves. In the second and third entries, it is the wives[245] of the men who have disappeared. It is the first entry, though, that claims our special attention and excites our interest.

The text begins by identifying a man of the town of Lubti who has gone missing from the Assyrian capital, Aššur.[246] It is not necessary to relate the contents of text #30 to the Assyrian campaigns[247] upon which we have been focusing to recognize the document's importance in the present context. This text may or may not touch on the Arrapḫan struggle in the east. What is important, emphatically so, is that someone from Lubti, at the eastern limit of Arrapḫan territory, could end up in Aššur, to the west of Arrapḫan territory, probably as a prisoner. That he later disappeared is, for our purposes, unimportant. Clearly it is not necessary to posit nearby Babylonia as the agent of Lubti's travails. Assyria, here explicitly so, made its presence known in Arrapḫan territory at the very border of Babylonia.

Obverse

1 ^{m}*E-ké-ké ša* URU *Lu-ub-ti*$_4$
2 *iš-tù* URU *Aš-šur iḫ-li-qa*
3 ^{m}*Ip-ša-ḫa-lu* ÌR É.GAL
4 *ša* URU *An-zu-kál-lì*
5 [DAM]-*sú Ar-ra-*<*ap*?>*-ḫa-i-ú*
6 [*ša*?*-ni*?*-tu*?]-*ú* DAM-*s*[*ú K*]*u-uš-šu-uḫ-ḫa-ú*
7 ⸢*iš-tù*⸣ URU *Šar-ni-ta-ki* [*iḫ-li-qa*]
8 ^{m}*Pu-ḫi-še-en-ni ša* U[RU X x x[248]]
9 1 DAM-*sú Ku-uš-š*[*u-uḫ-ḫa-ú*]
10 *iš-tù* URU *Mar-ta-*[*x iḫ-li-qa*]
11 *ša* ŠU ^{m}*Wa-an-ti-y*[*a*]

HSS XVI, 391

(1–2) Ekeke of the town of Lubti went missing from the city of Aššur.

(3–7) The Arrapḫan[249] wife … (and?) the [second?] Kassite wife of Ipšaḫalu of the town of Anzukalli, a palace slave, [went missing] from the town of Šarnitaki.

(8–10) The 1 wife, a Kassite, of Puḫi-šenni of the town of … [went missing] from the town of Marta-… .

(11) These were under the authority of Wantiya.[250]

Chapter Two
Corruption in City Hall

The following series of twenty-four texts describes assorted culprits and the charges leveled against them, all by means of various depositions and records of legal confrontations.[1] The core of this nexus of wrongdoing is the alleged official malfeasance by an erstwhile mayor of Nuzi, Kuššī-ḫarpe.[2] He did not hold this office at the time of the legal proceedings described in these texts. Artašenni and Ḫašip-apu were both mayors, probably after Kuššī-ḫarpe and before the time of these records (text #35:45; text #49:12).[3]

If the charges leveled in these documents are true, then Kuššī-ḫarpe stood at the center of a network of criminal activity ranging from misappropriation of government resources (text #37, to name one text) to, most spectacularly, the abduction and rape of a local woman.[4] This last act (texts ##53 and 54) has, by its nature, received the most attention, even in such non-scholarly media as the *National Geographic* (Speiser 1951: 88–89) and *The New York Times* (Kuntz 1998: 7), the latter recalling a more recent instance when a political leader adamantly denied having sex with "that woman."

All texts that can be connected to Kuššī-ḫarpe are included.[5] These range from the virtually complete to the highly fragmentary, a good illustration of both the depth of Nuzi documentation and the inadequate, sometimes tantalizing nature of the evidence.

The present order of the texts is not strictly chronological, but, rather, conceptual.[6] The centrality of Kuššī-ḫarpe in this affair is not immediately apparent. His henchmen are more frequently mentioned and at greater length. So to establish Kuššī-ḫarpe's position of criminal leadership, we begin with accusations of Kuššī-ḫarpe's sole culpability. Text #31 is a case where Kuššī-ḫarpe is accused of receiving the purchase price for land, yet failing to deliver the land. Kuššī-ḫarpe contends that the "price" was in fact a spontaneous gift. Importantly, the text says that the veracity of the contradictory assertions is to be determined by the water ordeal.[7] A second case, text #32, also involves Kuššī-ḫarpe alone. Here too, the accused is alleged to have received a sheep (the price of the land in the first case was a paltry two sheep), this time in exchange for the (illegal) exemption of an individual from the obligatory annual labor levy, the *ilku*.[8] This release, it is to be deduced, never took place. Two further, very fragmentary, documents, texts ## 33 and 34, also involve Kušši-ḫarpe. In both cases livestock and other items are involved. The former document twice mentions a mayor, but real context is lacking.

The next sequence of texts also testifies to the illegal acts of Kušši-ḫarpe. But, in addition, the deeds sometime involve subordinates of Kušši-ḫarpe, demonstrating that an organized system is at work here—a gang led by Kušši-ḫarpe. Text #35 records a series of depositions. Kušši-ḫarpe is accused of accepting a bribe and of not delivering a *quid pro quo* (ll. 1–5), of accepting a bribe, *quid quo pro* delivered (ll. 19–22), and of theft (ll. 23–26, 51–53). In addition, Zilip-tilla, one of Kušši-ḫarpe's henchmen,[9] also stands accused of theft (ll. 6–14), and of kidnapping (ll. 15–18). A similar crime is attributed to another cohort of Kušši-ḫarpe, Birk-ilišu (ll. 56–62). Ḫašip-apu[10] is twice accused of theft (ll. 54–55, 63–65) and once of kidnapping (ll.40–42). The same victim seems also to have been kidnapped on an earlier occasion by Šukri-tešup (ll. 36–39). Kipiya son of Abeya, a further subordinate of Kušši-ḫarpe, stole sheep (ll. 43–44), a commodity specially favored by him. Artašenni, the mayor who possibly succeeded Kušši-ḫarpe, seems also to have engaged in theft, transferring the proceeds to Kušši-ḫarpe (ll. 45–50). An anonymous gardener of Kušši-ḫarpe stood accused of extorting goods from a hapless citizen (ll. 27–35). Text #36, a fragmentary text, links Kušši-ḫarpe with Zilip-tilla in what may be a claim that a house was destroyed. Two towns are named, one of which appeared in text #37 as the location of a house of Kušši-ḫarpe. Text #37 describes six cases. Kušši-ḫarpe stands accused of misappropriation of government labor and of diverting government goods for his private use and enrichment. Furthermore, break and enter is alleged as well as the accepting of a bribe. In addition, three cohorts of Kušši-ḫarpe appear: Zilip-tilla, Šaḫlu-tešup, and an underling of Šaḫlu-tešup, Ḫašip-apu. As for the first, Kušši-ḫarpe claims that an act of which he was accused was performed by Zilip-tilla and that he, Kušši-ḫarpe, was unaware of any illegality associated with the act. Zilip-tilla, it may be argued, is being betrayed here by his "boss," Kušši-ḫarpe. And here, we may be witnessing the start of a second, chronologically posterior, stage of the proceedings, when the fabric of this united criminal front appears to unravel. Zilip-tilla is mentioned in another case as well, but the context is too broken to define his role there; but clearly he is an agent of Kušši-ḫarpe. Šaḫlu-tešup appears in this text as a Kušši-ḫarpe loyalist. His own underling, Ḫašip-apu, claims that Šaḫlu-tešup said that Kušši-ḫarpe authorized the (illegal) confiscation of raw material. Šaḫlu-tešup, followed by Kušši-ḫarpe, denies that claim. Text #38 possibly identifies another lackey of Kušši-ḫarpe,

Keliya (l. 7; cf. text #42:2). However, this Keliya may be a victim of Kuššiḫarpe. Similarly vague, one Tai-šenni appears in texts ## 39 and 40, possibly as a henchman of Kušši-ḫarpe. The latter text, especially, is too broken for this identification to be certain. The former is more suggestive.[11]

Having established the identities of most of Kušši-ḫarpe's known accomplices—and having established Kušši-ḫarpe's leadership—we continue by treating texts in the order according to which henchmen are involved. A Kuššiḫarpe loyalist is treated first, eventual "defectors" after. Interrelated texts are grouped together.

Of all Kušši-ḫarpe's accomplices, Birk-ilišu seems to have been the chief deputy, at least to judge from the charges leveled against him. Text #41 pertains to a failed bribe. Birk-ilišu was to have forwarded the bribe to Kušši-ḫarpe. The text establishes the connection between the two and Birk-ilišu's subordinate position. Text #42 confirms his function as go-between. More impressive, Birk-ilišu is charged with six separate offences, ranging from sheep rustling to breaking and entering. Text #43, the longest text in this dossier, implicates him in twelve further cases of types already described. Texts ##42 and 43 both focus on alleged crimes committed by Birk-ilišu with but scant mention of Kušši-ḫarpe. Text #44 is a fourth text pertaining to Birk-ilišu, here alleging one further offence.

Kipiya,[12] like Birk-ilišu, is linked with Kušši-ḫarpe. In text #45, he is the object of three charges, twice with theft of sheep (ll. 1–48, 49–56) and once with theft of barley (ll. 59–68). Text #46 has him involved with five further cases, all pertaining to seizure of livestock or barley. Text #47, possibly the record of a single case, links Kipiya with sheep, ostensibly for sacrifice at the *eššešu*-festival.[13] Last in this sub-series stands text #48, yet another text involving Kipiya's seizure of sheep for the *eššešu*-festival. This text is distinguished for Kipiya's denial of culpability.[14] Rather, he claims, it is Kušši-ḫarpe who is guilty of misappropriation, not himself (ll. 34–36).

If Kipiya eventually "rolls" on his boss, he is not the only subordinate to do so. Ḫašip-apu and Zilip-tilla[15] likewise break ranks with Kušši-ḫarpe.

Ḫašip-apu appears in text #49 (ll. 48–53) where he is alleged to have abused his office by retaining garments on temporary loan to the government.[16] Text #50, a broken text, likewise seems to involve Ḫašip-apu (and possibly other cohorts of Kušši-ḫarpe). In both these instances, Ḫašip-apu has (official?) dealings with foreigners in Nuzi. Text #51, highly fragmentary, further links Ḫašip-apu with Kušši-ḫarpe. Text #52 is very difficult, but what seems clear is that Ḫašip-apu places responsibility for wrongdoing upon Kušši-ḫarpe. Kuššiḫarpe diverts barley taxes to his personal store.

Finally, Zilip-tilla turns on Kušši-ḫarpe according to text #53. There, he deposes that he helped bring a female to Kušši-ḫarpe. He further asserts that

Kušši-ḫarpe then raped her. Kušši-ḫarpe vehemently denies the charge. The loyalty of Zilip-tilla to Kušši-ḫarpe, evident in text #35 but no longer so in text #37, is shattered here. Text #54 records a similar deposition on Zilip-tilla's part (ll. 8–13; cf. ll. 14–18). The same text records at least one further case (ll. 1–7).

If the logical order of texts as elucidated here corresponds to an accurate chronology, then the longer the legal proceedings continued, the more Kušši-ḫarpe was left isolated as his subordinates abandoned him. At the end, only Birk-ilišu of the major gang members remained loyal to Kušši-ḫarpe.[17]

These records of the prosecution of Kušši-ḫarpe and of his merry men raise troubling questions of function. Why do these records exist at all? If the complete set of records had survived, it would have shown either that a verdict ("verdicts," more likely) had been reached or that none was reached. If there were no verdict, why would these, surviving, records have been preserved? If a verdict had been reached, Kušši-ḫarpe would have been exonerated or convicted. If the former, why would these, surviving, records have been preserved? If he had been convicted, either there would have been a legal appeal or not.[18] If there were no appeal, then where is the record of a verdict? (With twenty-four surviving components of this dossier, evidence of a verdict should have survived.) If, on the other hand, an appeal had taken place, then it would probably have been heard in the city of Arrapḫa, the seat of the local king. These evidentiary records would have been transferred there. Why, then, were the depositions kept—and found—at Nuzi at all? And, given that the records *were* stored in Nuzi, where, again, is the verdict, the statement of exoneration or conviction?[19]

31. *EN* 9/1, 470 (SMN 855)

Findspot: Unknown
Publication: Lacheman, Owen, Morrison et al. 1987: 693–94
Edition: None[20]

Obverse

1[21] [*um-ma* ^{m}*Ḫu-ti-ya šum-ma* 2] ⌈UDU.MEŠ *a-n*⌉*a*
2 ⌈*i-ra-n*⌉*i*[22] *a-na* ^{m}*Ku-uš-ši-ḫar-pè*
3 *la ad-dì-nu-ma* 2$^{!}$ (=12$^{?}$) UDU.MEŠ
4 *ki-i il-qú-ú-ma*
5 *ù* AŠÀ.MEŠ *ka*$_4$*-du ze-ri-šu-nu-ma*[23]
6 *a-na* ^{m}*Qí-iš-te-e-ya it-ta-a-din*

S.I.

7 NA$_4$ ^{m}*Tar-mi-ya*
8 *um-ma* ^{m}*Ku-uš-ši-ḫ̮ar-pè-ma*
9 2 UDU.MEŠ ^{m}*Ḫ̮u-ti-ya*
10 *a-na ya-ši ka*$_4$*-am-ma*
11 *id-dì-i-na*
Lower Edge
12 *šum-ma a-na i-ra-na*
13 *ša* A.ŠÀ.MEŠ *ša*
Reverse
14 ^{m}*Za-pá-ki a-na-ku él-qú-*⸢*ú*⸣/-⸢*ma*⸣
15 *ù šum-ma* A.ŠÀ.MEŠ *ša*
16 ^{m}*Za-pá-ki a-na-ku a-na* NUMUN?-*šú*?
17 ^{m}*Qí-iš-te-e-ya*
18 *ú-še-él-mu-ma*
19 *ad-dì-nu-ma*
20 *aš-šum an-ni-ti-*[*m*]*a*?
21 *ḫ̮ur-ša-an* DU.MEŠ-*ku*

S.I.?
22 NA$_4$ ^{m}*Pa-*⸢*a*?*-a*⸣?
S.I.?
23 NA$_4$ ^{m}[ ]
S.I.?
24 NA$_4$ ^{m}[ ]
Left edge
25 ŠU ^{m}TI.LA-KUR DU[B.SAR (x)]

EN 9/1, 470

(1–6) [Thus Ḫ̮utiya: "I most certainly] gave to Kušši-ḫ̮arpe [2] sheep as a (purchase) price (or "gift"[24]), and the two sheep—which he took—and the land, together with its seed, he gave to Qîšteya."

---

(7) (*seal impression*) Seal impression of Tarmiya.

(8–19) Thus Kušši-ḫ̮arpe: "Ḫ̮utiya gave me 2 sheep, gratis. I most certainly did not take (them) as the (purchase) price for Zapaki's land. And I certainly did not measure and give Zapaki's land, together with its seed,[25] to Qîšteya."

(20–21) Concerning this (matter), they are undertaking the ordeal by water.

(22–25) (*seal impression*?) seal impression of Paya?; (*seal impression*?);

seal impression of …; (*seal impression*?); seal impression of … . Hand of Balṭu-kašid, the scribe.

32. *P-S* 13 (SMN 559)

Findspot: Room L2 or M2
Publication: Pfeiffer and Speiser 1936: 20[26]
Edition: None

Obverse

1 [*um-ma* ^{m}*A*]-*kap-ta-e-ma*
2 [ ] *a-ḫu-ya*
3 [ ]-*ma i-na il-ki*
4 [ ]-*ši*$^{?}$
5 [ ] 1 UDU *a-na*
6 [^{m}*Ku-/Ḫu-uš-ši*]-*ḫar-pè at-ta-din*
7 [*ù a-n*]*a-ku-ma it-ti*
8 [ ]-*né-en-mi ta-*...
9 [ ] KÙ.SIG$_{17}$ 1 UDU *il-*[*qè*]
10 [ ] *a-na ya-si it-*[ ]
11 [ ]-*ú* ZI *mi*...

P-S 13

(1–11) [Thus] Akap-tae: "… my brother … and in/for the *ilku* … I gave 1 sheep to Kušši-ḫarpe.[27] [And] I, together with … gold, he took 1 sheep … he …-ed to me … ."

33. *EN* 10/1, 59 (SMN 1641)

Findspot: Unknown
Publication: Fincke 1996: 460[28]
Edition: None

Obverse

.
.
.

1 [ ] ⌜*ú x*⌝ [ ]
2 [ ] UR I[Š?] ⌜x⌝ [ ]
3 [I]B? *i+na* ⌜É⌝ I⌜T⌝-[ ]
4 (erasure)[29]
5 [*-n*]*u a-na* ^{LÚ}*ḫa-za-an-ni*
6 [*-i*]*l*? / -I]B *-ti iš*!*-tu*$_4$
7 [ ]⌜*x*⌝*-ar* / *ù pa-am-pa-la*
8 [*i*]*š-tu*$_4$[30] É.GAL *la* ⌜*x*⌝[ ]

---

9 [ ]⌜*x*⌝ *il*[31]*-KI*
10 [*a*?*-n*]*a*? ^{m}*Ḫu-uš-ši-ḫar-pè*
11 [*-s*]*ú*
12 [*š*]*u*?*-un-du eš-ši-iš*
13 [ ]*-pu-ni-in-ni*
14 [AN] ŠE?.MEŠ*-šu-nu na-šu-ú-ma*
15 [ ]-⌜*a*⌝? *uš-te-ri-bu ù um-ma šu-nu-*[*ma*]
16 [ ]*-mi*[32] *ù ni-nu ki-i i+na il-k*[*i*??]
17 [ ] ⌜*x-m*⌝*a ù ni-il-la-ak*
18 [ ] ⌜*x*⌝ *i-ip-pu-šu ù šu-nu* [(x)]
19 [ ] ⌜*x-n*⌝*u a-na* ^{LÚ}*ḫa-za-*[*an-ni*]
20 [ ] ⌜x x⌝

.

.

.

Reverse

.

.

.

21 [ ]*-pu-uš*[33]

EN 10/1, 59

(1–8) … in the house … to the mayor … from … (a type of garment) … from the palace I(?) did not … .

(9–21) … he took(?) … to(?) Kušši-ḫarpe … at that time(?), anew … their donkeys(?) were carried off(?) … they brought (them?) (into …) and thus they (said): " … and we, as in … [we] … and we are going[34] … . They are making/doing … to the mayor … .

34. *EN* 10/1, 61 (SMN 1643A[35])

Findspot: Unknown
Publication: Fincke 1996: 463
Edition: None

Obverse (probably)

.
.
.

1 [ ] ⸢x⸣ [ ]
2 [ ] ⸢x⸣ *a-n*⸢*a*⸣ [ ]
3 [ ]-PA LÚ.MEŠ ⸢*a*?-*n*⸣[*a*?]
4 [*i*]*š*?-*tu*$_4$ É.GA⸢L⸣ [ ]
5 [*i*?-*le*?]-*eq-qú-ú ù* AŠ? [ ]
6 [^{m}]*Ku-uš-ši-ḫar-pa*
7 [ ] ⸢x⸣.MEŠ *ša* GIŠ.MAR.GÍD.[DA.MEŠ]
8 [ ] ⸢x⸣ ŠE BI DU 10 UDU.ME[Š]
9 [ ] ⸢*x*⸣-*ri-li i-ta-*⸢*x*⸣-[ ]
10 [-*l*]*i*? *i-ta-*⸢*x*⸣-[ ]
11 [⸢x⸣ [ ]

EN 10/1, 61

(1–11) … to … men to(?) … from(?) the palace … -ed and … Kušši-ḫarpe, x-s of wago[ns] … 10 sheep … .

35. *P-S* 3 + *EN* 10/1, 10 (SMN 348+1173[36])

Findspot: Room L2 or M2
Publication and edition: Pfeiffer and Speiser 1936:14–15, 67–69 (SMN 348 only)[37]

Obverse

1 *um-ma* ^{m}*Zi*-[(1) Í]B.LÁ *ša mar-dá-ti*
2 *ù* 1 UDU *a-na* [^{m}*Ḫu-uš-š*]*i-ḫar-pè at-ta-din*
3 *ù um-ma šu*-[*ma š*]*a-tù-um-ma*
4 *e-ep-pu-uš* [ ] *an-nu-ti il-te-qè*
5 *ù ya-ši-ma ša-t*[*ù*]*-um-ma la i-pu-ša-an-ni*

6 *um-ma* ^{m}*Ki-in-tar-ma* ša URU DINGIR-*ni-šu*
7 *il-te-nu-tu*$_{4}$ ^{GIŠ}MAR.GÍD.DA 5 GÍN KÙ.BABBAR *ṣar-pu*
8 1 *né-en-sé-tu*$_{4}$ *ša* 3 MA.NA 30 GÍN ZABAR
9 1 TÚG 2 UDU.MEŠ *bá-qít-tu*$_{4}$ *ù*$^{?}$ *an-nu-tu*$_{4}$
10 ^{m}*Zi-li-ip-til-la il-te-qè*
11 *ù* ^{m}*Zi-li-ip-til-la* ŠE.MEŠ *ša pu-ri*
12 *a-šar* ^{m}*Ki-ir-ru-ka-*[*az*]*-zi i-te-ri-iš*
13 1 UDU *il-te-qè ù* [ ] ANŠE ŠE.MEŠ *ša pu-ri*
14 AŠ$^{?}$ AN.ZA.KÀR *Tam-kà*[*r*(*-ra*)] *i-na* É-*šú it-ta-bá-ak* [(?)]
15 [*um-ma*] ^{m}*Ḫa-ni-ú-*[*ma* ^{m}*Z*]*i-li-ip-til-la*
16 [ ]*-ta-an-n*[*i*] *i-te-eš*$_{15}$*-ra-an-ni*
17 *um-ma šu-ma* 1 UDU *ša* [*mu*]*-ul-le-e bi-la-am-mi*
18 1 ŠAH *il-te-qè-ma ù* ŠEŠ-*ya un-te-eš-ši-ir*
19 *um-ma* ^{m}*Ni-nu-a-tal-ma* ^{m}*Ḫu-uš-ši-ḫar-pè*
20 *iš-tu*$_{4}$ *ma-aš-ka-ni-ya uš-te-ri-qà-an-*[*ni*]
21 2 GÍN KÙ.GI$_{17}$ 1 GUD *ù* 2 UDU.NITA.MEŠ
22 *a-na* ^{m}*Ḫu-uš-ši-ḫar-pè at-ta-din-ma ù u*[*t-t*]*e-er-ra-an-ni*
23 *um-ma* ^{m}*Te-hi-ya-ma* ŠE.MEŠ *ka-ru-ú*
24 *ša ma-la* ANŠE 5 ^{GIŠ}APIN A.ŠÀ *ù* IN.NU.UN.MEŠ
25 ^{m}*Ḫu-uš-ši-ḫar-pè e-mu-qà il-te-qè-ma*
26 *ù a-na* ^{m}*Ḫa-ma-an-na* ^{LÚ}NAGAR *it-ta-din*
27 *um-ma* ^{m}DUMU-^{d} X$^{?}$*-ma zi-ib-lu*^{MEŠ}
28 *ša* 1 ANŠE 5 ^{GIŠ}APIN A.ŠÀ ^{LÚ}NU.GIŠ.SAR
29 *ša* ^{m}*Ḫu-uš-ši-ḫar-pè il-te-qè-ma*
30 *ù um-ma a-na-ku-ma am-mi-ni*
31 *zi-ib-li te-le-eq-qè-mi*

Reverse

32 *ù um-ma šu-ma at-ta a-na ra-pa-sí*
33 *iq-bu-ka-mi ù* AN.ZA.KÀR*-ka a-na na-pa-li*
34 *iq-bu-k*[*a*]$^{?}$ *ù a-na-ku ap-ta-la-aḫ-ma*
35 *ù ir-te-eq*
36 *um-ma* ^{m}*Wa-ra-at-t*[*e*]*-ya-ma*
37 ^{m}*Šúk-ri-te-šup a-na r*[*e*]*-a-*[*ú*$^{?}$[38]]*-ti*
38 *iš-ta-ak-nu i-na* KÁ.GAL^{-li} *i-te-es-*[*ra*$^{?}$*-an*$^{?}$*-ni*$^{?}$]
39 1 UDU.NITA *il-te-qè-ma ù un-te-eš-ši-ra-an-ni*
40 ^{m}*Ḫa-ši-pa-pu i-na nu-pa-ri*
41 *it-ta-dá-an-ni* 1 UDU.NITA *il-te-qè-ma*
42 *ù un-te-eš-ši-ra-an-ni*
43 ^{m}*Ki-pí-ya* DUMU *A-be-ya* ^{LÚ}SIPA*-ya*
44 *ir-ta-pí-is* 2 UDU.MEŠ *ù* 1 MÁŠ *il-te-qè*

45 ^{m}*Ar-ta-še-en-ni a-n*[*a h̬*]*a-za-an-nu-*⸢*ti*⸣
46 *iš-ta-ka-an ù* [ ]⸢*x*⸣ DÙ URUDU *ša* 6 MA.NA
47 1 *zi-a-na-tu* 1 ⸢*x*⸣*-li-tu*$_4$ *ù* ^{GIŠ}NÁ
48 1 ⸢*x*⸣ [ ]⸢*x x*⸣ *il-te-qè-ma*$^!$
49 *ù* ⸢*x x x x*⸣*-ma a-na* ^{m}*H̬u-uš-ši-h̬ar-pè-mi*
50 *ù i*⸢*k-t*⸣*a-lu-ú*

---

51 *um-ma* ^{m}⸢*X*⸣*-*[*i*]*p*$^?$*-te-šup-ma* 5 UDU.HÁ *ku-ru-uš-tù-ú*
52 *ù* 1 ^{TÚG}⸢*x x*⸣*-ze-e* ^{m}*H̬u-uš-ši-h̬ar-pè*
53 *e-mu-qám-*[*ma*] ⸢*i*⸣*l-te-qè ù šu-ma ik-ta-la*

---

54 *um-ma* ^{m}*Um-*[*p*]*í-ya-ma* ^{m}*H̬a-ši-ip-a-pu*
55 *ir-ta-ap-sà-*[*an-n*]*i-ma ù* 1 UDU *il-te-qè*

---

56 *u*⸢*m-m*⸣*a* ^{m}*Pa-a-a-*[*ma*] ⸢*x*⸣ *aš-*⸢*ša*⸣$^{!?}$*-ti* ^{m}*Piš-ki-*DINGIR*-šu*
57 *i-na* [ ] *ka uš* [ ] *a-na-ku a-na*
58 *mu-uš-šu-hu* [*at*]*-ta-la-ak*
59 *iṣ-ṣa-ab-ta-an-ni ù* 40 *i-na*
60 ^{GIŠ}*h̬u-ṭá-ar-*[*ti*] *ir-ta-ap-sa-an-ni*
61 2 UDU.MEŠ *ù* 1 [MA.NA] AN.NA.MEŠ *at-ta-din*
62 *ù* DAM^{-ti} [*un-te*]*-eš-ši-ir*
63 ^{m}*H̬a-ši-pa-pu* [*i-na* (É) *nu*]*-pa-«ni»*$^?$*-ri*[39]
64 *i-na* [ ]*-ru-ub*
Edge
65 2 ANŠE ŠE 5 BÁN GIG.MEŠ *ù* 1 UDU.NITA *e-mu-qa il-te-qè*
66 ^{NA_4}KIŠIB ^{m}*H̬a-iš-te-šup*
67 ^{NA_4}KIŠIB ^{m}*Pa-a-a*

P-S 3 + *EN* 10/1, 10

(1–5) Thus Zi-…: "A (or: One) *mardatu*-type[40] sash and 1 sheep I gave to Kušši-h̬arpe. And thus he (i.e., Kušši-h̬arpe): 'I shall … (you).' He took these … . But, as for me, he did not … me."

(6–14) And thus Kintar of the town of Ila-nīšû: "One complete wagon, 5 shekels of refined silver, 1 washbowl (made) of 3 minas, 30 shekels of bronze, 1 garment, (and) 2 plucked sheep, now(?) these Zilip-tilla took. And Zilip-tilla demanded *pūru*-barley[41] from Kirrukazzi and took 1 sheep; he poured out … homer(s) of *pūru*-barley at the Tamkarra Tower, at his (own) house."

(15–18) [And thus] Ḫaniu : "Zilip-tilla …-ed me … he confined me." Thus he (i.e., Zilip-tilla): 'Bring to me 1 sheep as a fine.' And he took 1 pig and then released my brother."[42]

(19–22) And thus Ninu-atal: "Kušši-ḫarpe ousted me from my position, but I gave 2 shekels of gold, 1 ox, and two rams to Kušši-ḫarpe and he reinstated me."

(23–26) And thus Teḫiya: "Kušši-ḫarpe seized by force a heap of barley, (the yield) of a 1.5 homer field, and straw, and gave it to Ḫamanna the carpenter."

(27–35) And thus Mâr-ištar: "The gardener of Kušši-ḫarpe took the *ziblu*(s)[43] of/for a 1.5 homer field, and so I (asked): 'Why do you take the *ziblu*(s)?' And thus he (responded): 'They ordered you to be beaten and also ordered your tower to be toppled.'[44] Then I became afraid and slunk away."

(36–50) And thus Waratteya: "Šukri-tešup, having appointed (me?) to be (supervisor?) shepherd(??) (yet?) confined me(?) at the gate, then he took 1 ram and released me. Ḫašip-apu cast me into the workhouse; then he took 1 ram and released me. Kipiya son of Abeya beat my shepherd;[45] he took 2 sheep and 1 lamb. Artašenni was established in the mayoralty … of(?) copper, weighing 6 minas, 1 *ziyanatu*-blanket, 1…, and a bed, 1 … he took, and then … to Kušši-ḫarpe, who kept (these items)."

(51–53) And thus …-ip?-tešup: "Kušši-ḫarpe took by force 5 sheep-for-fattening and 1 … -garment and he himself kept it (*sic*)."

(54–55) And thus Umpiya: "Ḫašip-apu beat me and took 1 sheep."

(56–65) [And] thus Paya: " Birk-ilišu (…-ed?) my wife(??) … in …; I went in order to … . He seized me and hit me forty (times) with a rod. I gave 2 sheep and 1 [mina] of tin. He released my wife. Ḫašip-apu arrived(?) at … [in] the workhouse(?), … . . He took by force 2 homers of barley 5 seahs[46] of wheat and 1 ram.

(66–67) Seal of Ḫaiš-tešup; seal of Paya.

36. *EN* 10/1, 60 (*SMN* 1642)

Findspot: Unknown
Publication: Fincke 1996: 461–62[47]
Edition: None

Obverse

1 [ ] ⌜x⌝ *t*⌜*e* x⌝ [ ] ⌜x⌝ KU

2 [ ] ⌜É⌝$^{-it}$ ^{m}*A-k[a]-pu ša*[48]
3 [ ] ⌜*x*⌝-*ti*[49] *uš-te-es-sí-ik*
4 [ ] ⌜x⌝ É ^{m}*A-ka-pu ma* TA-AT
5 [-*n*]*a*$^{?}$ DUMU[50] *Ta-ak-ku*[51]
6 [ ]⌜*x*⌝ *is-sú-ku* ^{m}*Ḫu-uš-ši-ḫar-pè*
7 [ ]-⌜*x-s*⌝*ú-mi*$^{?}$[52]
8 [ ] ⌜^{m}⌝*Ḫu-uš-ši-ḫar-pè*
9 [ ]-⌜*x*⌝-*šu-nu pí-il-la-tu*$_4$
10 [*re*$^{?}$]-*eḫ*$^{?}$-*tu*$_4$⌜E⌝RIN$_2$.MEŠ *uṣ-ṣí-i*
11 [ ] ⌜É⌝$^{?\text{-it}}$
12 [*í*$^{?}$-*na*$^{?}$ URU]⌜A⌝$^{!}$-*ta-kál*
13 [*í*$^{?}$-*na*$^{?}$ URU A]*n-zu-kál-lì uš-te*-[ ]
14 [ ] ⌜x⌝

.

.

.

Reverse

.

.

.

15 [ ] ⌜*an-ti*⌝ [ ]
16 [ ]⌜*i*⌝+*na* É-*y*⌜*a*⌝
17 [^{L}]$^{\mathrm{Ú}?}$*ḫa-za-an-nu*
(erased line)
18 [ ]⌜*x*⌝-*mi*
19 [*a*]*š*$^{?}$-*šum*
20 [-*p*]*u-ru-uš*
21 [^{m}*Ḫu-uš-š*]*i-ḫar-pè*
22 [ ]-*ma*
23 [^{m}*Zi*]-*li-ip-til-la*
24 [-*m*]*a*$^{?}$
25 [^{m}]-*en-ni*

Upper Edge

26 [ ]⌜x⌝ *i-ti*$^{?}$
27 [G]E
28 [ ] x KU
29 [ ]-*l*[*a*]$^{?}$

EN 10/1, 60 (*SMN* 1642)

(1–29) ... the house of Akk-apu which .... he removed (i.e., razed) .... the house of Akk-apu was measured(??) ... the son of Takku .... they removed(?). Kušši-ḫarpe ... Kušši-ḫarpe ... (a noun of unknown meaning) ... the(?) rest(?) of(?) the task force goes out ... the house of ... [in? the town of] Atakkal .... [in? the town of] Anzukalli he ...-ed ... in my house .... the mayor ... concerning(?) .... Kušši-ḫarpe ... Zilip-tilla .... .

37. *P-S* 1 + *EN* 10/2, 70[53] (SMN 285 + 1647)

Findspot: Room L2 or M2 + findspot unknown
Publication and edition: Pfeiffer and Speiser 1936: 13–14, 65–67 (*P-S* 1 only)[54]
Publication: Fincke 1998a: 251 (*EN* 10/2, 70 only)

The sense of lines 27–39 is difficult to unravel. See below, notes 65 and 68.

Obverse

1 *um-ma* ^{m}*Tù-ra-ri-ma* 30 $^{\text{GIŠ.MEŠ}}$[*am-pá-an-na*]
2 *i-na* KÁ.GAL *šá-ak-nu-mi ù* ^{m}*Ku-u*[*š-ši-ḫar-pè il-te-qè-šu-nu-ti*]
3 *um-ma* ^{m}*Ku-uš-ši-ḫar-pè-*<*ma*?> *la él-te-qè-*[*šu-nu-ti*]
4 *um-ma* ^{m}*Tù-ra-ri-ma* 30 $^{\text{LÚ.MEŠ}}$*a-lik* [*il-ki*]
5 *ša* AN.ZA.KÀR.MEŠ ŠE.MEŠ *iš-tu* É.GAL$^{-lì}$ [[55]]
6 *ù a-na* ^{m}*Ku-uš-ši-ḫar-pè* ŠE.GIŠ.Ì[56] [.MEŠ? *ù du-u*]*ḫ-na e-*[*er-re-eš*$_{15}$][57]
7 *ù* $^{\text{GIŠ.MEŠ}}$*am-pá-an-na ú-pa-aḫ-ḫa-ru*
8 *um-ma* ^{m}*Ku-uš-ši-ḫar-pè-ma* ^{m}*Zi-li-ip-til-la aš-ta-*[*par-šu*]
9 *um-ma a-na-ku-ma* ŠE.GIŠ.Ì.MEŠ *ù du-uḫ-na e-ri-i*[*š*]
10 1 ANŠE ŠE.GIŠ.Ì.MEŠ *ù du-uḫ-nu i-ba-aš-ši ša ir-šu-*[ ]
11 *ù* $^{\text{GIŠ.MEŠ}}$*am-pá-an-na pu-uḫ-ḫi-ir-mi*
12 *ù* 30 $^{\text{LÚ.MEŠ}}$*a-lik il-ki ša* AN.ZA.KÀR.MEŠ *la i-de*$_{4}$*-šu-nu-*[*ti*]
13 *um-ma* ^{m}*Pal-te-ya-ma* 40 $^{\text{GIŠ.MEŠ}}$*ša-aš-šu-gu* [*ša* É.GAL$^{-lì}$]
14 ^{m}*Ḫu-ti-ya* ^{LÚ}NAGAR *il-te-qè-šu-nu-ti*
15 *ù* ^{GIŠ}IG *a-na* ^{m}*Ku-uš-ši-ḫar-pè* [[58]]$^{-uš}$
16 *ù* ^{GIŠ}IG *a-na* É ^{m}*Ku-uš-ši-ḫar-pè i-na* URU *An-zu-kál-li* [[59]]
17 [*ù a-na-ku*] GIŠ.MEŠ *ša-šu-nu az-bi-il-šu-nu-*<*ti*?>
18 *um-m*[*a* ^{m}*Ku*]*-uš-ši-ḫar-pè-ma* GIŠ.MEŠ [*a*]*t*?*-tu-ú-ya-ma*
19 *ù a-na* ^{GIŠ}IG *a-na e-pé-ši at-ta-din*
20 *ù* GIŠ.MEŠ *ša* É.GAL *a-na* ^{GIŠ}IG *a-na e-pé-ši la ad-dì-in*
21 *um-ma* ^{m}*Ḫu-ti-ya* ^{LÚ}NAGAR*-ma* ^{GIŠ}IG *e-pu-šu*

22 GIŠ.MEŠ *iš-tu* URU *An-zu-ka*$_4$*-al-li* ^{m}*Ša-aḫ-lu-te-šup*
23 *a-na ya-ši id-dì-na ú*[60] GIŠ.MEŠ *re-eḫ-tu*
24 *iš-tu* URU *Nu-zi id-dì-na ù* GIŠ.MEŠ *ša-a-šu-nu*
25 *a-na* É.GAL-*li*[61] *i-de*$_4$*-šu-nu-*[*ti*] *ù a-na* ^{GIŠ}IG
26 *ša* ^{m}*Ku-uš-ši-ḫar-pè e-te-pu-uš*
27 *um-ma* ^{m}*Ḫa-ši-pá-pu-ma* 2 *ṣí-mi-it-tù sa-dì-in-*[*ni*]
28 *ù* 2 ^{TÚG}*uš-pá-aḫ-ḫu* ^{m}*Ša-aḫ-lu-te-šup i-na* ŠU-*ya* [*it-ta*]*-din*
29 *um-ma šu-ma um-ma* ^{m}[*Ku*]*-uš-ši-ḫar-pè-ma-mi* Ì.MEŠ *a-*[*šar* LÚ].MEŠ
30 *ša* ŠU-*ka šu-ud-din-m*[*i*] *ù sa-dì-in-ni e-p*[*u-uš*]
31 *ù a-na-ku* Ì.MEŠ *a-šar* L[Ú].MEŠ *ša* ŠU-*ya*! (=E) *uš-te-ed-*[*din*]
32 *ù e-te-pu-us-sú-n*[*u*]*-ti*
33 *um-ma* ^{m}*Ša-aḫ-lu-te-šup-ma* 2 *ṣí-mi-it-tù sa-*[*dì-in-ni*]
34 *ša* ^{m}*Ku-uš-ši-ḫar-pè a-na ma-ha-ṣí a-na* ^{m}*Ḫa-ši-p*[*á-pu at-ta-din*]
35 *ù um-ma a-na-ku-ma i-na ra-ma-ni-ka*$_4$*-ma ma-ḫa-aṣ-mi t*[*a*]*-a*[*q*]*-bi*
36 Ì.MEŠ *a-šar* LÚ.MEŠ *ša* ⸢ŠU⸣-*ka šu-ud-din-mi ù e-pu-uš-mi*
37 *um-ma* ^{m}*Ku-uš-ši-ḫar-pè a-na* ^{m}*Ša-aḫ-lu-te-šup la aq-bi*
38 Ì.MEŠ *a-na sa-dì-in-né-e ù* ^{TÚG}*uš-*[*pá*]*-aḫ-ḫe-e*
39 *a-šar* URU ***šu-ud****-d*[*in*]*-mi*
40 *um-ma* ^{m}*Ḫa-ši-pá-pu-ma* ⸢É.**ME**⸣**Š** ***e-kál-la-a-ú*** *ik-ta-an-ku*
41 *ù* ^{m}*Ku-uš-ši-ḫar-pè* ^{NA_4}KIŠIB.**MEŠ** ***iḫ-te-pé-šu-n***[*u-ti*]
42 *ù* É.MEŠ *im-ta-šar*
43 *um-ma* ^{m}*Ku-uš-ši-ḫar-pè-ma* ^{NA_4}KIŠIB [*ša* É.MEŠ]
44 ^{m}*Ḫa-ši-pá-pu-*[*ma i*]*ḫ-pí ù* É-*s*[*ú im-ta-šar*]
45 *um-ma* ^{m}*Ḫa-ši-*[*pá-pu-m*]*a* ^{m}*Te-ḫu-u*[*p-še-en-ni*]
46[62] *ù* ^{m}*Ú-nap-t*[*a-e*] ŠAH *ma-ru-*[*ú*?]
47 *il-tar-qú ù* [AŠ *pa*]*-ni* DI.KU$_5$.ME[Š]
48 *ù* [^{m}*Ku*]*-uš-ši-ḫ*[*ar-pè*]

Reverse

49 ^{m}*Zi-li-ip-til-la* [ ] ZU-*ma*
50 *pí-i-šú ša* ^{m}*Tù-ra-*[*ri*]*-ru ù ṭà-as-s*[*ú*]
51 *ù* LÚ.MEŠ *ṣa-ru-ti ša* [ ]
52 ^{m}*Ku-uš-ši-ḫar-pè il-*[*te-qè*]
53 *um-ma* ^{m}*Ku-uš-ši-ḫar-pè-*[*ma* ^{m}*Te*]*-ḫu-up-še-en-ni* [*ù* ^{m}]*Ú-nap-ta-e*
54 *ṭà-as-sú-nu la al-*[ ]*-šu-nu-ti*

Edge

55 NA$_4$ ^{m}*Pár-ta-su-*[*a*]
56 NA$_4$ ^{m}*Bi-ri-aš-šu-ra*

P-S 1 + *EN* 10/2, 70

(1–2) Thus Turari: "Kušši-ḫarpe [took] 30 (fagots of?) [firewood[63]] (which had been) placed at the city gate."

(3) Thus Kušši-ḫarpe: "I did not take [them]."

(4–7) Thus Turari: "30 'goers of the [going]'[64] from the districts [take] grain from the palace and plant (this) flax [and] millet for Kušši-ḫarpe; and they gather the firewood (as well)."

(8–12) Thus Kušši-ḫarpe: "I dispatched Zilip-tilla, and I said (as follows): 'Plant flax and millet; there is 1 homer of flax and millet of/which … . And gather the firewood.' As for 30 'goers of the going' from the districts, I know nothing about them."

(13–17) Thus Pal-teya: "Ḫutiya the carpenter took 40 (pieces) of [palace] *šaššūgu*-wood and [fashioned] a door for Kušši-ḫarpe; [he fashioned] the door for Kušši-ḫarpe's house in the town of Anzukalli. [And it was I who] transported that wood."

(18–20) Thus Kušši-ḫarpe: "(That) wood is mine. I did give (it to the carpenter) to fashion a door. But I did not give palace wood to fashion a door."

(21–26) Thus Ḫutiya the carpenter: "I fashioned the door. Šaḫlu-tešup gave to me the wood from the town of Anzukalli. And he gave the rest of the wood from the town of Nuzi. And I know that that wood was palace (wood) and I used (it) for Kušši-ḫarpe's door."

(27–32)[65] Thus Ḫašip-apu: "Šaḫlu-tešup entrusted to me[66] 2 pairs of *saddinnu*-cloths/-bolts And 2 *ušpaḫḫu*[67]-garments. Thus he (viz. Šaḫlu-tešup) (said): 'Thus Kušši-ḫarpe: "Collect oil from the men under your authority and make *saddinnu*-garments."' So I collected oil from the men under my authority and I made them (viz. the garments)."

(33–36) Thus Šaḫlu-tešup: "[I gave] 2 pairs of *saddinnu*-cloths/-bolts of Kušši-ḫarpe to Ḫašip-apu for weaving. And thus I (say to you, Kušši-ḫarpe[68]): You yourself, 'Weave,' you said, 'and collect oil from the men under your authority, and make (this item).'"

(37–39) Thus Kušši-ḫarpe: "I did not say to Šaḫlu-tešup: 'Collect from the town oil for (finishing) *saddinnu*-cloths/-bolts and for *ušpaḫḫu*-garments.'"

(40–42) Thus Ḫašip-apu: "The buildings of the "palace"-workers(?)/dwellers(?) were sealed but Kušši-ḫarpe broke the seals and …-ed[69] the buildings."

(43–44) Thus Kušši-ḫarpe: "The seals of the buildings Ḫašip-apu broke and […-ed] his/its building."

(45–52) Thus Ḫašip-apu: "Teḫup-šenni and Unap-tae stole a fattened(?) pig and … before the judges. And Kušši-ḫarpe …. Zilip-tilla … the testimony of Turari … . And Kušši-ḫarpe took his bribe and the *ṣaruti*-men of … ."

(53–54) Thus Kuššhi-ḫarpe: "I did not … the bribes of Teḫup-šenni [and] Unap-tae."

(55–56) Seal impression of Partasua; seal impression of Biryaš-šura.

38. HSS XIII, 466 (SMN 466)

Findspot: Room L2 or M2
Publication: Pfeiffer and Lacheman 1942: 90[70]
Edition: None

Obverse
(Top destroyed)
1 *ù šu-ú* [x x x]
2 *um-ma* [x x x]
3 2 LÚ.M[EŠ x x x]
4 *la e-*[x x x]
5 BI TI [x x x]
6 *ku-ur-ri-wa im-*[x x x]
7 *um-ma* ^{m}*Ké-li-ya-*[*ma* x x x]
8 *a-na ku-la-al-li* [x x x]
9 ^{m}*Ku-uš-ši-ḫar-pè* [x x x]
10 *na-ki-ru* [x x x]
11 *um-ma* ^{m}Ku-[*uš-ši-ḫar-pè-ma*]
12 [x x] *la* [x x x x]
(Rest destroyed)

HSS XIII, 466

(1) …. and he …

(2–6) Thus …: "I did not …. 2 men …. he …-ed *kurriwa*."

(7–10) Thus Keliya: "Kušši-ḫarpe … *ana kulalli* … Kušši-ḫarpe … foreigner …

(11–12) Thus Kušši-ḫarpe(?): "… no(?) ….

39. *P-S* 2 (SMN 76)

Findspot: Room L2 or M2
Publication and edition: Pfeiffer and Speiser 1936: 14, 67[71]

This text poses conundrums at crucial points: lines 4, 11, and 12. Pfeiffer and Speiser 1936: 14, 67 undertake extensive restorations at lines 1–2 and a crucial alteration in line 5. But none of these, nor the guesses at lines 4, 11, and 12, result in a meaningful text. The most that can be asserted is that Kušši-ḫarpe is accused of taking gold, possibly as part of an intended or completed transaction.

Obv.
1 [ ]
2 [ ]
3 [*at-t*]*a-din ù i-na*
4 [*ma*]*-ag-ra-at-ti uš-te-ši-wa-an-ni*
5 [*um*]*-ma* ^{m} *Ku-uš-ši-ḫar-pè-ma*
6 2 GÍN KÙ.GI$_{17}$ *il-qè um-ma* ^{m}*Ni-nu-a-tal-ma a-n*[*a*]
7 ^{m}*Ta-i-še-en-ni ad-din-mi*
8 *um-ma* ^{m}*Ta-i-še-en-ni-ma*
9 2 GÍN KÙ.GI$_{17}$ *a-na* ^{m}*Ku-uš-ši-*[*ḫar-pè*]
10 *ad-din* 1 GUD 2 UDU.MEŠ
11 *a-na* BURU$_{15}^{-ri}$ *-ya iz-zi-i*[*z*$^{?}$]
12 *te-le-eq-qè-e ù le-qì*
Rev.
13 [N]A$_4$ ^{m}*Ḫa-iš-te-šup*

P-S 2

(1–4) .... "I gave, and he ...-ed me at the threshing floor."

(5–6a) Thus Kušši-ḫarpe; "He took 2 shekels of gold."

(6b–7) Thus Ninu-atal: "I gave (it) to Tai-šenni."

(8–12) Thus Tai-šenni: "I gave 2 shekels of gold to Kušši-ḫarpe. He ...-ed 1 ox (and) 2 sheep for my harvest. 'You take and it is taken.' (i.e., 'once and for all'?)"

(13) Seal of Ḫaiš-tešup.

40. *EN* 10/1, 63 (SMN 1644+1646[72])

Findspot: Unknown
Publication: Fincke 1996: 464–65
Edition: None

Obverse

1 [^{m}]-*te-y[a*!].MEŠ
2 [ ] ⸢x⸣ Ì.MEŠ [Š]AR?
3 [*u]š-te-*⸢*x*⸣[*-n]u*?
4 [*i*?*-na*?] *ka-ri* [ ] *it-ta-ab-ku-ma*
5 [^{m} *-e]n-ni* ⸢x⸣
6 [^{m}*Ku/Ḫu-u]š-ši-ḫar-[p]è*
7 [ ] ⸢*x*⸣*-e*-BI AŠ? *ši-ip-ri-šu*
8 [ ] ⸢x⸣ *ad-dì-[i]n*?

---

9 [*um*?*-ma*? ^{m}*Ku/Ḫu]-*⸢*u*⸣*š-ši-ḫ[ar]-pè-ma*
10 [^{m}]-⸢*x*⸣*-ya* ^{m}*A-*[ ] *ù* ^{m}*Ta-i-še-en-ni*
11 [ ]⸢x⸣[ ] ⸢x x x⸣ [G]AL

.

.

.

Reverse

.

.

.

12 [ ]⸢*x*⸣*-a-pu*[73] ⸢*x*⸣ [ ]
13 [ ]⸢*x x*⸣ *iš-tu*$_{4}$
14 [*i]l*?*-te-qè*![74]*-šu-nu-[ti*?]
15 [*a*?*-na*? ^{m}*Ku/Ḫu-u]š-ši-ḫar-pè*

---

16 [*um*?*-ma*? ^{m}*Ku/Ḫu-u]š-ši-ḫar-pè-ma*
17 [ ] BA? A[N]? ⸢TI⸣? *ša i+na*
18 [ ]*-li-ra-aš* [ ]
19 [^{m}]-⸢*x*⸣*-te-ya iq-[ta*?*-bu*?]*-*⸢*ú*⸣?
20 [ ] ⸢x⸣ *ka-ar*-WA *ša-a-šu*
21 [*um*?*-ma*? ^{m}]*-ya-ma š[u]-ú i+na* ^{NA_4}KIŠIB*-ya-ma*
22 [*-a]l*? *ù* 1 *šu-ši* GUN
23 [ ](-)*an-nu ša-a-šu el-te-qè-mi*

(blank)

EN 10/1, 63

(1–8) .... –teya .... oil .... were piled/stored [in?] a heap, and .... Kušši-ḫarpe ... his message ... I gave(?).

(9–11) [Thus?] Kušši-ḫarpe: " ...-ya, A-...., and Tai-šenni .... large ...."
(12–15) .... he took(?) them(?) ... from .... [to?] Kušši-ḫarpe.

(16–23) [Thus?] Kušši-ḫarpe: ".... which, in ... -teya said(?) ... that (one)." [Thus?] ...-ya: "It, by means of my seal(ing) ... and sixty talents ... I took that (one) .... ."

(blank)

41. *P-S* 9 (SMN 809)

Findspot: No room number
Publication and edition: Pfeiffer and Speiser 1936: 19, 74[75]

1 *um-ma* ^{m}*Ḫu-zi-ri-ma*
2 6 GÍN KÙ.BABBAR *ṣa-ar-pu*
3 *a-na* ^{m}*Bi-ir-ki*-DINGIR-*šu*[76]
4 *at-ta-din*
5 *um-ma a-na-ku-ma*
6 *a-na* ^{m}*Ku-uš-ši-ḫar-pè*
7 *i-din-ma ù*
8 *di-ni li-pu-uš*
8a[77] [*ù*$^?$ *a*$^?$-*na*$^?$ ^{m}]*Bi-ir-ki-li-šu*
9 1 *ka*$_4$-*ši-ir-na*
10 *ša* ^{GIŠ}GIGIR
11 *at-ta-din*
12 *di-ni la i-pu-šu*
13[78] 6 GÍN KÙ.BABBAR-*pí*?[79]
14 *ù* 1 *ka*$_4$-*ši-ir-nu*
15 *ša* ^{GIŠ}GIGIR ^{m}*Bi-ir-ki*-DINGIR-*šu*[80]
16 *ik-ta-la*

P-S 9

(1–16) Thus Ḫuziri: "I gave 6 shekels of refined silver to Birk-ilišu. Thus I (said): 'Give (the silver) to Kušši-ḫarpe, and let him dispose of my case.' I [also?] gave 1 chariot *kaširnu*[81] [to?] Birk-ilišu. They did not dispose of my case. Birk-ilišu kept the 6 shekels of silver and the 1 chariot *kaširnu*."

42. *P-S* 10 (SMN 319)

Findspot: L2 or M2
Publication and edition: Pfeiffer and Speiser 1936: 19, 74–75[82]

1 *um-ma* ^{m}*Ú-na-a-a-ma* 1 *en-zu* ^{m}*Ḫu-ti-y*[*a*]
2 *a-na ya-ši* SUM-*na ù* ^{m}*Ké-li-ya*
3 *iṣ-ṣa-bat ù ti-ik-ka*$_4$*-šu uk-te-en-ni-ku*
4 *di-na-ni iṣ-ṣa-bat-ma ù* ^{m}*Piš-ki*-DINGIR-*šu*
5 ^{NA_4}KIŠIB-*šu iḫ-te-pí-ma ù a-na* ^{m}*Ḫu-uš-ši-ḫar-pè* DÙ$^{-uš}$
6 ^{m}*Ta-a-a* DUMU *A-ra-a-a a-na* 3 GUN URUDU.MEŠ
7 *a-na ya-ši id-du-ú ù* ^{m}*Piš-ki*-DINGIR-*šu*
8 *e-mu-qa i-na ta-lu-uḫ-le-e il-te-qè*
9 *um-ma* ^{m}*Šu-mu-ut-ra-ma* 2 UDU.MEŠ-*ya*
10 ^{m}*Piš-ki*-DINGIR-*šu il-te-qè ù ik-ta-la*
11 ^{MÍ}*kál-la-ti il-te-qè ù a-na* 11 ITI
12 *i-na* É-*šú i-si-ir-šu*
13 *um-ma* ^{m}*Tù-ra-ri-ma* 2 UDU.MEŠ ^{m}*Piš-ki*-DINGIR-*šu*
14 *il-te-qè ša* ERIN2.MEŠ *il-ti-in-nu-ú*
15 *un-te-eš-ši-ru ù ut-tù-ya ik-ta-lu-ú*
16 *um-ma* ^{m}*Ip-ša-ḫa-lu-ma* ^{LÚ}UŠ.BAR 1 UDU ^{m}*Piš-ki*-DINGIR-*šu*
17 *il-te-qè ù ik-ta-la ù ša* LÚ.MEŠ *e-pí-iš* SÍG.MEŠ
18 UDU.ḪÁ.MEŠ-*šu-nu ú-me-eš-ši-ru*
19 *um-ma* ^{m}*Ar-ša-wa-ma a-na-ku i-na* URU *Túr-ša aš-bá-ak*
20 *ù* ^{m}*Piš-ki*-DINGIR-*šu i-na* É-*ya i-te-ru-um-ma*
21 ^{GIŠ}IG^{-ti} *it-ta-sà-aḫ-ma ù il-te-qè*
22 *ù* É$^{-ti}$ *ug-te-el-li-bu*

P-S 10

(1–8) Thus Unaya: "Ḫutiya gave 1 goat to me but Keliya seized (it) and sealed (i.e., placed a sealing on) its neck, and seized me myself. Now Birk-ilišu broke its seal and made it over to Kušši-ḫarpe. Taya son of Araya was consigned to me for 3 talents of copper. Now Birk-ilišu took (him) by force (from among?) the harem servants."[83]

(9–12) Thus Šumatra: "Birk-ilišu took 2 of my sheep and kept them. He took my daughter-in-law for 11 months, confining her in his house."

(13–15) Thus Turari: "Birk-ilišu took 2 sheep. The one belonging to the work force was released; but mine was kept."

(16–18) Thus Ipša-ḫalu, the weaver: "Birk-ilišu took one sheep (of mine?) and kept it. But he released the sheep (pl.) of the (other?) wool workers."

(19–22) Thus Ar-šawa: "I dwell in the town of Turša. Now Birk-ilišu entered my house, removed my door, and took it and (then) stripped my house bare."

43. *P-S* 8 (SMN 2693)

Findspot: No room number
Publication and edition: Pfeiffer and Speiser 1936: 18, 72–74[84]

Obverse

1 *um-ma* ^{m}*It-ḫi-iš-ta-ma* 1 ŠEŠ-*ya*
2 ^{m}*Piš-ki-il-li-šu il-te-qè*
3 *ù a-na ḫu-ša-ú-ru-ti i-na* URU *Ḫa-ši-⸢ik⸣-ku-we-ma*
4 *uš-te-ri-ib-šu i-na* 1 ITI-^{ḫi} *a-ši-ib*
5 *i-na ša-ni-i* ITI-^{ḫi} *la ú-me-eš-ši-ru-uš*
6 *ù i-na ša-aš-ši* ITI-^{ḫi} 2 ŠEŠ.MEŠ-*ya*
7 *ṣi-dì-ta il-te-qú-ma ù it-ta-at-la-ku*
8 *i-na* AN.ZA.KÀR *Ši-la-ḫi-iš ik-ta-al-du-ma*
9 *ù* 1 LÚ *ša* URU *Ar-ra-ap-ḫe i-ta-ag-ru*
10 1 ŠEŠ-*ya il-te-qè-ma ù i-na* URU *Ḫa-ši-ik-ku-we-ma*
11 *ṣi-dì-ta uš-te-ri-bu ù it-ta-ṣú-ú*
12 1 ŠEŠ-*ya ša ṣí-dì-ta ú-še-ri-bu*
13 LÚ KÚR.MEŠ *id-du-u[k]-šu ù* LÚ *ša* URU-DINGIR.MEŠ
14 *a-na ba-al-ṭú-ti-im-ma it-tab-lu-uš*
15 *ù a-bu-šu ša* LÚ *ša* URU-DINGIR.MEŠ *it-tal-ka*$_4$*-am-ma*
16 *ù* ŠEŠ-*ya ša* [*ir-te-eḫ*](?)[85] *iṣ-ṣa-bat ù iq-ta-bi*
17 DUMU-*ya ta-gu*$_5$*-u*[*r-mi*] *ù* KÚR.M[EŠ] *il-te-qè-mi*
18 3 UDU.MEŠ 1 TÚG *aš*-[n] M[A.N]A URUDU.MEŠ
19 *ù* 1 *né-en-sé-tu*$_4$ *ša* [ZABAR][86] *il-te-qè*
20 *ù* ŠEŠ-*ya un-te-eš-*[*ši-ir*]
21 *um-ma* ^{m}*Na-ni-ya-ma* ^{m}*It-ḫi-ip-a-tal* ŠEŠ-*ya*

22 *i-na* URU *Tù-ur-ta-ni-ya a-ši-ib*
23 *ù* ^{m}*Piš-ki-il-li-šu iš*-tu_4 *il-ki*
24 *un-te-eš-ši-ir-šu* 1 $GEME_2$ 1 KUŠ GUD *ša*(-)*li-mu*
25 *ù ša* 2 *ṣi-mi-it-ti* GIŠ.MEŠ *ḫa-al-wa-ad-ru*
26 *a-na ṭá-a-ti il-te-qè*
27 *um-ma* ^{f}*Ḫi-in-zu-ri-ma* DAM^{-at} ^{m}*Zi-li-ya*
28 1 UDU *a-na ṭá-a-ti a-na* ^{m}*Piš-ki*-DINGIR-*šu*
29 *at-ta-din ù um-ma a-na-ku-ma* A.ŠÀ.MEŠ-*ya*
30 *it-ti* ^{m}*Ka-ri-ru di-ni e-pu-uš-mi*
31 *di-ni la* DÙ$^{-uš}$ *aš-šum* UDU-*ya aq-ta-bi*
32 *ù ir-ta-ap-sà-an-ni-ma ù* UDU^{-ri}
33 *ik-ta-la ù iṣ-ṣa-ab-ta-an-ni-ma*

Reverse

34 *ù* 6 MA.NA URUDU.MEŠ *il-te-qè ù um-ma*
35 *šu-ma ki-mu-ú ša-ad-dá-ag-dì el-qè-mi*
36 *um-ma* ^{m}*Ḫu-ya-ma* 1 *šu-ú-du ša šar-ti*
37 ^{m}*Piš-ki*-DINGIR-*šu e-mu-qam-ma il-qè*
38 *um-ma* ^{m}*Ḫa-ši-ya-ma a-na ik-ka-ru-ti*
39 *a-na* ^{m}*Ḫu-uš-ši-ḫar-pè it-ta-ad-nu-ni-in-ni*
40 *i-na ka-lu-mé-e er-re-eš ù i-na mu-ši* (1 sign erased)
41 *i-na* É$^{-ti}$ *at-ta-la-ak ù* ^{m}*Ú-na-ap-ta-ar-ni*
42 ÌR *ša* ^{m}*Ḫu-uš-ši-ḫar-pè iṣ-ṣa-ab-ta-an-ni-ma*
43 *ù um-ma šu-ma am-mi-ni i-na* É$^{-ti}$-ka_4
44 *ta-al-li-ik-mi ù* 1 TÚG$^{-tù}$ *ša ši-ma* AN.$ZALAG_2$
45 *il-te-qè ù* ^{m}*Piš-ki*-DINGIR-*šu iṣ-ṣa-ab-ta*
:-*an-ni-ma*
46 *ù i-na* ŠU ^{m}*I-ni-ya a-na* 1 (PI) 2 BÁN ŠE.MEŠ
47 *it-ta-ad-na-an-ni ù* 1 (PI) 2 BÁN ŠE.MEŠ *iš*-tu_4
48 UGU$^{-ḫi}$-*ya il-te-qè*
49 *um-ma* ^{m}*Ut-ḫa-a-a-ma* 1 UDU *ù* 1 *en-zu*
50 *e-mu-qa* ^{m}*Piš-ki*-DINGIR-*šu il-qè*
51 *um-ma* ^{m}*Zi-ké-ma* 1 UDU *e-mu-qa*
52 ^{m}*Piš-ki*-DINGIR-*šu il-qè i-na ša-lu-uš-mu*
53 *um-ma* ^{m}*Pal-te-ya-ma* 1 UDU^{-ri} ^{m}*Piš-ki*-DINGIR-*šu* TI
54 *um-ma* ^{m}*Pa-li-ya-ma* 1 MA.NA AN.NA.MEŠ
55 1 ^{GIŠ}BANŠUR *ša* GÌR.MEŠ-*šú ša* ^{GIŠ}TÚG
56 *ù* 1 ^{GIŠ}NÁ ^{m}*Piš-ki*-DINGIR-*šu e-mu-qa il-qè*
57 *um-ma* ^{m}*Ḫa-na-ak-ka-ma* 1 ^{GIŠ}BAN *e-mu-qa*
58 ^{m}*Piš-ki*-DINGIR-*šu il-qè ù* 6 (PI) 1 BÁN ŠE
59 *a-šar* ŠEŠ-*ya a-na* [ ]-*ma-lu-ti il-qè*

60 *um-ma* ^{m}*Šúk-ri-te-*[*šup-ma* 1] UDU ^{m}*Piš-ki-*DINGIR-*šu*
61 *a-na ši-mi il-qè* [*ù*] *ši-im-šu la i-din*
62 *ù šum-ma* UDU *la* [*ut*]*-te-er i-na 3-lu-mu*[87]
63 *um-ma* ^{m}*Ḫa-tar-te-ma i-na* KUR *Ḫa-lì-gal-bat*
64 *at-ta-al-ka*$_4$ *ù aš-šum di-ni-ya i-na*
65 ŠU ^{m}*Piš-ki-*DINGIR-*šu it-ta-ad-nu-ni-in-ni*
66 1 UDU 1 *né-en-sé-tu*$_4$ *ša* ZABAR *ù* 2 $^{(\text{GIŠ}?)}$IG(.MEŠ?)[88]
67 ^{m}ŠEŠ-*mi-ša a-na ṭá-a-ti a-na*
68 ^{m}*Piš-ki-*DINGIR-*šu it-ta-din*

Left Edge

69 *ù di-ni la i-puš*
70 NA$_4$ ^{m}*Pa-a-a*
71 NA$_4$ ^{m}*Ḫa-iš-te-šup*

P-S 8

(1–20) Thus Itḫišta: "Birk-ilišu took one of my brothers and imprisoned him in the town of Ḫašikku. (There) he sat one month; nor in the second month was he released. Now in the third month two (other) brothers of mine took provisions and set out. They reached the *dimtu* of Šilaḫi where they hired[89] a man of the city of Arrapḫa. He took one of my brothers and they brought the provisions to the town of Ḫašikku. Then they left. My one brother who delivered the provisions was killed by enemies; and they carried off alive the man from Āl-ilāni.[90]

Now the father of the man from Āl-Ilāni came and seized my [remaining?] brother and said: 'You hired my son and (now) enemies have taken him away.' He accepted 3 sheep, 1 …-garment, n minas of copper and 1 [bronze] washing bowl and then released my brother."[91]

(21–26) Thus Naniya: "My brother Itḫip-atal, dwells in the town of Turtaniya. And Birk-ilišu released him from the *ilku*, accepting as bribe 1 maid-servant, 1 complete(?) oxhide and *ḫalmadru*-wood[92] for 2 yoke crosspieces."

(27–35)[93] Thus ^{f}Ḫinzuri wife of Ziliya: "I gave 1 sheep to Birk-ilišu as a bribe. And thus I (said): 'Deal with my lawsuit with Kariru (regarding) my land.' He did not deal with my lawsuit. I spoke to him regarding my sheep. And he beat me and kept my sheep. Further, he seized me and took 6 minas of copper. And thus he (said): 'I took (it) instead of (taking it) last year.'"

(36–37) Thus Ḫuya: "Birk-ilišu took by force 1 … made of hair."

(38–48) Thus Ḫašiya: "They made me farm for Kušši-ḫarpe. All day, I would sow and at night I went home. And Unap-tarni, the slave of Kušši-ḫarpe seized me and thus he (said): 'Why did you go to your house?' And he took 1 garment of ….[94] And Birk-ilišu (also) seized me and consigned me to Iniya's authority for 1 *pān* 2 *sât* (= .8 homers)[95] of barley. And he took the 1 *pān* 2 *sât* (= .8 homers) of barley against me."[96]

(49–50) Thus Utḫaya: "Birk-ilišu took by force 1 sheep and 1 goat."

(51–52) Thus Zike: "The day before yesterday(?) Birk-ilišu took by force 1 sheep."

(53) Thus Pal-teya: "Birk-ilišu took 1 sheep."

(54–56) Thus Paliya: "Birk-ilišu took by force 1 mina of tin, 1 table with legs of boxwood, and 1 bed."

(57–59) Thus Ḫanakka: "Birk-ilišu took by force 1 bow, and he (also) took from my brother's place 6 *pān* 1 *sūt*[97] of barley for ...-ing."

(60–62) Thus Šukri-tešup: "Birk-ilišu took [1] sheep for a price [but] failed to pay its price. And he certainly did not [lit: "did"] return (it) by the day before yesterday(?)."

(63–69) Thus Ḫatarte: "I went to the land of Ḫanigalbat, and, regarding my lawsuit, they entrusted it on my behalf to the care of Birk-ilišu. Aḫ-ummiša gave to Birk-ilišu 1 sheep, 1 bronze washing bowl, and 2 doors as bribe. But he failed to deal with my case."

(70–71) Seal of Paya; seal of Ḫaiš-tešup.

44. *EN* 9/3, 471 = *P-S* 14 (SMN 1048)

Findspot: Room L2 or M2
Publication: Pfeiffer and Speiser 1936: 20 (*P-S* 14)[98]
Publication: Lacheman and Owen 1995: 311 (*EN* 9/3, 471)[99]

Obverse
1 [*um*$^{?}$*-m*]*a*$^{?}$ ^{md}I⸢M⸣-[LUGAL[100]-*ma*]
2 [1 *en*]-*zù a-na* ^{m}*B*[*i*$_{4}$*-ir-ki-il-li-šu*]
3 [*a*]*t-ta-din ù um*-[*ma šu*$^{?}$*-ma*$^{?}$]
4 [ ] ⸢x⸣ *ša* UD *ku-mé-e* [ ]
5 *ù*$^{!}$ ^{m}*Mil-ka-a-a a-bi*-[*ya*$^{?}$] ⸢*un-te*⸣*-eš-ši-ra-an-ni*[101]
6 *AŠ*$^{?}$ *BA TA ki*$^{!?}$*-ma*$^{?}$
7 1 *en-zù i*[*l*]$^{!?}$*-t*[*e*]$^{?}$-[*qè*$^{?}$][102]
8 *ù i-*⸢*x*⸣[103][ ]
9 *ù* ^{m}*I-ri-*[*ri*]*-til-l*[*a*]⸢*e*⸣$^{?}$-[ ]
(blank space)
10 *um-ma* ^{m}*Bi*$_{4}$*-ir*$^{!}$ (=NI)-[*ki-i*]*l-l*[*i-šu*][104]
11 1 *en-zù* ^{md}IM-[LUGA]L[105] *id*-[*di*$_{1/3}$*-na*][106]
12 *um-ma šu-ma* ⸢x⸣ *a*[*p*$^{?}$*-l*]*a*$^{!?}$*-ku-mi*[107]

13 *ù ma-am-ma lu-ú* [ ]
14 *la* ⸢*i*⸣[108]-[*n*]*a* AN ZA MI
15 1 UDU *aš-šum a-lik it*-⸢*x*⸣[109] [ ]
Reverse[110]
.
.
.
S.I.
16 ^{NA_4}KIŠIB ^{m}*Tar-mi-ya*
S.I.?
17 [^{NA_4}KI]ŠIB ^{m}*Pa-a-a*

EN 9/3, 471 = *P-S* 14

(1–9) Thus(?) Adad-šarri: "I gave [1] goat to Birk-ilišu and thus [he?]: '. . . .' And he released to(?) me Milkaya, my(?) father. ... He took(?) 1 goat and ... and Iriri-tilla ... . "

(10–15) Thus Birk-ilišu: "Adad-šarri gave 1 goat. Thus he: 'I am satisfied(?).' And no one . . . . 1 goat regarding the one who went with(?) . . . . "

(16–17) (*seal impression*) Seal impression of Tarmiya; (*seal impression*?) seal impression of Paya.

45. *P-S* 6 (SMN 309)

Findspot: Room L2 or M2
Publication and edition: Pfeiffer and Speiser 1936: 16–17, 70–71[111]

Obverse
1 *um-ma* ^{m}*Ḫu-i-te-ma* 17 UDU.ḪÁ.MEŠ-*ya*
2 ^{m}*Ki-pí-ya a-na* 1 UD^{-mi}-*ma il-te-qè-šu-nu-ti*
3 *um-ma šu-ma* UDU.ḪÁ.MEŠ *ša* É.GAL^{-li}-*mi*
4 *šum-ma a-na ša* É.GAL^{-li} *la* SUM^{-din}-*šu-nu-ti*
5 *ù šum-ma a-na ya-ši la ú-te-er-šu-nu-ti*
6 *um-ma* ^{m}*Ki-pí-ya-ma* ^{m}*Ki-pa-a-a*
7 ^{LÚ}SIPA *ša* ^{m}*Ké-li-ya a-na mu-ru-ti*
8 *i-te-l*[*i ù u*]*m-ma šu-ma* 17 UDU.ḪÁ.MEŠ
9 *an-nu-*[*ti ša* É.G]AL^{-li}-*mi ù* ^{m}*A-ri-im-ma-at-ka*$_4$
10 [*i*]*t-ti* [^{m}*Ḫa*?-*ši*?-*ip*?]-*a-pu-ma iš-tap-ra-an-ni*
11 *ù* [UDU.ḪÁ.MEŠ]-*šu-nu nu-uṣ-ṣé-eb-bi-it*

12 *ù* $^{m?}$[^{m}*A-ri*]*-ma-at-ka*$_4$ *ik-ta-na-ak-šu-nu-ti-ma*
13 *ù i-*[*na* É$^?$.GAL$^?$] UL$^?$ *it-ta-din-šu-nu-ti*
14 *ù i-na* [17 UDU.ḪÁ].MEŠ *ša-a-šu-nu* 4 UDU.MEŠ
15 [*a*]*-šar* ^{m}*Šúk-r*[*i-y*]*a il-te-qè-šu-nu-ti*
16 *ù* ^{m}*Ki-pa-a-a* ^{LÚ}*mu-ru* 1 *na-am-si*$^?$*-ta*
17 [*a*]*-šar* ^{m}*Šúk-ri-ya il-te-qè ù* UDU.ḪÁ.MEŠ
18 [*un*]*-te-eš-ši-ru*
19 [*um*]*-ma* ^{m}*A-ri-im-ma-at-ka*$_4$*-ma*
20 [n UDU].ḪÁ.MEŠ ^{m}[*Ki*]*-pí-ya ú-bi-il-šu-nu-ti*
21 [ ] *ú ta* [ ] ^{m}*Ni-iḫ-ri-ya*
22 [ ] *ta na* [ ]*-ti ù i-na qa-ti*
23 [^{m} *-y*]*a-ma* [*it*]*-ta-din-šu-nu-ti*
24 [x$^?$+] 5 UDU.MEŠ *a-*[*šar* ^{m}]*Šúk-ri-ya*
25 [*il-te*]*-qè-šu-nu-ti i-*[*na*] [10+] 7 UDU.ḪÁ.MEŠ
26 [*ša ú*]*-me-eš-še*$_{20}$*-er-šu-*[*nu-ti*]
27 [*um*]*-ma* ^{m}*Šúk-ri-ya-ma* 4 UDU.MEŠ
28 ^{m}*Ki-pí-ya il-te-qè-šu-nu-ti*
29 *ù i-na* ŠÀ$^{-bi}$ UDU.MEŠ *ša-a-šu-nu* 2 [UDU.MEŠ]
30 *un-te-eš-ši-ir-šu-nu-ti ù* 2 UDU.MEŠ
31 *ik-ta-la-šu-nu-ti um-ma šu-ma-mi am-mi-ni-im-ma-mi* GA.MEŠ*-ka*$_4$ *a-na* A.MEŠ *še-qè-e tù-bi-il-šu-nu-ti-mi*
32 *um-ma* ^{m}*Ki-pí-ya-ma* ^{m}*A-ri-im-ma-at-*[*ka*$_4$]
33 *iš-tap-ra-an-ni ù um-ma šu-ma*
34 *am-mi-ni* GIŠ.MAR.GÍD.DA.MEŠ*-šu*
35 *ša* ^{m}*Ki-ri-ya i-na* A.ŠÀ A.GÀR.MEŠ

Reverse

36 *ša* É.GAL$^{-lì}$ *la ú-ri-du-mi*
37 *a-li-ik-ma-mi ù* 4 UDU.MEŠ*-šu*
38 *ṣa-ba-at-mi at-ta-la-ak-ma*
39 *ù* 4 UDU.MEŠ *aṣ-ṣa-bat-sú-nu-ti ù*
40 *a-na* ^{m}*A-ri-im-ma-at-ka*$_4$ *ú-bi-il-šu-nu-*[*ti*]
41 2 UDU.MEŠ*-šu un-te-eš-ši-ir ù* 2 UDU.MEŠ*-šu*
42 *i-na ma-ag-ra-at-ti ša* É.GAL$^{-lì}$ ^{m}*Ḫu-ti-ya* ^{L}[^{Ú}*in*$^?$*-k*]*a*$_4$$^?$*-ru*
43 *iṭ-ṭá-ba-aḫ-šu-nu-ti ù* $^{LÚ.MEŠ}$*za-bi-il*
44 GIŠ.MAR.GÍD.DA *i-ta-ak-lu-šu-nu-ti*
45 *um-ma* ^{m}*A-ri-im-ma-at-ka*$_4$*-ma*
46 *a-an-ni-mi aš-pu-*[*u*]*r-šu-mi*
47 *ù um-ma* $^{LÚ.MEŠ}$*za-bi-il* GIŠ.MAR.GÍD.DA.MEŠ*-šu*
48 *la ni-ku-ul-šu-nu-ti-mi*
49 *um-ma* ^{m}*Ip-šá-ḫa-lu-ma* ^{m}*Šúk-ri-ya*

50 ^{LÚ}*ṣa-bi-it* UDU.MEŠ *ù* 1 UDU-*ya il-te-qè*
51 ^{m}*Šúk-ri-ya ir-te-qú-šu-ma*
52 *ù i-na* ITI-^{ḫi} *ša-a-šu-ma*
53 ^{m}*Ki-pí-ya uš-te-ši-bu-uš ù ša-nu-ú* UDU
54 ^{m}*Ki-pí-ya il-te-qè*
55 *um-ma* ^{m}*Ki-pí-ya ú-la-mi*
56 1 UDU-*šu i-na* ITI-^{ḫi} *ša-a-šu la el-qè-mi*
57 *i-na ṭù-up-pu-ú-mi-šu* 1 UDU-*šu*
58 *el-te-qè-mi*
59 *um-ma* ^{m}*Zi-ka*$_4$*-an-ta-ma*
60 *iš-tu*$_4$ KUR *Ḫa-ni-gal-bat at-ta-al-ka*$_4$
61 *ù* ^{m}*Ki-pí-ya lu-ba-ri il-te-qè*
62 2 ANŠE ŠE.MEŠ *at-ta-din-ma ù* KU-*ri*[112]
63 *un-te-eš-ši-ir*
64 [*um-ma*] ^{m}*Ki-pí-ya-ma* 1 MÁŠ.TUR
65 [a-na] ^{m}*Tù-ul-tù-uk-ka*$_4$ *a-na* UR$_5$.RA
66 [*a*$^?$*-n*]*a*$^?$[113] $^{\text{<m?>}}$*Zi-ka*$_4$*-an-ta*
67 [*ù*$^?$ *a*$^?$*-na*$^?$ ^{m}*Tù*]*-ul-tù-uk-ka*$_4$ *at-ta-din*
68 [2 ANŠE Š]E.MEŠ *la el-qè*
Edge
69 ŠU ^{m}*Ḫu-ti-ya* DUB.SAR
70 NA$_4$ ^{m}*Ḫa-iš-te-šup*

P-S 6

(1–5) Thus Ḫui-te: "Kipiya was to take 17 sheep of mine for 1 day. But he (claimed): '(They are) "palace" sheep.' He certainly gave them to the palace's (flock?) and he certainly did not return them to me."

(6–18) Thus Kipiya: "Kipaya, Keliya's shepherd, acted as officer in charge of grazing"(?) (lit. "went up for "'grazing'?") [and] thus he (said): 'These 17 sheep are "palace" (sheep) and Arim-matka together with …-apu sent me and we seized those [sheep].' And further … Arim-matka tagged them and consigned them to [the 'palace'?]. And, of these [17 sheep], he (i.e., Arim-matka) took 4(?)[114] sheep to Šukriya, while Kipaya, the grazing officer(?) took from Šukriya 1 wash bowl(?),[115] and then released the (other?) sheep."[116]

(19–26) Thus Arim-matka: "Kipiya delivered [n sheep] …. Niḫriya …. and (he) placed them under the authority of ….. He gave to Šukriya x?+5 of the 17 sheep intended(?) for release (lit. "which? he was/is releasing")."[117]

(27–31) Thus Šukriya: "Kipiya took 4 sheep and, from amongst those sheep, he released 2 [sheep], and 2 sheep he kept. Thus he (i.e., Kipiya): 'Why did you bring your milk to dilute (it) with water?'"[118]

(32–44) Thus Kipiya: "Arim-matka sent me. Thus he (said): 'Why did Kirriya's carts not go down to the field of the "palace"'s land. Go and seize 4 of his sheep.'[119] So I went and seized 4 sheep and delivered them to Arim-matka. 2 of his sheep I released, and 2 sheep of his Ḫutiya, the (land) foreman(?), slaughtered at the palace threshing floor. Then the wagoners ate them."

(45–46) Thus Arim-matka: "Yes, I sent him (i.e., Kipiya)."[120]

(47–48) And thus his[121] wagoners: "We did not eat them."

(49–54) Thus Ipša-halu: "Šukriya, the sheep collector, took 1 of my sheep. Šukriya went away. And in that same month Kipiya put it back and Kipiya took another sheep."

(55–58) Thus Kipiya: "Not at all. I did not take 1 of his sheep that month. I did take 1 sheep of his at the appropriate time(?)."[122]

(59–63) Thus Zikanta: "I came back from the land of Ḫanigalbat, and Kipiya took away my clothes. I then gave 2 homers of barley and he gave back the clothes."

(64–68) [Thus] Kipiya: "I gave 1 kid [to] Tultukka as a loan—[to?] Tultukka [and? to?] Zikanta. I did not (simply?) take [2 homers of] barley."

(69) Hand of Ḫutiya, the scribe.

(70) Seal impression of Ḫaiš-tešup.

46. *EN* 10/3, 175 (SMN 350 [= HSS XIII, 350 = ERL 73] + NTF M 6 A [4 frags.])

Findspot: Room L2 or M2 (first fragment; others: findspots unknown)
Publication: Fincke 2002a: 200–201
Edition: cf. Fincke 2002b: 305–6[123]

Obverse

1 *um-ma* ^{m}*A-ta-a-a-ma* ^{m}*Ki-pí-ya*
2 *iṣ-ṣa-ab-ta-an-ni-ma um-ma šu-ma*
3 *e-eš-še-ša*[124] *bi-la-am-mi i+na* MU(-)*pa-ni-ri*
4 3 ANŠE A.ŠÀ ⸢*a-n*⸣*a ši-mi at-ta-din-ma*
5 ⸢*ù*⸣ 1 A⸢NŠE⸣ [ŠE$^{?}$.M]EŠ *el-te-qè*
6 [*a*]-*na* ^{m}*K*[*i-pí-y*]*a at*$^{!}$(=LA)-*ta-bal-ma ù i+na*
7 [Š]U ^{m}⸢*E*⸣-[*te-e*]*š-še-en-ni it-ta-ad-na-an-ni-ma*
8 ⸢*ù*⸣ ŠE.[MEŠ *ša n*]*a-šu-ú* ⸢*i*⸣*l-te-qè*

---

9 [*u*]*m-ma* ^{m}[*X-x*]*-ké-ma* [*ki*$^{?}$*-ma*$^{?}$] 1 A[NŠE$^{?}$] ⸢ŠE⸣$^{?}$

10 1 UDU ^{m}*K*[*i-p*]*í-ya il-t*⸢*e-q*⸣[*è-ma* 1 UD]U$^{!}$*-ya*
11 *im*$^{!?}$-[*ta*$^{?}$*-r*]*a*$^{?}$*-aṣ-ma ù* ANŠE.Š[E]*-ma*
12 *iṣ*-[*ṣa*$^{?}$*-bat*$^{?}$*-m*]*a*$^{?}$ *ù ša-na-am* UD[U *il-te-q*]*è*$^{!}$

——— (erasure)

13 *u*[*m-ma* ^{m}] ⸢*X*⸣*-li-ya* 1 *en-zu* DIŠ ⸢*x*⸣ [ ]
14 2 [UDU.MEŠ-*y*]*a uš-te-el-wu i+n*[*a*$^{?}$]-⸢*x*⸣*-ni-ma*
15[125] ⸢*ù*⸣ [*i-na* Š]U ^{m}*E-te-eš-še-en-ni* [*it-ta-a*]*d-na-an-ni*
16 ⸢*ù*⸣ [*i-na-a*]*n*-⸢*na*⸣ 2 UDU.MEŠ *i-ir-ri-*[*iš*]

---

17 *u*[*m-ma*] ⸢^{m}*N*⸣*i-in-te-y*⸢*a-ma x*⸣ *a*$^{?}$-[*n*]*a*$^{?}$ [(?)]
18 *k*[*a*]*-az-za-ur-n*⸢*i*⸣ [ ]
19 ⸢*ú*⸣*-še-et-te-eq* ⸢1⸣$^{?}$ *e*[*n*$^{?}$*-zu*$^{?}$*-ya a*]*t-ta-an-ni-ma*
20 ⸢*i*⸣*r-ta-ap-sà-an-ni-m*[*a*] ⸢*x*⸣*-ri*
21 *ù* 1 MÁŠ *il-te-q*⸢*è ù*⸣ *a-na-ku*
22 2 UDU.MEŠ *ki-i pu-ḫi ša* [1$^{?}$ M]ÁŠ *a-na* EN-*šú*
23 *un-te-el-li i+na* MU$^{-[t]i}$ *šu-ma*
24 [AŠ Š]U ^{m}⸢*N*⸣*a-an-te-šup i*[*t-ta-a*]*d-na-an-*[*ni*]
Lower Edge
25 *ù* 1 UDU$^{!?}$ ⸢*il*⸣$^{?}$*-te-qè-*[*mi*]
26 *um-ma* ^{m}*Tù-ra-ri-ma* [-B]U
Reverse
27 *ya-nu* ^{m}*Ki-pí-ya iṣ-ṣ*[*a-ab-t*]*a-*⸢*a*⸣*n-ni-ma*
28 *ù* 1 ŠAḪ *ki-ma* UDU *i*[*l-qè*]

(blank)

EN 10/3, 175 (SMN 350 [= HSS XIII, 350 = ERL 73] + NTF M 6 A [4 frags.])

(1–8) Thus Ataya: "Kipiya seized me. Thus he (said): 'Deliver (what you owe? for?) the *eššešu*-festival(?)!' I gave for a price (i.e., I sold) a 3 homer field. And I took 1 homer of [barley?] (and?) I carried (it) to Kipiya, and he gave me over to Eteš-šenni's authority. And he took the barley which was borne."[126]

(9–12) Thus …-ke: "Kipiya took 1 sheep [in? exchange? for?] 1(?) homer(?) of barley(?). My [1? sheep?] fell ill(?) and he seized(?) the homer of barley. And he took another one of my sheep."[127]

(13–16) Thus …-liya: "They caused 1 goat … 2 of my [sheep] to go in circles,[128] and …, and he gave me over to Eteš-šenni's authority and now he demands two sheep."

(17–25) Thus Nin-teya: " .... compensation to(?) .... he will hand over(?) .... he beat me ... and he took 1 lamb; and I paid 2 sheep as replacement for [the 1(?)] lamb to his master. In that (very) year, he gave me over to Nan-tešup's authority. And he(?) took 1 sheep(?)...."

(26–28) Thus Turari: "There is no .... Kipiya seized me and took 1 pig instead of a sheep."

---

47. *P-S* 12 (SMN 391)

Findspot: Room L2 or M2

Publication: Pfeiffer and Speiser 1936: 20[129]

Obverse

1 [ ].MEŠ [ ]

2 [ ] *šu* [ ]

3 [ ]-*lu il-li-*[*ik*]

4 [ ]-*šu lu* ^{m}*Zi-*[ ]

5[130] [ ]

6 *um-ma* ^{m}*Ki-pí-ya-ma*

7 *a-na ša-at-ta-an ša-at-*[*ta-an*][131]

8 1 UDU-*šu a-na eš*$_{15}$*-šé-ši*

9 *a-ṣa-ab-bat*

10 *um-ma* ^{m}*Be-la-a-bi-ma*

11 ^{m}*Ki-pí-ya iṣ-ṣa-ab-ta-*[ ]

12 *ù i-na* É *nu-pá-*[*ri*]

13 *ù* 1 UDU *il-te-qè* [ ]

14 *ša-nu-ú* ITI-^{ḫu} [ ]

15 *ù* UDU-*ya il-*[*te-qè*]

16 *ù lu-ba-ri* [ ]

17 *um-ma* ^{m}*Ki-*[*pí-ya-ma*]

18 1 UDU *a-na* [ ]

19 *ù ša-nu-ú* [ ]

20 *qà-as-sú*

21 ŠU ^{md}XXX$^{?}$[132]*-na-din-š*[*um*]

P-S 12

(1–5) ....-s .... he went(?) .... ^{m}Zi(?)-....

(6–9) Thus Kipiya: "Every year, I take 1 sheep for the *eššešu*-festival."

(10–16) Thus Bêl-abi: "Kipiya seized [me?[133]] and [put? me?] in the work-house; and he took 1 sheep... (for) a second month he also took a sheep of mine ... and my clothing ... ."

(17–20) Thus Kipiya: "1 sheep for ... and another/(a) second .... his hand/authority."

(21) Hand of Sin-nādin-šumi.

48. *P-S* 5 (SMN 346)

Findspot: Room L2 or M2
Publication and edition: Pfeiffer and Speiser 1936: 15–16, 69–70[134]

Text #48 is complicated and not entirely clear to me.[135] It deals with a single overriding issue, to be sure, but it seems to involve two, easily settled, minor points as well. The general issue is the disposition and possible misappropriation of overpayments of taxes. The taxpayer is a collectivity, the "task force of Nuzi." Whether this represents a group of individuals or a government bureau in charge of this group is unknown. In either case, sheep are paid by this "task force" in support of the *eššešu*-festival, a monthly religious rite. An individual, Kipiya, receives these sheep and is involved in their disbursal for the running of the festival. For some reason, overpayment of sheep is built into this system: ninety head of sheep in addition to the sixty required for the festival. The crux of the issue is the failure of the "task force" to receive back eventually the number of sheep paid exceeding sixty. Kipiya is accused of selling the excess for personal gain. He denies this, claiming that Kušši-ḫarpe confiscates the extra sheep and sells them for his own profit.[136]

The two minor points derive from the major point. The first is the (one-time?) retention of the ninety excess sheep as compensation for wagons or carts, presumably sold or rented to the "task force." Once the reason for the retention is given, the matter seems simply to have been dropped. The second point, stemming from the first, is the fate of seven of the ninety sheep retained. Three individuals eventually admit their consumption of the sheep, and, there too, the matter seems to have been dropped. Whether or not I have interpreted these matters correctly, these points seem irrelevant to the main issue and remain as uncomfortable loose ends.

Obverse

1 *um-ma* ERÍN.MEŠ *ša* URU *Nu-zi-ma*
2 92 UDU.MEŠ ^{m}[*Ki-pí*]-*ya il-te-qè-šu-nu-ti*
3 *šum-ma* AŠ É.GAL^{-li} *la ú-še-ri-ib-š*[*u-n*]*u-ti*
4 *ù šum-ma an-na-aš-ni*
5 *la ut-te-er-ru-šu-nu-ti*
6 *um-ma* ^{m}*Ki-pí-ya-ma*
7 90 UDU.MEŠ *a-na* *ka*$_{4}$*-az-za-ur-ni*
8 *ša* ^{GIŠ}MAR.GÍD.DA.MEŠ [(?)] *él-te-qè-ma*[137]
9 *ù* 7 UDU.MEŠ *i-na* ŠÀ$^{-bi}$-*šu-nu*
10 [*i*]-*na* GIŠ.SAR *i-te-ep-šu-nu-ti-ma*
11 [*ù*] ERÍN.MEŠ *ša* URU *Nu-zi-ma i-ta-kál-šu-nu-ti*
12 [*ù u*]*m-ma* ERÍN.MEŠ *ša* URU *Nu-zi-ma*
13 [UZU].MEŠ *la ni-ku-ul-mi*
14 *um-ma* ^{m}*Pa-a-a* ^{m}*Ú-ta-a-a*
15 *ù* ^{m}*Ka*$_{4}$*-wi-in-ni-ma ni-nu*
16 UZU.MEŠ *ni-ku-*[*ul*]*-mi*
17 *um-ma* ERÍN.MEŠ *ša* URU *Nu-zi-ma*
18 1 *ma-at* [50 UDU].MEŠ *a-na eš*$_{15}$*-šé-ší*
19 [^{m}*Ki-pí-ya*] *ú-ša-ad-dá-an*
20 [*ù im-ma-ti*]*-im-me-e* UDU.MEŠ-*šu*
21 [*ma-a-du*] *ù a-na* URUDU.MEŠ
22 [*ú-ša*]*-ad-dá-an*

Reverse

23 1 *šu-š*[*i*] UDU.MEŠ *i-n*[*a* ŠÀ$^{?\text{-}bi?}$-*šu*$^{?}$-*nu*$^{?}$[138]]
24 *a-na eš*$_{15}$-[*šé*]*-ší i-ip-pu-šu*
25 *ù* 90 UDU.MEŠ [ ] *ša-šu*
26 *i-ka*$_{4}$*-al-la-šu-nu-ti*
27 *um-ma* ^{m}*Ki-pí-ya-ma šum-ma*
28 UDU.MEŠ *eš*$_{15}$*-šé-ší* [*š*]*a*$^{?}$ *ú-ša-ad-dá-nu*
29 *ma-a-du ù a-na* [1 *ma*]*-at* UDU.MEŠ
30 *i-ka*$_{4}$*-aš-ša-du* [*ù*] *šum-ma mi-i-ṣú*
31 *a-na* 70 *a-na šu-*[*ši* UDU].MEŠ *i-ka*$_{4}$*-aš-ša-du*
32 *ù i-na* ŠÀ$^{-bi}$ [ ] *šu-ši* UDU.MEŠ
33 *ša in-ni-*i[*b-b*]*u* [*ù ša*$^{?}$ *a-n*]*a eš*$_{15}$*-šé-ší a-na-ku a-kál*
34 *ù ri-iḫ-ti* UDU.MEŠ
35 ^{m}*Ku-uš-ši-ḫar-pè i-ik-kál*
36 *ù i-na* URUDU.MEŠ *la ú-ša-ad-dá-as-sú-nu-ti*
37 ^{NA_4}KIŠIB ^{m}*Pa-*[*a*]*-a*
38 ^{NA_4}KIŠIB ^{m}*Ḫa-iš-te-šup*

P-S 5

(1–5) Thus the Nuzi task force: "Kipiya took 92[139] sheep. He most certainly brought them to the 'palace'. He certainly did not turn them over to us."

(6–11) Thus Kipiya: "I took 90 sheep as compensation[140] for the carts.[141] And of those, 7 sheep were prepared in the orchard [and] the Nuzi task force ate them."

(12–13) [And] thus the Nuzi task force: "We did not eat the meat."

(14–16) Thus Paya, Utaya, and Kawinni: "It was we who ate [the meat]."

(17–26) Thus the Nuzi task force: "[Kipiya] would make (us) give 1 hundred [50 sheep] for the *eššešu*-festival. [And] whenever his sheep would be [in excess[142]] he would have them (i.e., the excess) sold for copper. They prepare 60 [of? those?] sheep for the *eššešu*- festival and keep back those(?) … 90 sheep."

(27–36) Thus Kipiya: "If the *eššešu*-festival-sheep which I make (them) give are (too many), they get back [1] hundred sheep[143] [and] if they are too few they get back 70 or sixty [sheep].[144] And I appropriate (my share [or fee]) from among (those) … 60 sheep for the *eššešu*-festival, (just) mentioned(?[145]). And it is the remainder of the sheep that Kušši-ḫarpe expropriates. I do not have them sold for copper.[146]

(37–38) Seal impression of Paya; seal impression of Ḫaiš-tešup.

49. *P-S* 7 (SMN 356)

Findspot: Room L2 or M2
Publication and edition: Pfeiffer and Speiser 1936: 17, 71–72[147]

Text #49 describes four different situations. The first and longest (lines 1–38), stripped of its complications, amounts to a complaint by Akap-šenni that the government owed him two sheep. Failure to pay that amount resulted in his possibly permanent loss of eight homers of land. As best as I can understand it, the following is what happened. Akap-šenni owed two sheep for damaging public property.[148] He borrowed the sheep from Arim-matka (an agent of Kušši-ḫarpe, I assume) and used the sheep to compensate the government. A seemingly extraneous matter follows. Akap-šenni and another individual were ordered by Mayor Ḫašip-apu to deliver to the mayor twelve sheep he had had confiscated.[149] This they did. If this episode has relevance to the issue at hand—and how could it not?—it must be that Akap-šenni should have received as compensation for this work two sheep.[150] This datum, nowhere made explicit, makes sense in the light of what follows. First, note that I assume that Kušši-ḫarpe, his agent Arim-matka, Mayor Ḫašip-apu, and the soon-to-be-introduced Ehlip-apu are all acting in concert. To continue. Arim-matka duns Akap-šenni for the sheep he loaned to him. Akap-šenni applies to Kušši-ḫarpe for relief[151] but to no avail. Then, Eḫlip-apu indirectly (why indirectly?) gives two dying sheep, (erstwhile?) property of Kušši-ḫarpe, to Akap-šenni's brother. This act could have led to the discharge of the loan of the two sheep, for now Akap-šenni might have repaid Arim-matka. But the sheep died, leaving Akap-šenni still in debt, but now without prospect of further relief. At this point, he obtains two sheep by way of yet another loan, one secured by Akap-šenni's land. He gives the sheep to Eḫlip-apu, presumably Arim-matka's cohort, thus paying off that first loan. Eḫlip-apu denies it all, claiming that Ḫašip-apu (the mayor) both delivered the (sick) sheep and took back the (healthy) sheep.

A second reconstruction would have Akap-šenni involved in two cases, not one extended one. The first is the initial borrowing of two sheep to pay for the damaged bridge and his failed attempt to obtain an extension of the loan. The second case, introduced by a formula often signaling a fresh matter, would have Akap-šenni receiving two ailing sheep of Kušši-ḫarpe in order that he restore them to health. He fails and repays[152] with mobilia from another loan, secured by land. Two cases, two loans (the second more serious than the first: it is secured by land), indebtedness for four sheep to be paid to the government.

Though the latter reconstruction is simpler, it fails to account for the peculiar mention of the mission to bring to the mayor twelve recently seized sheep. In either case, or by any other interpretation, Akap-šenni finds himself in debt to government agents and, implicitly, argues the injustice of his situation.

The second case alleges that Kušši-ḫarpe stole building materials. The third case is somewhat vague. It appears that (Mayor) Ḫašip-apu borrowed garments from the citizenry to clothe "foreigners." One citizen claims he never got his clothing back. The fourth case alleges that an individual (known elsewhere to have been a government official) rustled private livestock.

Obverse

1 *um-ma* ^{m}*A-kap-še-en-ni-ma*
2 ^{LÚ}DUMU *ši-ip-ru ša* É.GAL$^{\text{-}li}$
3 *it-ta-al-ka ù iq-ta-bi*
4 *aš-šum ti-tu-ú-ri ša ḫe-pu-ú*
5 2 UDU.MEŠ *ka-az-za-ur-nu*
6 *ša* ^{LÚ}*ḫa-za-an-ni bi-la-am-mi*
7 *ù a-na-ku* 2 UDU.NITÁ.MEŠ *a-šar*
8 ^{m}*A-ri-im-ma-at-ka*$_4$ *a-na* UR$_5$.RA
9 *el-te-qè ù a-na* ^{m}*Ul-lu-ya šu-a-na-at-ḫi*

10 *at-ta-din ù a-na* É.GAL^{-li} *it-ta-bal-šu*
11 *ù ya-ši it-ti* ^{m}*Ké-li-ya-ma*
12 ^{m}*Ḫa-ši-ip-a-pu* ^{LÚ}*ḫa-za-an-nu*
13 *i-na* AN.ZA.KÀR *Ka-a-ri iš-tap-ra-an-ni*
14 *ù* 12 UDU.ḪÁ.MEŠ *uṣ-ṣé-eb-bi-it-ma*
15 *ù i-na* É$^{-it}$ ^{m}*Ḫa-ši-pa-pu*
16 *nu-uš-te-ri-ib ù aš-ra-nu-um-ma*
17 *ik-ta-lu-ú ù i-na-an-na*
18 ^{m}*A-ri-im-ma-at-ka*$_4$ *i-na* EGIR^{-ki} BURU
19 *aš-šum* 2 UDU.MEŠ *il-ta-na-as-sí*
20 *a-na* ^{m}*Ḫu-uš-ši-ḫar-pè e-ḫe-en-nu-ma*
21 *ù la i-ša-a-la-an-ni*
22 *um-ma* ^{m}*A-kap-še-en-ni-ma* 2 UDU.MEŠ
23 *en-šu-tu ša i-mu-ut-tù*
24 ^{m}*Eḫ-li-ip-a-pu a-na* ŠU ŠEŠ-*ya*
25 *it-ta-din ù um-ma šu-ma*
26 *ša* ^{m}*Ḫu-uš-ši-ḫar-pè-mi ù* [*b*]*u-ul-li-is-sú-nu-ti-mi*
27 *ù ki-i id-dì-nu-ma*
28 *ù im-tù-tù ù a-na-ku*
29 8 ANŠE A.ŠÀ *a-na ti*$_4$*-de*$_4$*-en-nu-t*[*i*]
30 *a-na* DUMU ^{m}*Ar-zi-iz-za*
31 *at-ta-din*

Reverse

32 *ù* 2 UDU.MEŠ *el-te-qè-*[*mi*]
33 *ù a-na* ^{m}*Eḫ-li-ip-a-*[*pu-m*]*a*
34 *at-ta-din*
35 *um-ma* ^{m}*Eḫ-li-ip-a-pu-ma*
36 *la ad-din a-na-ku*
37 ^{m}*Ḫa-ši-ip-a-pu-ma i-din-šu-nu-ti*
38 *ù* ^{m}*Ḫa-ši-ip-a-pu-ma il-qè*
39 *um-ma* ^{m}*Ḫa-na-tu*$_4$*-ma* É *ú-ṣa-al-la-al*
40 *ù bu-ú-ra i-na* UGU$^{-ḫi}$
41 $^{\text{GIŠ.MEŠ}}$*pa-ri-sà-ti ad-dì*
42 ^{m}*Zi-li-ip-til-la ù* 1 ^{LÚ}ÌR
43 *ša* ^{m}*Ḫu-uš-ši-ḫar-pè it-ta-al-ku*
44 *ù bu-ú-ra ga*$_{14}$$^{?}$*-am-ru*
45 É$^{-\text{ti}}$ *ka-wa-du-um-ma i-t*[*e-e*]*p-šu*
46 *ù bu-ú-ra a-na* ^{m}*Ḫu-uš-ši-ḫar-pè*
47 *il-te-qú-ú*
48 *um-ma* ^{m}*Te-ḫi-ip-til-l*[*a-ma*]

49 ^{m}*Ḫa-ši-ip-a-pu* [TÚG].HÁ.MEŠ
50 *a-na* LÚ.MEŠ *ú-ba-ra-[ti] uš-te-ed-dì-in*
51 *ša al-lu-ti* TÚG.HÁ.MEŠ *ut-te-er-ru*
52 *ù ut-tù-ya lu-ba-ri*
53 *ik-ta-la*
54 *um-ma* ^{m}*Um-pí-ya-ma*
55 1 UDU.NITA$_2$ ^{m}*Zi-il-ip-til-la*
56 *il-te-qè ù i-na* É-*šú iṭ-ṭá-ba-aḫ*
57 *ù i-ta-kál*
58 NA$_4$ ^{m}*Ḫa-iš-te-šup*
59 NA$_4$ ^{m}*Pa-a-a*

P-S 7

(1–21) Thus Akap-šenni: "The 'palace' messenger came and said: 'Bring 2 sheep, the mayor's (stipulated) compensation for the destroyed bridge.' And I borrowed 2 rams from Arim-matka and gave (them) to Ulluya, the *šuanatḫu*-official.[153] Then he delivered them (lit. it) to the 'palace'. And Mayor Ḫašip-apu sent me and Keliya to the 'Port' District; he seized 12 sheep and we brought them into Ḫašip-apu's house. And there they were kept. And now, since the harvest, Arim-matka has constantly been raising a claim regarding the 2 sheep. I have been pleading to Kušši-ḫarpe but he has not questioned me."[154]

(22–34) Thus Akap-šenni (further): "Eḫlip-apu transferred to my brother 2 emaciated, dying sheep. And thus he: 'These are Kušši-ḫarpe's; revive them.' And since he gave them,[155] and they did die, I gave 8 homers of land to the son of Ar-zizza in an antichretic loan[156] and I obtained (for that land) 2 sheep; and I gave (them) to Eḫlip-apu."

(35–38) Thus Eḫlip-apu: "I did not give (the sheep). Rather, Ḫašip-apu gave them, and Ḫašip-apu took them (back?)."

(39–47) Thus Ḫanatu: "In (the course of) roofing a house, I was placing the reed matting upon the wooden ribs (when) Zilip-tilla and a slave of Kušši-ḫarpe came and confiscated(?) all(?) the house's roof mats and took the matting to Kušši-ḫarpe."

(48–53) Thus Teḫip-tilla: "Ḫašip-apu had garments collected for the aliens. He returned the garments of the others, but kept my clothes.[157]

(54–57) Thus Umpiya: "Zilip-tilla took 1 ram, slaughtered it in his house, and ate (it)."

(58–59) Seal impression of Ḫaiš-tešup; seal impression of Paya.

50. HSS XIII, 430 (SMN 430)

Findspot: Room L2 or M2
Publication: Pfeiffer and Lacheman 1942: 83[158]
Edition: None

Obverse
Top destroyed
1 [*um-ma* ^{m}*Te*]-*ḫi-ya-ma*
2 [x x x x] ^{m}*Ki-pí-ya*
3 [x x ^{m}*Eḫ-l*]*i-pa-pu*
4 [x x x] *i-te-er-bu-ma*
5 [x x x x] QA-*ra-ni*
6 [x x x] 3 *ma-ti* [x x]-*šu*
7[159] [x x x]-*mu-ú*
8 [x x x] *ù nu-ut-t*[*a*-x]
9 [x x x x] -*ya ù* [x]-*mi*
10 [x x x]-*ti im-tù-ṭù*
11 [x x x]-*ma* ^{m}*Ḫa-ši-ip-a-pu*
12 [x x x]-*ta-an-ni*
13 [x x *at-ta*[160]]-*din-ma*
14 [x x x x]-*an-ni*
15 (destroyed)
Lower edge
16 $^{\text{L[Ú.MEŠ}}$*ú-bá*]-*ru-ti*
17 AN.ZA.KÀR *iḫ-te-pu-ú*
Reverse
18 4 $^{\text{TÚG.MEŠ}}$*zi-a-na-tu*$_{4}$
19 1 DAL Ì.MEŠ "6 ½" (*sic*) ŠE *an-nu-ti*
20 *il-te-qú-ú*
21 *um-ma* ^{m}*Ḫa-na-a-a-ma* 2 UDU.MEŠ
22 ^{m}*Eḫ-li-ip-a-pu a-na bi-ti* (*sic*)
23 *it-ta-dì i-na* É.MEŠ-*šu-ma*[161]
24 *im-tù-ṭá* 2 ANŠE A.ŠÀ
25 *a-na ši-mi at-ta-din*
26 2 UDU.MEŠ [*a-na* ^{m}]*Ḫa-ši-ip-a-pu*
27 *at-ta*-[*din*]
28 NA$_{4}$ ^{m}*Ḫa*-[*iš*$^{?}$-*te*$^{?}$-*šup*$^{?}$[162]]
(Rest destroyed)

HSS XIII, 430

(1–10) .... [Thus] Teḫiya: "..., Kipiya, ..., Eḫlip-apu arrived (pl.) .... its ... (was) 300 ... and we ...-ed .... they died."

(11–20) [Thu]s? Ḫašip-apu: "... me ... [I?] gave .... me. The foreigners destroyed the tower. They took these, (viz.) 4 felt blankets,[163] 1 jar of oil, and 6 ½ (homers? of) barley."

(21–27) Thus Ḫanaya: "He abandoned at home (*sic*) and he died in his house. I sold the 2-homer field for a price. I gave 2 sheep [to] Ḫašip-apu."

(28) Seal of Ḫa[iš?-tešup?] ...

51. *EN* 10/2, 117 (SMN 1735[164])

Findspot: Unknown
Publication: Fincke 1998a: 310
Edition: None

Obverse

.
.
.

1 [ ] ⸢x⸣ *ma mi* ⸢x⸣ [ ]
2 [ ]-⸢*x*⸣-IG-*mi ù* ⸢*i*⸣$^{?}$-[ ]
3 [ ] *e-te-ru-um-ma* $^{m?}$⸢X⸣-[ ]
4 [-*t*]*i ù mi-nu-um-me-*⸢*e*⸣ [ ]
5 [^{m}*Ḫa*$^{?}$-*ši*$^{?}$]-*ip-a-pu a-na ya-ši* [ ]

Lower Edge

6 [ ] *an*$^{!?}$-*nu-tu₄ nu*-UD DU$^{?}$ *i*-[ ]
7 [ ] ⸢x⸣ x *a-ta-ku ri*-⸢*x*⸣-[ ]
8 [ ] ⸢*x*⸣-*re-e* UD D[U$^{?}$/*n*[*a*$^{?}$]
9 [ ] ⸢x⸣ *a-na le-qè*

Reverse

10 [$^{m?}$ -*e*]*n*$^{?}$-*nu*-QA-*a*
11 [ ] BI *ù i+na-an-n*[*a*]
12 [ ]⸢*a-n*⸣*a* ^{m}*Ḫu-uš-ši*-[*ḫar*$^{?}$-*pè*$^{?}$]
13 [ ] ⸢x⸣ *a-na-ku-ma*
14 [ ]⸢x⸣ *ta*$^{?}$ lu$^{?}$ ⸢x⸣ [ ]
15 [ ] ⸢x⸣ [ ]

.

.

.

EN 10/2 117 (SMN 1735)

(1–15) .... I arrived, and ... and whatever .... Ḫašip(?)-apu .... to me ... these ... in order to take ... and now ... to Kušši-[ḫarpe?] ... I .....

52. HSS XIII, 286 (SMN 286)

Findspot: Room L2 or M2
Publication: Pfeiffer and Lacheman 1942: 48–49[165]
Edition: None

Obverse

1 [*um-ma* ^{m}*Ḫ*]*a-ši-ip-a-pu-ma*
2 [*i-na gi-ri-t*]*i*[166] *ša* LUGAL *it-ta-al-ka*$_4$
3 [*ù a-na*] LÚ.MEŠ *ša* ŠE.MEŠ TUK$^{\text{-šu}}$ *iq-ta-bu-ú*
4 [x x x] *ma-am-ma la ta-an-dì-na-mi*
5 [x x x]-*ú* ŠE.MEŠ *a-na* É.GÁL$^{\text{-lì}}$ *ú-za-ak-ki*[167]*-ma-mi*
6 [x x] ^{m}*Ku-uš-ši-ḫar-pè a-na* ^{m}MU-GÁL$^{\text{-ši}}$ DUMU *Ka*-[*x-x*]
7 [*iš*]*-pu-ra-an-ni-mi um-ma šu-ma*
8 [1 *m*]*a-at* ANŠE ŠE.MEŠ *e-ri-iš-mi*
9 *ù ki-na-an-na qí-bi-mi la-*[*am*]
10 [ŠE].MEŠ *na-di-na*[168]*-né-e ša* É.GAL$^{\text{-lì}}$
11 [*te-é*]*l-te-qú-ni-im-mi ù* ŠE.MEŠ *bi-la-am-mi*
12 *ù šum-ma* ŠE.MEŠ *te-le-eq-qè-mi*
13 *ù a-ḫi-ta-am-ma-mi tù-bu-uk-mi*
14 *ù ku-nu-uk-mi ù* ŠE.MEŠ *ma-aṣ-ṣa-re-e*
15 [*x*]*-ši-*[*x*][169]*-šu-nu-ti-mi ù šum-ma*
16 [*na-di-na*]*-a-né-e ša* ŠE.MEŠ
17 [[170]] *ù ki-na*[171]*-an-na qí-bi-mi*
18 [ŠE.MEŠ] *iš-tu*$_4$ *ša-ad-dá-ag-dá-am-mi*
19 [x x x] *at-ta ta-la-ak-ma*
20 [*ki-ma a*]*-wa-ti-šu an-nu-ti* DÙ$^{\text{-uš}}$*-mi*
21 [*u*]*m-ma* ^{m}*Ḫa-ši-ip-a-pu-ma šu-un-du*
22 [ŠE.ME]Š *a-na* ^{m}*Ku-uš-ši-ḫar-pè it-ta-ad-nu*
23 [*a-na gi-r*]*i-ti* LUGAL *iš-pu-ur-šu*
24 [*a-na*[172] ^{m}*Ku-u*]*š-ši-ḫar-pè qí-bi-mi*

25 [ŠE(.MEŠ) *ma-ṣa*]*-ar-ru-us-sú ša* URU *an-ni-i*
26 [x x] *ḫu-ul-li-iq-šu-mi*
27 [ŠE[173](.MEŠ) *ma-ṣa*]*-ar-ru-ti*
Lower Edge
28 [x x x]*-šu-nu-ti-ma*
29 [x x x]*-nu-ti*
30 [x x x]*-ma*
31 [*a-na gi-ri-ti it-ta-a*]*l-ka*$_4$
Reverse
32 [x x x] ^{LÚ}*a-lik*[174] *il-ki*
33 [x x x] *la* DÙ*-mi*
34 [x x x x x]*-ta*
35 [x x ^{LÚ}[175]*a-l*]*ik il-ki* ŠE.MEŠ
36 [x x x] *ù ši-pí-ir-šu*
37 (destroyed)
38 [x x ^{m}*Ku-uš*]*-ši-ḫar-pè*
39 [x x x]*-na-an-ni*
40 [x x x]-BI-*ka*
41 (destroyed)
42 [x x x]*-ul-li*
43 [x x x]*-ar-ti*
44 [x x x] *it-ta-al-ku*
45 [x x ^{m}*Ku-uš-ši-ḫar*]*-pè*
46 [x x x] LÚ.MEŠ *ša* ŠU^{-ti}*-ka*$_4$
47 [x x x] *ša* ŠU^{-ti}*-ya*
48 [x x x]*-nu-ti-ma*
49 [x x x]*-ak*
50 [x x x] 10 UDU.MEŠ
51 [x x x]*-ta-at-ta-nu*
52 [x x x *a*]*-na ni-ka-ti* DÙ*-šu*
53–55 (destroyed)
56 [x x x] *it-ta-al-ka*$_4$ *um-ma*
57 [x x x]*-ir-šu ša šar-ta-še-e-a*
58 [x x x] 2 ^{KUŠ}*lu-up-pá-tù*
Upper Edge
59 [x x x *uš*]*-ta-bi-la-an-ni-mi*
60 [x x x] *ya-nu-um-mi šum-ma šu-ma*
61 [x x x] *ya-nu-um-mi*
62 [x x x] *iš-tu*$_4$ É ^{m}*Ḫi-iš-mi-te-šup*

HSS XIII, 286

(1–20) [Thus] Ḫašip-apu: "He went [into? the? *girit*]*u*(?) of the king [and] said [to] the men who had barley: '… [176] …. has not cleared(??) barley for the "palace".' … Kušši-ḫarpe sent me to Šumu-libšī son of Ka-… . Thus he (said): 'Demand [1] hundred homers of barley and speak as follows: "Before you take [the barley] of the palace distributers, bring the barley." And if you take the barley, store it separately and seal (it off), station(?) watchmen over the barley. And if barley distributers …, state as follows: "Since last year [the barley] …, and you go. Act [according to] this, his order/word."'"

(21–62) Thus Ḫašip-apu: "On the occasion that they gave [the barley] to Kušši-ḫarpe, they sent it(?) [to] the *giritu*(?) of the king (They?? said??:[177]) '[178]Say [to?] Kušši-ḫarpe: "As for the barley, its guardianship is (the responsibility) of this city … remove it." The guardianship … [the barley] … went [to the *giritu*?]. The "goer of the going" … he did not do/act …the "goer of the going," the barley … and his message …. Kušši-ḫarpe … they went … [Kušši-ḫar]pe? … the men under your authority …. under my authority … these(?) … went(?) … 10 sheep … he made it … *ana nikati* … he went. Thus the message(?) of Šartašaya(?)[179] 2 leather bags …. he delivered me … there are none. If he … there are none … from the house of Ḫišmi-tešup."

53. *P-S* 4 (SMN 13)

Findspot: Room L2 or M 2

Publication and edition: Pfeiffer and Speiser 1936: 15, 69[180]

Obverse

1 *um-ma* ^{m} *Zi-li-ip-til-la-ma*

2 ^{f}*Pí-za-tu*$_{4}$ *i-na ša-ad-*[*d*]*á-ag-dá*

3 ^{f}*Ḫu-me-re-el-li ur-te-em-mi-šu-ma*

4 *a-na-ku ù* ^{m}*Ši-mi-til-la*

5 *i-na mu-ši ni-it-ta-la-ak-ma*

6 *ni-il-ta-sí-šu-ma a-šar*

7 ^{m}*Ḫu-uš-ši-ḫar-pé-ma ni-it-ta-bal-šu-ma*

8 *ù it-ti-ik-šu*

9 *um-ma* ^{m}*Ḫu-uš-ši-ḫar-pé la*

10 *ù*(-)*la-mi*[181] *la a-wa-tù-mi la a-ni-ik-šu-mi*

11 *um-ma* ^{m}*Pal-te-ya-ma*

12 ^{f}*Ḫu-me-re-el-li al-ta-sí-iš*

13 *i-na* É *ḫu-ri-za-ti ša* ^{f}*Ti-lu-un-na-a-a*
14 *uš-te-ri-ib-šu*
15 *ù* ^{m}*Ḫu-uš-ši-ḫar-pé it-ti-ik-šu*
16 *um-ma* ^{m}*Ḫu-uš-ši-ḫar-pé-ma*
17 *šum-ma* (erasure) ^{f}*Ḫu-me-re-el-li*
18 *i-na* É *ḫu-ri-za-ti*
19 *ša* ^{f}*Ti-lu-un-na-a-a*
20 ^{m}*Pal-te-ya ú-bi-il-šu-ma*
21 *ù a-na-ku a-ni-ik-šu-ma*
Reverse
22 ^{NA_4}KIŠIB ^{m}*Ar-ḫa-ma-an-na*
23 ^{NA_4}KIŠIB ^{m}*Te-ḫi-ip*-LUGAL
24 ^{NA_4}KIŠIB ^{m}*Pár-ta-aš-su*[182]*-a*
Edge
25 ŠU ^{md}*Ak-ka-dingir-ra*

P-S 4

(1–8) Thus Zilip-tilla: "Last year, ^{f}Pizatu released ^{f}Ḫumer-elli;[183] by night I and ^{m}Šimi-tilla went and summoned her and brought her to Kušši-ḫarpe's. Then he had illicit sex with her."

(9–10) Thus Kušši-ḫarpe: "No and no again! Not a word (is true).[184] I did not have illicit sex with her."

(11–15) Thus Pal-teya: "I summoned ^{f}Ḫumer-elli and brought her to the shed of ^{f}Tilun-naya. Then Kušši-ḫarpe had illicit sex with her."

(16–21) Thus Kušši-ḫarpe: "It is certainly not the case that Pal-teya brought ^{f}Humer-elli to the shed of ^{f}Tilun-naya[185] and that I had illicit sex with her."

(22–25) Seal impression of Ariḫ-ḫamanna; seal impression of Teḫip-šarri; seal impression of Partasua. Hand of Ak(ka)dingirra.

54. *EN* 10/1, 58 (*SMN* 1640)

Findspot: Unknown
Publication: Fincke 1996: 459[186]
Edition: None

Obverse
1 [ ] ⸢x⸣ [ ]
2 [ ] ⸢RU⸣ *ša* É G[AL?]

3 [ ] ⸢*a*⸣-*na ša-a-šu* ⸢12⸣? [ ]
4 [*a-n*]*a*? ^{m}*Ku-uš-ši-ḫar-pa* ⸢x⸣[187] [ ]
5 30 ^{GIŠ}GIGIR?/*ku*?-*pa-nu ša* ZI-[ ]
6 *a-na* É.GAL *ni*?-*ta-d*[*in*?]
7 ^{m}*Ku-uš-ši-ḫar-pa al*?- / *il*?-⸢*x*⸣[ ]
8 [*u*]*m-ma* ^{m}*Zi-li-ip-til-*[*la-ma*]
9 [*ša-a*]*d-dá-ag-dá* ^{f}*Pí-za-*[*tu*$_4$]
10 ⸢f⸣*Ḫu-me-re-el-li ú-*[[188]]
11 ⸢*a*⸣-*na-ku ù* ^{m}*Ši-mi-til-l*[*a*]
12 *ni-ta-la-ak ni-il*!-*t*[*a*!?-*si*?-*šu*?-*ma*?[189]]
13 *a-na* ^{m}*Ku-uš-ši-ḫar-p*[*a*]
14 ^{m}*Ši-mi-til-la* [ ]
15 *ša* É.GAL [ ]
16 *ša* ^{m} ⸢*X*⸣[190]-[ ]
17 ⸢*il*⸣-[ ]
18 ⸢x⸣ [ ]

.

.

.

EN 10/1, 58

(1–7) "… of the palace(?) … to him. 12(?) … to(?) Kušši-ḫarpe …. 30 (wooden objects) of … we gave(?) to the palace." Kušši-ḫarpe … .

(8–13) Thus Zilip-tilla: "Last year, ^{f}Pizatu released(?) ^{f}Ḫumer-elli. I and Šimi-tilla went and [summon?]ed [her?], (and) … to Kušši-ḫarpe."

(14–18) Šimi-tilla … of the palace … of (PN) … .

Chapter Three
A Legal Dispute over Land: Two Generations of Legal Paperwork

The seven documents comprising this dossier constitute an extended legal struggle over lawful ownership of a large tract of real estate. Spanning two generations, these records afford an extraordinary glimpse into the legal process—claims and counterclaims, affidavits, appeals, and courtroom proceedings—as practiced in a Late Bronze Age municipality.

Text #55 is a preliminary step towards a trial.[1] Five individuals declare that Ḫutiya son of Kuššiya represents their interests in real estate, as well as his own, in forthcoming legal proceedings.[2] They create, in effect, a class-action suit.[3]

Text #56 describes a trial, such as is envisioned in text #55. Ḫutiya and one Aštar-tilla (likely the individual identified as a witness in text #55:26, 36) take Bêlšunu and Šatu-kewi to court, claiming that the latter two are mere tenant farmers on their land, yet occupy the land as if they were owners. Bêlšunu and Šatu-kewi assert ownership, maintaining that, in effect, they bought the land (by means of real estate adoption). The remainder of the text is obscure, but a resolution was not reached.

Text #57 describes a subsequent stage of the proceedings initiated in text #56. It is a letter written to high royal court officials by the panel of judges who had heard the case,[4] requesting that the case, still unresolved, be referred to the king himself. Important details presented here overlap those of text #56: the same parties appear involved; assertion of tenancy is made; illegal occupancy is charged; and a counter-argument of ownership by adoption is made. But an important detail is added, and there is expansion and fleshing out, suggesting substantive change occurring in the time period between these two texts: (1) Ḫutiya claims title to the land and the tower in question because his ancestor, after whom this real estate is named, owned the land; (2) another "tenant" appears on the scene; and (3) the issue of the correct toponym (and hence implied legal ownership) is disputed. In addition to the earlier assertion of purchase by adoption, the three aver that they obtained the real estate from the government.

All three, furthermore, seem to charge the great-grandfather of Ḫutiya with theft of the land, so that, it is implied, all subsequent generations of that family hold that real estate illegally. The new, third, "tenant," claims that he obtained the land (legally), presumably from Bêlšunu and Šatu-kewi. The claim by the defendants that they purchased the real estate by adoption seems a strong argument: it is backed up by deeds of purchase. No verdict is mentioned—one hardly expects one, given the context of this missive—but the fact that, in subsequent texts from the next generation, Kel-tešup son of this Ḫutiya still fights to retain this land may suggest that the counter arguments of the three "tenants" failed to wrest the real estate from Ḫutiya's family.

The second chapter of this two-chapter tale involves the same core issue, which, through determination of the correct name of the *dimtu*-district (as is argued below), is rightful ownership. Three depositions, of sorts, somehow lead up to a trial. All four texts focus on the testimony of towns (or villages) located in the *dimtu*-district as to the correct name of the *dimtu*: Kizzuk or Ṭâb-ukur. It is the same question as was at issue in the earlier generation. In these latter texts, Kel-tešup son of Ḫutiya represents the interests of his family as had his father, Ḫutiya son of Kuššiya, in the previous generation.[5]

Text #58 is included here because this text shares with the others the focus on the correct name of a *dimtu*, and because the four towns whose testimony is taken reappear in the other texts. It also shares the archaeological context with two—probably all three—of the later tablets. However, the document has several features that do not fit comfortably with the other texts. None of the litigants is named. The *dimtu* name here, "Damqaya son of Waši," appears nowhere else on either side of the dispute. The key explanatory lines, 15 and 16, are damaged with the result that "Kizzuk" may not be mentioned at all, and, if it is, the last word in the matter may be that no one has heard of *this* name. In theory, that might work well for the opponents of the family of Kel-tešup son of Ḫutiya. But, if that is the case, why would such a useless text (useless at best; it might have been downright damaging) have been preserved in the Ḫutiya-Kel-tešup archive together with all the other texts, texts that at least point to a favorable outcome? Perhaps this deposition, with faulty data (i.e., the "wrong" *dimtu* name) was simply squirreled away, where it could do no damage. In the end, text #58 somehow pertains to the Kizzuk affair and so is included here as a cautionary tale regarding our continuing ignorance of all that goes on in these ancient archival documents.

The next text, #59, is less problematic. The document is cast as a legal declaration[6] made by high officials. The meaning of the document is somewhat obscured by a seeming promiscuous mixing both of singular and plural grammatical subjects in quotations and of verbal tenses. Nevertheless, the thrust of the document is reasonably clear. In the matter of Kel-tešup, the king[7] has ordered that seven villages be surveyed[8] regarding the name of the *dimtu* in which they are located. They testify that the name is Kizzuk—nothing else. Nevertheless, Wantari and Keliya[9] tell these officials that the *dimtu*'s name is Ṭâb-ukur (and not Kizzuk). Although this declaration is not referred to in the trial record, text #61 (on which see below), it points in the same direction as text #60, a series of declarations that did become part of the trial record as described in text #61. Perhaps text #59 was employed in a trial whose record is no longer extant.[10]

Text #60, the third in the series mentioning testimony of towns in the disputed *dimtu*, notes the testimony of nine towns, including all those mentioned in text #59, that the *dimtu* is called "Kizzuk" and nothing else.

Text #61 records, at long last, a verdict in the case of Kel-tešup son of Ḫutiya and of Ḫutiya before him regarding rightful ownership of a district, its towns, tower, and land. After seven surviving texts spanning two generations, implying limited failure for Ḫutiya in the first generation, appeals to the crown, and several indeterminate steps, Kel-tešup wins the land, rightfully bearing the name of his ancestor: "*dimtu* of Kizzuk." And, of course, these records ended up in *his* family archive, insurance against future spurious claims.

But a question persists. How can Bêlšunu and Šatu-kewi claim to have real estate titles attesting to their ownership of the disputed land and building(s), presumably actually able to produce them, and still lose the case? More pointedly, how could they actually produce acquisition documents—and, note, such a transaction is never disputed by the Ḫutiya/Kel-tešup Family—while the Ḫutiya/Kel-tešup Family could actually demonstrate that the land was ancestral *and remained within the family*.

A solution may be proposed. But it is to be emphasized that the hypothesized solution is helpful in explaining certain curiosities of this series but is not itself evidence: if the deduction is persuasive, it nevertheless remains just that, a mere deduction.

The background to this dispute appears to have been as follows. The Ḫutiya/Kel-tešup Family held the real estate as a patrimonial holding going back at least four generations from Ḫutiya back to one Kizzuk. For their part, Bêlšunu and Šatu-kewi bought the same land, possibly from the state (which somehow claimed title, according to them) before the appearance on the scene of Turi-kintar (a descendant of Kizzuk). They also claim that "Kizzuk" is not the key toponym. Rather, it is "Ṭâb-ukur," who once owned the land at issue.[11] They accuse Turi-kintar of having stolen the land. The descendants of Kizzuk emerged victorious, not because there was no such sale, but because the dynamic of inheritance was already in place when the sale took place and because such a sale could only legally have been undertaken by members of the family. The crux of the whole series (or *one* crux) was, *not* that the GN "Kizzuk" proves ownership, but that it proves that subsequent alienation by non-family individuals was *ipso facto* invalid. In short, the sale was illegal and, therefore, null. That is why the Ḫutiya/Kel-tešup Family's response to the claim of adoption (text #56) was, not that it had failed to take place, but that the land was theirs by inheritance, which claim they supported by asserting and demonstrating that the real estate was commonly known by the name of "Kizzuk," their ancestor (text #57, etc.).[12] The prolonged focus of the texts in this series on the correct toponym is thus explained: it is *the* point upon which Ḫutiya's and then Kel-tešup's case rests. Its correctness results in the utter irrelevance of the counterclaim of a deed of sale. Only a member of the Ḫutiya/Kel-tešup Family could have sold "Kizzuk" real estate, and such a sale is not the counterclaim.

To state the situation somewhat differently, if the "sale" were suspect on its face, the easiest way to neutralize the claim was, not to demonstrate falsity or irregularity in the sale itself, but to render it void *a priori*. That may be why, in the decisive trial, recorded in text #61, though Wantari claims legal ownership (he pays the *ilku*-tax, after all[13]), when he is asked to reply to Kel-tešup's demonstration of ancestral presence, he meekly surrenders: "I have no experts" (text #61:43).[14] The winning tactic appears to have been the defeat of an opponent's claim by undermining a premise to that claim.[15]

55. *JEN* VI, 644 (JENu 857)

Findspot: Room T10
Publication: Lacheman 1939a: pl. 585
Editions: H. Lewy 1942: 338–39; Hayden 1962: 127–29

Obverse

1 *u⸢m⸣-m⸢a⸣*[^{m}]⸢*Tar*⸣-[*m*]*i*-[*y*]*a-ma* DUMU *Ku-uš-ši-ya*
2 *um-ma* ⸢^{m}⸣*Ut-ta-a*[*z-z*]*i-na-ma* DUMU *Pu-i-ta-e*
3 *um-ma* ^{m}*Ak-ku-l*[*en-n*]*i-ma* DUMU *Pal-te-šup*
4 *um-ma* ^{m}*Ta-i-*⸢*te-šup-ma* DUMU⸣ *Ki-iz-zi-ḫar-pa*
5 *u*[*m*]-⸢*ma*⸣ ^{m}*Tù-um-ši-ma-na-ma* DUMU *T*⸢*ù-ri-k*⸣*i-in-tar*
6 [*um-ma*] 5 LÚ.MEŠ *an-nu-*tu_4*-ma*
7 [*mi-n*]*u-um-me-e* A.ŠÀ.MEŠ *ù* AN.ZA.KÀR *ša e-be-er-t*⸢*a*⸣*-an*
8 [*š*]*a* ^{m}*Ki-iz-zu-uk i+na* AN.ZA.KÀR
9 [*š*]*a* ^{m}*Ki-iz-zu-uk*
10 *i+na di-na-ti* ^{m}*Ḫu-ti-ya* DUMU *Ku-ši-ya*
11 *ni-it-ta-di-*<*in*$^{?}$> *šum-ma*
12 ^{m}*Ḫu-ti-ya i+na di-ni*

13 [*i*]*l-te-e-e*ʾ(/*sic*/) *i+na* A.ŠÀ.MEŠ ⸢*ù* AN.ZA.KÀR⸣ *ša-a-šu-nu*
14[16] 1^{-en} *pu-ru qa-tù*
15 ^{m}*Ḫu-*[*t*]*i-ya i-leq-qé*
16 *ù r*[*i-i*]*ḫ-tu*$_{4}$ A.ŠÀ.MEŠ *ù* AN.ZA.KÀR
17 *ki-i* [*qa-t*]*i-ni ni-za-az*
18 *um-m*[*a*] 5 LÚ.MEŠ *an-nu-tu*$_{4}$*-ma*
19 *šu*[*m-ma i-n*]*a a-wa-ti an-ni-t*[*i*]
20 [*ša*$^{?}$ *ni*$^{?}$*-id*$^{?}$]*-bu-*⸢*bu*⸣$^{?}$ *ni-ib-bá-*[*la*]*-ka*$_{4}$*-at*
21 [1 MA.N]A ⸢KÙ.BAB⸣BAR 1 MA.NA KÙ.SI[G$_{17}$]
Lower edge
22 [*a-na* ^{m}*Ḫ*]*u-ti-ya*
23 [*nu-ma-a*]*l-la ṭup-pu*
24 [*an-nu-ú*] ⸢*i*⸣*+na* EGIR *šu-du-t*[*i*]
25 [*a-šar* K]Á.GAL *ša* URU *Tú*[*r-ša*$_{1/2}$ *ša*$_{1/2/7}$*-ṭì*]*-ir*
Reverse
26 [IGI *Aš-tar-til-l*]*a* DUMU *Pu-i-ta-e*
27 [IGI *Ši-il-wa*]*-*⸢*a-a*⸣ DUMU *Pu-ur-šu-ru-u*⸢*t-ta*⸣
28 [IGI *Un*]*-te-*⸢*šup* DUMU *W*⸣*a-*⸢*at-wa*⸣
29 [IGI] *E-na-ma-*⸢*ti*⸣ DUMU *Ta-a-a*
30 IGI *A-kip-še-en-ni* DUMU *Ké-li-ya*
31 IGI *Ku-pár-ša* DUMU *Ur-ku-ti*
32 IGI ^{d}UTU SIG$_{5}$$^{-iq}$ DUB-SAR$^{-rù}$ DUMU *It-ha-pi-ḫe*
S.I.
33 NA$_{4}$ ^{m}*Ši-il-wa-a-a* DUMU *Pu-*⸢*ur-šu*⸣[17]*-ru-u*[*t-ta*]
S.I.
34 NA$_{4}$ ^{m}*Ku-pár-ša* DUMU *Ur-*[*k*]*u-ti*
S.I.
35 ⸢NA$_{4}$⸣ ^{m}*Un-te-šup* DUMU *W*[*a-at*]*-wa*
S.I.
36 $^{\langle NA_4 \rangle}$KIŠIB ^{m}[*Aš*]*-tar-til-la* DUMU *Pu-i-ta-e*
Upper edge

37 NA$_{4}$ ^{m}[*E-n*]*a-m*[*a*]*-*⸢*ti*⸣	[NA$_{4}$] ^{m}*A-kip-še-e*[*n*]*-ni*
[S.I.]	S.I.
38 DUMU *Ta-a*]*-a*	DUMU *Ké-li-ya*

Left edge
39 ^{NA_4}KIŠIB ^{d}UTU-⸢SIG$_{5}$$^{-iq}$⸣ DUB.SAR-*r*⸢*i*⸣
S.I.

JEN VI, 644

(1–17) Thus Tarmiya son of Kuššiya;[18] and thus Uttaz-zina son of Pui-tae; and thus Akkul-enni son of Pal-tešup; and thus Tai-tešup son of Kizzi-ḫarpa; and thus Tumšimana son of Turi-kintar; thus these 5 men:[19] "Whatever fields (there are) and the *dimtu*-tower of Kizzuk on the far shore, (all being) in the *dimtu*[20] of Kizzuk, we have given (to) Ḫutiya son of Kuššiya (for purposes of) the legal proceedings (to come). Should Ḫutiya win the case, Ḫutiya shall take 1 share from among those fields and the *dimtu*-tower, (all) to be at his disposal. And we shall divide the remaining fields and (the remaining part of the) *dimtu*-tower, (these) to be at our disposal."

(18–23) Thus these 5 men: "Should we violate this statement [that?] we have (just) made(?), we shall pay [to] Ḫutiya [1] mina of silver and 1 mina of gold."

(23–25) [This] tablet was written after the proclamation [at] the Town-of-Turša Gate.

(26–32) [Before] Aštar-tilla son of Pui-tae; [before] Šilwaya son of Pur-šurutta; [before] Un-tešup son of Watwa; [before] Enna-mati son of Taya; before Akip-šenni son of Keliya; before Kuparša son of Urkutu; before Šamaš-damiq, the scribe, son of Ith-apiḫe.

(33–39) (*seal impression*) Seal of Šilwaya son of Pur-šurutta; (*seal impression*) seal of Kuparša son of Urkutu; (*seal impression*) seal of Un-tešup son of Watwa; (*seal impression*) seal impression of Aštar-tilla son of Pui-tae; seal of Enna-mati (*seal impression*) son of Taya; seal of Akip-šenni (*seal impression*) son of Keliya; seal impression of Šamaš-damiq, scribe (*seal impression*).

56. *JEN* IV, 388 (JENu 167a+167b)

Findspot: Room T12
Publication: Chiera 1934a: pl. CCCLXXII
Editions: H. Lewy 1942: 341–42; Hayden 1962: 129–30

Obverse

1 ^{m}*Ḫu-ti-ya ù* ^{m}*Aš-tar-*[*til-la*]
2 *it-ti* ^{m}EN-*šu-nu*
3 *ù it-ti* ^{m}*Ša-tù-ké-wi*
4 *i+ na di-ni a-na pa-ni* DI.KU$_5$.MEŠ
5 *i*(!)*-te-lu-ma um-ma*
6 ^{m}*Ḫu-ti-ya ù um-ma*

7 ^{m}*Aš-tar-til-la-ma*
8 LÚ.MEŠ *an-nu-*tu_4
9[21] *aš-ša-bu-mi*(!) *ù*(!)
10 A.ŠÀ.MEŠ-*ni i+na e-mu-*[*qì-im-ma*[22]]
11 *ú-*ka_4*-al-šu-nu-ti-*[*mi*]
12 *um-ma* ^{m}EN-*šu-nu* ù
13 *um-ma* ^{m}KUR$^{-tù}$*-ké-* ⸢*wi*⸣!
14 *ù ni-i-nu* [ ] [23]
15 *a-na* A.ŠA *š*[*a-a-šu*[24]]
Lower Edge
16 *a-na ma-ru-ti*
17 *ip-šu* «*ù*»
18 *ù* DI.KU_5.MEŠ
Reverse
19 ^{m}EN-*šu-nu ù* ^{m}*Ša-tù-ké-*[*wi*]
20 *ir-ta-ak-sú-šu-nu-ti*
21 *i-na i-sí-ni*
22 *M*[*i*](!)*-ti-ru-u*[*n*]*-ni* AŠ [ ]AN[25]
22bis *lu-ú aš-bá-ni* [ ]
23 *ṣa-bit*(!?) A.ŠA ⸢*ki*?-*m*⸣ *a*?[26] ⸢x⸣ [(?)]
24 *šu-nu-ma* ⸢x⸣[ ]
25 ⸢*um-m*⸣*a* ^{m}KUR$^{-tù}$*-ké-w*[*i*]
26 A.ŠÀ.MEŠ ⸢*ša ir*⸣*-šu* ^{m}⸢*Ú*⸣*-ku-*[*ya*]
27 *a-na te-er-ḫa-ti a-na* ^{m}[ ][27]
28 *it-ta-di-*<*in*?>*-mi*
29 NA_4 ^{m}*Ar-ti-ir-wi*
30 NA_4 ^{m}*Ar-zi-iz-*[*za*]
31 NA_4 ^{m}*Ni-iḫ-ri-ya*
32 NA_4 ^{m}AN-GI
Left Edge
33 *ṭup-pí* [*ta*]*ḫ-sí*(!)*-il-ti*

JEN IV, 388

(1–5) Ḫutiya and Aštar-tilla took to court, before judges, Bêlšunu and Šatu-kewi.

(5–11) Thus Ḫutiya and thus Aštar-tilla: "These men are tenants; and they have been withholding our land by force."

(12–17) Thus Bêlšunu and thus Šatu-kewi: "But we … for that land … were adopted."[28]

(18–24) And the judges ordered Bêlšunu and Šatu-kewi to be present(?) at the festival of (the month of) Mitirunni … … seized, land as(?) … and they ….

(25–28) Thus Šatu-kewi: "Ukuya gave as a bride price to … the field under cultivation."

(29–32) Seal of Ar-tirwi; seal of Ar-zizza; seal of Niḫriya; seal of … .

(33) Memorandum tablet.

57. *JEN* IV, 325 (JENu 168)

Findspot: Room T12
Publication: Chiera 1934a: pl. CCCVII
Editions: H. Lewy 1942: 339–41; Hayden 1962: 126–27

Obverse
1 *a-na* S[UKKAL.MEŠ[29]]
2[30] *qí-b*[*i*!*-ma um-ma* ^{m}*Zi-li-y*]⌜*a*⌝
3 *ù* [*um-ma* ^{m}*Šúk-ri-ya*]
⌜*ù*⌝ [*um-ma* ^{m}*Ar-ti-ir-wi*]
4 ^{m}*Ḫu-t*[*i-ya* DUMU? *Ku*?-(*uš*?-)*ši*?-*ya*? *it-ti* ^{m}KUR(-*tù*)-*ké*[31]]-*wi*
5 *it-ti* ^{m}E[N-*šu-nu] it-ti* ^{m}*Z*]*i-li-pu-kùr*
6 AŠ ⌜*di*⌝-*ni a-na* [*pa-ni-ni i-te-lu*]-*ma*
7 *um-ma* ^{m}*Ḫu*-⌜*ti*⌝-*ya-ma* [AN.ZA.KÀR[32]] *ša Ki-iz-zu-uk*
8 *it-ti* A.ŠÀ.MEŠ-*šu-ma* [*ša* ^{m}*K*]*i-iz-zu-uk*
9 *am-ma-ti-ni ù* LÚ.MEŠ *an-nu-ti*
10 ⌜*a-n*⌝*a aš-ša-bu-ti-ma a-ši-ib*
11 [*ù*] *i+na-an-na* A.ŠÀ.MEŠ *ik-ta-la-šu-nu-ti-ma*
12 ⌜*ù*⌝ *i-te-ri-*⌜*i*⌝*š-mi*
13 *ù ni-nu* LÚ.MEŠ *al-ta-al-šu-nu-ti-ma*
14 *um-ma šu-nu-ma* URU *ša* É.GAL-*lì-mi*
15 *ù ni-i-nu ṣa-bi-*<*it*> A.ŠA-*mi*
16 *šu-un-*«*un*»*-šu ša* URU
Lower edge
17 *ša Ki-iz-zu-uk-we*
18 *l*⌜*a*⌝ *šu-ut-mi šu-un-šu*
19 ⌜*š*⌝*a* URU *ša Ṭá-ab-kúr*(!)
Reverse
20 ⌜*š*⌝*u-ut-mi ù* URU
21 ^{m}*Tù-ur-ki-in-tar*
22 *iš-ta*![33]*-ri-iq-mi*

23 *um-ma* ^{m}*Zi-li-pu-kùr-ma*
24 A.ŠA *a-na ya-ši*
25 *ḫi-šu-ru-mi ù e-te-ri-iš-mi*
26 *um-ma* ^{m}KUR-*ké-wi-ma*
27 *ù um-ma*
28 ^{m}EN-*šu-nu-ma ni-i-nu*
29 ^{m}*Ik-ti*-WI-*x ṣa-bit* A.⸢Š⸣À
30 *a-na ma-ru-ti*
31 *ni-te-pu-uš-mi ṭup-pi-ni*
32 *aš-bu-mi* [*ki*]-*ma*
33 URU *a-na* É *ša*
34 *iq-bu-uš a-nu-um-ma*
35 *ú-še-bi-la-ku a-na* LUGAL
36 *qi-bá-šu-nu-ti*
37 NA_4 ^{m}*Zi-li-ya* NA_4 ^{m}*Šúk-ri-ya*
38 NA_4 ^{m}*Ar-*[*ti*]*-ir-wi*

JEN IV, 325

(1–6) To the *sukkallu*s, say: "[Thus Ziliya] and [thus Šukriya] and(?) [thus Ar-tirwi]: 'Ḫutiya [son? of? Kuššiya?] took to court [before us] Šatu-kewi, Bêlšunu, [and] Zilip-ukur.

(7–12) "Thus Ḫutiya: '[The *dimtu*-tower] of Kizzuk together with the fields were (those) [of] Kizzuk, our ancestor.[34] And these men reside[35] (there) in tenancy. [Yet] now they are withholding the land and cultivating[36] (it on their own).'

(13) "So we summoned (those) men.

(14–22) "Thus they (responded): 'The town belongs to the "palace." And we are "holder" of the land. (As for) the name of the town being Kizzuk, that is *not* it. (As for) the name of the town being Ṭâb-ukur, that *is* it. And Turi-kintar[37] stole (i.e., illegally appropriated) the town.'

(23–25) "Thus Zilip-ukur: 'The land was given(?) to me and I cultivated it (accordingly).'

(26–32) "Thus Šatu-kewi and Bêlšunu: 'We were adopted (by) Ikti-WI-x, the "holder" of the land.[38] And our tablets exist.'

(32–36) "Since the town (is in the possession) of the household[39] of which they spoke, now he has brought (the case) to you. Tell these (things) to the king."

(37–38) Seal of Ziliya; seal of Šukriya; seal of Ar-tirwi.

58. *JEN* V, 512 (JENu 48)

Findspot: Room T12
Publication: Chiera 1934b: pls. CDLXXVIII–CDLXXIX
Editions: H. Lewy 1942: 344; Hayden 1962: 125–26

Obverse

1 ^{m}*Ar-ša-li* ^{m}*Zi-[li-ya]*
2 ^{m}*Ú-lu-uk-ka* 3 LÚ.MEŠ
3 *ša* URU *Ku-lu-ut-tù-e*

---

4 ^{m}*Te-ḫi-ip-til-la* ^{m}*Ku-un-ta-nu*
5 ^{m}*Ḫa-am-ti-še* ^{m}*Tù-ḫa-a-a*
6 4 LÚ.MEŠ *ša* URU *E-téš-še-ni-we*

---

7 ^{m}*Ḫa-ši-pu ša* URU *Ḫa-aš-lu-ni-a*

---

8 ^{m}*Ki-pa-li* ^{m}*Ni-iḫ-ri-ya*
9 ^{m}*Ta-e-na* ^{m}*Ta-i-še-en-ni*
10 ^{m}*Tar-mi-til-la* 5 LÚ.MEŠ
11 *ša* URU *Ez-ra*

---

12 13 LÚ.MEŠ *šu*$^{!}$*-nu ša*
13 *um-ma šu-nu-ma*
14[40]*šu-un-šu ša* AN.ZA.KÀR *ša*
^{m}*Dam*[41]*-qa-ya* DUMU *Wa-ši-i*

Lower Edge

15[42]x x *ša* ^{m}*Ki-x-x-x-we*
16 x URU x x TE MEŠ

Reverse

17 NA$_4$ ^{m}*Te-ḫi-ip-til-la* NA$_4$ ^{m}*Ta-e-na*
18 NA$_4$ ^{m}*Ḫa-ši-pu* NA$_4$ ^{m}*Ku-un-ta-nu*
19 NA$_4$ ^{m}*Zi-li-ya* NA$_4$ ^{m}*Tù-ḫa-a-a*
20 NA$_4$ ^{m}*Ù-lu-uk-ka*$_4$ NA$_4$ ^{m}*Ki-pa-li*
21 NA$_4$ DUB.SAR^{-ru} NA$_4$ ^{m}*Ni-iḫ-ri-ya*
22 NA$_4$ ^{m}*Tar-mi-til-la* NA$_4$ ^{m}*Ḫa-am-ti-še*
23 NA$_4$ ^{m}*Ta-i-še-en-ni* NA$_4$ ^{m}*Ar-ša-li*

JEN V, 512

(1–3) Ar-šali, Ziliya, Ulukka: 3 men of the town of Kuluttu.

(4–6) Teḫip-tilla, Kuntanu, Ḫamtiše, Tuḫaya: 4 men of the town of Eteš-šenni.

---

(7) Ḫašipu of the town of Ḫašluniya.

(8–11) Kipali, Niḫriya, Taena, Tai-šenni, Tarmi-tilla: 5 men of the town of Ezira.

(12–16) 13 men; they are the ones who "thus they (said)": "The name of the *dimtu* (is that) of Damqaya son of Waši ... of Ki-... ... town .... .

(17–23) Seal of Teḫip-tilla; seal of Taena; seal of Ḫašipu; seal of Kuntanu; seal of Ziliya; seal of Tuḫaya; seal of Ulukka; seal of Kipali; seal of the scribe; seal of Niḫriya; seal of Tarmi-tilla; seal of Ḫamtiše; seal of Tai-šenni; seal of Ar-šali.

59. *JEN* II, 135 (JENu 50)

Findspot: Room T12
Publication: Chiera 1930: pl. CXXXII
Editions: Gordon 1936: 3–5; H. Lewy 1942: 342–43; Hayden 1962: 123–24; Jankowska 1969: 263–64

Obverse

1 ⸢*um*⸣-*ma* ^{m}*Ḫu-ti-pa-pu š*[*a*$^{!}$-*ki-in*[43]] *ma-ti*
2 *ù* ^{m}*A-ki-ya* ^{LÚ}SUKKAL *iš-t*[*a-ap-r*]*u*[44]-*ú*
3 *aš-š*[*um*] *ša* ^{m}*Ké-el-te-šup u*[*m-ma*] ⸢*š*⸣*u-nu-ma*
4 *a-lik-mi* URU.MEŠ-^{ni} *ša* AN.ZA.KÀR
5 *ša* ZAG-*šu-nu ù* K⸢A⸣B-$^{mé-li}$-*šu-nu*
ša AN.ZA.KÀR
6 *iš-ta-lu-uš ù a-na-ku* URU.MEŠ
ḫe-wa-⸢*du*⸣-*um-ma* DÙ-$^{⸢u⸣š}$
7 URU *E-zi-ra* URU *Ḫa-aš-lu-ni-a*
8 URU *E-te-eš-še-ni-we*
9 URU *Ku-lu-ut-tù* URU *Ú-a-ak*-⸢*ka*⸣$^{?}$[45]-*a*
10 URU *Ti-lu-ša*-^{GIŠ}TUKUL$^{?}$

11 URU *I-re-ma-dá-ad-we*
12 7 URU.MEŠ$^{-ni}$ *an-nu-ú*
13 *ni-iš-ta-lu-uš um-ma* [*šu-nu-ma*] *šu-un-šu*
14 AN.ZA.KÀR *ša* ^{m}*Ki-iz-zu*$^{!}$*-u*[*k*] [ ] *š*⸢*a*⸣
^{m}*Ki-iz-zu-uk*
15 *ù ša-nu-ú la i-de*$_4$[*-e*$^?$]
16 *um-ma* ^{m}*Wa-an-ta-ri*
17 *ù um-ma* ^{m}*Ké-li-ya-ma*
18 AN.ZA.KÀR *ša* ^{m}DÙG.GA-*bu-*<*ku*>*-ur*
19 *ù* ^{m}*Ṭá-bu-ku-ur iṣ-ṣa-ab-bat*$^{-at}$
20 *šu-un-šu ša* AN.ZA.KÀR *ša*(!) *Ṭá-bu-kùr-ma*
Reverse
21 NA$_4$ ^{m}*Ḫu-ti-pa-pu*

JEN II, 135

(1–2) Thus Ḫutip-apu, the regional governor, and Akiya, the *sukkallu*:

(2–3) "They[46] dispatched (a message). Thus they (said) concerning the matter of Kel-tešup:

(4–6) "'Go[47] and question (lit. 'they questioned it/him') the towns of the *dimtu*-district, those of the right (part) and of the left (part) of the *dimtu*.'[48]

(6–13) "So I (*sic*) made a survey(?) of the towns. We questioned these 7 towns: the town of Ezira, the town of Ḫašluniya, the town of Eteš-šenni, the town of Kuluttu, the town of Uak-k?a, the town of Tillu-ša-kakki(?), the town of Irēm-adad.

(13–15) "Thus [they] (said): 'Its name is the *dimtu* of Kizzuk … after (the man called) Kizzuk.' And no one knows another (name for the *dimtu*).

(16–20) "Thus Wantari and thus Keliya: '(It is) the *dimtu* of Ṭâb-ukur, for Ṭâb-ukur held it all along. The name of the *dimtu* is that of (the man called) Ṭâb-ukur.'"

(21) Seal of Ḫutip-apu.

60. *JEN* II, 184 (JENu 44)

Findspot: Room T12
Publication: Chiera 1930: pls. CLXVI–CLXVII
Editions: Gordon 1936: 5–6; H. Lewy 1942: 343–44; Hayden 1962: 124–25

Obverse

1 *um-ma* LÚ.MEŠ *ša* URU *Ez-r*[*a*]
2 *um-ma* LÚ.MEŠ *ša* URU *Ši-mé-*[*ru-un-ni*]
3 *um-ma* LÚ.MEŠ *ša* URU *E*(!)*-téš-*[*še-en-n*]*i-we*
4 *um-ma* LÚ.MEŠ *ša* URU *A-šu-*[*ri*]
5 *um-ma* ⸢LÚ⸣.MEŠ *ša* URU *Til-*^{GIŠ}T[UKUL]$^{?}$
6 *um-ma* ⸢LÚ⸣.[MEŠ] *ša* URU [*Ḫ*]*a-*[*aš*]*-lu-*⸢*ni-ya*⸣
7 *um-ma* [LÚ.MEŠ *š*]*a* URU *Ku-lu-ut-tù-e*
8 [*um-ma* LÚ.MEŠ *ša*] URU *K*[*u*]*m*$^{!}$*-ri*
9 *um-*[*ma* LÚ.MEŠ *ša* URU] *Wu-ul-tù-ku-ri-a*
10 9 URU.MEŠ *an-nu-ti iš-ta-lu-uš-mi*
11 *um-ma šu-*⸢*nu*⸣*-ma šu-*[*u*]*n-šu*
12 *š*[*a* AN.ZA.KÀR *ša* ^{m}*Ki*]*-iz-zu-uk-we-ma*
13 *šu-*[*ut-mi*]
14 *š*[*u*]*-un-šu ša-nu-ú*
15 *ya-a-nu*

Reverse

16 NA$_4$ ^{m}*Tù-uḫ-mi-ya* NA$_4$ ^{m}*Šur-*[ ]
17 NA$_4$ ^{m}*Kàr-ra-te* NA$_4$ ^{m}[ ]*-kam-*⸢*ma*⸣
18 NA$_4$ ^{m}*Ut-ḫap-ta-e* NA$_4$ *I-*[ ]
19 NA$_4$ ^{m}*A-kap-ta-e* NA$_4$ ^{m}*Zi-li-ya*
20 NA$_4$ ^{m}*Ḫa-na-ak-ka*$_4$

JEN II, 184

(1–15) Thus the men of the town of Ezira; thus the men of the town of Šimerunni; thus the men of the town of Eteš-šenni; thus the men of the town of Ašuri; thus the men of the town of Tillu-ša-kakki(?); thus the men of the town of Ḫašluniya; thus the men of the town of Kuluttu; thus the men of the town of Kumri; thus the men of the town of Wultukuriya—they questioned these 9 towns—thus they (said): "(As for) the name of the [*dimtu* being] Kizzuk, that is its name. There is no other name."

(16–20) Seal of Tuḫmiya; seal of Šur-…; seal of Karrate; seal of …-kamma; seal of Utḫap-tae; seal of I-…; seal of Akap-tae; seal of Ziliya; seal of Ḫanakka.

61. *JEN* II, 321 (JENu 191a and 191b)

Findspot: Room T13 (*sic*)[49]
Publication: Chiera 1934a: pls. CCCI–CCCII
Editions: H. Lewy 1942: 344–47; Hayden 1962: 120–23; Jankowska 1969: 260–61

This is a double artifact: an inscribed clay envelope enclosing a tablet. That the case contains the scribe's name only (and sealing, probably) suggests that trial tablets (some at least) were filed according to the name of the writer or that this tablet was specially enveloped to ensure the legal integrity of its contents, contents decisively favorable to the family in whose archive the tablet was found.

Case
[NA$_4$] ^{m}*Ur-ḫi-te-šup* DUB.SAR
Obverse
1 ^{m}*Ké-el-te-šup* DUMU ^{m}*Ḫu-ti-ya*
2 *it-ti* ^{m}*Wa-an-ta-ri* DUMU *Ú-ku-ya*
3 AŠ *di-ni a-na pa-ni* DI.KU$_5$.MEŠ *i-te-lu-ma*
4 *um-ma* ^{m}*Ké-el-te-šup-ma* AN.ZA.KÀR-*ya*
5 *ša* ^{m}*Ki-iz-zu-uk ša e-be-er-ta it-ti*
6 A.ŠÀ.MEŠ-*ya* ^{m}*Wa-an-ta-ri e-mu-qam-ma*!
7 *ú-ka$_4$-al i+na* EGIR-*šu al-ta-na-as-sí*
8 *a-na* LUGAL *uš-tu-ḫé-ḫi-in ù a-na*
9 ^{m}*Ḫu-ti-*⸢*pa*⸣*-pu* GAR KUR *iš-tap-ru iq-ta-bu-ú*
10 URU.MEŠ *ša* ZAG-*šu ù ša* KAB-*šu ša* AN.ZA.KÀR
11 ša ^{m}*Ki-iz-zu-uk-we ša-al-šu-nu-ti-mi* [*ù*]
12 *ṭe$_4$-e-ma te-er* URU.MEŠ ^{m}*Ḫu-ti-pa-pu* GAR KUR
13 *il-ta-al-šu-nu-ti a-ma-ti$_7$-šu-nu*
14 *i+na ṭup-pí il-ta-ṭar* ^{NA_4}KIŠIB.MEŠ-*šu-nu*
15 *ša* LÚ.MEŠ *ša* URU.MEŠ *i+na ṭup-pí šu-gi-ir-ri-ru*
16 DI.KU$_5$.MEŠ ^{m}*Wa-an-ta-ri iš-ta-lu-uš*
17 *um-ma* ^{m}*Wa-an-ta-ri-ma* AN.ZA.KÀR *ša* ^{m}*Ki-iz-zu-uk*
18 *it-ti* A.ŠÀ.MEŠ-*šu a-bu-ya ú-ka$_4$-al-lu a-na-ku*
19 *i-na* EGIR *a-bi-ya ú-ka$_4$-al-lu-ma aš-šum*
20 A.ŠÀ.MEŠ *ša-a-šu-nu ù* AN.ZA.KÀR *ša-a-šu a-lik*
il-ki a-na-ku-mi
21 *ù* ^{m}*Ké-el-te-šup ṭup-pu ša* URU.MEŠ
22 *ša* ^{m}*Ḫu-ti-pa-pu* GAR KUR *il-ṭù-ru a-na pa-ni*
23 DI.KU$_5$.MEŠ *uš-te-li ki-na-an-na il-ta-sí*

24 *um-ma* LÚ.MEŠ-*ma ša* URU *Kum-ri-ma*
25 *um-ma* LÚ.MEŠ-*ma ša* URU *Wu-ul-tù-ku-ri-a*
26 *um-ma* LÚ.MEŠ-*ma ša* URU *E-zi-ra*
27 *um-ma* LÚ.MEŠ-*ma ša* URU *Ku-lu-ut-tu-e*
28 *um-ma* LÚ.MEŠ-*ma ša* URU *Ši-me-ru-un-ni*
29 *um-ma* LÚ.MEŠ-*ma ša* URU *E-te-eš-še-en-ni*
30 *um-ma* LÚ.MEŠ-*ma ša* URU *A-šu-ri*
31 *um-ma* LÚ.MEŠ-*ma ša* URU *Ti-li-ša*-^{GIŠ}⸢TUKUL⸣$^{?}$
32 *um-ma* LÚ.MEŠ-*ma ša* URU *Ḫa-aš-lu-ni-a*
33 *ù um-ma* 9 URU.MEŠ-*ma ša* ZAG-*šu ù*
34 *ša* KAB-*šu ša* AN.ZA.KÀR *Ki-iz-zu-uk-we*
35 AN.ZA.KÀR *ša* ^{m}*Ki-iz-zu-uk-we*
Lower Edge
36 *it-ti* A.ŠÀ.MEŠ-*šu ša* ^{m}*Ki-iz-zu-uk-ma*
37 *ša at-ti-ḫu*[50] *ù a-na* ^{m}*Wa-an-ta-ri*
la ni-de$_4$*-mi*
Reverse
38 DI.KU$_5$.MEŠ *a-na* ^{m}*Wa-an-ta-ri iq-ta-bu-ú*
39 *a-nu-um-ma* 9 URU.MEŠ *a-na pa-la-aḫ-ḫi*
40 *a-na* ^{m}*Ké-el-te-šup im-ta-nu-ú ù*
41 LÚ.MEŠ *mu-de*$_4$*-ka*$_4$ *ša at-tù-ka*$_4$ *bi-lam-mi*
42 *um-ma* ^{m}*Wa-an-ta-ri-ma* LÚ.MEŠ *mu-du-ya*
43 *ya-nu-mi ki-me ṭup-pu ša* ^{m}*Ḫu-ti-pa-pu* GAR KUR
44 *a-na pa-ni* DI.KU$_5$.MEŠ *il-ta-sí* 9 URU.MEŠ
45 *a-na pa-la-aḫ-ḫi a-na* ^{m}*Ké-el-te-šup im-ta-nu-ú*
46 ^{NA_4}KIŠIB.MEŠ *ša* LÚ.MEŠ *ša* 9 URU.MEŠ *ù ša*
47 ^{m}*Ḫu-ti-pa-pu i+na ṭup-pí šu-gi-ir-ri-ru*
48 *ù mu-du-šu ša* ^{m}*Wa-an-ta-ri ya-nu*
49 DI.KU$_5$.MEŠ *di-na ki-i pí-i ṭup-pí i-te-ep-šu*
50 AŠ *di-ni* ^{m}*Ké-el-te-šup il-te-e*
51 AN.ZA.KÀR *ša* ^{m}*Ki-iz-zu-uk-we ka*$_4$*-dú* A.ŠÀ.MEŠ
52 AŠ *šu-pa-al mi-iṣ-ri ša*
53 URU *E-te-eš-še-en-ni-we i+na il-ta-na-ni*
54 *mi-iṣ-ri ša* URU *E-zi-ra*
55 *i+na e-le-ni* AN.ZA.KÀR *ša* ^{m}*Ul-lu-ya*
56 ^{m}*Ké-el-te-šup il-te-qì*
57 ŠU ^{m}*Ur-ḫi-te-šup* DUB.SAR
58 NA$_4$ ^{m}*Til*[51]*-ta-aš-šu-ra* SUKKAL NA$_4$ ^{m}*A-ki-ya* SUKKAL
59 NA$_4$ ^{m}*A-ri-pa-pu* DUMU *Te-ḫi-pa-pu*
60 NA$_4$ ^{m}*Ni-iḫ-ri-te-šup* DUMU *Pu-i-ta-e*

61 NA$_4$ ^{m}*Šur-ki-til-la* DUMU *A-kip-ta-še-ni*
62 NA$_4$ ^{m}*Wa-aḫ-ri-ta-e* DUMU *Tar-mi-te-šup*
63 NA$_4$ ^{m}*Ḫu-ta-an-ni-a-<pu>* DUMU *Tar-mi-til-la*
64 NA$_4$ ^{m}*Te-ḫi-ip-til-la* DUMU *Ḫa-šu-ar*
65 NA$_4$ ^{m}[*T*]*ù-ra-ar-te-šup* DUMU *Eḫ-li-te-šup*
Upper edge
66 NA$_4$ ^{m}*Šu-ur-te-šup* DUMU *Ta-an-te-a*
67 NA$_4$ ^{m}*Zi-li-pa-pu* DUMU *Šur-kum-a-tal*
68 NA$_4$ ^{m}*Ar-ru-um-ti*[52] *DUB.SAR*
Left edge
69 NA$_4$ ^{m}*En-na-mu-ša* DUMU *Ka$_4$-an-na-pu*
70 NA$_4$ ^{m}*Ša-ar-te-šup* DUMU *Ut-ḫap-ta-e*
71 NA$_4$ ^{m}*Ḫu-ti-pa-pu* DUMU *Tar-mi-til-la*
72 NA$_4$ ^{m}*Mu-uš-te-*⸢*e*⸣/[*y*]*a* DUMU *Pil-maš-še*
73 ŠU ^{m}*Ur-ḫi-te-šup* DUB.SAR

JEN IV, 321

(Tablet case) [Seal of] Urḫi-tešup, scribe.

(1–3) Kel-tešup son of Ḫutiya took to court, before judges, Wantari son of Ukuya.

(4–15) Thus Kel-tešup: "Wantari, by force, withholds the *dimtu*-tower of Kizzuk (standing) on the far bank, which is mine, together with my fields. I have been continually raising claim against him, and have appealed[53] to the king. They (viz. the royal court) replied to Ḫutip-apu, the regional governor, saying: 'Question the towns in the right (part) of and in the left (part) of the *dimtu* of Kizzuk [and] report back.'[54] Ḫutip-apu, the regional governor, questioned the towns, recording on a tablet their testimony. The cylinder seals of the men from (those) towns were rolled on the tablet."[55]

(16–20) The judges questioned Wantari. Thus Wantari: "My father held the *dimtu*-tower of Kizzuk together with its fields and I hold (them) following my father. I bear (i.e., pay; lit. "go") the *ilku* for those fields and for that *dimtu*-tower."

(21–37) Then Kel-tešup produced before the judges the document regarding the towns, (the one) that Ḫutip-apu, the regional governor, recorded. He read aloud as follows: "Thus the men of the town of Kumri; thus the men of the town of Wultukuriya; thus the men of the town of Ezira; thus the men of the town of Kuluttu; thus the men of the town of Šimerunni; thus the men of the town of Eteš-šenni; thus the men of the town of Ašuri; thus the men of the town of Tillu-ša-kakki(?); thus the men of the town of Ḫašluniya; thus the 9 towns in the right (part) and in the left (part) of the *dimtu* of Kizzuk: 'The *dimtu*-tower with its fields is patrimonial[56] (property going back) to Kizzuk. And we know nothing about Wantari.'"

(38–41) The judges said to Wantari: "Now 9 towns have testified for Kel-tešup with respect[57] (i.e., to his benefit). So bring your own experts (i.e., expert witnesses)."

(42–43) Thus Wantari: "I have no experts."

(43–56) Inasmuch as he (viz. Kel-tešup) read aloud before the judges the tablet of Ḫutip-apu, the regional governor, (that) 9 towns testified for Kel-tešup with respect (and that) the cylinder seals of the men from the (same) 9 towns and of Hutip-apu were rolled on the tablet; and (further, that) Wantari had no experts, the judges reached a verdict in accordance with the tablet. Kel-tešup won the case. Kel-tešup took the *dimtu*-tower of Kizzuk together with (those) fields to the west of the border of the town of Eteš-šenni, to the north of the border of the town of Ezira, (and) to the east of the *dimtu* of Ulluya.

(57) Hand of Urḫi-tešup, scribe.

(58–73) Seal of Tiltaš-šura, *sukkallu*; seal of Akiya, *sukkallu*; seal of Arip-apu son of Teḫip-apu; seal of Niḫri-tešup son of Pui-tae; seal of Šurki-tilla son of Akip-tašenni; seal of Waḫri-tae son of Tarmi-tešup; seal of Ḫutanni-apu son of Tarmi-tilla; seal of Teḫip-tilla son of Ḫašuar; seal of Turar-tešup son of Eḫli-tešup; seal of Šur-tešup son of Tanteya; seal of Zilip-apu son of Šurkum-atal; seal of Aril-lumti, the scribe; seal of Enna-muša son of Kannapu; seal of Šar-tešup son of Utḫap-tae; seal of Ḫutip-apu son of Tarmi-tilla; seal of Muš-teya son of Pilmašše. Hand of Urḫi-tešup, scribe.

Chapter Four
The Decline and Fall of a Nuzi Family

The story of Ḫišmeya son of Itḫišta and his family illustrates the progressive impoverishment of the free peasantry of Nuzi at the hands of large landlords. In this case, a scion of the family of Teḫip-tilla son of Puḫi-šenni, his first-born son Enna-mati, is the main beneficiary. Though other activities are attested, for the most part Enna-mati purchases plot after plot from the widow of Itḫišta, Uššen-naya (Itḫišta himself never appears; Uššen-naya is a widow not a wife, therefore, and powerful in her own right), Itḫišta's first-born son (probably), Ḫišmeya, and Ḫišmeya's brothers.

Although the chronological order of the texts cannot be precisely determined,[1] the following ordering represents a logical course of events, supported by some circumstantial evidence.[2] Text #62 seems to be the first text of this series of ten.[3] It has the appearance of an equal exchange by Enna-mati and Ḫišmeya, a *quid pro quo* of slave for slave. But, if so, what would then be the point of the transaction? More likely, there was a qualitative difference in the slaves. Given the weighting of all the other nine texts, the exchange probably redounded to the benefit of Enna-mati.

The family's fortunes are clearly in decline, though not radically so, as demonstrated by a loan text, text #63. Ḫišmeya borrows seed-grain from Enna-mati. The loan is to be repaid with interest at or just after the harvest. Note that title to agricultural land (implicitly) remains in the possession of the borrower. It is only later, presumably as a last resort, that family land itself is alienated to obtain grain (this time for food) and other mobilia. Thus text #63 should represent an early stage in the decline of the family of Ḫišmeya son of Itḫišta.

All subsequent texts directly or indirectly deal with the alienation of family real estate holdings. Probably, the earliest of these are texts ##64, 65, and 66, not necessarily in that order. The family members alienating land in the first two contracts are Ḫišmeya and his mother, Uššen-naya. In the third, these two are joined by a brother of Ḫišmeya, Šarra-šadûni. Apart from these three instances, Uššen-naya appears in no other documents. She may no longer have been alive at the time of the later transactions. The family's land appears to have been concentrated in the region of the town of Tente, east of the road to the town of Natmane. Thus is it described in texts ##64, 66 (more or less), 67 (in part), 70, and 71 (in part). Since text #71 seems to describe comprehensively the family holdings, it is likely that all the remaining texts refer to land in this general vicinity.

If the three Uššen-naya texts are the earliest of the contracts of real estate alienation, as seems plausible, and since Ḫišmeya appears as a co-contractor with his mother in all three, then texts ##67 and 68 may well be the next contracts in this desultory family history. In those two documents (again, in no particular order), Ḫišmeya alone contracts to alienate land to Enna-mati. In the absence of Uššen-naya (by death?), Ḫišmeya alone would have continued the dissolution of the family fortune.

Text #69 is a receipt most likely based on a prior real estate adoption whereby Ḫišmeya ceded land to Uzna, Enna-mati's wife.[4] The receipt describes partial payment for land being ceded to Uzna. Uzna is to pay the balance on a later occasion. That she is the purchaser and not Enna-mati could, in theory, suggest that her husband has died and that she is acting as an economically independent agent. If this were so, this transaction must have taken place after all those in which Enna-mati appears as a principal party. But this cannot be. For, the next two documents of the series as here reconstructed definitely suggest a wrapping up of affairs, involving a final plot of land ceded by a younger brother and a final, general waiving of rights by the youngest brother. And Enna-mati is clearly alive at both of these events. It, therefore, would seem that in text #69 Uzna acts as an independent economic agent during the lifetime of her husband.[5] For whatever reason, she is the principal party here,[6] perhaps in the final stages of the economic absorption of the Ḫišmeya Family.

As for the remaining documents, text #70 must be either the last or next to last. Here, Akiya, the youngest (probably) of the three brothers alienates land. Further, the contract alludes to prior alienation of land by Ḫišmeya (lines 9, 23–27) and mentions an undertaking by Akiya not to raise claims against any(?) of the land alienated by Ḫišmeya (lines 23–27). (The contract thus makes best sense at a time when Ḫišmeya had no more land to cede. And so text #70 is best placed after the last of the Ḫišmeya documents.) This latter clause is closely analogous to the written obligation, text #71, whereby Šarra-šadûni (the other, middle, brother) undertakes not to raise claims against land alienated by Ḫišmeya *and* Akiya.

That document, text #71, is most probably the last tablet of this series. The list of sorts of real estate appears general and comprehensive. The document itself seems designed to tie up an important loose end: Šarra-šadûni's potential opposition to all the real estate alienated by his two brothers to Enna-mati. To forestall this possibility, Enna-mati gives this brother a small "gift," presumably the price of his acquiescence The required acquiescence is put in writing (lines 2–14), the ratification of which is the sealing of the document by Šarra-šadûni (line 32).[7]

The family's members almost certainly stayed on at least some of their former land as tenants. This would be the case whether or not they bore legal responsibility for the *ilku*. *De facto*, they probably bore it: the landlords could hardly have performed this annual labor on all their holdings. The now landless peasants bore it in return for some of the crops they raised. For further on the dynamic of the *ilku*, see chapter five.

62. *JEN* III, 280 (JENu 1005a)

Findspot: Room T15
Publication: Chiera 1931: pls. CCLXI–CCLXII
Editions: Saarisalo 1934: 50; cf. Maidman 1987: 166

Obverse
1 [*ṭup-pí*] *šu-pè-ul-ti*
2 *ša* ^{m}*Ḫi-iš-me-ya* DUMU *It-ḫi-iš-ta*
3 *ù ša* ^{m}*En-na-ma-ti* DUMU [*Te-ḫi-ip-til-la*]
4 *i+na bi*$_4$*-ri-šu-nu* ^{LÚ}[ÌR.MEŠ *uš-pè-i-lu*]
5 ^{m}*Ta-am-pu-up-še-en-ni* [ÌR]
6 ^{m}*Ḫi-iš-me-ya a-na* ^{m}*En-na-ma-ti* SUM
7 *ù* ^{m}*En-na-ma-ti*
8 ^{m}*El-ḫi-ip-til-la* ÌR *a-na*
9 ^{m}*Ḫi-iš-me-ya* SUM [*ša*] *ma-an-ni-im-mé*
10 LÚ-*šu pa-qí-ra-na* TUK-*ši*
11 *ù ma-an-nu* LÚ-*šu-ma ú-za-ak-ka*$_4$
12 *ma-an-nu ša* BAL-*kat-tu*
13 2 $^{LÚ.MEŠ}$ÌR *ša* KUR *Nu-ul-*[*lu-a*]*-ú*
14 *ú-ma-al-la*
Reverse
(lines destroyed)
15 NA$_4$ ^{m}[*It-ḫa*]*-pí-ḫé* NA$_4$ ^{m}*Ḫi-iš-me-ya*

JEN III, 280

(1–4) [Tablet] of exchange of Ḫišmeya son of Itḫišta and of Enna-mati son of [Teḫip-tilla. They exchanged] slaves between them.

(5–9) Ḫišmeya gave to Enna-mati Tampup-šenni, a slave. And Enna-mati gave to Ḫišmeya Elḫip-tilla, a slave.

(9–11) Whose man has claimants, it is he who shall clear (the man).

(12–14) He who abrogates (this contract) shall pay 2 slaves from the land of the Lullubians.

(lines destroyed)

(15) Seal of Ith-apiḫe; seal of Ḫišmeya.[8]

63. HSS XIII, 62 (SMN 62)

Findspot: Room T19
Publication: Pfeiffer and Lacheman 1942: 11[9]
Edition: None

Obverse
1 3 ANŠE ŠE *ša* ᵐ*En-na-ma-ti*
2 *a-na* MÁŠ-*šú a-na*
3 ᵐ*Ḫi-iš-me-ya* DUMU *It-ḫi-iš-ta*
4 *il-qì* AŠ *e-bu-ri*
5 ŠE.MEŠ *qa-du* MÁŠ-*šú*
6 ᵐ*Ḫi-iš-me-ya*
Lower Edge
7 *a-na* ᵐ*En-na-ma-ti*
Reverse
8 *ú-ta-ar*

HSS XIII, 62

(1–8) 3 homers of barley belonging to Enna-mati were delivered on interest to Ḫišmeya son of Itḫišta. Ḫišmeya shall return the barley at harvest time, interest included, to Enna-mati.

64. *JEN* I, 68 (JENu 622)

Findspot: Room T15
Publication: Chiera 1927: pls. LXVIII–LXIX
Editions: Gordon 1935: 120–22; Cassin 1938: 197–200

Obverse

1 *ṭup-pí ma-ru-ti ša* ^{m}*Ḫi-iš-me-ya*
2 DUMU *It-ḫi-iš-ta ù ša* ^{f}*Uš-še-en-na-a-a*
3 DUMU.MÍ *En-na-mil-ki*
4 ^{m}*En-na-ma-ti* DUMU *Te-ḫi-ip-til-la*
5 *a-na ma-ru-ti i-pu-šu-*[*uš*]*-ma*
6 1 ANŠE 6 ^{GIŠ}APIN A.ŠÀ.MEŠ *i+n*[*a e-le*]*-en*
7 KASKAL.MEŠ *ša* URU *Na-at-ma-né-*⸢*e*⸣
8 *i+na il-ta-na-nu ša* ⸢A⸣.[ŠÀ].MEŠ *ša* ^{m}AN-[ ]
9 *ù i+na šu-pa-a*[*l*] *ša ú-sú-ur-tu*
10 *i+na* URU *Te-*[*en-te(-we)*] ⸢^{m}⸣*Ḫi-*⸢*i*⸣*š-me-ya*
11 *ù* ^{f}*U*[*š-še-e*]⸢*n*⸣*-na-a-a ki-ma*
12 ḪA.LA-*šú* [*a-na*] ^{m}*En-na-ma-ti* SUM-*nu*
13 *ù* ^{m}*E*[*n-n*]*a-ma-ti* 1 TÚG 1 ^{KUŠ}*zi-ya-na-tù*
14 *ù* 5 [+n? U]DU.MEŠ *an-nu-tù* ^{m}*En-na-ma-ti*
15 *ki-mu* NÍG.BA-*šu-nu a-na* ^{m}*Ḫi-iš -me-ya*
16 *ù a-na* ^{f}*Uš-še-en-na-a-a it-ta-ad-nu*
17 *šum-ma* A.ŠÀ.MES *an-nu-ú pá-qí-ra-na i-ra-aš-ši*
18 [*ma*]*-an-nu-ú i+na* ŠÀ-^{bi}-*šu-nu a-ši-ib*
19 ⸢*ù*⸣ A.ŠÀ *an-nu-ú ú-za-ak-ka*
20 *a-na* ^{m}*En-na-ma-ti i-na-an-dì-nu*
21 *ma-an-nu-um-me-e i+na* bi_4*-r*[*i-š*]*u-nu*

Lower Edge

22 [*ša* (KI.)B]AL-^{kat}-*tu* 2 MA.NA KÙ.BAB[BAR]
23 [2 MA.N]A KÙ.SIG_{17} SI.A.MEŠ

Reverse

24 IGI *Ar-te-eš-še* DUMU *Ša-aḫ-*[*-y*]*a*?
25 IGI *Tu-ra-ri* DUMU *En-ša-ru*
26 IGI *Ta-e* DUMU *Ni-ik-ri-ya*
27 IGI *A-*⸢*ḫ*⸣*u-um-ma* DUM⸢U *Ḫu*⸣*-u*[*r*]*-pí-še-en-ni*
28 IGI *Ak-ku-le-en-ni* DUMU *Ar-ni-ya*
29 IGI ^{d}UTU-RI DUMU *Sí-la-*⸢ku_8⸣*-bi*
30 IGI *Ḫa-na-a-a* DUMU *A-ri-ip-*LUGAL
31 [2+]5 LÚ.MEŠ *an-nu-tù ša* A.ŠÀ *mu-še-el-wu-ú*
32 *ù šu-nu-ú-ma ša* TÚG.MEŠ <*ša*?> $^{KU[Š]}$*zi-ya-na-ti*
33 *ù ša* UDU.MEŠ *na-dì-na-n*[*u*]
34 *ù qà-an-na-š*[*u š*]*a* ^{m}*En-na-ma-ti*
35 *a-na pa-ni ši-bu-t*[*i*] *an-nu-*⸢*ti*⸣ *im-ta-šar*
36 IGI *Zu-un-zu* DUMU *In-ti-ya* DUB.SAR-^{rù}
37 ^{NA_4}KIŠIB ^{f}*Uš-še-en-na-a-a* ^{NA_4}KIŠIB ^{m}*Ta-e*

38 $^{\text{NA}_4}$KIŠIB ^{m}*Ḫi-iš-me-ya* $^{\text{NA}_4}$KIŠIB ^{m}*Ar-te-eš-še*
39 $^{\text{NA}_4}$KIŠIB ^{m}*Ḫa-na-a-a* $^{\text{NA}_4}$KIŠIB ^{m}*Tù-ra-ri*
40 $^{\text{NA}_4}$KIŠIB ^{m}⸢*A-ḫ*⸣*u-um-ma* $^{\text{NA}_4}$KIŠIB $^{\text{m d}}$UTU-RI
41 *ṭup-pí* AŠ KÁ.GAL *ša* URU
42 *T*[*úr*]*-šá ša-ṭì-ir*

JEN I, 68

(1–5) Tablet of adoption of Ḫišmeya son of Itḫišta and of Uššen-naya daughter of Enna-milki. They adopted Enna-mati son of Teḫip-tilla.

(6–12) Ḫišmeya and Uššen-naya gave [to] Enna-mati as his inheritance share a 1.6 homer field in the town of Tente, to the east of the road to the town of Natmane, to the north of the field of [Šamaš-RI?[10]], and to the west … of the enclosure.

(13–16) And Enna-mati gave to Ḫišmeya and to Uššen-naya as their gift 1 garment, 1 leather *ziyanātu*-blanket, and 5[+n?] sheep.

(17–20) Should this field have claimants, (then) whichever amongst them (i.e., the adopters) is present shall clear this field (and) give (it) to Enna-mati.

(21–23) Whoever amongst them abrogates (this contract) shall pay 2 minas of silver (and) [2] minas of gold.

(24–33) Before Ar-tešše son of Šaḫ-…-ya?; before Turari son of En-šaru; before Tae son of Nikriya; before Aḫumma son of Ḫurpi-šenni; before Akkul-enni son of Arniya; before Šamaš-RI son of Silakku-abi; before Ḫanaya son of Arip-šarri; these [2+]5 men are the ones who are the measurers of the land and, as well, they are the ones who are the givers of the garments (*sic*), <of?> the leather *ziyanātu*-blanket, and of the sheep.

(34–35) Enna-mati dragged(?) his hem in the presence of these witnesses.[11]

(36) Before Zunzu son of Intiya, scribe.

(37–40) Seal impression of Uššen-naya; seal impression of Tae; seal impression of Ḫišmeya; seal impression of Ar-tešše; seal impression of Ḫanaya; seal impression of Turari; seal impression of Aḫumma; seal impression of Šamaš-RI.

(41) The tablet was written at the city gate of the town of Turša.

65. *JEN* VI, 597+ JENu 1035g (JENu 226+1035g)

Publication: Lacheman 1939a: pl. 546 (JENu 226); Maidman 2005: 62, 108 (JENu 1035g)
Room numbers: T15 + findspot unknown
Edition: None

Obverse

1 *ṭ[up-pí ma-ru]-ti ša*
2 ^{m}*Ḫi-i*⸢*š*⸣-[*me-y*]⸢*a*⸣ DUMU *It-ḫi-iš-ta*
3 *ù ša* ^{f}*Uš-še-en-na-a-a*
4 *aš-ša-at* ^{m}*It-ḫi-iš-ta*
5 ^{m}*En-na-ma-ti DUMU Te-ḫi-ip-til-l*[*a*]
6 *a-na ma-ru-ti i-pu-šu-uš*
7 1 ANŠ[E] A.ŠÀ *i+na mi-in-dá-ti* [GAL$^{?}$]
8 *š*[*a* É$^{?}$.GAL$^{?-li?}$] *ù mi-in-dá-as-s*[*ú*]
9 [*ša* A$^{?}$.ŠÀ$^{?}$ 1 *ma*]-⸢*a*⸣*t* GÌR.MEŠ *ši-id-du-ú*
10 [*ù* 80$^{?}$ GÌR$^{?}$.MEŠ$^{?}$] *pí-ir-ki ša* A.ŠÀ
11 [A.Š]À *ša* ^{m}*El-ḫi-ip-til-*[*la*]
12 [ ] A.ŠÀ *ša* ^{m}*Ki-pí-y*[*a*$^{?}$]
13 [ ]⸢x⸣ A.ŠÀ *ša* 9 [ ]
14 [^{m}*Ḫi*]-*iš-me-ya*
15 [ ] *ki-ma* ⸢ḪA⸣.[LA]

.

.

.

left edge

16 [ ]⸢x⸣[ ]

S.I.

JEN VI, 597+ JENu 1035g

(1–6) Tablet of adoption of Ḫišmeya son of Itḫišta and of Uššen-naya wife of Itḫišta. They adopted Enna-mati son of Teḫip-tilla.

(7–15) Ḫišmeya ... [gave to Enna-mati] as [his] inheritance share a field, 1 homer by the [large? palace?] standard. And the measurements of [the field?] (i.e., the homer): the length 100 *purīdu* (lit. "feet") [and] the width of the field [80? *purīdu*?].[12] (The field is) ... the field of Elḫip-tilla, ... the field of Kipi-ya?, ... field of 9 ... .

.

.

.

.

(16) [Seal ....] (*seal impression*).

66. *JEN* VI, 603 (JENu 267) (+?) JENu 1041f[13] (in bold)

Findspot: Room T15 + findspot unknown
Publication: Lacheman 1939a: pl. 551 (JENu 267 only)
Edition: None

Obverse

1 [*ṭup-pí ma-ru*]***-ti š[a*** ^{m}*Ḫi-iš-me-ya* DUMU *It-ḫi-iš-ta*]
2 [*ša* ^{m}*Šar-r*]***a**$^{?}$**-aš-š*⸢*a*⸣**-[*du-ni*]
3 [DUMU] ⸢*It*⸣$^{?}$-[*ḫi-iš-t*]***a ù š[a]***
4 ^{f}*Uš-š*[*e-en-**n***]***a-a-a*** **DUMU.MÍ** [*En-na-mil-ki*]
5 *aš-ša-a*[*t It*]-⸢***ḫ***⸣***i-iš-ta*** [(?)]
6 3 LÚ.ME[Š *an-nu-**t***]***i*** ^{m}***En***-[*na-ma-ti* DUMU *Te-ḫi-ip-til-la*]
7 *a-na ma-r*[*u-ti i-te*$^{?}$***-e***]⸢***p***⸣***-š[u***(*-uš*)]
8 5 ANŠE A.Š[À]⸢x⸣[ ]
9 KASKAL.MEŠ *ša* [URU] *Na-a*⸢*t*⸣*-m*[*a-ne-e*]
10 A.ŠÀ *ša* ^{m}*A-a-*⸢*x*⸣*-ú ù i+*⸢*n*⸣*a* AŠ$^{?}$ [ ]
11 A.ŠÀ *ša* ^{m}*E-ni-iš-ta-e* ⸢x⸣[*ša-nu-ú*]
12 *aš-lu* 3 ANŠE ⸢1⸣$^{?}$+4 ^{GIŠ}APIN A.ŠÀ [*i-na*]
13 ⸢*su-ta*⸣*-an* URU *Te-en-te-we i+n*[*a*]
14 [A$^{?}$.ŠÀ$^{?}$ *ša* ^{m}*A-ka*]*p-tuk-ké ù i+na šu-pa-*[*al* A$^{?}$.ŠÀ$^{?}$]
15 *š*⸢*a*⸣ ^{m}*E*⸢*l*⸣*-ḫi-ip-til-la ù ša-aš-*[*šu aš-lu*]
16 9 ^{GIŠ}APIN A.ŠÀ *i+na šu-pa-al* A.ŠÀ *š*[*a* ^{m}]
17 *ù* <AŠ> *e-le-en* A.ŠÀ *ša* ^{m}*El-ḫi-*⸢*ip*⸣-[*til*$^{?}$*-la*$^{?}$]
18 ŠU.NIGIN$_{2}$ 10 ANŠE A.ŠÀ.MEŠ *i+na* A.GÀR *š*[*a*$^{?}$]
19 ^{m}*Ḫi-iš-me-ya* ^{m}LUGAL-KUR^{-ni} *ù* ^{f}*Uš-še-en-*[*na-a-a*]
20 [*k*]*i-ma* ḪA.LA-*šú a-na* ^{m}*En-na-ma-ti* SUM-*nu*
21 *ù* ^{m}*En-na-ma-ti* 5 ANŠE.ŠE.MEŠ 4 ANŠE *dú-u*⸢*ḫ*⸣-[*nu*]
22 10 UDU.MEŠ *ki-ma* NÍG.BA.MEŠ-*šu-nu a-na*
23 3 LÚ.MEŠ *an-nu-ti* SUM-*na-šu-nu-ti*
24 *šum-ma* A.ŠÀ.MEŠ *an-nu-ú pá-qí-ra-na* TUK-*ši*
25 *ù ma-an-nu-me-e* ⸢*i*⸣*-na* ⸢ŠÀ$^{-bi}$-*šu*⸣$^{?}$-[*nu*$^{?}$]
26 *ša* 3 LÚ.MEŠ *a*⸢*n*⸣*-nu-ti a-ši-i*⸢*b* x⸣ [ ]

Lower Edge

27 *ù* A.ŠÀ *an-*[*n*]*u-ú*$^{!}$(=UM) *ú-za-ak-ka*$_{4}$
28 *a-na* ^{m}*En-na-ma-ti i+*⸢*n*⸣*a-an-di-nu*
29 *il-ka ša* A.ŠÀ.MEŠ [*a*]*n-ni-ti*
30 3 LÚ.MEŠ$^{!}$(=AN) *an-nu-ti-ma na-*⸢*šu-ú*⸣

Reverse

31 *ù* ^{m}*En-na-ma-ti la na-š*[*i*]

32 *ma-an-nu-um-me-e i+na bi$_4$-ri-šu-nu*
33 *ša* KI.BAL$^{\text{-}kat\text{-}tu}$ 2 MA.NA ⸢K⸣Ù.BABBAR ⸢2⸣ [MA.NA KÙ.SIG$_{17}$]
34 *ú-ma-al-la*

---

35 IGI *A-pu-uš-ka$_4$* DUMU *It-ḫi-ip*-LUGAL ^{LÚ}*sà-su-uk-ku*
36 IGI *E-ni-iš-ta-e* DUMU *Ú-ṣú-ur-me-šu*
37 IGI *Al-ki-ya* DUMU *Ú-na-ap-ta-e*
38 IGI *Ké-li-ip*-LUGAL DUMU *A-ri-ik-ka$_4$-ni*
39 IGI *Ip-šá-ḫa-lu* DUMU *A-ri-ip*-LUGAL
40 IGI *I-ka$_4$-ti-ya* DUMU *Ta-ku-uš-ki*
41 IGI *Ta-ú-ka$_4$* DUMU *Zi-ku-*⸢*r*⸣[*a*]
42 IGI *Mu-kà-ru* DUMU *Ú-na-*[*ap-ta-e*]
43 IGI *Ḫa-na-a-a* DUMU *Pu-*[ ]
44 IGI *Be-le-e-a* DUMU [ ]
45 IGI *A-ḫu-um-ma* [DUMU *Ḫu-ur-pí-še-en-ni*]
46 IGI *Um-pí-y*[*a* DUMU *Ú-na-ap-ta-e*]
47 IGI ⸢*Ḫ*⸣*a-ši*$^?$-[DUMU]
48 IGI *Z*[*i-* DUMU]
49 13 L[Ú.MEŠ *ša* URU *Te*]*-en-te-we*
50 ⸢*ù* x⸣ [ ]
51 *um-ma* ⸢f⸣[*Uš-še-en-na-a-a um-ma*]
52 ^{m}*Ḫi-iš-me-*[*ya ù um-ma* ^{m}LUGAL-KUR$^{\text{-}ni}$]
53 *ša* URU [ ]
54 *ù a-*⸢*x*⸣ [ ]

S.I.

55 NA$_4$ ^{m}*E-*[*ni-iš-ta-e*]

Upper Edge

56 [NA$_4$ ^{m}*Ḫi*$^?$*-i*]*š*$^?$*-me-*[*ya*$^?$]

Left Edge

57 *ṭup-pí i+na* EGIR *šu-du-ti*
58 *i+na* KÁ.GAL (erasure)
59 *ša* URU *Túr-*⸢*š*⸣*a ša-ṭì-ir* | S.I. | S.I.
60 | NA$_4$ ^{m}*A-*⸢*ḫu*⸣*-um-ma* | N[A$_4$ ^{m}]*Ké-li-i*[*p*-LUGAL]

JEN VI, 603(+?)JENu 1041f

(1–7) [Tablet of] adoption of [Ḫišmeya son of Itḫišta, of] Šarra-šadûni(??) [son of] Itḫišta(?), and of Uššen-naya daughter of [Enna-milki] (and) wife of Itḫišta. These 3 people adopted Enna-mati [son of Teḫip-tilla].

(8–20) Ḫišmeya, Šarra-šadûni, and Uššen-naya gave to Enna-mati as his inheritance share a 5 homer field (or: "5.6![14] homer [field]") ... the road to [the town of] Natmane ... the field of Ay-...-u ... the field of Eniš-tae; [a second] plot: a 3.4 +.1(?) homer field ... [to] the south of the town of Tente, to the ... [the field? of] Akap-tukke, and to the west of [the field?] of Elḫip-tilla; and a third plot: a .9 homer field to the west of the field of ..., and to the east of the field of Elḫip-[tilla?]; a total of 10 homers of land in the town green of(?) ... .

(21–23) And Enna-mati gave to these 3 people as their gift 5 homers of barley, 4 homers of millet, (and) 10 sheep.

(24–28) Should this land have claimants (*sic*), and whoever is present from them(?), (i.e.,) these 3 people ..., then he/she shall clear this land (and) give it to Enna-mati.

(29–31) These 3 people shall bear the *ilku* of this land; and Enna-mati shall not bear (it).

(32–34) Whoever between them abrogates (this contract) shall pay 2 minas of silver (and) 2 [minas of gold].

(35–50) Before Apuška son of Itḫip-šarri, bookkeeper; before Eniš-tae son of Uṣur-mêšu; before Alkiya son of Unap-tae; before Kelip-šarri son of Arik-kani; before Ipša-ḫalu son of Arip-šarri; before Ikatiya son of Takuški; before Tauka son of Zikura; before Mukaru son of Unap-tae; before Ḫanaya son of Pu-...[15]; before Bêliya son of ...; before Aḫumma [son of Hurpi-šenni[16]]; before Umpiya [son of Unap-tae[17]]; before Ḫa-ši(?)-... [son of] ...; before Zi-...[son of] ...; 13 (*sic*) men ... [of the town of] Tente, and [they? ...]

(51–54) Thus [Uššen-naya, thus] Ḫišmeya, [and thus Šarra-šadûni ...?] of the town of ... and to(?) ... .

(55–56) (*seal impression*) Seal of Eniš-tae;

.

.

.

[seal of] Ḫišmeya(?).

(57–59) The tablet was written at the city gate[18] of the town of Turša after the (royal) proclamation.

67. *JEN* II, 212 (JENu 464)

Findspot: Room T15
Publication: Chiera 1930: pls. CXC–CXCI
Edition: Cassin 1938: 202–4

Obverse
1 *ṭup-pí ma-ru-ti ša* ^{m}*En-na-ma-ti*
2 DUMU *Te-ḫi-ip-til-la ù* ^{m}*Ḫi-iš-mé-ya*
3 DUMU *It-ḫi-iš-ta a-na ma-ru-ti*
4 *i-te-pu-ús-sú* 2 ANŠE A.ŠÀ
5 *i+na* URU *Te-en*$_{6}$*-te-we i+na šu-ta-an*
6 URU *i+na le-et* KASKAL^{-ni}
7 *ša* URU *Bu-ra-dá-ad-we i+na* ⌜*ša*⌝*-pa-at* x
8 A.ŠÀ.MEŠ *ša* ^{m}*Ḫu-lu-uk-ka*$_{4}$ *il-ta-wu-šu*
9 ^{m}*Ḫi-iš-mé-ya ki-i* ḪA.LA.MEŠ-*šu*
10 *a-na* ^{m}*En-na-ma-ti it-ta-din*
11 *šum-ma* A.ŠÀ *pí-ir-qa*$_{4}$ *ir-ta-ši*
12 ^{m}*Ḫi-iš-mé-ya ú-za-ak-ka*$_{4}$*-ma*
13 *a-na* ^{m}*En-na-ma-ti i+na-an-din*
14 *šum-ma* A.ŠÀ *ma-ad la i+na-ki-is*
15 *šum-ma ṣé-hé-er la ú-ra-ad-dá*
16 *il-ka ša* A.ŠÀ.MEŠ *an-ni-<ì>*
17 ^{m}*Ḫi-iš-me-ya-ma na-ši*
18 *ù* ^{m}*En-na-ma-ti* 1-*nu-tu*$_{4}$ ^{GIŠ}*ma-gàr-re-e*
19 *ša šu-du-a-ti ša še-ni*
20 1 TÚG 3 UDU.NITA.MEŠ 3 UDU.SAL<.MEŠ$^{?}$>
21 *ki-i-ma* NÍG.BA-*šu a+na*
22 ^{m}*Ḫi-iš-mé-ya it-ta-din*
Lower Edge
23 *šum-ma* ^{m}*Ḫi-iš-mé-ya it-ta-bal-ka-at*
24 2 MA.NA KÙ.BABBAR 2 MA.NA KÙ.SIG$_{17}$
Reverse
25 *ú-ma-al-la ṭup-pu an-nu-ú*
26 *i+na* EGIR^{-ki} *šu-du-ti i+na*
27 KÁ.GAL *ša* URU *Túr-šá ša-ṭì-ir*
28 IGI *Ša-ma-aš*-RI DUMU *Sí-la-ka-bi*
29 IGI *Ak-ku-le-en-ni* DUMU *Ar-ni-ya*
30 IGI *A-ḫu-um-ma* DUMU *Ḫu-ur-pí-še-en-ni*
31 IGI *Um-pí-ya* DUMU *Ú-nap-ta-e*
32 IGI *Ḫa-na-a-a* DUMU *A-ri-ip*-LUGAL
33 IGI *A-ki-ya* DUMU *It-ḫi-iš-ta*
34 IGI *A-pu-uš-ka* DUMU *It-ḫi-ip*-LUGAL
35 IGI *Zi-li-ip-til-la* DUMU *Wa-ar-ta-a-a*
36 IGI *Wa-al-la-ka-a-a* DUMU *Ke-en*$_{6}$*-na-bi*
37 9 LÚ.MEŠ *an-nu-tu*$_{4}$ *ša* A.ŠÀ *ú-še-el-wu-ú*

38 *ù* KÙ.BABBAR.MEŠ *id-di-nu*
39 IGI *Wa-aq-ri-ya* DUMU *Ú-a-az-zi*
40 IGI *It-ḫi-til-la* DUMU *Qí-iš-te-ya*
41 ŠU ^{m}*Ki-in-ni-ya* DU[B.SAR]
42 DUMU *Ar-teš-še*
43 NA$_4$ ^{m}*Ḫi-iš-mé-ya* NA$_4$ ^{m}*A-ḫu-um-ma*
44 NA$_4$ ^{m}*A-pu-uš-ka* NA$_4$ ^{m}*Ki-in-ni-ya*
45 NA$_4$ ^{m}*Ša-ma-aš*-RI NA$_4$ ^{m} *A-ki-ya*
46 NA$_4$ ^{m}*Wa-al-la-ka-a-a*

JEN II, 212

(1–4)Tablet of adoption of Enna-mati son of Teḫip-tilla. Now, Ḫišmeya son of Itḫišta adopted him.

(4–10) Ḫišmeya gave to Enna-mati as his inheritance share a 2 homer field in the town of Tente, to the south of the town, adjacent to the road to the town of Būr-Adad, by the bank … the land of Ḫulukka surrounds it.[19]

(11–13) Should the field have a claim (against it), Ḫišmeya shall clear (the field) and give (it) to Enna-mati.

(14–15) Should the field prove large(r than estimated), it shall not be diminished; if it prove small(er than estimated), it shall not be augmented.

(16–17) Ḫišmeya shall bear the *ilku* attaching to this field.

(18–22) And Enna-mati gave to Ḫišmeya as his (i.e., as Ḫišmeya's) gift 1 set of … (chariot) wheels "of (the) shoes(??),"[20] 1 garment, 3 rams, and 3 ewes.

(23–25) If Ḫišmeya shall have abrogated (the contract), he is to pay 2 minas of silver (and) 2 minas of gold.

(25–27) This tablet was written at the city gate of the town of Turša after the (royal) proclamation.

(28–40) Before Šamaš-RI son of Silakku-abi; before Akkul-enni son of Arniya; before Aḫumma son of Ḫurpi-šenni; before Umpiya son of Unap-tae; before Ḫanaya son of Arip-šarri; before Akiya son of Itḫišta[21]; before Apuška son of Itḫip-šarri; before Zilip-tilla son of Waratteya; before Pallakaya son of Kên-abi. These are the 9 men who measured the field and gave the money (lit. "silver"[22]). Before Waqriya son of U̯azzi; before Itḫip-tilla son of Qîšteya.

(41–42) Hand of Kinniya, scribe, son of Ar-tešše.

(43–46) Seal of Ḫišmeya; seal of Aḫumma; seal of Apuška; seal of Kinniya; seal of Šamaš-RI; seal of Akiya; seal of Pallakaya.

68. *JEN* VII, 776+ JENu 1127d+1173+1174 (JENu 92+1127d+1173+1174)

Findspot: Rooms T15+T12$^{!}$+ two unknown findspots
Publication and edition: Maidman 1998: 98–104

Obverse
1 ṭu[p-p]í m⸢a⸣-ru-ti š⸢a⸣
2 ^{m}Ḫi-⸢iš⸣-me-ya DUMU ⸢It⸣-ḫi-iš-[ta]
3 ^{m}En-na-ma-ti DUMU Te-ḫi-i[p-til-la]
4 a-na ma-ru-ti i-pu-u[š -(ma)]
5 2 ANŠE A.ŠÀ i-na mi-in-d[á-ti (GAL)]
6 ša É.GAL$^{-lì}$ 30 ši-id$^{!?}$(=A)-d[u]
7 ù pí-i⸢r-ku$^{?}$ 80 i$^{?}$-na⸣$^{?}$ [ ]
8 ša URU [(GN) A$^{?}$.ŠÀ$^{?}$]
9 ša ^{m}En-[na-ma-ti ša ^{m}Ḫi-iš-me-ya ša]
10 a-na ^{m}E[n-na-ma-ti]
11 i[d-di-nu (?)]
(2 lines missing)
12 ⸢a-n⸣a ^{m}E [n-na-ma-ti SUM-nu]
13 ù ^{m}E[n]-na-ma-[ti n$^{?}$ UDU$^{?}$]
14 1 ^{UDU}pu-ḫ[a-lu n] UDU 2 en-z[u$^{?}$]
15 ŠU.NIGÍN 8 ⸢U⸣[DU].MEŠ ⸢ù⸣ (erasure?) en-⸢za⸣ [ù$^{?}$]
16 10 MA.NA AN.[NA.ME]Š$^{?}$ ù 1 TÚG [(?)]
17 an-nu-tù ^{m}[En-na]-ma-ti
18 ki-ma NÍG.⸢B⸣[A-šú] ⸢a⸣-na ^{m}Ḫi-iš-me-[ya SUM-nu]
19 š⸢u⸣m-ma A.Š[À(.MES) an$^{?}$-nu$^{?}$]-ú pa-qí-ra-na [i-ra-aš -š i]
Lower Edge
20 [^{m}Ḫ]⸢i⸣-iš-m[e-ya ú-z]a-⸢ak-k⸣a_4-ma
21 [a-na ^{m}En-n]a-m[a-ti i-na-an-dì-nu]
Reverse
22 [ma-an-nu-ú i-n]a bi_4-⸢r ⸣[i-šu-nu]
23 [ša KI.BA]L^{-kat}-tu 1 [+1 MA.NA KÙ.BABBAR]
24 ⸢2 MA⸣.NA KÙ.SIG_{17} ú-ma-a[l-la]

---

25 IGI Al-ki-ya DUMU Ú-na-ap-ta-e
26 IGI Um-pí-ya ŠEŠ-šu-ma
27 IGI Ta-ú-ka DUMU Zi-ku-ra
28 IGI E-ké-ké DUMU Ki-li-li-ya
29 IGI A-ḫu-um-ma DUMU Ḫu-ur-pí-še-en-ni

30 IGI *Zi-li-ip-til-la* DUMU ÌR-*te-ya*
31 IGI *Zu-un-zu* DUB.SAR
32 IGI *Pa-al-la-ka*$_4$-*a-a* DUMU *Ké-en-na-bi*
33 8 LÚ.MEŠ *an-nu-ti* ⸢x⸣?
34 *ša* A.ŠÀ.MES *mu-še-el-wu ù* KÙ.BA[BBAR!? SUM?-*nu*?]
35 ⸢x⸣[ ]

S.I.

S.I.

36 NA$_4$ ^{m}*Ta-ú-ka*

S.I.

37 NA$_4$ ^{m}*Zi-li-ip-til-la*

upper edge

S.I. S.I.

38 NA$_4$ [^{m}]-*x-x* NA$_4$ ^{m}*E-ké-ké*

Left Edge

39 ⸢*ṭup-pí*⸣ [*i-n*]*a* ⸢EGIR-*k*⸣*i* *šu-du-ti* S.I. | S.I.
40 AS K⸢Á.G⸣[AL *ša* UR]U *Túr-šá* |
41 [*ša-ṭì*]-⸢*i*⸣*r* NA$_4$ ^{m}*Pa-al-la-ka*$_4$-*a-a* NA$_4$ DUB.SAR-*rù*

Right Edge

42 [D]I? *na-aš* ⸢x x⸣
43 [ ] ⸢x⸣

JEN VII, 776+ JENu 1127d+1173+1174

(1–4) Tablet of adoption of Ḫišmeya son of Itḫišta. He adopted Enna-mati son of Teḫip-tilla.

(5–12) [Now Ḫišmeya gave] to Enna-mati [as his inheritance share this field], a field 2 homers by the [large?] standard of the palace—(a homer being) 30! (*purīdu*) on [its?] long side,[23] (its) short (lit. "transverse") side (being) 80 (*purīdu*)—[to? the (north/south/etc.)] of the town of [Natmane?/Tente?, to? the (north/south/etc.) of (another) field?] of Enna-mati [which Ḫišmeya] had (already) given to Enna-mati.

(13–18) And Enna-mati, [n? …-sheep], 1 breeding ram, [n] sheep, 2 goats—total: 8 sheep and … goat (*sic*) [and?] 10 minas of tin and 1 …?-garment, these Enna-mati [gave] to Ḫišmeya as [his (i.e., Ḫišmeya's)] gift.

(19–21) Should this? field [have] claimants, Ḫišmeya shall clear (it) and [give (it) to] Enna-mati.

(22–24) Whoever between [them] abrogates (this contract) shall pay 2 minas of gold.

(25–34) Before Alkiya son of Unap-tae; before Umpiya his brother, as well; before Tauka son of Zikura; before Ekeke son of Kilīliya; before Aḫumma son of Ḫurpi-šenni; before Zilip-tilla son of Waratteya; before Zunzu, the scribe; before Pallakaya son of Kên-abi. These eight men are the measurers of the field and [distributors?] of the money.

(35–38) Seal? [impression of …] (*seal impression*); (*seal impression*) seal impression of Tauka; (*seal impression*) seal impression of Zilip-tilla; (*seal impression*) seal impression of …; (*seal impression*) seal impression of Ekeke.

(39–41) (This) tablet was written after the proclamation [at] the city gate of the town of Turša.

(41) (*seal impression*) Seal impression of Pallakaya; (*seal impression*) seal impression of the scribe.

(42–43) ….

69. HSS XIII, 232 (SMN 232)

Findspot: Room T19
Publication: Pfeiffer and Lacheman 1942: 40[24]
Edition: None

Obverse
1 *um-ma* ^{m}*Ḫi-iš-mé-*⸢*ya* DUMU *It-ḫi-iš-ta*⸣
2 1 TÚG *a-šar*
3 ^{f}*Uz-na el-te-qè-*[*mi*]
4 *ù a-na-ku* (erasure)
5 4 ANŠE A.ŠÀ
6 *a-na* ^{f}*Uz-na*
7 *a-na-an-din-mi*
8 *ù* KÙ.BABBAR.MEŠ *ri-iḫ-tu*$_{4}$
9 *ša* A.ŠÀ.MEŠ
10 *a-šar* ^{f}*Uz-na*
11 *i-le-qè*
(rest destroyed)

HSS XIII, 232

(1–11) Thus Ḫišmeya son of Itḫišta: "I have taken 1 garment from Uzna. And (in return) I am giving to Uzna 4 homers of land. And I shall be taking the remaining payment for the land from Uzna." ….

70. *JEN* IV, 415 (JENu 98)

Findspot: Room T15
Publication: Chiera 1934a: pls. CCCXCVIII–CCCXCIX
Edition: Cassin 1938: 204–5

Obverse

1 *ṭup-pí ma-ru-ti ša*
2 ^{m}*A-ki-ya* DUMU *It-ḫi-iš-ta*
3 ^{m}*En-na-ma-ti* DUMU *Te-ḫi-ip-til-la*
4 *a-na ma-ru-ti i-pu-úš*
5 2 ANŠE A.ŠÀ *mi-in-dá-*[*as-sú*]
6 *ša* A.ŠÀ *a-x*[25] *1 ma-at š*[*i-id-dá-šu*]
7 *ù* 80 *pí-ir-ka-šu* [(?)]
8 AŠ *e-le-en* Ú[26] KASKAL.MEŠ *ša* [URU *N*]*a-at-ma-né*
9 *i+na su-ta-an* A.ŠÀ *ša* ^{m}*Ḫi-iš-me-ya*
10 *ša a-na* ^{m}*En-na-ma-ti id-di-nu*
11 *ù i+na šu-pa-al* A.ŠÀ *ša* ^{m}*Ḫa-i-iš-te-šup*
12 *ù* AŠ *e-le-en* URU *Te-en-te-we*
13 *ù* A.ŠÀ *an-nu-ú* ^{m}*A-ki-ya*
14 *ki-i-ma* ḪA.LA-*šú a-na* ^{m}*En-na-ma-ti* SUM-*nu*
15 *ù* ^{m}*En-na-ma-ti* 5 UDU.MEŠ 5 *en-zu*^{MEŠ}
16 *ù* 20 MA.NA AN.NA.MEŠ *ki-ma*
17 NÍG.BA-*šú a-na* ^{m}*A-ki-ya* SUM-*nu*
18 *šum-ma* A.ŠÀ *an-nu-ú pí-ir-qa*$_4$ *ir-ta-ši*
19 ^{m}*A-ki-ya ú-za-ak-ka*$_4$*-ma*
20 [*a-na* ^{m}]*En-na-ma-ti i-na-an-dì-nu*
21 [*il-ka*] *ša* A.ŠÀ *an-ni-ti*
22 [^{m}*A-ki-ya-m*]*a na-ši*
23 [*aš-šum ka*$^{?}$*-le*$^{?}$]*-e* A.ŠÀ.MEŠ ḪA.LA-*šú*
24 ⌜*ša* ^{m}*Ḫi-iš*⌝*-me-ya ša a-na*

Lower Edge

25 ^{m}*En-na-ma-ti i-di-nu*
26 ^{m}*A-ki-ya i+na* EGIR-^{ki}-*šu-nu*

Reverse

27 *la i-ša*$_{10}$*-as-sí*
28 *ma-an-nu-ú i+na bi*$_4$*-ri-šu-nu*
29 *ša* KI.BAL-$^{kat-tu}$
30 2$^{!}$ MA.NA KÙ.BABBAR 2$^{!}$ MA.NA KÙ.SIG$_{17}$ SI.A.MEŠ
31 IGI *Al-ki-ya* DUMU *Ú-na-ap-ta-e*

31a IGI *Mu-ka*$_4$*-ru* DUMU *Ú-na-ap-ta-e*
32 IGI *Ak-ku-le-en-ni* DUMU *Ar-ni-ya*
33 IGI *Ta-ú-ka* DUMU *Zi-ku-ra*
34 IGI *Zi-li-ip-til-la* DUMU ÈR-*te-e*
35 [IGI] *Ta-a-a* DUMU *A-ri-ip*-LUGAL
36 [IGI] *Ki-iš-me-ya* DUMU *It-ḫi-iš-ta*
37 [IGI] *A-pu-uš-ka* DUMU *It-ḫi-ip*-LUGAL
38 [IGI] *Zu-un-zu* DUMU *In-ti-ya* DUB.SAR
39 8 LÚ.MEŠ *ša* A.ŠÀ *mu-še-el-wu*
40 *ù šu-nu-ú-ma* UDU.MEŠ *ù en-zu*^{MEŠ} SUM-*nu*
41 IGI *Ki-in-[k]i-a* DUMU *Na-al-tù-uk-ka*$_4$
42 IGI *Ni-iḫ-ri-ya* DUMU *Na-ḫi-šal-mu*
42a IGI *Ḫu-lu-uk-ka*$_4$ DUMU *Zi-in-na-a-a*
43 NA$_4$ ^{m}*A-ki-ya* EN A.ŠÀ
44 NA$_4$ ^{m}*Mu-ka*$_4$*-ru* NA$_4$ ^{m}*Ta-a-a*
45 NA$_4$ ^{m}*Zi-li-ip-til-la* NA$_4$ ^{m} *Al-ki-ya*
46 NA$_4$ ^{m}*Ḫi-iš-me-ya*
Upper Edge
47 *ṭup-pí* AŠ EGIR *šu-du-ti*
48 AŠ *a-bu-ul-li ša* URU *Túr-šá ša-ṭì-ir*$^{!}$ (=NI)

JEN IV, 415

(1–4) Tablet of adoption of Akiya son of Itḫišta. He adopted Enna-mati son of Teḫip-tilla.

(5–14) Now Akiya gave to Enna-mati as his inheritance share this land: a 2 homer field—the measurements of the … field: [its (i.e., a homer's)] length is 100 (*purīdu*) and its width, 80 (*purīdu*)—to the east of the road to the [town of] Natmane, to the south of the land of Ḫišmeya, which he had given to Enna-mati, and to the west of the land of Ḫaiš-tešup, and to the east (*sic*) of the town of Tente.

(15–17) And Enna-mati gave to Akiya as his (i.e., Akiya's) gift 5 sheep, 5 goats, (and) 20 minas of tin.

(18–20) Should this field have a claim, Akiya shall clear (the field) and give (it) [to] Enna-mati.

(21–22) As well, [Akiya] shall bear [the *ilku*] of this field.

(23–27) [Regarding] all(?) the land, Ḫišmeya's inheritance share, which he had given to Enna-mati, Akiya shall not raise a claim against them (i.e., those lands/fields).

(28–30) Whoever amongst them abrogates (this contract) shall pay 2! minas of silver (and) 2! minas of gold.[27]

(31–42a) Before Alkiya son of Unap-tae; before Mukaru son of Unap-tae; before Akkul-enni son of Arniya; before Tauka son of Zikura; before Zilip-tilla son of Waratteya; [before] Taya son of Arip-šarri; before Ḫišmeya son of Itḫišta;[28] [before] Apuška son of Itḫip-šarri; [before] Zunzu son of Intiya, scribe: 8 (*sic*) men who are the measurers of the field; and they also gave the sheep and goats.[29] Before Kikkiya son of Naltukka; before Niḫriya son of Naḫiš-šalmu; before Ḫulukka son of Zinnaya.

(43–46) Seal of Akiya, (erstwhile) owner of the land; seal of Mukaru; seal of Taya; seal of Zilip-tilla; seal of Alkiya; seal of Ḫišmeya.

(47–48) The tablet was written at the city gate of the town of Turša after the (royal) proclamation.

71. *JEN* II, 101 (JENu 502)

Findspot: Room T15
Publication: Chiera 1930: pl. CI
Edition: Jankowska 1962: 230 (partial)

Obverse

1 *um-ma* ^{m}*Ša-ar-ra-ša-du*$^{!}$*-ni-ma* DUMU *It-ḫi-iš-ta*
2 *mi-nu-um-me-e*
3 A.ŠÀ.MEŠ *a-wi-i-ru mi-nu-um-me-e*
4 *qà-aq-qa-ru pa-i-ḫu*
5 *ù qà-aq-qa-ra ša* É.MEŠ *ep-šu*
6 *i+na* ŠÀ$^{-bi}$ URU *ša Te-en-te-we*
7 *ma-ag-ra-at-tù* GIŠ.SAR
8 *ù qà-aq-qa-ru ḫa-la-aḫ-wu*
9 *i+na ṣe-re-e-ti i+na* URU *ša Te-en-te*
10 *ša* ^{m}*Ḫi-iš-me-ya ù ša*
11 ^{m}*A-ki-ya* ŠEŠ.MEŠ*-ya a-na*
12 ^{m}*En-na-ma-ti* DUMU *Te-ḫi-ip-til-la i-din-nu*
13 *a-na-ku i+na* EGIR^{-ki}*-šu-nu*
14 *la a-ša*$_{10}$*-as-sí-mi*
15 *šum-ma* ^{m}LUGAL-KUR*-ni* AŠ EGIR^{-ki}
16 A.ŠÀ.MEŠ *ša pí-i ṭup-pí an-ni-ti*
17 *i-ša-as-sí* 1 MA.NA KÙ.BABBAR 1 MA.NA KÙ.SIG$_{17}$
18 *a-na* ^{m}*En-na-ma-ti ú-ma-al-la*

19 *ù* ^{m}*En-na-ma-ti* ⌜1? UDU⌝? SIG$_5$-*qà*
Lower Edge
20 *ki-ma* NÍG.BA-*šu a-na* ^{m}LUGAL-KUR-*ni* SUM-*na*
21 IGI *Zu-un-zu* DUMU *In-ti-ya*
22 IGI *A-pu-uš-ka*$_4$ DUMU *It-ḫi-ip*-LUGAL
23 IGI *Pu-ḫi-še-en-ni* DUMU *Ša-ma-ḫul*
Reverse
24 IGI *Zi-li-ip-til-la* DUMU ÈR-*te-ya*
25 IGI *Er-ḫa-na-tal* DUMU *Ur-ḫi-ya*
26 IGI *Ḫa-na-tù* DUMU *A-kip*-LUGAL
27 IGI ⌜*A*⌝-[*m*]*ur*-GAL DUMU *Ṣil-lí-ya-we*
28 IGI *It-ḫi-til-la* DUMU *Qí-iš-te-ya*
29 ^{LÚ}*ma-ṣar* KÁ.GAL-*lì*
30 IGI *Ni-iḫ-ri-ya* DUMU *Na-ḫi-iš-šal-mu*
31 NA$_4$ ^{m}*A-mur*-GAL NA$_4$ ^{m}*Zi-li-ip-til-la*
32 NA$_4$ ^{m}*Ni-iḫ-ri-ya* NA$_4$ ^{m}LUGAL-KUR-*ni*
33 NA$_4$ ^{m}*It-ḫi-til-la* NA$_4$ ^{m}*Zu-un-zu* DUB.SAR
Left Edge
34 *ṭup-pí i+na* KÁ.GAL *ša* URU *Túr-šá ša-ṭì-ir*

JEN II, 101

(1–14) Thus Šarra-šadûni son of Itḫišta: "I shall not raise a claim against them, (to wit) whatever *awīru*[30]-land, whatever (empty?) building plot and built-up plot (lit. "a plot of built structures") in the midst of the town of Tente, (whatever) threshing floor, orchard, and *ḫalaḫwu*-plot in the hinterland,[31] in the town(ship) of Tente, which Ḫišmeya and Akiya, my brothers, have given to Enna-mati son of Teḫip-tilla."

(15–18) Should Šarra-šadûni raise a claim against land described in (lit. "according to the mouth of") this tablet, he shall pay to Enna-mati 1 mina of silver (and) 1 mina of gold.

(19–20) And Enna-mati has given to Šarra-šadûni as his (i.e., as Šarra-šadûni's) gift 1(?) fine sheep(?).

(21–30) Before Zunzu son of Intiya; before Apuška son of Itḫip-šarri; before Puḫi-šenni son of Šamaḫul; before Zilip-tilla son of Waratteya; before Erḫan-atal son of Urḫiya; before Ḫanatu son of Akip-šarri; before Amur-rabī son of Ziliya; before Itḫip-tilla son of Qîšteya, gatekeeper; before Niḫriya son of Naḫiš-šalmu.

(31–33) Seal of Amur-rabī; seal of Zilip-tilla; seal of Niḫriya; seal of Šarra-šadûni;[32] seal of Itḫip-tilla; seal of Zunzu, scribe.

(34) The tablet was written at the city gate of the town of Turša.

Chapter Five
The Nature of the *Ilku* at Nuzi

In the introduction to this volume, I stressed that the issue of the Nuzi tax called *ilku* is especially important because of its immediate connection to real estate and to its alienation (particularly its alienation through sale). This impost is tied up with other features of the Nuzi economic landscape, most notably (and also mentioned above) the contract called *ṭuppi mārūti*, "tablet of adoption [lit. 'sonship']," a contract used to achieve, not only legal integration of an outsider into a family unit, but—more important here—the transfer of real estate from one party to another party from a different family. The *ilku* appears in many such "tablets of adoption" of this second variety as well as in other contexts to be examined below. This kind of "tablet of adoption" constitutes a crux, many scholars have argued, whereby Nuzi's economic structure may be defined. Such definitions vary wildly, ranging from feudalism[1] to primitive communalism in the classic Marxist paradigm.[2] This is *not* the appropriate forum to detail the different interpretations and definitions[3] and the assorted correct and incorrect conclusions of other scholars. The *ilku*, the *ṭuppi mārūti*, and other characteristics of Nuzi's economic life may well be parts of a very complicated phenomenon, as argued by others. However, I think it has been made more complicated than necessary. In keeping with the aim of this volume and of the series as a whole, I present in this chapter key texts[4] pertaining to the *ilku*. The purpose of presenting these texts is to lay out indisputable facts regarding the *ilku* and important contexts in which the *ilku* appears.[5] This elucidation lays the foundation for a more extensive, more closely argued, and appropriately documented monograph for scholars wishing to take up the phenomenon anew. Any interpretation, whether my own or those of others,[6] *must* consider the data contained in the documents in this chapter.

And so, we begin by inducing basic characteristics of the *ilku* and then continue with less basic features. First the word itself: *ilku* is a noun derived from a verbal root meaning to walk, go, come, and so on.[7] It is possible that the term originally implied "a going (to perform the tax obligation)." One fulfills the obligation by "going (i.e., performing) the *ilku*" or by "bearing the *ilku*" or by "doing the *ilku*." The term is attested from the Old Babylonian period (2000–1600 B.C.E.) down to the Persian period (559–333 B.C.E.). Derivations of Akkadian *ilku* appear in biblical Aramaic (Ezra 4:13, 20; 7:24) and other languages.

In the Nuzi texts, since performing this service (below we shall see that it is a tax to be paid in labor, not goods) is called "to go the going" (awkward in English but not in Akkadian), the one who performs the service is called the "goer of the going," Akkadian *ālik ilki*. This could raise a problem since *ālik ilki* is also the name of one of the four chief social classes in the kingdom of Arrapḫa. A brief notation of these classes is thus in order here.

The main social classes are, in descending order of social status: *rākib narkabti* ("charioteer," lit. "rider of a chariot"), *nakkuššu* (meaning unknown), *ālik ilki*, and *aššābu* ("tenant," lit. "habitual dweller," "inhabitant").[8] The portrait of these social classes, their status, occupations, and other points of comparison with each other, is too complex (and partially irrelevant) for elucidation here.[9] It should be stressed, though, that the names of these classes do not directly describe their most salient characteristics. Rather, their names seem to go back to original, not current, features. Thus, "charioteers" are not necessarily tied to the chariotry. Nor are "goers of the going" the only ones performing the *ilku*-tax. Since classes other than the *ālik ilki*[10] also perform the *ilku*-service, it is clear that the service is not confined to this class. Nor is it necessarily the case that all members of this class perform the *ilku*. Now context virtually always determines which definition of *ālik ilki* is meant in a given case: *ilku*-tax payer or member of the *ālik ilki* class. Nevertheless, this constitutes a ragged edge in our reasoning. Ambiguity is possible. And one always dislikes a single expression with more than one real meaning. Self-serving choice is always a risk.

We return now to the *ilku* per se, shifting from the term itself to its meaning. *ilku* is one tax amongst several levied in the Nuzi region. Not all these taxes are clearly understood. Nevertheless, it appears certain that some taxes were payable in goods, while others were paid in labor. Obligatory military service is implicit throughout the Nuzi corpus, although a term for this service is curiously lacking. The *ilku* has been seen as involving such military service, at least some of the time.[11] However, the only specific descriptions of the *ilku* are agricultural labor for the government (text #37), the manufacture of textiles (text #72), and other non-military labor (text #37). Another text, text #73, may even imply that the *ilku* is specifically non-military in nature.[12] Thus, the *ilku* is a labor tax, predominantly—probably exclusively—of a non-military sort. The *ilku*, in short, is a corvée.

There is a bureaucratic nicety here. Such labor has connection with local, municipal jurisdiction (texts ## 37, 43[13]). That is, the tasks of which the *ilku* is comprised are probably administered by local governments. Indeed, the *ilku* is partly defined by *where* it is performed, not merely *what* is actually done and by whom.

The geographical jurisdiction is most often the town (texts ##73, 74, 75, 76?) where the *ilku* is supposed to be performed. It is once defined by the *dimtu*-district in which it is performed (text #37).[14]

However, though it is administered by the mayor's office, it is probably owed to the Arrapḫan crown[15] (text #76) which then redirects it to the towns. This is suggested by instances where individuals perform the *ilku* in one jurisdiction despite the expectation that it was supposed to be performed in another (text #74, implicitly; and so too texts ##75, 76). Such mobility of execution makes best sense if the obligation were ultimately owed to a super-municipal authority, that is, to the state. Also, text #76 may represent another example of state control, describing a possible royal exemption from the *ilku*.

On what is the *ilku* owed? The answer, in a word, is real estate. Moreover, real estate of all sorts (possibly every sort; see text #77) is the basis of this obligation: fields (text #67), buildings or other structures (text #78), urban building lots (text #79), urban buildings (text #80), rural towers (i.e., *dimtu*s; text #81, including a well and other specialized real estate), and other types of real estate (texts ## 82, 83).[16] Thus, *ilku* is closely tied to realia per se. Clearly, the one who owes this obligation has ties to real estate as well. But a crucial question now comes to the fore. Does the *ilku*-bearer owe this obligation because he *once* owned land (or, of course, other real estate) or because he is the current owner? In other words, does the corvée attach to "original" land owners or to the land itself, adhering to whoever owns the land at the moment? The answer to that question, though, presupposes the answer to another one: is real estate indeed alienable?[17] Can it be sold? Can it be transferred outside the family? Also, does title reside with individuals and not, say, with the crown? The answers to these questions are uniformly affirmative.

Any number of texts describe land transferred for a "price," or—much the same thing for our purposes—land not transferred (in a particular case) for a "price" (texts ##31, 46, 50, for example). One text (text #84), an early one (this is important in establishing the fact throughout Nuzi's history), is an actual contract whereby land is sold. Thus, land is alienable, and therefore the presupposition mentioned earlier is correct. This brings us back to the question of whether the *ilku* stays with the land's "original" owner or is transferred to subsequent owners of real estate. The answer parallels that of the previous question: as real estate is alienable, so is the corvée attaching to it. New owner, new taxpayer. Logical.[18] And factually verifiable (text # 80, for example[19]). From a slightly different perspective, we can conclude that *ilku*-land is alienable. Thus the land is neither a feoff nor part of a commune's property. From an earlier period and from farther south, the principle was already articulated in CH §40: "a *nadītu*, a merchant, or any holder of *ilku* real estate may sell his field, orchard, or building; the buyer performs the *ilku* of the field, orchard, or house that he buys."[20]

The clarity of this straightforward situation has unfortunately been muddied owing to a peculiarity of Nuzi contract formulation mentioned above. Many real estate transfers are effected by means of adoption formulary. Such "adoption" contracts[21] are cast in the following form. A father (= seller) adopts someone to be his son (= buyer) and bequeaths to him real estate. (The inheritance share is "bequeathed" immediately, not eventually, after the "father"'s death.[22]) The "son" usually tenders to the "father" a "gift," amounting (again, usually) to the market value of the real estate. With this his filial obligation is entirely discharged.[23] This contract form has been taken to indicate that real estate was formally *in*alienable from the family circle. Hence, an outside purchaser was (fictively) adopted of necessity. But clearly, as we have seen, this is not the case. Outright sale (text #84), donation (text #80), and exchange (text #78) (to name but three vehicles) show that real estate could be alienated without the device of adoption. Thus "real estate adoption" accomplishes what it appears to accomplish: land sale.[24]

But if that is the case, why the fiction of adoption at all? I believe that the answer lies in the "prehistory" of the Nuzi period, when legal formulation was being forged.[25] But whatever the origin, the function, the *current* function, is clearly land sale[26] with no connection to family law or status at all. "Adoption" in this context has no more to do with family than shaking hands in our day has to do with ensuring that one's fellow is not holding a sword.

The issue was further confused because of how the *ilku* was mentioned in these "adoption" and similar contexts. In many cases, the son (= buyer) is said to bear the *ilku*, and this is what we would expect. We also find the heir bearing the *ilku* in genuine family-law contexts (texts ## 77, 85[27]). This too is what is expected. However, what is surprising is that, often, the father (= seller) is said to bear the *ilku* despite the cession of land to which it attaches. See texts ## 66, 67, 70. This would seem to indicate that the *ilku* and the land were separable and that the *ilku* stayed with the "original" owner regardless of the disposition of the land. If *that* were so, then (a) one could interpret the agrarian regime at Nuzi as feudal or communal; and (b) one could then consider the ubiquity of real estate adoption as a reflex of (a).

I hypothesize (for there is no explicit indication) that those "adoptions" asserting that the "father" continues to bear the *ilku*[28] state this to ensure that legal responsibility remains with the seller for that tax year, in instances where the sale takes place late in the tax year or after the harvest.[29] Both income and tax thus remain with the seller for that year only. This would be both logical (see immediately below) and economically reasonable. Now this idea unsupported would remain a nice hypothesis only and a blatant example of special pleading to uphold my notion of the *ilku* at Nuzi: the solution would lack evidence. I could appeal to logic in support of my position. Separation of the *ilku* from the real estate to which it attaches leaves us with a serious problem. How can the seller and his family continue to bear the impost permanently while lacking the economic grounding for its performance? Logic, however compelling, is no substitute for evidence. But whether or not my specific solution to the problem is correct, there is evidence—and not isolated evidence—that even when the *ilku* is said to remain with the seller, it in fact legally shifts to the buyer sooner or later.[30] This evidence takes the form of three pairs of texts (texts ## 86–87; 88–82; 89–90). (President Lyndon Johnson, a Democrat, was reputed to have once said about Republican electoral victories that once was an accident, twice a coincidence; three times, however, was a habit. Applying these criteria here, transfer of the *ilku* with land is, at Nuzi, habitual.) In each of the three pairs, the first text documents the movement of real estate while the *ilku* remains with the seller. In the second, the same real estate moves again, and the seller (i.e., the former buyer) is said to bear the *ilku*. In other words, the first *ilku* statement notwithstanding, legal responsibility for the *ilku* shifts to the buyer by the time the second contract was written. Other documents point in the same direction (texts ##83, 91), but these pairs of texts are the clearest indication of the alienation of land and of the *ilku* attaching to that land.

Thus legal title to land and *ilku*-bearing are tightly bound.[31] In fact, there are cases where title to real estate is claimed based on the assertion that the claimant bears legal responsibility for the *ilku* of the land and, therefore, is the legal owner of the land (texts ##61, 74; cf. text #85). (This too is evidence but not as compelling as the actual documentation of the shift in *ilku*-bearing.)

Who actually, that is, physically, performs the *ilku*, the corvée? This is a different question from who bears the legal responsibility for it. Clearly, an individual such as the large landowner, Teḫip-tilla son of Puḫi-šenni, adopted many scores of times and legal bearer of many scores of *ilku*s, cannot have performed these tasks himself.[32] Others, such as women bearers of this tax (text #66[33]), probably cannot have borne substantial parts of it themselves. It is most likely that the erstwhile owners of the land stayed on that land as tenants, tilling the soil, harvesting its bounty, keeping a share, tendering a share to the new owners, *and* physically performing the *ilku* in place of their landlords who themselves bore legal responsibility for it.[34] A few texts clearly show the separation of *ilku* performance from land ownership (for example, text #92). Other texts, such as texts ##56, 57, 61, presuppose this state of affairs. In each of these latter cases, a legal dispute pits party A, claiming he was adopted (and thus obtained title to land), and party B, who claims that party A is a mere tenant and is now distraining that land illegally.

As for the classes bearing the *ilku*, it appears that members of all classes able to own land were liable for this tax. A "son of the king" (probably both a status and a biological reality) bears it (text #80). A (local) queen is responsible likewise for its execution (text #93[35]). (Other women are also responsible for the *ilku*; see text #77.) And of the remaining classes, the *ilku* attaches to land owned by charioteers (texts ##75;[36] text #85, based on a datum from text #94 [see line 33]), *ālik ilki* (of course; text #86 [see line 6] and text #87, based on a datum from text #95 [see line 42]), and even landholding slaves (text #96).[37]

Excursus

The issue of the *ilku*'s meaning and function is not limited to Nuzi. Documentation is especially rich (and, therefore, the discussion is especially vigorous) in the Old Babylonian period (ca. 1800–1600, to the south of Nuzi), the Middle Assyrian period (yet it is a sufficiently small amount of material, so that it is difficult to interpret convincingly; ca. 1350–1100, among Nuzi's western neighbors), and the Neo-Assyrian period (ca. 745–630).

This is not the forum to view the *ilku* panoramically, though I could not resist citing above the Old Babylonian Code of Hammurabi.[38] For the Middle Assyrian evidence, see the useful summary of Postgate 1982. Note, however, that Postgate lumps Nuzi together with Assyria proper, though Nuzi was never part of the Assyrian economic regime. This leads him down several false paths. He incorrectly considers Nuzi's *ilku* to include military service.[39] He further judges that this impost was, not a tax attaching to real estate, but an obligation to the state remaining with a given family that once was given access to land. The *ilku* was heritable, whether or not the family continued to have the land (Postgate 1982: 307). Finally, I would disagree with Postgate that Nuzi's *ilku* has little or nothing to do with the Old Babylonian *ilku* but *is* linked to Hurrian or Mittannian practice (Postgate 1982: 312). For this last, there is not a shred of evidence.

With respect to the Neo-Assyrian evidence, the herculean and masterful labors of Simo Parpola in publishing and editing the Neo-Assyrian royal archives in the series SAA has opened up much of this late period to historical scholarship as never before. And this includes rich data on the workings of the *ilku* in the first millennium, especially in northern Mesopotamia. To give only a sampling, note the following. The *ilku* is performed (SAA VIII, 296; XIII, 182; cf. SAA I, 223; XII, 82, 92), even by scribes (SAA X, 143) and physicians (SAA X, 324). The *ilku* seems linked to particular real estate (SAA VI, 31, 191 [stated negatively; that is, *not* in these two cases]). Other texts reveal still other aspects of the *ilku* (e.g., SAA VII, 45; XI, 49, 97; XV, 67).

72. HSS XIII, 369 (SMN 369)

Findspot: No room number
Publication: Pfeiffer and Lacheman 1942: 69[40]
Edition: None

This is a list of barley disbursements. The first three entries represent rations given to *ilku*-tax payers working at textile production. The fourth and sixth entries involve relatively large quantities; the barley is meant for processing, once for malt and once for flour. The fifth entry is meant for further disbursement, perhaps rations for three unnamed individuals.

Obverse
1 [1] ANŠE ŠE ^{m}*Ḫa-na-a-a* ^{LÚ}[x]
2 1 ANŠE ŠE ^{m}*Wi-in-ni-ke*
3 1 ANŠE ŠE ^{m}*A-ti-ka*$_{4}$*-ti-il*
4 3 LÚ.MEŠ *an-nu-tu*$_{4}$ *ù*
5 *il*$_{5}$*-ku ša ḫul-la-an-na-ti i-pu-šu*
6 10 ANŠE ŠE *a-na* MUNU$_{x}$ (=BULUG$_{3}$) *a-na* ^{m}*Zi-ir-ru na-ad-nu*
7 3 ANŠE ŠE *šu-ku-ni a-na* ^{f}*Am-mi-na-a-a*
8 15 ANŠE ŠE *a-na* ZÍD.DA.MEŠ *a-na ni-iš* É.GAL
9 *a-na di-a-ni na-din*

"Rest not inscribed"

HSS XIII, 369

(1–5) [1] homer of barley, Ḫanaya, the …-man; 1 homer of barley, Winnike; 1 homer of barley, Atikkatil. Now these 3 men performed the *ilku* of (i.e., "by making") blankets/wraps.

(6) 10 homers of barley for malt (production), given to Zirru.

(7) 3 homers of barley (for) distribution, ^{f}Amin-naya.

(8–9) 15 homers of barley for flour, given to palace personnel for …[41].

73. *JEN* V, 498 (JENu 860a)

Findspot: Room T10
Publication: Chiera 1934b: pl. 471
Editions: Chiera and Speiser 1927: 56; Jankowska 1981: 195; Fadhil 1983: 339

In this letter, the recipient is told that the brothers of Kurpa-zaḫ are alive and well, though serving with the chariotry. As for Kurpa-zaḫ himself (the initial focus of the letter), he resides in the town of the (i.e., his?) *ilku*. I understand a kind of contrast here: Kurpa-zaḫ is in his (home) town, that is, where he normally fulfills his *ilku*-tax obligation. It need not be said (and is not said) that he is well. His brothers are well too (and this *is* noted), although they are *not* at home but with the chariotry.

It is possible, though not certain, that *ilku* labor contrasts here with military service. If so, then the *ilku* is a civilian corvée, not a military obligation with which it contrasts.

Obverse
1 *a-na* ^{m}*Šu-ur-te-šup*
2 *qí-bí-ma*
3 *um-ma* ^{m}*Šèr-ši-y*[*a-ma*]
4 ^{m}*Kùr*$^{!}$*-pa-zaḫ i+na*
5 URU *il-ki a-ši-im-mi*
6 *ù* ŠEŠ.MEŠ-*šú a-na*
7 ^{GIŠ}GIGIR.MEŠ *aš-bu-mi*
8 *ù bal-ṭe*$_{4}$*-mi*
Reverse
9 $^{\text{NA}_4}$KIŠIB ^{m}*Šèr-ši-ya*

JEN V, 498

(1–8) Say to Šur-tešup[42]: "Thus Šeršiya: Kurpa-zaḫ is present in the town of (his) *ilku*,[43] while his brothers are present among the chariots, and they are safe and sound."

(9) Seal impression of Šeršiya.

74. *JEN* IV, 327 (JENu 715)

Findspot: Room T16
Publication: Chiera 1934a: pl. 309
Edition: None

"Should this field have claimants/a claim (against it), PN_1 (i.e., the adopter/vendor) shall clear it (i.e., the field) and give (it) to PN_2 (i.e., the adoptee/purchaser)."

This is a "clear title" clause, and it appears (with expected variations) in case a future claim should arise. It is found in assorted contracts whereby real estate is alienated. See, for example, texts ## 64, 66. The present text, a record of a trial, represents just such a claim, resulting in the clearing of the title: the vendors fend off a challenge to their sale of land and, having won their case, cede (again) the land to the purchaser. It happens that the probable[44] original contract giving rise to this trial has survived as the somewhat damaged *JEN* 798 (publication: Lacheman and Maidman 1989: 207–8; edition: Maidman 2002: 71–77).

This particular trial text helps shed light on the nature of the *ilku* obligation. Teḫiya claims (lines 9–13) that he has not ceded his ownership rights to the disputed land, and—in what must be an extension of that claim—that he bears the *ilku* of the land in the town of Apena. Two points emerge. First, *ilku*-bearing points to ownership of real estate. Second, and this is less straightforward, bearing the *ilku* in Apena somehow buttresses his claim. It does, when the following is considered. The land at issue is located in the town of Zizza.[45] When Teḫiya avers that he bears the *ilku* in Apena, he must be claiming that the *ilku* is his but is borne, unexpectedly, in a jurisdiction other than Zizza. This argument would be effective only if he believes (and we assume) that the court would seek evidence of his ownership in the Zizza tax rolls (or equivalent evidence). Teḫiya thus explains why his name does not appear in the expected place. The state, it appears, assigned him tasks elsewhere in the kingdom of Arrapḫa.[46]

And how does the court respond? It seems to reply that it does not care. And to this illogical reaction, Teḫiya admits that, as a matter of fact, he *did* cede his land rights to his current adversaries. Illogic piled on illogic. Teḫiya ends up contradicting himself (cf. lines 16–19 with lines 10–11). This troubling state of affairs vanishes when it is recognized that this document, as other trial documents, does not represent a transcript, but at best a sketchy summary. Illogic abounds in these texts with parties first claiming one thing and then, without explanation, confessing its opposite. The accurate recording of proceedings is secondary (if that) to the statement of the verdict and outcome. These records are always found in private archives, not government offices. They were written to serve the interests of the winners (Maidman 1993b: 47–56).

But data such as personal and geographical names, boundaries, amounts of land, and, here, *where* the *ilku* is borne, are likely to be accurate. Such data, if falsified or sloppily recorded, would diminish the authority of the document. It is otherwise with testimony and detailed judicial response to testimony.

To summarize, the salient points of this text are (a) that it is an example of clearing title to real estate in the process of alienation; (b) that the *ilku* implies ownership of land; (c) that the *ilku* is typically, but not always, borne in the jurisdiction where the land in question is located; and (d) trial records are not to be construed as literal records of proceedings. Rather, they are evidence of the successful claims of trial victors and are stored in *their* archives, not the government's.

Obverse
1 [^{m}]*Še-en-na-a-a* DUMU *Ḫa-ši-ip-a-pu*
2 *ù* ^{m}*Ik-ki-ri* DUMU *Tu-ra-ri*
3 (erasure) *it-<ti>*[47] ^{m}*Te-ḫi-ya* (erasure) DUMU *Ḫa-ši-pa-pu*
4 AŠ *di-*⸢*ni*⸣ [*a-n*]*a p*[*a*]*-ni* DI.KU$_5$.MEŠ
5 *aš-šum* 12 A[NŠE] A.Š[À].MEŠ *i+na* AN.ZA.KÀR
6 *ša pí-ir-ša-ni* [*i+n*]*a bi*$_4$*-ri-ít*
7 AN.ZA.KÀR ḪA.LA-*ni* [*i-n*]*a* AN.ZA.KÀR *pí-ir-ša-ni*
^{m}*Ik-ki-ri*
8 ⸢*ù*⸣ ^{m}*Še-en-na-a-a ša a-na* ^{m}*Te-ḫi-ip-til-la*
9 SUM-*nu i-te-lu-ma ù um-ma*
10 ^{m}*Te-ḫi-ya* A.ŠÀ *ša-a-šú a-na* ^{m}*Še-na-a-a*
11 *ù a-na* ^{m}*Ik-ki-ri la a-na-din*
12 *a-na-ku il-ka*$_4$ AŠ URU *A-pè-na-aš*
13 *na-ša-ak ù um-ma* DI.KU$_5$.MEŠ-*^{nu}-ma*
14 *a-na* ^{m}*Te-ḫi-ya aš-šum il-ki*
15 *at-tù-ka*$_4$ *mi-nu-ka*$_4$ *ù um-ma*
16 ^{m}*Te-ḫi-ya-ma* 12 ANŠE A.ŠÀ *ša-a-šú*
17 *a-na* ^{m}*Še-en-na-a-a ù a-na*
18 ^{m}*Ik-ki-ri un-te-eš-ši-ir*
19 *a-šar* SUM-*nu-ma ù li-*⸢*x*⸣-[ ]
20 *ù* AŠ *di-ni* ^{m}*Še-en-*[*na-a-a*]
Lower Edge
21 *ù* ^{m}*Ik-ki-ri i*[*l-tu-ú-ma*]
22 *ù* 12 ANŠE A.ŠÀ *ša* AŠ [AN.ZA.KÀR]

Reverse

23 *pí-ir-ša-ni il-te-q*[*ú*?-*ú*?]

24 *ù a-na* ^{m}*Te-ḫi-ip-til-la*

25 DUMU *Pu-ḫi-še-en-ni it-ta-ad-*[*nu*]

26 *ù uš-tu* UD^{-mi} *an-ni-im*

27 *aš-šum* A.ŠÀ *ša-a-šú* ^{m}*Te-ḫi-ya i+na*

28 EGIR^{-ki} ^{m}*Še-en-na-a-a ù* AŠ EGIR$^{\mathrm{-ki}}$

29 ^{m}*Ik-ki-ri la i-ša*$_{10}$*-as-sí*

30 $^{\mathrm{NA_4}}$KIŠIB ^{m}*Ḫa-iš-te-šup* DUMU *Pu-ḫi-še-en-ni*

31 $^{\mathrm{NA_4}}$KIŠIB ^{m}*Ké-e-li-ya* $^{\mathrm{NA_4}}$KIŠIB ^{m}ÌR-DINGIR-*šu*

32 $^{\mathrm{NA_4}}$KIŠIB ^{m}*Ú-ta-a-a*

33 $^{\mathrm{NA_4}}$KIŠIB ^{m}*Ar-te-eš-še* DUMU *E-ka*$_{4}$*-am-me-šu*

34 ŠU ^{m}*Ḫu-ti-ya* DUB.SAR DUMU ^{d}*Uta-ma-an-sì*

35 $^{\mathrm{NA_4}}$KIŠIB ^{m}*Tar-mi-ya* DUMU *En-na-ma-ti*

JEN IV, 327

(1–9) Šennaya son of Ḫašip-apu and Ikkiri son of Turari took to court, before judges,[48] Teḫiya son of Ḫašip-apu, concerning a 12 homer field in the *piršanni dimtu*[49] within the *dimtu*, our (*sic*) inheritance share in the *piršanni dimtu*, and which Ikkiri and Šennaya had given to Teḫip-tilla.

(9–13) Now thus Teḫiya: "I did not give (over) that land to Šennaya and to Ikkiri. I (still) bear the *ilku* (pertaining to that land), (but) in the town of Apena."

(13–15) Then thus the judges to Teḫiya: "As for your *ilku*, what of it (lit. "what is it to you")?

(15–19) Then thus Teḫiya: "I released and(?) gave that 12 homer field to Šennaya and to Ikkiri and … ."

(20–25) Now Šennaya and Ikkiri won the case. And they took(?) the 12 homer field of the *piršanni dimtu* and gave it to Teḫip-tilla son of Puḫi-šenni.

(26–29) Now from this day (forward) Teḫiya shall not raise a claim against Šennaya and against Ikkiri regarding that land.

(30–35) Seal impression of Ḫaiš-tešup son of Puḫi-šenni; seal impression of Keliya; seal impression of Ward-ilišu; seal impression of Utaya; seal impression of Ar-tešše son of Ekammešu. Hand of Ḫutiya, scribe, son of Uta-mansi. Seal impression of Tarmiya son of Enna-mati.

75. *EN* 10/2, 170 (ERL 49 + 1 unnumbered fragment)

Findspot: Room A23![51] + findspot unknown
Publication: Fincke 1998a: 368–69[50]
Edition: None

This badly broken tablet is, happily, best preserved where the data are most informative. It is a list of at least eleven charioteers who are distinguished by two features. Only one of these is recoverable: they do not perform the *ilku* in their own town(s).

Obverse

.
.
.

1 [^{m} DUMU$^{?}$]-⌜*te*$^{?}$/*li*$^{?}$-*x*⌝
2 [^{m} DUMU$^{?}$]-⌜*na*⌝$^{?}$[52]-UD-DU
3 [^{m} DUMU *X*]-*ri-ya*
4 [^{m} DUMU *Ar*$^{?}$]-*zi-iz-za*
5 [^{m} -B]E$^{?}$ DUMU *Ta-ú-ka*
6 [^{m} DU]MU *A-kap-tùk-ké*
7 [^{m} DUM]U [*Ḫu-ti* (or: *A-ri*) -*p*]*u-ú-ra-áš-še*
8 [^{m} -*m*]*a*$^{?}$ DUMU *N*[*a*$^{?}$-*an*$^{?}$-*t*]*e*$^{?}$-*šup*
9 [^{m} -*t*]*a*$^{?}$-*ak* DUMU [*X-t*]*i-ya*
10 [^{m}]-*a ša* AN.[ZA.KÀ]R$^{?}$ *ša Ak-ku-*[ ]
11 [^{m}]-*ya ša* UR[U]$^{!?}$ *A-pa-we*
(space)
12 [n ^{L}]$^{Ú.MEŠ}$ *ra-kib* ^{GIŠ}⌜G⌝IGIR *an-nu-tu*$_{4}$
13 [x$^{?}$-*š*]*a*$^{?}$ *i+na ṭup-pa*^{MEŠ}-*t*[*i*]
14 [ ] ⌜x x⌝ *ta ma* [(?)] AŠ
Lower edge.
15 *i-ša-as-sú-ú*
16 *ù it-ti* ⌜U⌝RU-*šu-nu*
17 *il-ka*$_{4}$ *la na-šu-ú*

EN 10/2, 170

(1–11) [PN? son of?] PN?; [PN? son of?] …-uttu; [PN son of] …-riya; [PN son of Ar?]-zizza; …-BE? son of Tauka; [PN] son of Akap-tukke; [PN] son of

[Ḫuti/Ari]p-urašše; …-ma(?) son of Nan(?)-te(?)-šup; …-ta?-ak son of …-tiya; …-a of the *dimtu*(?) of Akku-…; …-ya of the town(?) of Apa.

(space)

(12–17) These [n] charioteers, who(?) … in the tablets, call (out) and do not bear the *ilku* with their town(s?).

76. HSS XIV, 9 (SMN 3626)

Findspot: Room G29[53]
Publication: Lacheman 1950: pl. 8
Edition: None

This is a difficult text: essential data were written on the right side of the tablet, now effaced and even broken off. The fact that the document is not a contract or other formulaic, predictable context means that the surviving text remains somewhat obscure. However, what is decipherable is important. The tablet is an announcement of a royal proclamation, certainly from the king of Arrapḫa. In it, the king may be exempting the residents of a certain town—and them alone—from the *ilku*. In addition, he appears to be paying them two oxen apiece. The crucial point in the present context is that the king clearly exercises authority over the *ilku*. Therefore, the *ilku* is a state, not a local, impost.

Obverse
1 *ki-na-an-na* LU[GAL-*ma a-na*]
2 LÚ.MEŠ *ša i+na* U[RU? -*l*]*u*?-*ú*
3 *uš-te-dì um*?-[*ma*?]
4 *lu-ú* LUGAL-*ma-m*[*i*]
5 LÚ.MEŠ *ša i-na* UR[U]-*lu-ú*
6 *ù il-ka*$_4$ *i+na* U[RU?]
7 *ma-aš-ka*$_4$*-an aš-bu* ⸢x⸣ [ ]
8 *i-lik-šu-nu ša* L⸢Ú⸣? ⸢MEŠ⸣!
9 *ù šá-nu-ú ya-nu*
10 *ma-a*[*n*]-*n*[*u*]-⸢*um*⸣-*me-e*!
11 LÚ *ša* URU LUGAL
Lower Edge
12 ⸢*i*⸣-*na il-ki* ⸢*ù*⸣?
13 *ú-še-eṣ-ṣí*
Reverse
14 2 GUD.MEŠ *a-na* LÚ[.MEŠ]

15 *ša* URU LUGAL SI.A
S.I.
16 NA_4 ᵐ*A-ki-ya* SUKKAL
Left Edge
17 ⌜NA_4? *A*⌝*k-ku-le-en-*⌜*n*⌝*i*
: DUB.SAR

HSS XIV, 9

(1–3) The king proclaimed as follows [to] the men, who in the town(?) [of?] … .

(3–13) Thus(?) … the king, indeed: "… the men who, … in the town and [who? perform?] the *ilku* in the town(?) … the location where they reside …, the *ilku* of (these?) men and no others—whichever man of the town—the king exempts from the *ilku*.[54]

(14–15) The king will pay 2 oxen to the men of the town.

(16–17) (*seal impression*) Seal of Akiya, *sukkallu*; seal of Akkul-enni, scribe [(*seal impression*?)].

77. HSS XIX, 51 (SMN 3502)

Findspot: Room F24
Publication: Lacheman 1962: pl. 83
Edition: None[55]

This document is a type of genuine adoption and belongs in the realm of family law rather than strictly business law. A man is adopted and then his adoptive father marries him off to his daughter. Two separate issues are involved here.[56] The adoption solves the problem of the failure of the father to have sired a son. The new son inherits and keeps the property in the family. The father also wishes his daughter to inherit real property. Her marriage would normally mean that the property she inherits would devolve to her husband's family. By having the daughter marry the adopted son, they both inherit and *all* the real property stays within the family. That, no doubt, was the adoptive father's motivation all along.

The *ilku* of the real property is inherited along with the real estate. Man and wife both are responsible for the *ilku*, since both have title to real estate, he receiving a double share and she, implicitly, receiving a single share.

Obverse

1 *ṭup-pí m*[*a-r*]*u-ti ša* $^{m?}$*Pá-i-til-la* DUMU *Na-i-te-šup*
2 DUMU-*šu* ^{m}*A-ri-im-ma-a*[*t*]-*ka*$_4$ *a-na ma-ru-ti*
3 *a-na* ^{m}*Ké-li-pu-kùr* DUMU *Ḫa-na-tu*$_4$ ⸢*i*⸣*t-ta-din*
4 *ù Ké-li-pu-kùr* DUMU.MÍ-⸢*sú*⸣ ^{f}⸢*T*⸣*a-*[*tù-n*]*i*
5 *a-na aš-šu-ti a-na* ^{m}*A-ri-im-m*[*a*]-*a*[*t-ka*$_4$ *it-t*]*a-din*
6 *um-ma* ^{m}*Ké-li-pu-kùr* ^{m}*A-ri-i*[*m*]-*ma-a*[*t-ka*$_4$]
7 *a-na m*[*a-r*]*u-ti i-te-pu-uš* [A.Š]À.ḪÁ$^{!}$-*ya*
8 É.ḪÁ-[*ya*] *ma-na-ha-ti-ya* ⸢*ù*⸣ *šá-a-ši i-*[*s*]*é-em-me-hu*
9 *il*-⸢ku⸣ [*ša* A.Š]À *ù* ^{m}*A-ri-ma-a*[*t*]-*ka*$_4$ *it-ti* [D]UMU.<MÍ>$^{-ti}$-*ya*
10 ⸢x⸣ [ ]-ŠI *na-ši šum-ma* DUMU-*šu ša Ké-*[*l*]*i-pu-kùr*
11 [ ]⸢x x⸣ [ ] ⸢x⸣-*še-li i-bá-aš-ši* GAL 2-*šu*$^{!}$ ḪA.LA-*šu*
12 [*i*]-⸢*l*⸣*eq-*[*qè*] *šum-ma* DUMU-*šu ša Ké-li-p*[*u*]-*kùr*
13 [*y*]*a-nu* [D]UMU.MÍ (erasure)-*ti it-ti* ^{m}*A-*[*ri*(*-im*)]-*ma-at-ka*$_4$
14 *iz-zi-*[*iz-z*]*u šum-ma* ^{m}*A-*[*r*]*i-im-ma-a*[*t*]-*ka*$_4$ GAL 2-*šu* ḪA.LA *i-leq-qè*
15 [^{m}*A*]-*ri-ma-at-ka*$_4$ *a-na* ⸢É⸣$^{-ti}$ A.[ŠÀ] ḪA.LA *i-leq-qè*
16 [*šum-m*]*a* ^{f}[*T*]*a-tù-ni* DUMU^{-ra} *ú-la-ad*
17 [*ù*] ^{m}*A-ri-im-ma-at-ka*$_4$ *aš-ša-ta*
18 [*ša*]-*ni-ta i-leq-qè qa-an-na-šu*
19 [*i-na-a*]*k-ki-su i+na* É$^{-ti}$-*ša* ⸢x x⸣
20 [-*m*]*a*$^{?}$ ^{m}*A-ri-im-ma-a*[*t-ka*$_4$]
21 [ ] ⸢x x⸣ [ ]
.
.
.

Reverse
.
.
.
22 [ ] ⸢x⸣ [ ]
23 [KÁ].GAL^{-li} *ša*$_{10}$-*ṭì-ir*
24 [IGI] ⸢*Ši*⸣-[*m*]*i-ka*$_4$-*tal* DUMU *Še-el-la-pa-*⸢*i*⸣
25 IGI *A-*[*w*]*i-iš-ta-e* DUMU [*U*]*t-ḫa-ap-ta-e*
26 IGI *Tar-mi-ip-ta-še-en-ni* DUMU *Wi-ir-ri-*<*iš*/*eš*>*-ta-ni*
27 IGI *Ḫa-ni-ú-*⸢*y*⸣*a* DUMU *E-ḫé-el-te-šup*
28 IGI *Ḫa-ši-ip-*[*ti*]*l-la* DUMU *Šu-ma-li-ya*
29 IGI *Ul-mi-t*[*il*]*-la* DUMU *Ma-te-šup*
30 IGI *Ḫa-šu-ar* DUMU *Ḫu-i-til-la*
31 ŠU *Ḫi-ip*-LUGAL[57] DUB.SAR$^{-rù}$

S.I.$^{?}$

32 NA$_4$ ^{m}DUB.SAR$^{-rù}$

S.I.$^{?}$ S.I.$^{?}$

33 NA$_4$ ^{m}*Ḫa-ši-ip-til-la* NA$_4$ *Ul-mi-til-la*

S.I.$^{?}$

34 NA$_4$ ^{m}*A-wi-iš-ta-e*

Upper Edge

S.I.$^{?}$ S.I.$^{?}$

35 NA$_4$ ^{m}*Tar-mi-ip-ta-*[*še-en*]*-ni* [N]A$_4$ *Ši-mi-ka$_4$-tal*

Left Edge

S.I.

36 NA$_4$ ^{m}*Pa-i-til-la*

HSS XIX, 51

(1–3) Tablet of adoption of Pai-tilla son of Nai-tešup. He gave his son Arim-matka for adoption to Kelip-ukur son of Ḫanatu.

(4–5) Now Kelip-ukur gave his daughter ^{f}Tatuni in marriage (lit. "into wife-ship") to Arim-matka.

(6–10) Thus Kelip-ukur: "I (lit. "He") adopted Arim-matka. He will share in my fields, [my] buildings, the things I've labored to make—(all) these aforementioned (things). And the *ilku* of the land Arim-matka together with my daughter … shall bear."

(10–15) Should Kelip-ukur have a son …, (he shall be the) senior (son, and) will receive a (lit. "his") double inheritance share. Should Kelip-ukur not have a (lit. "his") son, (then his) daughter and Arim-matka shall divide (the estate). Arim-matka would be the senior; he would receive a (lit. "his") double inheritance share. Arim-matka shall take house and land as his inheritance share.

(16–21) Should ^{f}Tatuni bear a son [but] Arim-matka (still) take another wife, they shall clip the hem of his (garment),[58] and he shall [exit] her house …. And(?) Arim-matka ….

(22–23) …. (this tablet) was written at the gate.[59]

(24–30) [Before] Šimika-atal son of Šellapai; before Awiš-tae son of Utḫap-tae; before Tarmip-tašenni son of Wirriš-tanni; before Ḫaniuya son of Eḫli-tešup; before Ḫašip-tilla son of Šumaliya; before Ulmi-tilla son of Mat-tešup; before Ḫašuar son of Ḫui-tilla. Hand of Ḫ<u(t)?>ip-šarri, scribe.

(31–35) (*seal impression*?) Seal of the scribe; (*seal impression*?) seal of Ḫašip-tilla; (*seal impression*?) seal of Ulmi-tilla; (*seal impression*?) seal of Awiš-tae; (*seal impression*?) seal of Tarmip-tašenni; (*seal impression*?) seal of Šimika-atal; (*seal impression*) seal of Pai-tilla.

78. *EN* IX/3, 482 (SMN 997x)

Findspot: No room number
Publication: Lacheman and Owen 1995: 323
Edition: None

This text is a remnant of a tablet of real estate exchange. Structures are exchanged for their equivalents. Most of this section of the document is lost in the missing top part of the tablet. One party "sweetens" the deal (thus defining who initiated the transaction) by adding an excess payment, probably consisting of barley. The *ilku* attaches to the buildings of both parties.

Obverse

.

.

.

1 ⸢DIŠ x⸣ [ ]

2 *a-na ḫu-*⸢*pí*⸣?-[ ] ⸢x x⸣ [ ]

3 *a-na* ^{m}*Ur-ḫi-til-la* ⸢*i*⸣?-[ ]

4 *ù* ^{m}*Ḫa-ši-ya* 5 AN[ŠE ŠE.?MEŠ?]

5 *i+na* UGU É.MEŠ *ša* ^{m}[*Ḫa-ši-ya*]

6 *a-na* ^{m}*Ur-ḫi-til-la i*[*t-ta-din*]

7 *il-ka ša* É.MEŠ *š*[*a* ^{m}]

8 ^{m}*Ur-ḫi-til-la-ma na-ši* [(?)]

9 *il-ka ša* É.MEŠ *ša* ^{m}⸢x⸣-[ ]

Lower Edge

10 ^{m}*Ḫa-ši-ya-ma na-ši* ^{m}*Ur-ḫ*[*i-til-la*]

11 *la na-ši šum-ma* É.MEŠ *ša* ^{m}[*Ur-ḫi-til-la*]

12 *pá-qí-ra-na* TUK-^{ši} É.MEŠ *ša-a-š*[*u-nu*]

Reverse

13 ^{m}*Ur-ḫi-til-la ú-za-ak-ka*$_{4}$!*-m*[*a*]

14 *a-na* ^{m}*Ḫa-ši-ya i+na-an-din* [*šum-ma*]

15 É.MEŠ *ša* ^{m}*Ḫa-ši-ya p*[*á-qí-ra-na* TUK-^{ši}]

16 É.MEŠ *ša-a-šu-nu-ma* ^{m}*Ḫ*[*a*!*-ši-ya ú-za-ak-ka*$_{4}$(*-ma*)]

17 *a-na* ^{m}*Ur-ḫi-til-la i+na-a*[*n-din*]

18 *ša ma-an-ni-im-me-e* ⸢É⸣.[MEŠ]

19 *ma-ad la i+na-ak-ki-*[*is*]

20 *mi-iṣ ù la* ⸢*ú*⸣-[*ra-ad-dá*]

21 *ša* ^{m} ⸢*Ur-ḫi*⸣*-til-l*[*a*]

.

.

.

Left Edge

22 NA_4 DUB.SAR NA_4 ᵐ*Ur-ḫi-til-l*[*a*]

S.I.? S.I.?

23 EN É.MEŠ

EN IX/3, 482

(1–6) … to … [he gave?] to Urḫi-tilla and Ḫašiya gave to Urḫi-tilla 5 homers [of barley?] as excess payment (in addition to) the structures of [Ḫašiya].

(7–11) The *ilku* for the structures of … Urḫi-tilla shall bear …(?); the *ilku* of the structures of … and Ḫašiya shall bear—Urḫi-tilla shall not bear (it).

(11–17) Should the structures of [Urḫi-tilla] have claimants, Urḫi-tilla shall clear those structures and(?) give (them) to Ḫašiya. [Should] the structures of Ḫašiya [have] claimants, Ḫašiya [shall clear] those structures and give (them) to Urḫi-tilla.

(18–20) Whosever structures are large(r than estimated) he shall not diminish (them), (if) small(er than estimated), he need not augment (them).

(21) … of Urḫi-tilla …

(22–23) Seal of the scribe; seal of Urḫi-tilla

S.I.? S.I.?

owner of the structures

79. *EN* 9/1, 7 (SMN 2630)

Findspot: Room K465[61]

Publication: Lacheman, Owen, and Morrison 1987: 399–400[60]

Edition: None

This is a typical real estate adoption text, notable here because it demonstrates that small, valuable, urban building plots were subject to the *ilku* just as was other real estate.

Obverse

1 *ṭup-pí ma-ru-ti ša* ᵐ*A-ri-ip-a-pu*

2 DUMU *E-ni-iš-ta-e* ᵐ*Be-li-ya*

3 DUMU *Ra-ap-še-ya a-na ma-ru-ti*

4 *i-te-pu-us-sú-ma qà-aq-qa-ru*

5 *p*⌜*á-i*⌝*-ḫu i+na* URU *Ḫu-ra-ṣí-na ṣé-éḫ-ri*

6 *i+na* [x]-⌜x⌝ *ti-il* ⌜x⌝-[ ]-⌜*ti*⌝$^?$

7 ⌜x⌝ [ ] ⌜*i-x ù*⌝ [ ]

8 *a-*⌜*dì*⌝*-i i+na* É.Ḫ[Á(.MEŠ)]

9 *ù a-dì-i i+na* KASKAL ⌜x x⌝ [(?)]

10 *ša* ⌜x x⌝ *bi*$_4$*-ri-šu-nu* ⌜x x⌝

11 *k*[*i-ma* ḪA.L]A-*šu* ^{m}*A-ri-ip-*⌜*a*⌝-[*pu*]

12 ⌜*a*⌝-[*na* ^{m}*Be-lí*]-*ya* SUM^{-in} *ù*

13 22 MA.⌜N⌝A URUDU.MEŠ 2 ANŠE 5 BÁN Š[E.MEŠ]

14 *ù ma-la ku-du-u*[*k-t*]*i* SÍG [*ki-ma*]

15 NÍG.BA-*šu a-na* ^{m}*A-*[*r*]*i-ip-a-*[*pu*]

16 *it-ta-ad-na-aš-*[*šu*] ⌜*šum-ma*⌝

17 *qà-aq-qà-ru p*[*á-i-ḫu pí-ir-qà* / *pá-qí-ra-na*]

18 *i-ra-aš-šu-ú* ^{m} ⌜*A*⌝-[*ri-ip-a-pu*]

19 *ú-za-ak-ka-ma a-na* ^{m}[*Be-li-ya* SUM^{-in}]

Lower Edge

20 *il-ka ša q*[*à-aq-qa*$_{1/3}$*-ru* (*pá-i-ḫu*)]

21 ^{m}*A-ri-ip-a-pu n*[*a-ši*]

22 *ša i+na bi*$_4$*-ri-šu-nu* K[I.BAL$^{-at?}$]

23 ⌜10$^?$⌝ SAL.MEŠ ⌜SIG$_5$⌝$^?$*-ti ú-ma-a*[*l-la*]

Reverse

24 [IGI] *A-kap-še-en-ni* DUMU *Na-*⌜*x-x*⌝

25 IGI *Ik-kí-ya* DUMU *Ḫa-ta-*[*ar*$^?$*-te*$^?$]

26 IGI *Šúk-ra-pu* [DUMU] *A-ri-i*⌜*p-a-p*⌝*u*

27 IGI *Ké-en-na-bi* DUMU *A-ḫa-a-*⌜x⌝-*ri-*⌜x⌝

28 IGI *Wa-at-*[*wa*] DUMU *Še-en-*[*za-a*]*ḫ*

29 IGI *Ḫi-t*]*i-i*[*m-pá*] DU[MU *Š*]*e-le-bu*

30 IGI AN ⌜*ni*⌝$^?$-[DUM]U ^{d}XXX-*iš-ma-a*[*n-ni*]

31 [*an*]-⌜*nu*⌝-[*ti* LÚ$^?$.MEŠ$^?$]-*ti* ⌜*š*⌝*a qà-aq-*[*qa*$_{1/3}$*-ru* (*pá-i-ḫu*)]

32 *ú-še-*[*el-m/wu-ú ù*] KÙ.BABBAR.MEŠ SUM [(?)]

33 *um-m*[*a*] ^{m}*Ar-na-p*[*u*]

34 *i+na* ⌜x⌝ [ ] AK [ ]-*ti-*⌜*x*⌝

35 ⌜IGI⌝$^?$ [ ]-*a* DUMU [ ]-*ni*

.

.

.

.

[S.I.]

36 ^{NA_4}KIŠIB ^{m}*Šúk-*⌜*r*⌝*a-pu* [S.I.]

37 ^{NA_4}KIŠIB *Ik-kí-ya*

Left Edge

38 NA4KIŠIB m*Ḫi-ti-im-pá* S.I.? NA4KIŠIB m*Ké-en-na-bi* S.I.?

EN 9/1, 7

(1–4) Tablet of adoption of Arip-apu son of Eniš-tae. He adopted Bêliya son of Rapšeya.

(5–12) Arip-apu gave to Bêliya, as his inheritance share, ground, a building lot[62] in the town of Ḫurāṣina-ṣeḫru, withḫin ... and ... up to in (*sic*) the buildings of ..., and up to in (*sic*) the road ... which ... between them ... .

(12–16) And he (i.e., Bêliya) gave to Arip-apu [as] his gift 22 minas of copper, 2.5 homers of [barley], and a full *kuduktu*[63] of wool.

(16–19) Should the ground, the building lot, have [a claim/claimants], Arip-apu shall clear (the lot) and [give (it)] to [Bêliya].

(20–21) Arip-apu shall bear the *ilku* of the ground [(the building lot)].

(22–23) Who amongst them should abrogate (this contract) shall pay 10(?) fair women.

(24–32) [Before] Akap-šenni son of Na-...; before Ikkiya son of Ḫata[rte?]; before Šukr-apu [son of] Arip-apu; before Kên-abi son of Aḫā-...-ri-...; before Watwa son of Šien-zaḫ; before Ḫitimpa son of Šêlebu; before AN-ni(?)-... son of Sin-išmânni. These are the ...(?) men(?) who measured the ground [(, the building lot,) and] who gave the price (lit. "silver").

(33–35) Thus ... Arn-apu ... in ... . Before(?) ...-a son of ...-ni.

(36–38) ([*seal impression*]) Seal impression of Šukr-apu; ([*seal impression*]) seal impression of Ikkiya; seal impression of Ḫitimpa (*seal impression*?); seal impression of Kên-abi (*seal impression*?).

80. HSS IX, 35 (SMN 133)

Findspot: Room A26[64]
Publication: Pfeiffer 1932: pls. 32–33
Edition: None

This document records a transfer of real estate, but in an unusual way. It starts with a statement by the current owner rather than with a title ("tablet of ...") followed by a third-person description of the transaction. The owner describes the location of the urban buildings to be transferred with respect to what adjoins them on the four sides.[65] On two sides lie structures of the very prince who will be obtaining the buildings at hand. This explains why the prince wants these structures: he would be establishing or expanding his own contiguous urban property.[66] It is to be noted that the structures were located in Āl-ilāni, the "City of the Gods," a quarter in Arrapḫa, the capital city of the kingdom of Arrapḫa. On the third side of the structures are structures owned by another individual, and on the fourth there lies a road, apparently a major, named, thoroughfare. The owner states that, sometime in the past, he had obtained this land by way of exchange or compensation of some other sort.

The owner continues by stating that now he undertakes to donate this property to the prince, together with its relevant documentation. Those records probably recorded (at least) the exchange by which the current owner received the structures in former times. He further notes that he has received a present from the prince in return, probably mobilia. In short, this text documents a sale of real estate. And, just as real estate adoption texts couch such transactions in terms of inheritance within a family, so this text masks the sale as something else, a donation which calls forth a donation in return.

The text turns from the actual transaction to ancillary matters. The prince, not the old owner, shall bear the *ilku*. The old owner is enjoined from legal challenges to this donation of structures. And, in a peculiar departure from the normal pattern, the prince (rather than the old owner) undertakes to clear up potential outstanding claims on the property.

The text continues with a sort of date formula: the contract was concluded after a (royal) proclamation. This was important to note because the edict, not the first of its kind (line 29: "a new proclamation"), probably affected real estate transactions entered into before the proclamation's issuance. The text concludes with a list of sealers of the tablet, ending with the very person giving up his buildings.

Obverse

1 *um-ma* ^{m}*Ḫa-ši-ya-ma*
2 DUMU *Al-ki-te-šup a-ni-n*⸢*a*⸣
3 É.MEŠ *ša* ŠÀ URU-DINGIR
4 *ša il-ta-an ù ša šu-pa-al*
5 É.MEŠ *ša* ^{m}*Ši-il-wa-te-šup* DUMU LUGAL
6 *ša su-ta-na-an* É.MEŠ
7 *ša* ^{m}*Wa-an-ti-ya* DUMU *Al-ki-til-la*
8 *ša* AN.TA KASKAL *ša Nu-ul-ta-aḫ-ḫé*
9 *ša a-na pu-ḫu-ka-ri* (erasure)

10 *ša a-šar* ^{m}*Ur-hi-til-la*
11 DUMU *Aš-tar-til-la ša el*$^{!}$*-qú-ú*
12 *ù i+na-an-na a-na-ku* É.MEŠ *ša-a-šu-nu*
13 *it-ti ṭup-pí-šu-nu-ma*
14 *a-na ma-ka-an-nu-ti*
15 *a-na* ^{m}*Ši-il-wa-te-šup* DUMU LUGAL
16 *at-ta-din-šu-nu-ti*
17 *ù a-na-ku ma-ka*$_4$*-an-nu-ya*
Lower Edge
18 *a-šar* ^{m}*Ši-il-wa-te-šup*
19 *el-te-qè i-lik-šu-nu*
20 *ša* É.MEŠ ^{m}*Ši-il-wa-te-šup-ma*
Reverse
21 *na-ši* ^{m}*Ḫa-ši-ya*
22 *la na-ši šum-ma* ^{m}*Ḫa-ši-ya*
23 *i+na* EGIR É.MEŠ *i-ša-as-sí*
24 *ù* É.MEŠ ^{m}*Ḫa-ši-ya a-na* 10*-šu*
25 *ú-ma-al-la a-na* ^{m}*Ši-il-wa-te-šup*
26 *i+na-an-din šum-ma* É.MEŠ
27 *pá-qí-ra-na* TUK$^{-\check{s}i}$ *ù* ^{m}*Ši-il-wa-te-šup*
28 *ú-za-ak-ka*$_4$ *ṭup-pí* AŠ EGIR
29 *šu-du*$_4$*-ti eš-ši* AŠ URU-DINGIR
30 *ša-ṭì-ir*

31 NA$_4$ ^{m}*A-ri-ik-ka*$_4$*-ni*	NA$_4$ *Muš-te-šup*
32 DUMU *Še-ḫu-ur-ni ši-bu*	DUMU *Na-i-te-šup*
33 NA$_4$ ^{m}*Ši-ip-ki-te-šup*[67]	*NA*$_4$ ^{m}*Ur-ḫi-ya*
34 DUMU *Šúk-ri-ya*	DUMU *Muš-te-šup*

Upper Edge

35 NA$_4$ ^{m}*Ši-pí-*⌜*i*⌝*š*-LUGAL	NA$_4$ ^{m}*Ni-ik-ri-ya*
36 DUMU *Ut-ḫap-ta-e*	DUMU *Šur*$^{!}$*-kip*-LUGAL

Left Edge

37 NA$_4$ ^{m}*Šar-til-la*	NA$_4$ ^{m}*Ḫa-ši-ya*
38 DUB.SAR DUMU DINGIR-*ya*	EN É.MEŠ

HSS IX, 35

(1–16) Thus Ḫašiya son of Alki-tešup: "Structures of (i.e., in) (the town of) Āl-ilāni, to the north and west of structures of Šilwa-tešup son of the king, to the south of structures of Wantiya son of Alki-tilla, (and) to the east of the road of (i.e., to) Nultaḫḫe, (these structures) which I once received from Urḫi-tilla son of

Aštar-tilla by way of an exchange, I have now given together with their tablet(s) (i.e., documentation) to Šilwa-tešup son of the king as a donation.

(17–19) “And I have taken my present from Šilwa-tešup.”

(19–22) The *ilku* of the structures Šilwa-tešup shall bear; Ḫašiya shall not bear (it).

(22–26) Should Ḫašiya hail (Šilwa-tešup into court) over the structures, then Ḫašiya shall pay to Šilwa-tešup 10-fold (the value of) the structures.

(26–28) Should the structures have claimants, then Šilwa-tešup[68] shall clear (the structures).

(28–30) (This) tablet was written after the new proclamation[69] in Āl-ilāni.

(31–38)[70] Seal of Arik-kani son of Šeḫurni, witness; seal of Muš-tešup son of Nai-tešup; seal of Šipki-tešup son of Šukriya; seal of Urḫiya son of Muš-tešup; seal of Šipiš-šarri son of Utḫap-tae; seal of Nikriya son of Šurkip-šarri; seal of Šar-tilla, scribe, son of Iluya; seal of Ḫašiya, (erstwhile) owner of the structures.

81. *EN* 9/1, 4 (SMN 2684)

Findspot: No room number
Publication: Lacheman, Owen, and Morrison 1987: 393–94
Edition: Koliński 2001: 5–6[71]

This real estate adoption text is notable for several distinctive features. The size af a *dimtu*-tower is reported, together with the kinds of real estate contained within its confines. (The entire complex is subject to the *ilku*.) The actual month of purchase is noted, juxtaposed with a previous month in which a royal edict was issued—mentioned, no doubt, because that edict does not apply to the current transaction. Scribal practice is peculiar also. The writer employs atypical pronunciations (in writing, of course; especially in rendering personal names), unusual choice of signs to depict certain phonetic realizations, and idiosyncratic phraseology.[72]

Obverse

1 [*ṭup-pí*] DUMU-*ti ša* ^{m}*Te-ḫi-pa-pu*
2 [DUMU]-⌜x⌝-*ki*$^{?}$-*ya ù* ^{m}*Eḫ-li-ya*
3 [DUMU] ⌜*E*⌝-*ze-e-ra a-na* DUMU-*ti*
4 [*i-t*]*e-pu-uš ki-ma* ḪA.LA-*šu*
5 [AN.ZA.KÀ]R PÚ ^{GIŠ}*zi-iq-pu*
6 [GIŠ.S]AR *ḫa-la-aḫ-wu*

7 [*i-n*]*a li-mi-is-sú ša* AN.ZA.KÀR
8 [n$^{?}$+] 2 *ma-ti* 20 *i+na am-ma-ti*
9 *li-mi-is-sú i-na il-ta-na-an-nu*
10 AN.ZA.KÀR *ša* ^{m}*Ú-na-áp-ta-e*
11 *i-na su-ta-an-nu* A.ŠÀ
12 *ša* ^{m}*Šu-ru-ka*$_4$*-a-a*
13 *i-na šad-dá-an-nu ša* ^{m}*Ú-na-áp-ta-e*
14 *i+na šu-pa-li ša* ^{m}*Ú-na-áp-ta-e-ma*
15 ^{m}*Te-ḫi-pa-pu a-na* ^{m}*E-ḫe-li-ya i-din*$^{-in}$
16 *ù* ^{m}*E-ḫe-li-ya ki-ma* NÍG$^{!}$.BA-*šu*
17 [ ] ⌜x⌝ SIG$_5$$^{-qá}$ *na-aš-qú-ú*
18 [n M]A.NA *an-na-ku* 3 ANŠE ŠE.MEŠ
19 [UDU$^{?}$ *b*]*á-aq-nu* SAL 1 *en-zù* SAL 1 *ga*$_5$*-zi-iz*
20 [^{m}*E*]*ḫ-li-ya*
21 [*a-na* ^{m}*Te-ḫi-pa*]-*pu i-din*$^{-in}$

Lower Edge

22 [*il-ka ša* A]N.ZA.KÀR
23 [^{m}*Te-ḫi-pa-p*]*u na-ši-i*
24 [^{m}*E*]*ḫ-li-ya la na-a-*[*ši*]

Reverse

25 [*šum-ma* A]N.ZA.KÀR *pí-ir-qa* TUK-*šu*
26 [^{m}*Te-ḫi-pa*]-*pu ú-za-ak-ka*$_4$*-a-ma*
27 [*a-n*]*a* ^{m}*E-ḫe-li-ya*
28 ⌜*i*⌝*-na-an-din*$^{-in}$
29 *ma-an-nu i+na bi*$_4$*-ri-šu-nu*
30 KI.BAL$^{!}$-*tù* 5 MA.NA KÙ.BABBAR
31 5 MA.NA KÙ.SIG$_{17}$ SI.A
32 *um-ma* ^{m}*Te-ḫi-pa-pu*
33 *ṭup-pu ša* AN.ZA.KÀR *ša-šu-ú*
34 *a-na* ^{m}*E-ḫe-li-ya-ma at-ta-din*
35 *ṭup-pí* <*i-na*> EGIR^{-ki} *šu-du-ti*
36 *eš-ši ki-me-e qí-bi-i-ti ša* LUGAL
37 *ša* ITI$^{-ḫi}$ *Ke-nu-na-ti ša* URU-DINGIR.MEŠ
38 *i+na* ITI$^{-ḫi}$ *Mi-ti-ru-ni i-na* URU *Nu-zi*
39 *ša*$_{10}$*-ṭi*$_4$*-ir*
40 IGI *Ka*$_4$*-i-te-šup* DUMU *Ša-ti-ki-tar*
41 IGI *Pa-i-*LUGAL DUMU *Ké-el-te-šup*
42 IGI *Tù-ra-ri-te-šup* DUMU *Ḫu-ur-pu*
43 IGI *Ké-ra-ri-te-šup* DUMU *Tup-ki-ya*
44 4 LÚ *an-nu-tù mu-še-el-mu*$^{!}$ (=BU)

45 *ša* AN.ZA.KÀR *šu-nu-ma na-di-na-nu*
46 *ša*$^{!}$ KÙ.BABBAR
Upper Edge
47 IGI *A-kap-še-en-ni* DUMU *Ḫa-šu-ma-tal*
48 [IG]I *Mi-iš-ša* DUMU *Te-ḫi-ip-til-la*
49 [IGI *M*]*a-at-te-e* DUMU *Na-a-a*
50 [N]A$_4$ *Te-ḫi-pa-pu* EN^{-li} A.ŠÀ
seal impression
seal impression[73]
Left Edge

51 [NA$_4$]-*a* [S.I.$^?$]	NA$_4$ *Pa-i*-LUGAL S.I.	NA$_4$ *Ma-at-te-e* S.I.	N[A$_4$] [S.I.]

EN 9/1, 4

(1–4) [Tablet of] adoption of Teḫip-apu [son of] ...-ki?-ya. He adopted Eḫliya [son of] Ezera.

(4–15) Teḫip-apu gave to Eḫliya as his inheritance share a *dimtu*-tower (with) a well, a plant nursery(??),[74] an orchard, (and) *ḫalaḫwu*-land within the perimeter of the *dimtu*-tower—its perimeter is n?+2 hundred 20 cubits. (The *dimtu*-tower) is to the north of the *dimtu*-tower of Unap-tae, to the south of the field of Šurukkaya, to the east of Unap-tae (*sic*), (and) to the west of Unap-tae (*sic*) as well.

(16–21) And Eḫliya gave ... [to] Teḫip-apu, as his gift, fine, chosen(??) ..., n minas of tin, 3 homers of barley, 1 ewe(?), plucked, (and) 1 she-goat, shorn.

(22–24) The [*ilku* of] the *dimtu*-tower Teḫip-apu shall bear; Eḫliya shall not bear (it).

(25–28) [Should] the *dimtu*-tower have a claim (against it), Teḫip-apu shall clear (the *dimtu*-tower) and give (it) to Eḫliya.

(29–31) Whoever between them abrogates (this contract) shall pay 5 minas of silver (and) 5 minas of gold.

(32–34) Thus Teḫip-apu: "I have also given to Eḫliya the tablet of (i.e., pertaining to) that *dimtu*-tower."

(35–39) (This) tablet was written in the month of Mitirunni (i.e., January/February)[75] in Nuzi, after the new proclamation, in accordance with the king's command of the month of Kenūnati (i.e., possibly November/December)[76] of/in Āl-ilāni.

(40–49) Before Kai-tešup son of Šati-kintar; before Pai-šarri son of Kel-tešup; before Turar-tešup son of Ḫurpu; before Kerar-tešup son of Tupkiya. (These) 4 men are the measurers of the *dimtu*-tower; and they are the givers of the silver.[77] Before Akap-šenni son of Ḫašum-atal; before Mišša son of Teḫip-tilla; before Mat-teya son of Naya.

(50–51) Seal of Teḫip-apu, (erstwhile) owner of the land[78] (*seal impression*); (*seal impression*);[79] [seal of] …-a [(*seal impression*?)]; seal of Pai-šenni (*seal impression*); | seal of Mat-teya (*seal impression*); | seal of … [(*seal impression*)]

82. *JEN* II, 206 (JENu 481)

Findspot: Room T15
Publication: Chiera 1930: pl. 184
Edition: Cassin 1938: 155–57

This text is one of many in the Nuzi corpus closely related to other documents. In the present instance, four documents appear tightly bound. Text #88 records that A adopted B and thereby sold real estate to B. *JEN* IV, 400 (not treated in the present volume) has B[80] selling, again through adoption, the same property to C. The present text, text #82, is an adoption text, most likely completing the sale recorded in *JEN* IV, 400. Finally, *JEN* V, 521 (also absent from this volume) describes the receipt of tablets (and, implicitly, the land defined in those tablets) by a grandson of C. Among the tablets are two identified as B's.[81]

The *ilku* obligation here applies to several types of specialized real estate: stables(?), *ḫalaḫwu*-land, and an orchard.

The scribe of this text has committed several errors in wording and spelling. For more on text # 82, see below at text #88.

Obverse

1 *ṭup-pí ma-ru-ti ša* ^{m}*Zi-l*[*i-ya* DUMU *Mil-ki-te-šup*]
2 *ša* ^{m}*Al-ki-ya* DUMU Mil-ki-t[*e-šup*(*-ma*)]
3 *ù ša* ^{m}*Ša-an-ḫa-ri* DUMU *E-en-*[*ša-ku*]
4 [1+]2 $^{LÚ.MEŠ}$ŠEŠ.MEŠ *an-nu-tu*$_{4}$ ^{m}*Te-ḫi-ip-*[*til-la*]
5 DUMU *Pu-ḫi-še-ni a-na ma-ru-ti i-te-ep-*[*šu-uš*]
6 [1$^{?}$+]2 É.ḪÁ.MEŠ *ku-pa-*⸢*ti*⸣ *ri-ḫu-ti*$_{4}$
7 1 ^{GIŠ}APIN A.ŠÀ *ḫa-la-aḫ-wu ri-*⸢*iḫ*⸣*-tu*$_{4}$ *ša* A.ŠÀ.MEŠ
8 *ša ḫa-la-aḫ-wi-ma ša ip-pa-*⸢*na*⸣*-tu*$_{4}$*-*[*ma*]
9 [*š*]*a a-na* ^{m}*Te-ḫi-ip-til-la-ma* SU[M]*-nu*
10 1 ^{GIŠ}APIN GIŠ.SAR *ga*$_{5}$*-bu-um-ma i+na šu-pa-*[*al*]
11 É.ḪÁ.MEŠ *ša* ^{m}*Te-ḫi-ip-til-la-ma*
12 *i+na ša-pa-at a-*⸢*ta*⸣*-ap*$^{!}$*-pí ša* ^{m}*Ki-il-*[*l*]*i*

13 É.ḪÁ.MEŠ *ga*$_{5}$*-bá-ši-na-ma* A.ŠÀ ḪA.LA
14 *ga*$_{5}$*-bá-šu-ma ù* GIŠ.SAR *ga*$_{5}$*-bá-šu-ma*
15 GÌR.MEŠ-*šu-nu uš-te-lu-ma*
16 *ù* GÌR.MEŠ-*šú ša* ^{m}*Te-ḫi-ip-til-la it-ta-ar-*[*ma*$^{?}$] *a-na* ^{m}*Te-ḫi-ip-til-la* SUM-*nu*
17 2 GUD.MEŠ 4 DAL Ì MEŠ *ù* 1 GUN URUDU.MEŠ
18 ^{m}*Te-ḫi-ip-til-la a-na* ^{m}*Zi-li-ya*
19 *a-na* ^{m}*Al-ki-ya ù a-na* ^{m}*Ša-an-ḫa-ri*
20 *ki-i-ma* NÍG.BA.MEŠ-*šu-nu id-di-in* É.ḪÁ.[MEŠ]
21 *šum-ma* A.ŠÀ.MEŠ *ḫa-la-aḫ-wu ù* GIŠ.SAR.MEŠ
22 *pa-qí-ra-na ir-ta-ši* ^{m}*Zi-li-*ya
23 ^{m}*Al-ki-ya ù* ^{m}*Ša-an-ḫa-ri*
24 *ú-za-ak-ku-ma a-na* ^{m}*Te-ḫi-ip-til-la*

Lower Edge

25 *i+na-an-dì-nu il-ka*$_{4}$ *ša* É.ḪÁ.[MEŠ]
26 *ša* A.ŠÀ.MEŠ *ḫa-la-aḫ-wi*
27 *ù ša* GIŠ.SAR.MEŠ ^{m}*Al-ki-ya*

Reverse

28 ^{m}*Zi-li-ya ù* ^{m}*Ša-an-ḫa-ri*
29 *na-a-šu šum-ma* ^{m}*Zi-li-ya*
30 *šum-ma* ^{m}*Al-ki-ya ù šum-ma*
31 ^{m}*Ša-an-ḫa-ri* KI.BAL-*tu*
32 4 MA.NA KÙ.SIG$_{17}$.MEŠ *a-na* ^{m}*Te-ḫi-ip-til-la*
33 *ú-ma-al-lu*

---

34 IGI *A-ri-ḫar-pa* DUMU *E-na-mil-ki*
35 IGI *Te-ḫi-ip-til-la* DUMU *Ḫa-ši-ya*
36 IGI *It-ḫi-zi-iz-*<*za*> DUMU *E-na-mil-ki*
37 IGI *Ḫa-ni-ya-aš-ḫa-ri* DUMU *A-ri-ya*
38 IGI *Šúk-ri-te-šup* DUMU *Kip-ta-li-li*
39 IGI *Še-ka*$_{4}$*-ru* DUMU *Še-el-wi-na-tal*
40 IGI *Wa-an-ti-iš-še* DUMU *Še-el-wi-na-tal*
41 *an-nu-tu*$_{4}$ $^{LÚ.MEŠ}$*mu-še-le-mu ša* É.ḪÁ.MEŠ
42 *ša* A.ŠÀ.MEŠ *ḫa-la-aḫ-wi ù ša* GIŠ.SAR.MEŠ
(an erased line)
43 IGI *A-ka*$_{4}$*-la-a-*<*a*> DUMU *Ké-en-ni* IGI *Tup-ki-iz-z*[*a*]
44 IGI DINGIR-*ma*-ŠEŠ DUMU *Ḫa-na-an-na-a-*<*a*$^{?}$> : DUMU *Ar-zi-*[*iz-za*]
45 IGI *It-ḫa-pí-ḫe* DUMU *Ta-a-a* DUB.SAR
46 *an-nu-tu*$_{4}$ IGI.MEŠ-*tu*$_{4}$ *ga*$_{5}$*-bá-šu-nu-ma*
47 GUD.MEŠ Ì.MEŠ URUDU.MEŠ *i-di-nu*

48 $^{\mathrm{NA_4}}$KIŠIB ^{m}*Tup-ki-iz-za* DUMU *Ar-zi-iz-za*
49 $^{\mathrm{NA_4}}$KIŠIB ^{m}*I-li-ma-hi* DUMU *Ḫa-na-<an-na>-a-a*
50 $^{\mathrm{NA_4}}$KIŠIB ^{m}*Te-ḫi-ip-til-la* ^{LÚ}NUN.⸢Z⸣A-*tu*$_4$
51[82] $^{\mathrm{NA_4}}$KIŠIB ^{m}*It-ḫi-zi-iz-za* DUMU *E-na-mil-ki*
52 $^{\mathrm{NA_4}}$KIŠIB DUB.SAR

JEN II, 206

(1–5) Tablet of adoption of Ziliya [son of Milki-tešup], of Alkiya son of Milki-tešup, and of Šamḫari son of En-[šaku]. These [1+] 2 brothers[83] adopted Teḫip-tilla son of Puḫi-šenni.

(6–16) They gave to Teḫip-tilla the [1? +] 2 remaining stables(?),[84] .1 homer of *ḫalaḫwu*-land, (being) the remainder of the *ḫalaḫwu*-land which had already been given to Teḫip-tilla, (and) a .1 homer orchard, all (of these) (?) (lying) to the west of the buildings of Teḫip-tilla too (i.e., like the real estate already given), by the bank of the Killi Canal, having ceded their own claim (lit. "they lifted their foot") and confirmed Teḫip-tilla's claim (lit. "Teḫip-tilla's foot returned [i.e., came down]") (to) all the structures, all the land (comprising) the inheritance share,[85] and the entire orchard.

(17–20) Teḫip-tilla gave to Ziliya, to Alkiya, and to Šamḫari as their gifts, 2 oxen, 4 pots[86] of oil, and 1 talent of copper.

(20–25) Should the structures, *ḫalaḫwu*-land (lit. "the structures, should the *ḫalaḫwu*-land"[87]), (and) orchard have claimants, Ziliya, Alkiya, and Šamḫari shall clear (these properties) and give (them) to Teḫip-tilla.

(26–29) The *ilku* of the structures, of the *ḫalaḫwu*-land, and of the orchard Alkiya, Ziliya, and Šamḫari shall bear.

(29–33) Should Ziliya, should Alkiya, and should Šamḫari abrogate (this contract), they shall pay to Teḫip-tilla 4 minas of gold.[88]

(34–47) Before Ariḫ-ḫarpa son of Enna-milki; before Teḫip-tilla son of Ḫašiya; before Itḫi-zizza son of Enna-milki; before Ḫaniašḫari son of Ariya; before Šukri-tešup son of Kip-talili; before Šekaru son of Šelwin-atal; before Wantiš-še son of Šelwin-atal. These are the measurers of the structures, of the *ḫalaḫwu*-land, and of the orchard.

(erased line)

Before Akalaya son of Kenni; before Tupkiya son of Ar-zizza; before Ilima-aḫi son of Ḫanannaya; before Itḫ-apiḫe son of Taya, scribe. These are all the witnesses, and they gave the oxen, the oil, (and) the copper.

(48–52[89]) Seal impression of Tupkizza son of Ar-zizza; seal impression of Ili-ma-aḫi son of Ḫanannaya; seal impression of Teḫip-tilla, the …; seal impression of Itḫi-zizza son of Enna-milki; seal impression of the scribe.

83. HSS XIII, 143 (SMN 143)

Findspot: No room number
Publication: Pfeiffer and Lacheman 1942: 24[90]
Edition: None

This is another real estate adoption demonstrating that still more kinds of real estate are subject to the *ilku*. Here the categories are similar to those found in text #81, but privately owned threshing floors are here attested as well. Of interest as well, though not directly germane to the theme of this chapter, the seller alienates the property on behalf of his still-living father. This seems to be stated in lines 11–17. Further, the *ilku* is defined as attaching to land belonging to the seller's father (lines 24–26). The father may be incapacitated though. This is shown by the following. Not only is it the son who alienates the real estate, but, in stating that the purchaser is to bear the *ilku*, the text further specifies that the son (i.e., the seller) shall not bear it. The father's legal status of *ilku*-bearer has somehow been compromised.

Obverse

1 *ṭup-pí ma-ru-ti ša* [^{m}*E-wa-a-a*]
2 DUMU *Ar-zi-iz-za ù* [^{m}*Ni-iḫ-ri-ya*]
3 DUMU *Ḫu-zi-ri a-na ma-*[*ru-ti i-te-pu-uš*]
5 *um-ma* ^{m}*E-wa-a-a-*[*ma*]
5 *mi-nu-um-me-e* A.ŠÀ.MEŠ-*ya*
6?[91] É.ḪÁ.MEŠ-*ya ma-ag-ra-at-tù-ya*
7 *ḫa-wa-al-ḫu-ya* PÚ.MEŠ
8 GIŠ.SAR-*ya* AN.ZA.KÀR-*ya*
9 *i-na* URU *Nu-zi ù i-na* URU.DIDLI.MEŠ
10 *ki-ma* ḪA.LA-*šu a-na* ^{m}*Ni-iḫ-ri-ya*
11 [*at-ta*]-*din-mi ù* GÌR-*ya*
12 [*iš-tu* A.ŠÀ.MEŠ] *ù iš-tu* [É.ḪÁ.MEŠ]
13 [*ša* ^{m}*Ar-zi*]-*iz-za a-*[*bi-ya*]
14 *uš-te-li-mi ù* GÌR-*šu*
15 *ša* ^{m}*Ni-*[*iḫ*]-*ri-ya i-na* A.ŠÀ.MEŠ
16 *ù i-na* É.ḪÁ.MEŠ *ša* ^{m}*Ar-*[*zi-iz*]-*za a-bi-ya*

17 *aš-ta-ka*$_4$*-an-mi ù mi-nu-um-me-e*
18 A.ŠÀ.MEŠ É.ḪÁ.MEŠ AN.ZA.K[ÀR-*š*]*u*
19 *ma-ag-ra-at-*[*tù-šu*]
20 PÚ-*šu* GIŠ.SAR-*šu ù ḫa-*[*al*]*-wa-ḫi-šu*
21 *ša* ^{m}*Ar-zi-iz-za a-bi-ya*
22 *i-na* URU *Nu-zi ù i-na* URU.DIDLI.MEŠ
23 *a-na* ^{m}*Ni-iḫ-ri-ya at-ta-din*
24 *ù il-ku ša* A.ŠÀ.MEŠ *ù ša* É.MEŠ
25 *ša* ^{m}*Ar-zi-iz-za* ^{m}*Ni-iḫ-ri-ya-ma*
26 *na-ši ù* ^{m}*E-wa-a-a-ma la* [*na-ši*]
Lower Edge
27 *um-ma* ^{m}*E-wa-a-a-ma*
28 *ṭup-pu ša ši-mu-*<*ma*>*-ki*
29 *ša* ^{m}*Ar-zi-iz-za a-bi-ya*
Reverse
30 *a-na* ^{m}*Ni-iḫ-ri-ya-ma*
31 *at-ta-din-mi*
32 *ma-an-nu-um-me-e i-na bi*$_4$-[*ri-šu-nu*]
33 *ša* KI.BAL$^{-kát}$ 5 MA.NA [KÙ.BABBAR]
34 5 MA.NA KÙ.SIG$_{17}$ *ú-ma-al-la*
35 *ṭup-pí i-na* EGIR^{-ki} [*šu*]*-du-ti*
36 *i-na* KÁ KÁ.[GAL *š*]*a* URU *Nu-zi ša*$_{10}$*-ṭi*$_4$*-ir*
37 IGI *Pal-*[*te-e-a* DUMU]*-ip-pí-ya*
38 IGI *Ta-*[x x x] DUMU *Zi-iz-za-e*
39 IGI *Zi-*[*líp-*LUGAL] DUMU *A-ku-še-en-ni*
40 IGI *Ak-*[*ku*]*-ya* DUMU *Mu-uš-te-e-a*
41 IGI *Ša-ma-ḫul* DUMU *It-ḫi-ip-*LUGAL
42 IGI ^{d}[XXX]*-a-bu* IGI *Še-ka*$_4$*-an*
43 ⸢DUMU⸣.[MEŠ]*-ki-til-la*
44 [IGI] *Ḫa-ni-ku-*[*u*]*z-zi* DUMU *Na-an-te-šup*
45 [IGI] *Ḫé-er-ri-*[*ya*] DUMU *Ša-a*[*r-ri-ya*]
46 [IGI] *Nu-ul-lu* [DUMU] *Ḫa-na-tu*$_4$
47 IGI *Tù-ra-ar-*[*te*]*-šup* DUB.SAR$^{-rù}$ DUMU *Ké-e*[*l-t*]*e-šup*
48 IGI *Pu-ḫi-še-en-ni* DUMU ⸢*A*⸣*-i-ti-ya*
49 ^{LÚ}*ma-ṣar* KÁ.GAL
50 NA$_4$ ^{m}*Pu-ḫi-še-en-ni* ^{LÚ}*ma-ṣar* KÁ.GAL
51 NA$_4$ ^{m}*Še-ka*$_4$*-an* NA$_4$ ^{m}*Nu-ul-lu*
52 NA$_4$ ^{m}*Pal-te-e-a* NA$_4$ ^{m} *Ša-*[*ma*?*-ḫul*?]
Upper Edge
53 NA$_4$ ^{md}[XXX*-a-bu*]

Left Edge

54 NA_4 ᵐ *Ak-ku-ya* NA_4 ᵐ*Ḫa-ni-ku-uz-zi*

55 NA_4 ᵐ*Zi-líp*-LUGAL NA_4 ᵐ*Ša-ma-ḫul*

HSS XIII, 143

(1–3) Tablet of adoption of [Ewaya] son of Ar-zizza. Now he adopted [Niḫriya] son of Ḫuziri.

(4–11) Thus Ewaya:[92] "I have given to Niḫriya as his inheritance share all my fields, my structures, my threshing floors, my *ḫawalḫu*-land, wells, my (entire) orchard, my (whole) *dimtu*-tower, (all) in (i.e., in the jurisdiction of) the town of Nuzi, and in (its) outlying(?) settlements.

(11–17) "And I have ceded my claim (lit. "I have lifted my foot") [to the fields] and to [the structures of] Ar-zizza, my father, and I have confirmed Niḫriya's claim to (lit. "I have set Niḫriya's foot upon") the fields and the structures of Ar-zizza, my father.

(17–23) "I have (therefore) given to Niḫriya all the fields, the structures, his (i.e., my father's) *dimtu*-tower, [his] threshing floor, his well, his orchard, and his *ḫalwaḫu*-land, (that is, the properties) of Ar-zizza, my father, in the town of Nuzi and in (its) outlying(?) settlements."

(24–26) Now the *ilku* of the fields and of the structures of Ar-zizza, Niḫriya shall bear, and Ewaya shall not [bear].

(27–31) Thus Ewaya: "I have also given to Niḫriya the tablet containing the testamentary dispositions of Ar-zizza, my father."[93]

(32–34) Whoever between them (i.e., between Ewaya and Niḫriya) abrogates (this contract) shall pay 5 minas of gold.

(35–36) The tablet was written after the proclamation at the city gate of Nuzi.

(37–49) Before Pal-teya son of …-ippiya; before Ta-… son of Zizzae; before Zi-… son of Aku-šenni; before Akkuya son of Muš-teya; before Šamaḫul son of Itḫip-šarri; before [Sin]-abu (and) before Šekan son[s] of …-ki-tilla; before Ḫanikuzzi son of Nan-tešup; before Ḫerriya son of Šarriya; before Nullu [son of] Ḫanatu; before Turar-tešup, scribe, son of Kel-tešup; before Puḫi-šenni son of Aitiya, gatekeeper.

(50–55)[94] Seal of Puḫi-šenni, gatekeeper; seal of Šekan; seal of Nullu; seal of Pal-teya; seal of Ša[maḫul??];[95] seal of [Sin-abu];[96] seal of Akkuya; seal of Ḫanikuzzi; seal of Zilip-šarri; seal of Šamaḫul.

84. *JEN* V, 552 (JENu 447)

Findspot: Room T15
Publication: Chiera 1934b: pl. 505
Edition: None[97]

This document is among the oldest of the Late Bronze Age Nuzi texts. It was commissioned by the father of Nuzi's most prosperous landlord, Teḫip-tilla son of Puḫi-šenni. In it he buys a large amount of land. He acquires the real estate for the eventual benefit of his children by his wife Winnirke. Those children were Teḫip-tilla and his younger brother, Ḫaiš-tešup (at least).

The simplest interpretation of this text is that it is a straight sale.[98] To be sure, a key term, *irana*, representing the amount of money given over in exchange for the land, is not entirely clear. It is either "gift" or "price."[99] In the present context, the difference is immaterial.[100] This is a cash-for-land transaction. Wilhelm 1992b: 504 maintains that this is a false adoption text, albeit of an idiosyncratic kind. It is atypical because it is early and the later standard formulary is not yet in place. However, this is not a reasonable interpretation. The standard formulary of adoption is already present in very early texts.[101] That this document has absolutely none of the terminology of a real estate adoption or, for that matter, any other kind of adoption, means that none was implicitly intended. A later generation may have especially preferred the verbal garb of adoption to expedite land transfer, but that says nothing about the format of our document.

Obverse

1 ^{m}*Pu-ḫi-še-ni* DUMU *Tu-ri-še-ni*
2 1 GÍN KÙ.SIG$_{17}$ *i-ra-na*
3 *a+na Ú-na-ap-ta-e*
4 *a+na Al-pu-ya*
5 *a+na A-ri-ma*$^{!}$*-at-ka*$_{4}$
6 3 DUMU.MEŠ *Ḫa-nu-ya*
it-ta-ad-na-šu-nu-ti-ma
7 1 *ma-a-at* ANŠE A.ŠÀ.ḪÁ
8 [*a-ša*]*r* D⸢UM⸣ [U.MEŠ] *Ḫa-nu-ya il-te-qè*
9 *ù* ⸢*Pu-ḫi-še-ni*[102] *a*⸣-[*n*]*a* DUMU.MEŠ-*šu*
10 [*ṣ*]*e-ḫe-ru-t*⸢*i š*⸣*a* ^{f}*Wi*$_{4}$*-ni-ir-ké*
11 A.ŠÀ.ḪÁ GIŠ.ŠAR *i+na Na-at-ma-né* SUM
12 IGI ^{d}MAR.TU-LUGAL-DINGIR DUB.SAR
13 IGI *A-nu-pir-ra* DUMU ÌR-É-*ti*
14 IGI *Ar-nu-úr-ḫe* SANGA

DUMU *Ar-ta-še-ni*
15 IGI *Wa-ar-*˹*di*˺?*-ya*
DUMU *Nu*?-˹*i*˺?-[*še*?-*r*]*i*?
Reverse
16 IGI *A-kà-wa*$_6$*-ti*$_4$*-il*
DUMU *Pí-zi-ya*
17 IGI *Šu-ma-li-a*
DUMU *Pa-am-ku*$_8$*-rù*
18 IGI DINGIR-KAM DUMU *Tá-an-n*[*a*]-˹*tàš*˺*-ši*[103]
19 IGI *In-bi*-DINGIR-*šu*
DUMU *Ta-ri-ba-tu*$_4$
20 IGI *Ar-ra-ap-ḫa-tal*
21 DUMU *Ar-*˹*ša*˺!*-lì*
22 IGI *A-kà-we*$_4$
DUMU *Ku-un-nu*
23 IGI *Ta-ri-ba-tu*$_4$ *ma-la-ḫu*
24 IGI *Ip-ša-ha-lu* DUMU É.GAL

JEN V, 552

(1–6) Puḫi-šenni son of Tur-šenni gave to Unap-tae, to Alpuya, (and) to Arim-matka, 3 sons of Ḫanuya, 1 sheqel of gold, (as) the price (or "gift").

(7–11) He (i.e., Puḫi-šenni) took 1 hundred homers of land from the sons of Ḫanuya. And Puḫi-šenni gave fields and orchard-land in (the town of) Natmane to his sons, the youngsters of ^{f}Winnirke.[104]

(12–24) Before Amurru-šarr-ilī, scribe; before Anupirra son of Warad-bîti (or: "son of a palace slave"); before Arn-urḫe, (chief?) temple administrator, son of Artašenni; before Wardiya(?) son of Nui-šeri(?); before Akawatil son of Piziya; before Šumaliya son of Pamkuru; before Ilu-êriš son of Tanna-tašši; before Inb-ilišu son of Tarîbatu; before Arrapḫa-atal son of Ar-šali; before Akawe son of Kunnu; before Tarîbatu, a boatman; before Ipša-ḫalu "son of the palace."

85. HSS V, 57 (SMN 335)

Findspot: Room A34
Publication: Chiera 1929: pl. 52
Editions: Speiser 1930: 37[105]; Cassin 1938: 294–95

Fincke 1993: 345 calls this a false adoption. This is incorrect. The document has the typical hallmarks of a genuine adoption: filial service to the adopting father, eventual (not immediate) inheritance as a post-mortem provision, and so on. The *ilku* here is an inherited obligation attaching to inherited real estate. Note that the adopted son may choose not to bear the *ilku*. However, should he exercise this option, he forfeits the land he otherwise would inherit (lines 11–14). For further on the *pater familias*, Bêlaya son of Kip-tae, see below, text #94.

Obverse

1 *ṭup-pí ma-ru-ti ša* ^{m}*E-te-eš-še-en-ni*

2 DUMU *Na-ni-ya* DUMU-*šu* ^{m}*Pal-te-šup*

3 *a-na ma-ru-ti a-na* ^{m}*Be-la-a-a*

4 DUMU *Kip-ta-e* SUM-*nu ù* ^{m}*Be-la-a-a*

5 ^{m}*Pal-te-šup* DAM *ú-ša-aḫ-*<*ḫa*>*-az-zú*

6 *ù a-du*$_4$ ^{m}*Be-la-a-a bal-ṭù*

7 *ù* ^{m}*Pal-te-šup i-pal-la-aḫ-šu*

8 *im-ma-ti-me-e* ^{m}*Be-la-a-a im-tù-ut*

9 *ù* ^{m}*Pal-te-šup* DAM-*sú ka*$_4$*-dù še-er-ri-šu*

10 *ù* 2 ANŠE A.ŠÀ.MEŠ AŠ URU *Za-mi-te i-le-eq-qè*

11 *ù šu-ú il-ka*$_4$ *it-ti* DUMU.MEŠ ^{m}*Be-la-a-a*

12 *na-ši ù šum-ma la na-ši*

13 DAM-*sú ù še-er-ra-šu i-le-eq-qè*

14 *ù* A.ŠÀ.MEŠ *i-iz-zi-ib ù ú-uṣ-ṣí*

15 [*ma*]*-an-nu-um-me-e* AŠ *bi*$_4$*-ri-šu-nu*

16 [KI].BAL-*tù* 6 GUD.MEŠ SIG$_5$-*qá ú-ma-al-la*

17 [*ṭu*]*p-*⸢*p*⸣*í* AŠ EGIR *šu-du-ti*

18 [AŠ] URU *Nu-zi* AŠ *bá-ab* KÁ.GAL

19 *ša-ṭì-ir*

20 IGI ^{d}XXX^{-ir}*-ra-me-ni* DUMU E-⸢*ri*⸣*-šu*

21 IGI DÙG.GA-*Ar-*«*ar*»*-ra-ap-ḫé*
DUMU *Ka*$_4$*-pí-in-ni*

Lower Edge

22 IGI *Ku-un-nu-ya a-bu-ul-ta-nu*

23 IGI *E-ḫé-el-te-šup* DUMU *Ta-i-še-*[*en-ni*]

Reverse

24 IGI *Ku-uš-ši-ya* DUMU *Ki-iz-zi-ri*

25 IGI *A-kap-še-en-ni* DUMU *Zi-ké*

26 IGI *Šúk-ri-ya* DUMU XXX-*nap-šìr* DUB.SAR

27 NA$_4$ ^{m}*Ku-uš-si-ya* NA$_4$ ^{m}*E-ḫé-el-te-šup*

28 NA$_4$ ^{m}*Ku-un-nu-ya* NA$_4$ ^{md}XXX^{-ir}*-ra-me-ni*

29 NA$_4$ ^{m}DÙG.GA-*ar-ra-ap-ḫé* NA$_4$ ^{m}*A-kap-še-en-ni*
30 NA$_4$ ^{m}*Š*⌈*úk*⌉*-ri-ya* DUB.SAR

HSS V, 57

(1–4) Tablet of adoption of Eteš-šenni son of Naniya. He gave his son, Pal-tešup, into adoption to Bêlaya son of Kip-tae.

(4–5) And Bêlaya shall obtain a wife (for) Pal-tešup.

(6–7) And as long as Bêlaya shall live, Pal-tešup shall "fear"[106] him.

(8–10) When Bêlaya shall have died, Pal-tešup shall take his wife (i.e., his own wife), together with his children , and a 2 homer field in the town of Zamite.

(11–14) Also *he*[107] shall bear the *ilku* together with the (other) sons of Bêlaya. But if he does not bear (it), he shall take (only) his wife and his children. But he shall forfeit the field and he shall leave (Bêlaya's household).

(15–16) Whoever amongst them abrogates (this contract) shall pay six fine oxen.

(17–19) The tablet was written after the proclamation [in] the town of Nuzi at the (city) gate.

(20–26) Before Sin-rêmēnī son of Êrišu; before Ṭâb-arrapḫe son of Kap-inni; before Kunnuya, a gatekeeper; before Eḫli-tešup son of Tai-šenni; before Kuššiya son of Kizziri; before Akap-šenni son of Zike; before Šukriya son of Sin-napšir, scribe.

(27–30) Seal of Kuššiya; seal of Eḫli-tešup; seal of Kunnuya; seal of Sin-rêmēnī; seal of Ṭâb-arrapḫe; seal of Akap-šenni; seal of Šukriya, the scribe.

86. *JEN* V, 467 (JENu 139)

Findspot: Room T16
Publication: Chiera 1934b: pls. 444–445[108]
Edition: None

This agreement establishes the following. The sale of land to five individuals stands. The son of the vendor raised objections to the sale, a sale which he admits had taken place. Subsequently he dropped his claim. The *ilku*, he declares, is still his to bear.[109]

Text #86 is, in terms of legal formulas, a rather freewheeling document. It contains multiple declarations (by one party), including quotation within quotation, interspersed with background information (see especially lines 9–11). To the extent that a court case is involved, the claimant is said to offer no corroborating evidence; nor does he consent to undergo an ordeal to establish his truthfulness. This is not a transcript. Rather it is primarily an account of the result, and the trial process itself is inadequately represented. This is typical of Nuzi "trial texts." See, for example, text #61. For more on Keliya son of Un-tešup (line 6), see text #95.

Obverse

1 *ṭu*[*p-pí*] *tam-gu*$_5$*-ur-ti ša*
2 ^{m}*M*[*i*]*-na-aš-šúk* DUMU *Za-zi-ya*
3 *it-*[*t*]i ^{m}*Še-eḫ-li-ya* DUMU *A-ka*$_4$*-*[*a-a*]
4 ⸢*ù*⸣ *it-ti* ^{m}*Zi-ké* DUMU *Ta-m*[*ar*]*-ta-e*
5 *it-ti* ^{m}DINGIR-*ni-šu* DUMU *E-ni-y*[*a*]
6 *it-ti* ^{m}*Ké-li-ya* DUMU *Un-te-š* [*up*]
7 *ù it-ti* ^{m}*Šúk-ri-ya* DUMU *Ma-*⸢*li-ya*⸣
8 *it-ta-am-*⸢*ga*$_{14}$⸣*-ru*
9 5 ANŠE A.ŠÀ.MEŠ *i+na ša-pát a-tap-pí Ni-ra-aš-*[*še*$_{20}$]
10 *i+na le-et* A.ŠÀ ^{m}*Ḫu-ti*$_4$*-ya* DUMU *Me-le-ya*
11 *i+na* ^{IM}*su-ti-it* KASKAL *ša* URU *Tar-ku-*[*ul-l*]*i*
12 *um-ma* ^{m}*Mi-na-aš-šúk-ma*
13 ^{m}*Za-zi-ya-ma a-bu-ya* 5 ŠEŠ.MEŠ *an-nu-ti*
14 *a-na ma-ru-ti* ⸢*i*⸣*-pu-us-sú-nu-ti*
15 *ù* 5 ANŠE A.ŠÀ.MEŠ *ša-a-šu ki-ma* ḪA.LA-*šu id-din*
16 *ù um-ma* ^{m}*Mi-na-aš-šúk-ma*
17 *ù i+na-an-na a-na-ku i+na* EGIR A.ŠÀ *ša-a-šu*
18 *al-ta-sí ù a-na pa-ni* DI.KU$_5$.MEŠ
19 *e-te-li* (erasure) *ù* DI.KU$_5$.MEŠ *a-na ya-ši*
20 *iq-ta-bu-ú* (erasure)
21 $^{LÚ.MEŠ}$*mu-de*$_4$*-e-ka le-qà-am-mi*
22 [*k*]*i-me-e i+na* EGIR A.ŠÀ *ta-al-t*[*a-sí*]
23 ⸢*ù*⸣ $^{LÚ.MEŠ}$*mu-du-ú-ya ya-nu*
24 ⸢*ù*⸣ D[I.K]U$_5$.MEŠ *iq-ta-bu-ú* A.ŠÀ [ ]
25 *šu-ku*$^{!}$*-*⸢*un*⸣$^{?}$*-mi ù i+na* ^{Í}⸢^{D}⸣*ḫur-ša-*[*a*]*n*
26 *a-li-*[*i*]*k-mi* (erasure) [EME-*šu*[110]]
27 *ša* ^{m}*Mi-na-aš-šúk a-na pa-*⸢*ni*⸣

Lower Edge

28 IGI.MEŠ [*i*]*q-ta-bi a-na* [^{ÍD}*ḫur-ša-an*[111]]
29 *a-na a-*[*l*]*a-ki qa-ba-ku* ⸢*ù*⸣
la a-al-la-a[*k*]

Reverse

30 *i-te* A.[Š]À$^{?}$.MEŠ⸢*ki*⸣*-ma a-na* 5 ŠE[Š.MEŠ *iddin*[112]]

31 [*ù*] *i+na-an-na* ᵐ*Mi-na-aš-šúk* ⌈*a*⌉?-[*na pa-ni*]

32 IGI.MEŠ *it-tam-gàr-ma* A.ŠÀ.MEŠ *a-na* ŠEŠ.[MEŠ]

33 *ša i+na* DAL.BA.NA-*šu-nu* KI.BAL-*t*[*u*]

34 2 MA.NA KÙ.BABBAR 2 MA.NA KÙ.SIG₁₇ ⌈*ù*⌉?-[*ma-al-la*/-*lu*]

35 *ù* ⌈EME⌉-*šu ša* ᵐ (followed by an erased DIŠ) *Mi-na-aš-šúk iq-t*[*a-bi il-ku*/*a*]

36 *ša* A.ŠÀ *ša-*⌈*a*⌉-*šu a-na-ku-ma na-ša-ak-šú*

37 IGI *Ni-ir-ḫi-til-la* DUMU *Ar-ru-u*[*m-*]

38 IGI *Tù-ra-ri* DUMU *E-mu-ya*

39 IGI *Zi-li-ya* DUMU *Tup-ki-ya*

40 IGI *A-al-te-šup* DUMU *Šu-um-mi-*[*ya*]

41 IGI *Ut-ḫap-ta-e* DUMU *Zi-ké*

42 IGI *Na-aš-wi* DUMU *Ka₄-lu-li*

43 IGI *Wa-qar*-EN DUMU *Ar-te-ya*

44 IGI *Wa-an-ti₄-ya* DUMU *Na-ḫi-a-šu*

45 IGI *Ké-eš₁₅-ḫa-a-a* DUMU *Ki-in-ni-ya*

46 IGI *Ta-a-a* DUMU *Ni-nu-a-tal*

47 IGI *Ni-iḫ-ri-ya* DUMU *Ka-lu-li*

48 IGI *Ḫa*¹¹³-*na-ak-ka₄* DUMU *Še-ka₄-ru*

49 IGI *Ḫé-šal-la* DUMU *Zu-ú-me*

50 IGI *Sí-ir-ra-me-ni* DUMU *E-ri-*⌈*š*⌉*u*

51 IGI *Ma-at-te-šup* DUMU *Pa-zi-ya*

52 IGI LUGAL-XXX DUMU *Ta-ak-ka₄-r*[*a*]-⌈*a*⌉-*a*

53 IGI MU-GÁL-*ši* DUMU *Ta-a-a* DUB.SAR

54 NA₄ ᵐ*Ni-ir-ḫi-til-la* NA₄ ᵐ*Ma-at-te-šup*

55 NA₄ ᵐ*Zi-li-ya* NA₄ ᵐ*Tù-ra-ri*

56 ᴺᴬ⁴KIŠIB ᵐ MU-GÁL-*ši* DUB.SAR

57 ᴺᴬ⁴KIŠIB ᵐ*Ḫa-na-ak-ka₄*

58 ᴺᴬ⁴KIŠIB ᵐ*Wa-an-ti₄-ya*

59 NA₄ ᵐ*Ut-ḫap-ta-e*

JEN V, 467

(1–8) Tablet of agreement of Minaš-šuk son of Zaziya. He (lit. they) reached an agreement with Šeḫliya son of Akaya, and with Zike, son of Tamar-tae, with Ila-nîšū son of Eniya, with Keliya son of Un-tešup, and with Šukriya son of Maliya.

(9–11) (The issue is) a 5 homer field by the bank of the Nirašše Canal, adjoining a field belonging to Ḫutiya son of Meleya to the south(!)[114] of the road of (i.e., leading to) the town of Tarkulli.

(12–29) Thus Minaš-šuk: "My father adopted these 5 brothers.[115] And he gave as his inheritance share (to them) that 5 homer field."

And thus Minaš-šuk, further: "But just now I raised a claim against that field and went to court (lit. went up before the judges). And the judges said to me: 'Summon your expert witnesses inasmuch as you have raised a claim against the field.' But I had no expert witnesses. Then the judges said: 'Settle(?) (the matter of) the ... field by going to the "ḫuršan" river[116].'"

[The declaration] of Minaš-šuk before witnesses. He said: "I am ordered[117] to go to the ['ḫuršan' river], but I shall not go."

(30–32) Since he gave the border(??) of the land to the 5 brothers, [so] now Minaš-šuk has agreed (to this) [before] witnesses: The land is (indeed) the brother[s]'.

(33–34) Who amongst them abrogates (this agreement) shall pay 2 minas of silver (and) 2 minas of gold.

(35–36) And (this is) a declaration of Minaš-šuk. He said: "It is I who bears [the *ilku*[118]] of that field."

(37–53) Before Niḫri-tilla son of Arrum-...; before Turari son of Emuya; before Ziliya son of Tupkiya; before Al-tešup son of Šummiya; before Utḫap-tae son of Zike; before Našwi son of Kalūli; before Waqar-bêli son of Ar-teya; before Wantiya son of Naḫi-ašu; before Kešḫaya son of Kinniya; before Taya son of Ninu-atal; before Niḫriya son of Kalūli; before Ḫanakka son of Šekaru; before Ḫešalla son of Zume; before Sin-rêmēnī son of Êrišu; before Mat-tešup son of Paziya; before Šarru-sin son of Takkaraya; before Šumu-libšī son of Taya, scribe.

(54–59)[119] Seal of Niḫri-tilla; seal of Mat-tešup; seal of Ziliya; seal of Turari; seal impression of Šumu-libšī, the scribe; seal impression of Ḫanakka; seal impression of Wantiya; seal of Utḫap-tae.

87. *JEN* ,VII, 699 (JENu 65)

Findspot : Room T15
Publication : Lacheman and Maidman 1989: 87–88
Edition : Maidman 1994: 100–107[120]

Text #87 is a complicated document with connections to text #86 (see immediately below) and to *JEN* V, 508. Further elucidation of these texts and their complexities are found in Maidman 1994: 100–107. And *those* remarks far from exhaust the implications and possibilities contained in these texts.[121]

The text focuses on a pair of declarations. In the first, a group of men state that their "fathers" gave land to Teḫip-tilla son of Puḫi-šenni.[122] They themselves appear to reconfirm that transaction. The second declaration, by one man, is similar. Since this man had once been a co-owner of that land, one wonders why he was not included in the first declaration.[123] Then witnesses are noted. Atypically, only after the witnesses are named is there an *ilku* clause and a clear-title clause. Then, sealings and the names of the sealers appear. The identity of the scribe ends the document.

Although text #87 is badly damaged, enough is preserved (and more is amenable to reconstruction) to demonstrate important connections to text #86. The same land is involved. And the recipients of the land in text #86 are, *for the most part*, those who cede their rights to the land in text #87.[124] (Both tablets were recovered from the family archive of the ultimate recipient of the land, mentioned in text #87, the aforementioned Teḫip-tilla.) And for the purposes of this chapter, note well that, despite the assertion in text #86 that Minaš-šuk (son of Zaziya) retains the *ilku* impost for that land (text #86:35–36), by the time the land is transferred again, it is not Minaš-šuk who bears the *ilku* but those to whom his father had sold (and to whom he himself ratified the sale of) the land (text #87:46–47). The *ilku* was alienated as was the land to which it was linked.

Obverse

1 [EME-*šu ša* ^{m}*Še-eḫ-li*]-⸢*y*⸣*a* DUM⸢U⸣ *A*$^{!?}$-*k*[*a*$^{?}$-*a-a*]
2 [EME-*šu*] ⸢*ša*⸣ [^{m}]*Ḫu-ti-*[*ya ù* EME]- ⸢*š*⸣*u* ⸢*ša*⸣ [^{m}*Ar-te-ya*]
3 [EME-*šu*] *ša* ^{m}*Zi-k*[*é ù* EM]E-*šu* [*ša* ^{m}*A-ta-a-a*]
4 [(*ù*) EME-*šu ša* ^{m}*Ki-pí*]-*ya* DUMU.MEŠ ^{m}*T*[*a-mar-t*]*a*-⸢*e*⸣
5 [EME-*šu*] *ša* ^{m}*Šúk-ri-ya* ⸢*ù*⸣ [E]ME-*šu*
6 [*ša* ^{m}*Ḫ*]*a-ip*-LUGAL DUMU.MEŠ ^{m}*Ma-*[*l*]*i-ya*
7 [(*ù*) EME]-*šu ša* ^{m}*Eḫ-l*[*i*]-⸢*y*⸣*a* DU[MU] *Ak-ku-*[*le-en-ni*]
8 [*um-ma*]⸢ŠEŠ⸣.MEŠ *an-nu-tu*$_{4}$-[*m*]*a*
9 [*i-na pa*]-*na-nu-ma a-bu-ni-*[*m*]*i* 5 ANŠE [A.ŠÀ.MEŠ]
10 [*ša* ^{m}*M*]*i-na-aš-šúk* [D]UMU ⸢*Za*⸣-[*z*]*i-ya*
11 [*i-na š*]*a-pá-at a-tap-p*[*í N*]*i-ra-aš-*[*še*$_{20}$]
12 [*i-na le*]-*et* A.ŠÀ.MEŠ [*ša* ^{m}]*Ḫu-ti-ya*
13 [DUMU *Me-l*]*e-ya i-na* KASKAL.MEŠ-[*n*]*i ša* URU
14 [*Ta-a*]*r-ku-ul-li* ⸢*i-n*⸣*a*$^{\ulcorner \mathrm{IM} \urcorner ?}$ *sú*$^{!?}$-*ta*$^{!?}$-*ni*[125]
15 [*a-na* ^{m}*T*]*e-ḫi-ip-til-l*[*a*] DU[MU *P*]*u-ḫi-še-en-ni*
16 ⸢*i*⸣*t-ta-ad-nu* ⸢*ù i*⸣$^{?}$-[*na*$^{?}$-*an*$^{?}$-*na*$^{?}$] ⸢*ni*$^{?}$⸣-[*i*$^{?}$-*nu*$^{?}$]
17 *ni*-⸢*it*⸣-*ta-d*[*in šum-ma*] ⸢*i*⸣+*na* EGIR

18 A.ŠÀ.MEŠ *an-*⸢*ni*⸣-[*i ni-š*]*a-as-sí*
19 *ù* 10 MA.NA K[Ù.SIG$_{17}$.MEŠ *a-n*]*a* ^{m}*Te-ḫi-ip-til-la*
20 ⸢*ni-m*⸣*a-a* ⸢*l*⸣-[*la-m*]*i um-ma* ^{m}*Ké-li-ya-m*[*a*]
21 [DUMU] ⸢*Un-te*⸣-[*šup*] A.ŠÀ.MEŠ *an-ni-i*
22 [ ]⸢*ù*⸣ *a-na-ku i+na* EGIR
23 [A].ŠÀ.M[EŠ *a*]*n-ni-*⸢*i*⸣ *ša* ŠEŠ<.MEŠ>- ⸢*y*⸣*a*
24 [*a-na* ^{m}*T*]*e-ḫi-i*⸢*p*⸣*-til-la in-dì-nu*
25 [*i-na* EG]IR ^{m}*Te-ḫi-ip-til-la*
26 [*l*]*a* [*a*]*-ša-as-sí šum-ma a-ša-as-sí*
Lower Edge
27 [10$^{?}$ MA.N]A KÙ.SIG$_{17}$.MEŠ *a-na* ^{m}*Te-ḫi-ip-til-la*
28 [*ú*]*-ma-al-la-mi*
29 [IGI] ⸢x x⸣ [D]UMU *Pu-ḫi-ya*
30 [IGI DUMU *K*]*u-ri-iš-ni*
Reverse
31 [IGI DUMU *En-n*]*a-ma-ti*
32 [IGI] ⸢x x⸣ [DUMU]- ⸢*x*⸣*-a-ni*
33 [IGI] ⸢*Ḫa*⸣*-na-ak-kà* DUMU [*Še-ka*$_{4}$*-rù*]
34 I[G]I ŠU-^{d}IM DUMU *Zu-*[*ú-me*]
35 IGI *Ma-i-it ta* DUMU [ ]
36 IGI ⸢*Ḫu*⸣*-ti-ip-*LUGAL DUMU *Te-*[ ]
37 ⸢IGI⸣*Ḫé-šal-la* DUMU *Zu-ú-me*
38 [IG]I *Ḫa-aš-har-pá* DUMU *Mil-ku-ya*
39 [IG]I *Ḫa-*⸢*n*⸣*a-a-a* DUMU *Ta-e*
40 [IG]I *Še-*⸢*k*⸣*a*$_{4}$*-rù* DUMU DINGIR-ŠEŠ
41 [IGI *Ḫ*]*a-na-a-a* DUMU *Na-al-tùk-ka*$_{4}$
42 [IGI *U*]*r-ḫi-te-šup* DUMU *Kál-ma-aš-šu-ra*
43 [IGI *U*]*r-ḫi-ya* DUMU *Še-ka*$_{4}$*-rù*
44 [IG]I *Ḫu-ti-ya* DUMU *Zi-li-ḫar-pè*
45 [IGI] *Ki-in-ki-ya* DUMU *Ši-mi-ka*$_{4}$*-tal*
46 [*i*]*l-ku ša* A.ŠÀ.MEŠ *an-ni-i šu-nu-*[*ma*]
47 [*na*]*-šu-ú šum-ma* A.ŠÀ.MEŠ *pa-qí-*⸢*r*⸣*a-na*
48 [*i*]*-ra-aš-ši* ⸢*šu-nu-m*⸣*a ú-za-ak-ku-ma*

S.I.

49 [^{N}]^{A4}KIŠIB ^{m}*Ur-ḫi-ya*

S.I.

50 [^{NA4}KIŠI]B [^{m}]

S.I.

51 ^{NA4} KIŠIB ^{m}*Ḫa-na-ak-kà*
52 ŠU ^{m}*I-ni-ya*

53 DUMU ˹*Ki*˺-[*a*]*n-ni-pu*

JEN VII, 699

(1–7) [Declaration of] Šeḫliya son of Akaya; [declaration] of Ḫutiya [and declaration] of [Ar-teya], [declaration] of Zike [and] declaration of [Ataya] [(and) declaration of] Kipiya sons of Tamar-tae; [declaration] of Šukriya and declaration [of] Ḫaip-šarri sons of Maliya; [(and) declaration] of Eḫliya son of Akkul-enni.

(8–20) [Thus] (declared) these brothers: "Formerly, our fathers gave [to] Teḫip-tilla son of Puḫi-šenni a 5 homer [field of (i.e., which had previously belonged to)] Minaš-šuk son of Zaziya, (located) on the bank of the Nirašše Canal, adjacent to a field of Ḫutiya [son of] Meleya on the road of (i.e., leading to) the town of Tarkulli, to the south(?). And now(?), we have given (it again). [If] we (hereafter) lodge a formal complaint regarding this field, then we shall pay to Teḫip-tilla 10 minas of gold."[126]

(20–28) And thus (declared) Keliya [son of] Un-tešup as well: "… this field … and I shall not (hereafter) lodge a formal complaint against Teḫip-tilla regarding … this field which my brother<s> gave [to] Teḫip-tilla. If I lodge (such) a complaint, I shall pay to Teḫip-tilla [10?] minas of gold."

(29–45) [Before] … son of Puḫiya; [before] … [son of] Kurišni; [before] … [son of] Enna-mati; [before] … [son of] …-ani; [before] Ḫanakka son of [Šekaru]; before Gimill-adad son of Zume; before Maitta son of …; before Ḫutip-šarri son of Te-…; before Ḫešalla son of Zume; before Ḫaš-ḫarpa son of Milkuya; before Ḫanaya son of Tae; before Šekaru son of Ili-aḫi; [before] Ḫanaya son of Naltukka; [before] Urḫi-tešup son of Kalmaš-šura; [before] Urḫiya son of Šekaru; [before] Ḫutiya son of Ziliḫ-ḫarpa; [before] Kikkiya son of Šimika-atal.

(46–47) [And] they (i.e., the declarers) shall bear the *ilku* of this field.

(47–48) And should the field have claimants, they (i.e., the declarers) shall clear (it).

(49–51) (*seal impression*) seal impression of Urḫiya; (*seal impression*) seal impression of …; (*seal impression*) seal impression of Ḫanakka.

(52–53) Hand of Iniya son of Kiannipu.

88. *JEN* VII, 707 (JENu 941a)

Findspot: Room T16
Publication: Lacheman and Maidman 1989: 97
Edition: Maidman 1994: 127–31[127]

Text #88 is a straightforward tablet of real estate adoption. It is chronologically the first of four closely related documents concerning the same property. Text #82 and its introductory comments should be consulted for context and for details regarding particular parties and individual words. Of particular importance for our purposes, note that the vendor of real estate here is said to continue bearing the *ilku* of the alienated property (lines 14–15). The purchaser of the property[128] here, excluded from bearing the *ilku*, reappears in text #82 as one of three vendors of the same property (or part of it). In that text, the three vendors are said to bear the *ilku* (lines 25–29). Despite what text #88 asserts, the *ilku* here passed from vendor to purchaser. This pair of texts demonstrates, along with the other two pairs treated here, that, sooner or later, the *ilku* obligation pertaining to real estate follows the owner of that property and does not remain with some "original" owner.

Obverse

1 *[ṭ]up-pí ma-r[u-ti ša* ^{m}*Te-eš-šu-a-a* DUMU]
2 ^{m}*Al-ki-y[a* DUMU *Mi]l-[ki-te-šup]*
3 *a-na ma-ru-[t]i i-te-p[u-uš]*
4 É.HÁ.MEŠ GI[Š].SAR.MEŠ ù *ḫ[a-la-aḫ-wa]*
5 *i+na šu-pa-al ku-pa-ti [ša*]
6 *i+na* ⸢*ša-pa-at*⸣ *a-ta-pi [ša* ^{m}*Ki-il-li]*
7 ^{m}*Te-[eš-šu-a]-*⸢*a*⸣ *a+na* <m>*A[l-ki-ya]*
8 ⸢x⸣ [ ]-šu TUR$^{?}$ ⸢x⸣ [ ]
9 [ ] ⸢x x⸣ [ ] ⸢x⸣ [(?)]
10 [ ] ⸢x x x x⸣[(?)]
11 *šum-[ma* É.ḪÁ.MEŠ-*t]u*$_4$ GIŠ.SAR.MEŠ *[ù ḫa-la-aḫ-wu]*
12 *di-[na ir-t]a-šu-ú* ^{m}*T[e-eš-šu-a-a]*
13 *ú-z[a-ak-ka*$_4$*]* ⸢*ù*⸣ *a-na* ^{m}*Al-[ki-ya i-na-di-in]*
14 *i[l-ka*$_4$ *ša* É].HÁ.MEŠ GIŠ.S[AR.MEŠ É.HÁ.MEŠ *ù ḫa-la-aḫ-wi]*
15 ^{m}*T[e-eš-šu-a]-*⸢*a-m*⸣*a na-ši*
16 *šum-m[a* ^{m}*Te-e]š-šu-a-a* KI.[BAL($^{-at}$)]
17 2 MA.NA K[Ù.BAB]BAR 2 MA.NA KÙ.SIG$_{17}$ *[a-na]*
18 ^{m}*Al-ki-ya i-na-di-[in]*

Lower Edge
19 $^{\text{NA}_4}$KIŠIB ^{m}*A-ri-ḫ*[*ar-pa*$_{12}$]
S.I.

Reverse
20 $^{\text{NA}_4}$KIŠIB ^{m}*Ur-ḫi-ya* DUMU *A-*⸢*ru*⸣-[*um-pa*$_{12}$]
S.I.
21 IGI *Ar-zi-iz-za* DUMU *Mil-*⸢*ku*$^{!}$⸣-[*y*]*a*$^{!}$
22 IGI ⸢*Ki-li*⸣-*li-ya* DUMU *Šur*$^{!}$*-ri-*[ ]
23 IGI *Ur-ḫi-ya* DUMU *A-ru-um-pa*$_{12}$
24 IGI *A-ri-ḫar-pa*$_{12}$ DUMU *E-na-mil-ki*
25 [IGI] *Ḫa-ni-a-aš-ḫa-ri* DUMU *A-ri-ya*
26 [IGI *I*]*t-ḫi-zi-iz-za* DUMU *E-na-mil-k*[*i*]
27 [IGI *A-k*]*ip-til-la* DUMU *Tu-ra-ri*
28 [IGI *W*]*u-ur-tù-ru-*⸢*uk* DUMU *Ma*⸣-[*li-ya*]
29 [IGI]-*in*-[DUMU]
.
.
.
S.I.
.
.
.

Left Edge
S.I.
30 $^{\text{NA}_4}$KIŠIB *A*$^{?}$-[ ]

JEN VII, 707

(1–3) Tablet of adoption [of Teššuya son of] … . He adopted Alkiya [son of] Milki-tešup.

(4–8) Teššuya [gave] to Alkiya … structures, orchards, and *ḫalaḫwu*-land to the west of the stables(?) [of] …, on the bank of the [Killi] Canal.

(8–10) … .

(11–13) Should the structures, orchards, [and *ḫalaḫwu*-land] have a case (against them), Teššuya shall clear (the real estate) and [give] (it) to Alkiya.

(14–15) Teššuya shall also bear the *ilku* [of] the structures, orchards, [and *ḫalaḫwu*-land].

(16–18) Should Teššuya abrogate (this contract), he shall give [to] Alkiya 2 minas of silver (and) 2 minas of gold.

(19–20) Seal impression of Ariḫ-ḫarpa (*seal impression*); seal impression of Urḫiya son of Arrumpa (*seal impression*).

(21–29) Before Ar-zizza son of Milkuya; before Kilīliya son of Šurri-...; before Urḫiya son of Arrumpa; before Ariḫ-ḫarpa son of Enna-milki; [before] Ḫaniašḫari son of Ariya; [before] Itḫi-zizza son of Enna-milki; [before] Akip-tilla son of Turari; [before] Wur-turuk son of Maliya; [before] ...-in-... [son of] ....

(30) .... (*seal impression*); ... (*seal impression*) seal impression of A?-... .

89. *JEN* VII 782 (JENu 28a)

Findspot: Room T13
Publication: Lacheman and Maidman 1989: 187
Edition: Maidman 1999: 336–40[129]

Text #89 is a simple tablet of real estate adoption. Lines 17–20 emphatically assert (with peculiar syntax) that the vendors are to bear the *ilku* and the buyer is *not* to. The distinction of this text lies in the fact that, together with text #90, this pair is probably the clearest of the three sets here presented illustrating the mobility of the *ilku* despite explicit contractual statements to the contrary. Texts ##89 and 90 are not unusually formulated or idiosyncratic (as some of the other texts are), and they are relatively well preserved. At a more general level, these pairings demonstrate that the significance of a text may increase and even change qualitatively when juxtaposed with other documents from the same archive and corpus. The Nuzi texts are especially rich in this respect, containing scores of groups of interrelated texts.

Obverse

.
.
.

1 [(*ù*) ^{m}*Ka-na-a-a* D]UM[U]$^{?}$ ⸢X⸣-[ ]
2 [^{m}*Ut-ḫap-t*]*a*-⸢*e*⸣ DUMU *Mu-u*⸢*š*⸣-[*te-e*]
3 [*a-na ma-r*]*u-ti e-pu-u*[*š*(*-ma*)]
4 [2[130] ANŠ]E A.ŠÀ *mi-ṣí-ir-šu ú*-[*ka-al*]
5 [*i-na s*]*u-ta-an* A.ŠÀ *ša* ^{m}*Aš-š*[*u-ra*-[131]]
6 [*i-na*] *ša-ad-dá-an mi-iṣ-ri* [*ša* URU KÙ$^{?}$.SI]$G_{17}$$^{?}$-GAL
7 [*i-n*]*a šu-pa-al* A.ŠÀ *ša* ^{m}*Ḫu-i-t*[*e-e*]
8 [*i*]-*n*[*a*] *il-ta-an-ni* A.ŠÀ *ša* ^{m}*Tar-mi-ya*

9 [*k*]*i-m*⸢*u*⸣ ḪA.LA-*šu* ^{m}*Tù-ra-ri-i-a*
10 [*ù*] ^{m}*K*⸢*a*⸣*-na-*⸢*a*⸣*-a a-na* ^{m}*Ut-ḫap-ta-e* DUMU *Mu-uš-te-e it-ta-*[*di*]*n*
11 *ù* ^{m}*Ut-*⸢*ḫáp*⸣*-ta-e* 1 GUD.SAL 9 MA.NA AN.NA
12 [n$^{?}$ +] 1 UDU 2 *en-zu* 15 ANSE ŠE *ki-ma* NÍG.BA *a-na* ^{m}*Ka-*<*na*>*-a-a*
13 *ù* ⸢*a-n*⸣*a* ^{m}*Tu-*⸢*ra*⸣*-ri-i-a it-ta-din*
14 *šum-ma* ⸢A.ŠÀ⸣ [*pí*]- ⸢*ir*⸣*-qà i-ra-aš-ši*
15 *ù* ^{m}*Ka-n*⸢*a-a*⸣*-*[*a it-t*]*i* ^{m}*Tu-*[*r*]*a-ri-i-*[*a*]
16 *ú-za-ka-ma* ⸢*a*⸣*-*[*na* ^{m}] ⸢*Ut*⸣$^{?}$-[*ḫap-ta-e i-na-an-din*]
17 ⸢*ù*⸣$^{?}$ *il*$^{!}$*-k*⸢*a ša*⸣ [A].⸢ŠÀ⸣ [ ] ⸢x⸣ [ ]
18 *a-na* ^{m}*Tu-ra-ri-y*⸢*a*⸣ *ù a-na*
19 ^{m}*Ka-na-a-a* ⸢*na-ši*⸣$^{!}$
20 *ù* ^{m}*Ut-ḫap-ta-e* ⸢*l*⸣*a na-š*[*i*]

Lower Edge

21 *ma-an-nu-um-me-e*
22 *i-na bi*$_{4}$*-ri-šu-nu i-*⸢*bala*⸣*-ka-tu*

Reverse

23 1 MA.NA KÙ.BABBAR 1 MA.NA KÙ.SIG$_{17}$
24 *ú-ma-al-la-šú*
25 *ṭup-pu a*[*n-nu-ú i-n*]*a* EGIR-^{ki} *šu-du-ti*
26 *i+na* K[Á.GAL *š*]*a* URU *Ar-ša-li-pè*
27 [*š*]*á-*⸢*ṭì*⸣*-*[*ir*]
28 IGI ⸢*En*⸣-[DUMU]-⸢*a*⸣$^{?}$*-ya* ⸢x⸣$^{?}$
29 [IGI] ⸢x x⸣ [DUMU] ⸢x x⸣*-ku*
30 [IGI *Ši*]*-la-ḫi* DUMU ⸢X⸣ [ ]-LUGAL
31 [IGI]*-ki-y*[*a* DUMU]*-en-ni*
32 [IGI] ⸢DUMU⸣$^{?}$
33 [(?)] *Pu-un-ni-*⸢*y*⸣*a*$^{!}$
34 [IGI]- ⸢*x-a*⸣*-a* DUMU *It-ḫi-ip-*LUGAL
35 [*an-nu-tu* LÚ.MEŠ *š*]*a mu-še-el-wu* A.ŠÀ
36 [IGI DUM]U *Ar-ta-še-e*[*n-ni*]
37 [IGI$^{?}$] ⸢x⸣ [ ]
38 [IGI$^{?}$] ⸢x x⸣ [ ]

.

.

.

Left Edge

39 [^{NA_4}KIŠIB] ⸢x⸣ [ ]
S.I.
40[132] [^{N}]^{A_4}⸢KIŠ⸣IB] ⸢*Šu*⸣$^{?}$*-ul-*[ ]
[S.I.$^{?}$]

JEN VII, 782

. . . .[133]

(1–3) [(and) Kanaya] son of… . They (lit. "He") adopted Utḫap-tae son of Muš-teya.

(4–10) Turariya [and] Kanaya gave (lit. "he gave") to Utḫap-tae son of Muš-teya as his inheritance share a [2] homer field; they (lit. "he") will hold (it up to) its border: [to] the south of the field of Aššur-a-…, to the east of the border [of the town of] Ḫurāṣina(?)-rābu, to the west of the field of Ḫui-te, to the north of the field of Tarmiya.

(11–13) And Utḫap-tae gave to Kanaya and to Turariya as a gift 1 cow, 9 minas of tin, n?+1 sheep, 2 goats, (and) 15 homers of barley.

(14–16) Should the field have a claim, then Kanaya with Turariya shall clear (the field and) [give (it)] to Utḫap-tae.

(17–20) And(?) the *ilku* of … field is for Turariya and for Kanaya to bear(?); Utḫap-tae shall not bear (it).

(21–24) Whoever amongst them abrogates (this contract) shall pay to him (i.e., to the other party) 1 mina of silver (and) 1 mina of gold.

(25–27) This tablet was written after the proclamation at the gate of the town of Ar-šalipe.

(28–38) Before En-… [son of] …-aya(?); [before] … [son of] …-ku; [before] Šilahi son of …-šarri; [before] …-kiya [son of] …-enni; [before] … son(?) of(?) […?] Punniya; [before] …-aya son of Itḫip-šarri . [These are the men] who are the measurers of the field. [Before] … son of Artašenni ; [before?] …; [before?] … .

(39–40) [seal impression of] … (*seal impression*); seal impression of Šu?-ul-… [(*seal impression*?)].

90. *JEN* VI, 599 (JENu 274a)

Findspot: Unclear[134]
Publication: Lacheman 1939a: pl. 547
Edition: None

The three pairs of texts demonstrating the mobility of the *ilku* concludes with this document, text #90. It is paired with text #89. Like the other pairs, the first text claims that the *ilku* is to be borne by the seller of the real estate. The second text asserts that, in alienating real property, the seller (once again) is to bear the *ilku*. Thus it is clear that, despite written claims to the contrary, the *ilku* for land shifts from owner to owner. But texts ##89 and 90 actually go even further. The description of the real estate is almost identical in these two cases.[135] By itself, this suggests that the scribe of the latter text may have actually seen the former text. This suggestion is strengthened by a clause in text #90. Lines 24–27 state that the vendor gave to the purchaser, not only land, but a tablet involving an earlier legal stage in the history of that land. From the description given of that tablet, there can be no doubt that this earlier tablet is none other than text #89. The match is perfect. Now all this would be interesting and informative regarding the mechanisms of transferring legal title to real property. Having in hand a tablet actually mentioned in another tablet is also pleasing in an aesthetic way; there is a certain sense of wholeness to all this. But of especial importance in the present context is the probability that the scribe of text #90 really did read text #89. For, if he did, then he must have understood, as did both of the principal parties to text #90, that the *ilku* clause of text #89 attached the *ilku* to the vendors in that document while the same impost on the same property was being assigned to someone else in the current transaction. Thus, the *ilku*, not only shifted, but was perceived to have shifted.

And no difficulty was sensed by the co-contractors or the scribe.

Obverse

1 [*ṭup-pí ma-ru-t*]*i ša*
2 [^{m}*Ut-ḫap-ta-e*] DUMU *Mu-uš-t*[*e-e/ya*]
3 [^{m}*Tar-mi-til-la*] DUMU *Šur-ki-til-la*
4 [*a-na ma-r*]*u-ti* ˹*i*˺*-te-pu-uš*
5 [2 A]NŠE A.ŠÀ *mi-ṣí-ir-šu ú-ka-a*[*l*]
6 [*i-n*]*a su-ta-an-ni* A.ŠÀ *ša* ^{m}*Aš-šu-ra-*[ ]
7 [*i-na*] *e-le-ni mi-i*˹*ṣ*˺*-ri ša* URU [KÙ?.SIG$_{17}$?-GAL]
8 [*i-n*]˹*a šu-pa-a*˺*l* A.ŠÀ *š*[*a*] ^{m}*Ḫu-i-te-e*
9 *i+na il-*˹*ta-an-ni* A.ŠÀ˺ [*š*]*a* ^{m}*Tar-mi-ya*
10 *ki-ma* ḪA.˹LA˺-[*š*]*u* [^{m}*Ut-ḫap-t*]*a-*˹e˺
11 *a-na* ^{m}*Tar-mi-t*[*il-la* SU]M-*nu ù*
12 ^{m}*Tar-mi-til-la* [1? A]NŠE.SAL
13 *ù* 3 MA.NA [AN.N]A *ki-ma* NÍG.BA-*šu*
14 *a-na* ^{m}*Ut-ḫap-*[*ta*]-˹*e*˺ *it-ta-din*
15 *šum-ma* A.ŠÀ [GAL] *la i+na-ki-is*
16 *šum-ma* A.[ŠÀ T]UR *la ú-ra-ad-dá*
17 *šum-ma* [A].ŠÀ *pa-qí-ra-na* TUK$^{-ši}$
18 ^{m}*U*˹*t-ḫap*˺*-ta-e ú-za-ak-ka*$_{4}$*-ma*
19 *a-na* ^{m}*Tar-mi-til-la i+na-an-din*

20 *il-ku ša* A.ŠÀ ^{m}*Ut-ḫ̮ap-ta-e na-ši*
21 ^{m}*Tar-mi-til-la la na-ši*
22 ⸢*i*⸣*-na* ŠÀ-*bi* A.ŠÀ *ka*$_{4}$*-aš-ka*$_{4}$
Lower Edge
23 ^{m}*Ut-ḫ̮ap-ta-e la i-leq-qè*
24 *ù* ^{m}*Ut-ḫ̮ap-ta-e ṭup-pu ša ma-ru-ti*
25 *ša* 2 ANŠE A.ŠÀ *ša* ^{m}*Tù-r*[*a*]*-ri-ya*
Reverse
26 *ù ša* ^{m}*Ka-na-a-a a-na*
27 ^{m}*Tar-mi-til-la it-ta-din*
28 *ma-an-nu-um-me-e* AŠ *bi*$_{4}$*-ri-šu-nu*
29 KI.BAL-*tu*$_{4}$ 1 MA.NA KÙ.BABBAR 1 MA.NA
30 KÙ.SIG$_{17}$ SI.A *ṭup-pu i-na* EGIR
31 *šu-du-ti a-šar ma-ḫ̮i-ri ša* GAL
32 *i-na* URU *Nu-zi ša*$_{10}$*-ṭì-ir*
33 EME-*šu ša* ^{m}*Ut-ḫ̮ap-ta-e a-na pa-ni* $^{LÚ.MEŜ}$
34 IGI.MEŜ *iq-ta-bi* ANŠE *ù* AN.NA.MEŜ
35 *a-šar* ^{m}*Tar-mi-til-la el-te-qè-mi*
36 IGI *Ši-mi-ka*$_{4}$*-a-tal* DUMU *Te-ḫ̮i-ip-til-la*
37 IGI *Ké-ra-ar-til-la* DUMU *En-na-ma-ti*
38 IGI *Ar-ti-ir-wi* DUMU *Al-ki-te-šup*
39 [IG]I *Šá-ma-*[DUMU]

.
.
.

Left Edge
40 NA$_{4}$ ^{m}*Ké-ra-ar-til-la*

S.I. S.I.

41 NA$_{4}$ ^{m}*Ši-mi-*[*ka*$_{4}$$^{?}$*-a*$^{?}$*-tal*$^{?}$]

JEN VI, 599

(1–4) Tablet of adoption of Utḫ̮ap-tae son of Muš-teya. He adopted [Tarmi-tilla] son of Šurki-tilla.

(5–11) Utḫ̮ap-tae gave to Tarmi-tilla as his inheritance share a [2] homer field; he will hold (it up to) its border: to the south of the field of Aššur-a-…, [to] the east of the border of the town of [Ḫ̮urāṣina?-rabû], to the west of the field of Ḫ̮ui-te, to the north of the field of Tarmiya.

(11–14) And Tarmi-tilla gave to Utḫ̮ap-tae as his gift [1?] jenny and 3 minas of tin.

(15–16) Should the field prove large(r than estimated), it shall not be diminished; should the field prove small(er than estimated), it shall not be augmented.

(17–19) Should the field have claimants, Utḫap-tae shall clear (it) and give it to Tarmi-tilla.

(20–21) Utḫap-tae shall bear the *ilku* of the field; Tarmi-tilla shall not bear (it).

(22–23) In the midst of the field is (a?) *kaška*.[136] Utḫap-tae shall not take it.

(24–27) And Utḫap-tae has given to Tarmi-tilla the tablet, pertaining to adoption, of the 2 homer field of Turariya and of Kanaya.

(28–30) Whoever amongst them abrogates (this contract) shall pay 1 mina of silver (and) 1 mina of gold.

(30–32) The tablet was written after the proclamation at the great(?)[137] market place in the town of Nuzi.

(33–35) Declaration of Utḫap-tae before the witnesses. He said: "I have taken the donkey and the tin from Tarmi-tilla."

(36–39) Before Šimika-atal son of Teḫip-tilla; before Kerar-tilla son of Enna-mati; before Ar-tirwi son of Alki-tešup; before Šama-… [son of] …; … . .

(40–41) Seal of Kerar-tilla (*seal impression*); (*seal impression*) seal of Šimi[ka?-atal?].

91. HSS V, 58 (SMN 99)

Findspot: Room A34
Publication: Chiera 1929: pl. 53
Edition: Speiser 1930: 41–42[138]

This tablet of real estate adoption notes that the purchaser, not the vendor, is to bear the *ilku* (line 11). The *ilku* moves. It is of interest that the purchaser is also to pay a debt (line 12), certainly owed by the vendor. Zaccagnini 1984a: 88 correctly links this debt to an otherwise unknown separate prior transaction.[139] Discharging the debt must have constituted the *quid pro quo* in this transaction: the usual gift clause benefiting the vendor is here absent.

Obverse

1 *ṭup-pí ma-ru-ti ša*
2 ^{m}*Er-wi-šar-ri* DUMU *Na-ḫi-iš-šal-mu*
3 *ù* ^{m}*Zi-ké* DUMU *Ak-ku-ya*
4 *a-na ma-ru-ti i-te-pu-uš*
5 *mi-nu-um-me-e* ḪA.LA-*šu*

6 *ša* ^{m}*Er-wi-šar-ri i+na* É
7 ^{m}*Na-ḫi-iš-šal-mu ša i-le-qú-ú*
8 *ù a-na* ^{m}*Zi-ké it-ta-di*$_{4}$*-in*
9 GÌR-*šu ul-te-li ù* GÌR-*šu*
10 *ša* ^{m}*Zi-ké il-ta-ka-an*
11 *ù il-ka*$_{4}$ ^{m}*Zi-ké-ma na-ši*
12 *ù ḫu-ub-bu-ul-tu*$_{4}$ ^{m}*Zi-ké-ma*
ú-ma-al-la
13 *ma-an-nu-um-me-e ša i+na*
14 *bi-ri-šu-nu i-ba-la-ka-tu*$_{4}$
15 1 MA.NA KÙ.BABBAR *ù* 1 MA.NA KÙ.SIG$_{17}$
16 *ú-ma-al-la*

Lower Edge
17 IGI *Ta-e* DUMU *Še-el-la-pá-i*
18 IGI *Ip-ša-a-a* DUMU *E-ra-ti*
19 IGI *Te-ḫu-up-še-en-ni* DUMU *Na-ni-ya*
Reverse
20 IGI *Ta-e-na* DUMU ⸢*E*⸣*-ra-ti*
21 IGI *Ú-na-ap-ta-e* DUMU *A-ri-wa-kál-še*
22 IGI *Kàr-ra-te* DUMU *Ki-pá-an-ti-il*
23 IGI *Ur-ḫi-ya* DUMU *Ta-e*
24 IGI *A-ri-ka-ma-ri* DUMU *Ka-ri-ru*
25 IGI *Al-ki-te-šup* DUB.SAR$^{-rù}$ DUMU *Wa-qàr*-EN

26 ^{NA_4}KIŠIB ^{m}*Ta-e*
27 ^{NA_4}KIŠIB ^{m}*Ta-e-na*
28 ^{NA_4}KIŠIB ^{m}*Ú-na-ap-ta-e*
29 ^{NA_4}KIŠIB ^{m}*Kàr-ra-te*
30 ^{NA_4}KIŠIB ^{m}*Al-ki-te-šup*

HSS V, 58

(1–4) Tablet of adoption of Erwi-šarri son of Naḫiš-šalmu. Now he adopted Zike son of Akkuya.

(5–8) Whatever constitutes Erwi-šarri's inheritance share taken from (lit. "in") the household of Naḫiš-šalmu (i.e., Erwi-šarri's father), (*that*) he has given to Zike.

(9–10) He (i.e., Erwi-šarri) has ceded his claim (lit. "he has lifted his foot") (from the property) and confirmed Zike's claim (lit. "he has set Zike's foot") (to the property).

(11) And Zike shall bear the *ilku* too.

(12) And Zike shall pay the debt.

(13–16) Whoever amongst them who abrogates (this contract) shall pay 1 mina of silver and 1 mina of gold.

(17–25) Before Tae son of Šellapai; before Ipšaya son of Erati; before Teḫup-šenni son of Naniya; before Taena son of Erati; before Unap-tae son of Ari-wakalše; before Karrate son of Kipantil; before Urḫiya son of Tae; before Arik-kamari son of Kariru; before Alki-tešup, scribe, son of Waqar-bêli.

(26–30)[140] Seal impression of Tae; seal impression of Taena; seal impression of Unap-tae; seal impression of Karrate; seal impression of Alki-tešup.

92. *EN* 9/1, 165 (SMN1067)

Findspot: No Room number
Publication: Lacheman, Owen, Morrison et al. 1987: 496–97[141]
Edition: None[142]

Text #92 is an antichretic loan contract. In such a loan, the lender tenders mobilia to the borrower and establishes a minimum or indefinite length of time for that loan. At the end of a minimum period or at any time thereafter, the mobilia, the principal of the loan, is returned to the lender. No interest on the loan is paid on that occasion. In a personal antichretic loan, such as is described in text #92, the borrower enters the household of the lender and works there. The borrower's labor during the period of the loan constitutes the interest on the mobilia.

In another type of antichretic loan, it is real estate, not a person, that goes to the lender for the duration. The produce of the land (rather than the work of the borrower) constitutes the interest on the loan.

A personal antichretic loan is obtained, clearly, when the borrower is in dire economic straits. In economic terms, such a transaction approaches a kind of limited-term slavery.[143] A real estate antichretic loan probably represents a less desperate situation for the borrower, since, in addition to his own person, he owns real estate that he can exploit before reaching the ultimate stage of using himself as a commodity. The borrower in a personal antichretic loan probably owns little more than himself. That is the situation behind text #92.[144]

Now text #92 contains many problems of interpretation, but the basics of the transaction are clear. The borrower receives mobilia (lines 9–17) for an indefinite period until the loan's return (lines 18–23). By way of interest, the borrower enters the lender's household (lines 4–8) to perform work and guarantees this performance (lines 24–33).

Lines 24–29 are difficult to understand, but one thing is clear and stands out: as part of his work, it is envisioned that the borrower may do the actual performance of the *ilku*, however obscure the circumstances may appear to us. Thus, performance of the *ilku* here does not imply ownership of the real estate to which it attaches. (Indeed, it is performed for one Kirip-šarri, probably the landowner to whom the lender in this text seems himself somehow indebted.) It is part, at least potentially, of the *šipru*, the "work," owed by the borrower as interest on his loan. This document, in other words, offers a rare written record pinpointing a plausible performer of the *ilku*, an *ilku* actually belonging to someone else.[145]

Thus text #92 demonstrates, in passing, that physical performance of the *ilku* may be done by one who does not own the real estate.

Obverse

1 *ṭup-pí ti-de*$_4$*-en-nu-ti*

2 *ša* <^{m}>*Šu-ul-lu-ma*-^{d}IM

3 DUMU ^{m}*Tù-uḫ-mi-te-šup*

4 *ù ra-ma-an-šu ù*

5 ^{m}*Šu*$^{!}$*-ul-lu-ma*-^{d}IM

6 *a-na ti-de*$_4$*-en-nu-ti a-na*

7 É.HÁ.MEŠ-^{ti} *ša* ^{m}*Ip-ša-ḫa-lu*

8 DUMU *Ú-na-a-a i*$^{!}$*-te-ru-ub*

9 *ù* <^{m}>*Ip-šá-ha-lu* 4 UDU.SAL 2-*ni-šu bá-aq-nu*

10 1 UDU.NITA *ṣa-ri-pu* 1 UDU.SAL *ṣa-ri-pu*

11 1 UDU.NITA 1 *bá*-⸢*aq*⸣-*nu* 1 UDU.SAL 1 *bá-aq-nu*

12 2 *en-zu ḫu*-⸢*x*⸣-*šu*-BA-*te*-UŠ

13 1 *en-zu*.SAL 2-*ni-šu ga*$_5$*-az-zu*

14 ŠU.NIGIN$_2$ 11 UDU 2 MA.NA 30 GÍN

15 ZABAR«*ù*»[146] (erasure) *ù*

16 ^{m}*Ip-ša-ḫa-lu a-na*

17 ^{m}*Šu-ul-lu-ma*-^{d}IM SUM-^{nu}

18 *im-ma-ti-me-e* KÙ.BABBAR

19 *ša pí*-<*i*> *ṭup-pí an-nu-tu*$_4$

Lower Edge

20 *ù* ^{m}*Šu-ul-lu-ma*-^{d}⸢IM⸣

21 *a*-⸢*n*⸣*a* <^{m}>⸢*Ip*⸣*-ša-ḫa-lu*

Reverse

22 *ú-ta-ar*

23 *ù ra-ma-an-šu ú-*⸢*u*⸣*ṣ-ṣí*

---

24 *šum-ma* ^{m}*Šu-ul-lu*$^{!}$*-ma-*^{d}IM

25 *a-na il-ka ša* ^{m}*Kí-ri-ip-*LUGAL

26 *ša-at-te-ta-um-ma e-pu-uš*

27 *ù* ^{m}*Nu-ul-za-ḫi ù* $^{<m>}$*Wu-ur-ta*$^{?}$*-ri*

28 ^{m}*Ut-ḫáp-ta-e ú-za-ak-ka*$_{4}$

29 *a-na* <^{m}>*Ip-šá-ḫa-lu ina-an-din*$^{!}$

30 *šum-ma ši-pí-ir-šu ša*

31 ^{m}*Ip-šá-ḫa-lu ù* $^{<m>}$*Šu-ul-lu-ma-*$^{<d>}$IM

32 *ú-a-šar* 1 M[A.N]A URUDU *ú-ri-ḫul*

33 *a-na* $^{<m>}$*Ip-šá-ḫa-lu* SI.A-⸢*m*⸣*a*

34 IGI *Ši-na-me-til-la* DUMU *Na-an-te-šup*

35 IGI *Ḫu-pí-ta* DUMU *Tar-mi-še-*⸢*ni*⸣$^{!?}$

36 IGI *A-kip-til-la* DUMU *Ú-na-ap-ta-e*

37 IGI *Eḫ-li-te-šup* DUMU *Ku-ni-na*

38 IGI *Ša-ar-te-*[*š*]*up* DUMU *Ú-na-*<*ap*>*-ta-e*

39 IGI *Ma-at-te-šup* DUMU *Pur-na-an-zi*

40 ŠU *Ḫu-ur-pí-te-šup* DUB.SAR

S.I. S.I.

41 NA$_{4}$ *Ši-na*$^{!}$*-me-til-la* NA$_{4}$ *Ḫu-pí-ta*

S.I. S.I. S.I.

42 NA$_{4}$ *A-kip-til-la* NA$_{4}$ *Eḫ-li-te-šup*

43 NA$_{4}$ ^{m}*Šá-ar-te-šup*

Upper Edge

S.I. S.I.

44 NA$_{4}$ *Ma-at-te-šup*

45 NA$_{4}$ *Šu-ul-lu-ma-*^{d}IM

Left Edge

46 *ṭup-pu* AŠ EGIR *šu-du-ti* AŠ URU BÀD-*ub-la* [ ]

47 *a-bu-ul-li ša-ṭì-ir* MU.MEŠ^{ti} *ša Ši-ya-ḫu-ur* [(?)]

EN 9/1, 165

(1–3) Tablet of antichretic loan of Šullum-adad son of Tuḫmi-tešup.

(4–8) Now Šullum-adad himself entered, in antichretic status, into the household of Ipša-ḫalu son of Unaya.

(9–17) Now Ipša-ḫalu gave to Šullum-adad 4 twice-plucked ewes, 1 dyed ram, 1 dyed ewe, 1 once-plucked ram, 1 once-plucked ewe, 2 … goats, 1 twice-shorn she-goat—a total of 11 sheep and goats[147]—(and) 2 minas, 30 sheqels of bronze (did) Ipša-ḫalu (give).

(18–23) Whenever Šullum-adad returns to Ipša-ḫalu the value[148] according to (i.e., as spelled out in) this tablet, then he himself may leave (Ipša-ḫalu's household).

(24–29) Should Šullum-adad …[149] for the *ilku* of Kirip-šarri, then Utḫap-tae[150] shall clear Nula-zaḫi and Wur-ta(?)-ri,[151] (and) give (them?) to Ipša-ḫalu.

(30–33) Should Šullum-adad abandon(?) the work of (i.e., due to) Ipša-ḫalu, he shall pay to Ipša-ḫalu 1 mina of copper, the equivalent wage.

(34–40) Before Šiname-tilla son of Nan-tešup; before Ḫupita son of Tarmi-šenni(?); before Akip-tilla son of Unap-tae; before Eḫli-tešup son of Kunina; before Šar-tešup son of Unap-tae; before Mat-tešup son of Pur-nanzi. Hand of Ḫurpi-tešup, the scribe.

(41–45) (*seal impression*) Seal of Šiname-tilla; (*seal impression*) seal of Ḫupita; (*seal impression*) seal of Šar-tešup; (*seal impression*) seal of Akip-tilla; (*seal impression*) seal of Eḫli-tešup; (*seal impression*) seal of Mat-tešup; (*seal impression*) seal of Šullum-adad.

(46–47) The tablet was written after the proclamation in the town of Dūr-ubla [at] the (town) gate, in the year of Šiyaḫur[152](?).

93. HSS XIV, 110 = 604 (SMN 604)

Findspot: Room K32

Publications: Lacheman 1950: pl. 53 (# 110; copy);[153] 1950: 29 (# 604; transliteration)

Edition: None

This tablet of real estate adoption is unusual insofar as the recipient has a special status. She is a "queen," that is a local consort of the king of Arrapḫa. She obtains land in her own right. In this case, her new field lies between land she already owns and land owned by the local or state government (lines 7–9).

Of note in the present context, the *ilku* clause (lines 26–28) specifies that the vendor of the land is to bear this impost, not the purchaser. This implies that, if this were not stated, ᶠTarmen-naya, a female and a queen besides, could be expected to bear responsibility for the *ilku*.[154]

Obverse

1 *ṭup-pí ma-ru-ti ša* ^{m}*Wa-ar-za*
2 DUMU *Ḫa-ši-ip-til-la ù*
3 ^{f}*Tar-mé-en-na-a-a* SAL.LUGAL
4 DUMU.MÍ ^{m}[155]*Te-ḫi-ip-til-la a-na*
5 *ma-ru-ti i-te-pu-uš ki-ma*
6 ḪA.LA^{-ti}-*šu* 1 ANŠE A.ŠÀ *ši-qú-ú*
7 *i+na ú-ga*$_5$*-ri ša* URU *A-ták-kál i-na*
8 *su-ta-an* A.ŠÀ *ša* SAL.LUGAL
9 *i-na il-ta-an* A.ŠÀ *ša* É.GAL$^{-lì}$
10 *i-na e-le-en* KASKAL^{-ni} *ša* URU *Nu-zi i-na*
11 *šu-pa-al* A.ŠÀ *ša* ^{m}*Tar-mi-ya*
12 *an-nu-tu*$_4$ A.ŠÀ ^{m}*Wa-ar-za*
13 *a-na* ^{f}*Tar-mé-en-na-a-a* SUM^{-din}
14 *ù* ^{f}*Tar-mé-en-na-a-a*
15 3 ANŠE 5 BÁN ŠE.MEŠ *ki-ma* NÌG.BA^{-ti}-*šu*
16 *a-na* ^{m}*Wa-ar-za* SUM^{-din}
17 *šum-ma* A.ŠÀ *pí-ir-qa*$_4$ *ir-ta-ši*
18 ^{m}*Wa-ar-za* A.ŠÀ *šu-ú-ma*
19 *ú-za-ak-ka*$_4$*-mi a-na*
20 ^{f}*Tar-mé-en-na-a-a i+na-an-din*
21 *šum-ma* A.ŠÀ GAL *ù la i+na-ak-ki-is*
22 *ù* ^{m}*Wa-ar-za ka*$_4$*-aš*$_x$(= AS)-*ka*$_4$
23 *iš-tu* A.ŠÀ *an-nu-ú ù*
24 *la i-na-ak-ki-is ù a-na*

Lower Edge

25 *ma-am-ma la i+na-an-din*
2 *il-ku ša* A.ŠÀ *Wa-ar-za-ma*
27 *na-ši ù* ^{f}*Tar-mé-en-na-a-a*

Reverse

28 *la na-ši ma-an-nu-um-me-e*
29 *i-na bi*$_4$*-ri-šu-nu ša* KI.BAL$^{-ak-ka_4-tu_4}$
30 1 MA.NA KÙ.BABBAR 1 MA.NA KÙ.SIG$_{17}$ *ú-ma-al-la*
31 *ṭup-pí i+na* EGIR^{-ki} *šu-du-ti*
32 *i-na bá-ab a-bu-ul-li ša* URU
33 *A-ták-kál ša-ṭì-ir*
34 IGI *Ḫa-an-ta-ka*$_4$ DUMU *A-ka*$_4$*-a-a*
35 IGI *Ta-i-iz-zu-un-ni* DUMU *Ḫa-lu-ut-ta*
36 IGI *Na-am-ḫé-e-a* DUMU *Ar-zi-ib-ni*
37 IGI *Te-ḫi-ya* DUMU *Ar-ša-*⌜*l*⌝*ì*

38 *an-nu-tu*$_4$ $^{\text{LÚ.MEŠ}}$*mu-šal-mu-ú*
39 *ša* A.ŠÀ *na-dì-na-nu ša* ŠE.MEŠ
40 IGI *Ú-lu-ti* DUMU *N/na-ar-tu*$_4$
41 IGI *Eḫ-li-pa-pu* DUMU *Ar-ša-ḫa*-RI
42 IGI *Ut-ḫáp-ta-e* DUMU *Še-er-ši-ya*
43 ŠU ^{m}*Šúk-ri-te-šup* DUB.SAR
44 DUMU *Tù-ra-ri*

S.I.
45 NA$_4$ ^{m}*Wa-ar-za* EN A.ŠÀ NA$_4$ ^{m}*Ta-i-iz-zu-un-ni*
S.I.
46 NA$_4$ ^{m}*Ut-ḫáp-ta-e*
S.I.

Upper Edge
47 || NA$_4$ ^{m}*Ḫa-an-ta-ka*$_4$
S.I. || S.I.
48 NA$_4$ ^{m}*Na-am-ḫé-e-a*

Left Edge
49 NA$_4$ ^{m}*Te-hi-ya*
S. I. || S.I. | S.I.
50 NA$_4$ ^{m}*Ú-lu-ti* NA$_4$ ^{m}*Šúk-ri-te-šup* DUB.SAR

HSS XIV, 110 = 614

(1–5) Tablet of adoption of Warza son of Ḫašip-tilla. Now he adopted Tarmen-naya, queen, daughter of Teḫip-tilla.[156]

(6–13) Warza gave to Tarmen-naya as her (lit. "his") inheritance share this one, a field: a 1 homer irrigated field in the town green of the town of Atakkal, to the south of the queen's field, to the north of palace land, to the east of the road of (i.e., leading to) the town of Nuzi, (and) to the west of the field of Tarmiya.

(14–16) And Tarmen-naya gave to Warza as his gift 3 homers, 5 seahs[157] of barley.

(17–20) Should the field have a claim (against it), Warza shall clear that very field and give it to Tarmen-naya.

(21) Should the field prove large(r than estimated), it shall not be diminished.

(22–25) And Warza shall not cut (off?; away?) (the) *kaška*[158] from/in this field. Nor shall he give it to anyone.

(26–28) Warza shall bear the *ilku* of the field; and Tarmen-naya shall not bear (it).

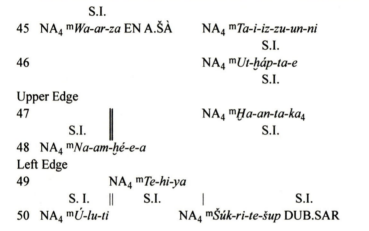

(28–30) Whoever amongst them who abrogates (this contract) shall pay 1 mina of silver (and) 1 mina of gold.

(31–33) The tablet was written at the gate of the town of Atakkal.

(34–44) Before Ḫantaka son of Akaya; before Taizzunni son of Ḫalutta; before Namḫeya son of Ar-zipni; before Teḫiya son of Ar-šali. These are the measurers of the field (and) the givers of the barley. Before Uluti son of Nartu (or: "son of a female musician/singer"); before Eḫlip-apu son of Ar-šaḫari (or: "Aršaḫ(a)-atal"); before Utḫap-tae son of Šeršiya. Hand of Šukri-tešup, scribe, son of Turari.

(45–50) (*seal impression*) Seal of Warza, (erstwhile) owner of the field; seal of Taizzunni (*seal impression*); seal of Utḫap-tae (*seal impression*); seal of Ḫantaka (*seal impression*); (*seal impression*) seal of Namḫeya; seal of Teḫiya (*seal impression*); (*seal impression*) seal of Uluti; (*seal impression*) seal of Šukri-rešup, the scribe.

94. HSS XIII, 212 (SMN 212)

Findspot: Room A34
Publication: Pfeiffer and Lacheman 1942: 33–34[159]
Edition: Dosch 2009: 109–11 (#30)

Texts ##94 and 95 are the most pedestrian of records. They are basically just lists of persons, that is, names and patronymics. Little else is mentioned. However, some of what *is* mentioned gives these documents an importance out of all proportion to their apparently modest contents. They identify these individuals as either "charioteers" (text #94) or as "charioteers" or "goers of the going" (text #95), two of the four main social classes of Nuzi as discussed in the introduction to the present chapter.

To appreciate the significance of these texts, one must understand that any combination of personal name and patronymic in the Nuzi texts most usually (and by far, at that) defines a single individual. While "Joe" or "Fred" may be the names of scores of men, it is extremely rare that "Joe son of Fred" is applied to more than a single individual.[160] Thus, when "Joe son of Fred" is qualified as a member of the "charioteer" class, it may safely be assumed that, wherever that pair of names appears as son and father in the Nuzi corpus, the same person, a member of the same class, is meant. When one recalls that the Nuzi texts are rich, that they are very numerous and teem with names in assorted bureaucratic contexts, then one begins to appreciate the value of texts such as texts ##94 and

95. For each of these many names (over four score) may potentially appear many times throughout the corpus.[161] And some actually do. And this means that, by tracing these names in their assorted contexts, one, in effect, traces the social activities and characteristics of these two social classes. One such description of these classes is included as part of Maidman 1993a. The utility of such an exercise is self-evident.

In the present instance, text #94 is employed to extract an important datum. Members of the "charioteer" class may legally be responsible for performing the *ilku*. Text #85 establishes that one Bêlaya son of Kip-tae owns real estate and that that real estate is subject to the *ilku* which must be borne by Bêlaya's sons when Bêlaya dies (lines 3–4, 8–10, 11–12). (That is, Bêlaya's sons inherit the land.) Thus, Bêlaya bore it during his lifetime. This same Bêlaya is, according to text #94:33, 35, a member of the "charioteer" class.

As to the ancient function of text #94, it is somewhat obscure. Two groups of "charioteers" are distinguished (lines 1–24, 25–37). The latter group is defined as not having abandoned fields designated as *iškaru*. Much ink has been spilled over this term; its functional meaning remains unclear. See, for example, Dosch 1993: 39–40. It seems likely that *iškaru* refers to palace property, real estate and non-real property alike. Further, it involves public work on such real property or creation and or contribution of such non-real property as a kind of tax. Thus, the latter group of "charioteers" seems to be defined as not being tax evaders. One might then expect the first of the two groups to be contrasted with the second, that is, that they be defined as tax delinquents. In accordance with this idea, Dosch 2009: 110, interprets lines 23–24 something like: "They most certainly were thrown out of their houses; they abandoned their *iškaru*(-fields?)."[162] Pfeiffer and Lacheman, 1942: 33, however, read differently.[163] A translation based on their reading might be: "They most certainly divided their houses; they most certainly harvested their *iškaru*(-fields)." However, this does not stand in contrast with the description in lines 36–37, nor does the first part make clear sense to me. Yet, although a contrast would be sensible in this text, it is not, strictly speaking, necessary. What is most attractive about the Pfeiffer-Lacheman translation, though, is that it echoes HSS XIII, 300:9–11, 19–21, where men are also classified according to *iškaru* performance. There they clearly "did not harvest" and "did harvest" (the verb is the same as the one Pfeiffer and Lacheman read in our text).

So neither solution satisfies, even though each has its points: I have left the problematical lines untranslated below.

But what is important for our purposes, let it be recalled, is not which "charioteers" did what, but that the individuals singled out *were* "charioteers."

Obverse

1 ^{m}*Ḫu-ti-ya* DUMU *Zi-li-ya*
2 ^{m}*Ú-na-ap-te-šup* DUMU *Ar-ku*
3 ^{m}*Ši-la-ḫi* DUMU *Šur-kip*-LUGAL
4 ^{m}*Ar-ta-še-en-ni* DUMU *A-ri-ya*
5 ^{m}*Pil-maš-še* DUMU *Eḫ-li-te-šup*
6 ^{m}*Tu-ra-ri* DUMU *Pa-a-a*
7 ^{m}*Pa-li-ya* DUMU *A-kap-ta-e*
8 DUMU.MEŠ *Ḫa-i-iš-te-šup*
9 DUMU.MEŠ *Pu-ú-ra-a-sa*
10 ^{m}*Ša-ḫi-ni* DUMU [*Mu*]-*uš-te-šup*
11 ^{m}*Te-ḫi-pa-pu* DUMU *Ké*-[*el*]-*šá-pu*
12 ^{m}*Tup-ki-til-la* DUMU *Be-la-a-a*
13 ^{m}*Šúk-ri-te-šup* DUMU *Ar-ru-um-ti*
14 ^{m}*Ur-ḫi-ya* DUMU *Ḫu-ti-ya*
15 ^{m}*Ḫu-ti-ya* DUMU *A-kip*-LUGAL
16 DUMU.MEŠ *Ta-a-a* [ ] *up-pu-tù*
17 ^{m}*Še-en-na-a-a ša* URU *Zi-im-ḫal-še*
18 ^{m}GI-[ ][164] DUMU *Ḫa-ma-an-na*
19 [^{m}x x x[165] DUMU] *It-ḫi-pa-pu*
20 ^{m}GI-[ ][166] DUMU *Tu-ra-ri*
21 ^{m}*Tup-ki-ya* DUMU *Ta-a-a*
22 ŠU.NIGIN 22 (*sic*) $^{LÚ.MEŠ}$*ra-kib* ^{GIŠ}GIGIR
23 *šum-ma iš-tu* É-*šu-nu-ma ša la ú-zi-iz-zu-ú*
24 *šum-ma iš-ka-ri-šu-nu la i-ṣí-*⌈*du*⌉$^{?}$
(blank space)

Reverse

25 ^{m}*Pa-li-ya* DUMU *Me-le-ḫar-pè*
26 ^{m}*Ḫu-ti-ya* DUMU *Zi-li-iḫ-ḫar-pè*
27 ^{m}*A-ri-ya* DUMU *Te-ḫi-ya*
28 ^{m}*Te-eš-šu-ya* DUMU *Zi-il-li-ya*
29 ^{m}*Zi-li-ip-šèr-ta* DUMU *Ma-šar-ta-nu*
30 ^{m}*Al-pu-ya* DUMU *Ma-šar-ta-nu*
31 ^{m}*En-na-ma-ti* DUMU *Na-aš-wi*
32 ^{m}*Te-ḫi-ip-til-la* DUMU *Te-eš-šu-ya*
33 ^{m}*Be-la-a-a* DUMU *Kip-ta-e*
34 ^{m}*Te-ḫi-ip*-LUGAL DUMU *Ni-iḫ-ri-ya*
35 (erasure) ^{LÚ}*ra-kib* ^{GIŠ}GIGIR.<MEŠ$^{?}$>
36 *šum-ma* A.ŠÀ *iš-ka*$_{4}$*-ri-šu-nu*
37 *it-te-zi-ib ù it-ta-bi-it-šu-nu-ti*

HSS XIII, 212

(1–21) Ḫutiya son of Ziliya, Unap-tešup son of Arkun, Šilaḫi son of Šurkip-šarri, Artašenni son of Ariya, Pilmašše son of Eḫli-tešup, Turari son of Paya, Paliya son of Akap-tae, the sons of Ḫaiš-tešup, the sons of Purusa, Šaḫini son of Muš-tešup, Teḫip-apu son of Kelš-apu, Tupki-tilla son of Bêlaya, Šukri-tešup son of Aril-lumti, Urḫiya son of Ḫutiya, Ḫutiya son of Akip-šarri, the sons of Taya ... *upputu*, Šennaya of the town of Zimḫalše, GI-... [son of] Ḫamanna, ... [son of] Itḫip-apu, GI-... son of Turari, Tupkiya son of Taya.

(22–24) Total: 22 (*sic*) charioteers; they most certainly..... .

(25–34) Paliya son of Mele-ḫarpa, Ḫutiya son of Ziliḫ-ḫarpa, Ariya son of Teḫiya, Teššuya son of Ziliya, Zilip-šerta son of Mâšartānu, Alpuya son of Mâšartānu; Enna-mati son of Našwi, Teḫip-tilla son of Teššuya, Bêlaya son of Kip-tae, Teḫip-šarri son of Niḫriya.

(35–37) (erasure) charioteer<s?>; they most certainly did not abandon their *iškaru*-fields and flee.

95. HSS XIII, 6 (SMN 6)

Findspot: Room A34
Publication: Pfeiffer and Lacheman 1942: 1[167]
Edition: Dosch 2009: 105–8 (#28)[168]

Text #95 records, as does text #94, persons of particular social classes (here, two, in the former text, one) who are traceable throughout the Nuzi text corpus.[169] And, in turn, some of those persons, in other contexts, shed light on otherwise invisible features of text #95.[170] The importance of text #95 for this chapter lies with Keliya son of Un-tešup. In text #86, Keliya is one of the purchasers of land, and it is asserted that the vendor is the one bearing the *ilku*. But text #87 implies that the *ilku* had passed to Keliya and his fellow purchasers. Text #95:42, 51 identifies the same Keliya as a member of the *ālik ilki* (the "goers of the going") class. This constitutes a neat, if unsurprising, proof, that members of this class were at times legally liable for the *ilku*-impost.

The function of this text is almost transparent, but not quite. It is a list of persons divided into two groups, "charioteers" and "goers of the going." They, or their interests, are somehow the responsibility of one Akap-šenni, who alone seals the tablet (line 52). The first three entries of the first group assign barley to the individuals. Thus, I consider this list a ration distribution roll. However, a question nags: why is the mention of barley limited to the first three parties only?

Perhaps all the others were given the same, uniform amount, and the scribe felt that, having noted it three times and having established a pattern, further mention was superfluous.[171]

A further matter. Note that the second part of the document lists twenty-eight individuals. And the sum total given on line 51 is twenty-eight. Good! However, the first part of the list is more complicated. The sum is given as 27 "charioteers" (line 28). But there are more than that number counting "son*s* of PN (son of PN$_2$)" (lines 11, 17, 21). Deller apud Dosch 2009: 108, suggests that the first three entries not be included (they are the only ones to whom rations are explicitly assigned) and that the three entries where "sons of ..." are mentioned mean that, in each case, two sons are implied. The result is the desired number, 27. But the omission of the first three entries seems arbitrary. Furthermore, at least in the case of the sons of Teḫip-tilla son of Puḫi-šenni (line 21), they are known to number three, not two.

I believe, on the other hand, that all entries are to be counted, all twenty-seven of them. In the four instances (lines, 11, 17, 21, noted above, *and* line 1—now to be counted), where "son*s* of PN (son of PN$_2$)" appear, they are joint recipients of a single ration for unknown reasons. Note that the two sons of Ḫampate (and perhaps other possible brothers in this list) each receive an individual ration (lines 2–3).

Obverse

1 1 ANŠE ŠE *ša* DUMU.MEŠ ^{m}*Ku-ri-iš-ni*
2 1 ANŠE ŠE *ša* ^{m}*E-ké-ké* DUMU *Ḫa-am-pa-te*
3 1 ANŠE ŠE *ša* ^{m}*Ta-a-a* DUMU KI.MIN
4 ^{m}*Šúk-ri-te-šup* DUMU *Ḫa-ip*-LUGAL
5 ^{m}*Zi-líp-še-er-ta* DUMU *E-ḫé-el-te-šup*
6 ^{m}*Um-pí-ya* DUMU *Ḫu-ti-ya*
7 ^{m}*Ta-in-šu-uḫ* DUMU *Še-ka*$_4$*-ru*
8 ^{m}*Ni-iḫ-ri-ya* DUMU *A-kap-tùk-ké*
9 ^{m}*Tu-ra-a-ri* DUMU *Pá-a-a*
10 ^{m}*Še-ḫé-el-te-šup* DUMU *Ku-tùk-ka*$_4$
11 DUMU.MEŠ ^{m}*Ḫa-iš-te-eš-šup*
12 ^{m}*Na-an-te-šup* DUMU *Ar-te-ya*
13 ^{m}*Pu-ru-sa* DUMU *Ni-iḫ-ri-ya*
14 ^{m}*Ku-ul-mi-ya* DUMU *Ké-li-ya*
15 ^{m}*Šúk-ri-te-šup* DUMU *Ar-ru-um-ti*$_4$
16 ^{m}*Ur-ḫi-ya* DUMU *Ḫu-ti-ya*
17 DUMU.MEŠ *ša* ^{m}*Te-ḫi-ip-til-la* DUMU *Eḫ-li-te-šup*
18 ^{m}*Ur-ḫi-ya* DUMU *Ar-ru-um-pa*

19 ^{m}*Ḫa-ši-ip-til-la* DUMU *I-ri-ri-til-la*
20 ^{m}*Na-i-til-la* DUMU *Te-eš-šu-ya*
21 DUMU.MEŠ *ša* ^{m}*Te-ḫi-ip-til-la* DUMU *Pu-ḫi-še-ni*
22 ^{m}*A-kap-tùk-ké* DUMU *Ka*$_{4}$*-ak-ki*
23 ^{m}*A-mur*-GAL DUMU *Ḫ*[*u*]*-ti-ya*
24 ^{m}*Ut-ḫap-ta-e* DUMU *Zi-ké*
25 ^{m}*A-kip-til-la* DUMU *Šur-kip*-LUGAL
Lower Edge
26 ^{m}*Wa-qar*-EN DUMU *Ta-a-a*
27 ^{md}*Ak-dingir-ra* DUMU ^{d}XXX*-nap-šìr*
Reverse
28 27 $^{LÚ.MEŠ}$*ra-kib* ^{GIŠ}GIGIR.MEŠ

---

29 ^{m}*Te-ḫi-pá-pu* DUMU *Ké-el-ša-pu*
30 ^{md}XXX*-re-me-ni* DUMU *E-ri-šu*
31 ^{m}*Ḫa-ši-pá-pu* DUMU *A-ki-pá-pu*
32 ^{m}*Ḫu-zi-ri* DUMU *A-ri-ik-ka*$_{4}$*-a-a*
33 ^{m}*Ta-ḫi-ri-iš-ti* DUMU *Ta-ri-ba-as-sú*
34 ^{m}*Te-ḫi-ya* DUMU *Ḫa*$^{!}$(=ZA)*-ma-an-na* ^{m}*It-ḫe-ki* DUMU ^{d}IM*-te-ya*
35 ^{m}*Ar-šá-an-ta* DUMU *Šur-kip*-LUGAL
36 ^{m}*Ni-iḫ-ri-ya* DUMU *Ta-ú-ka*$_{4}$
37 ^{m}*Ḫu-pí-ta* DUMU *Ḫa-ma-an-na*
38 ^{m}*Pa-a-a* DUMU *Ar-te-eš-še*
39 ^{m}*Eḫ-li-pa-pu* DUMU *Nu-pá-na-a-a*[172]
40 ^{m}*Ḫa-na-a-a* DUMU *Še-eš-we* ^{m}*A-kip-še-ni* DUMU *Ki-ri-ya*
41 ^{m}*Ka*$_{4}$*-wi-in-ni* DUMU *Šúm-mi-ya* ^{m}*It-ḫa-pu* DUMU *Wa-an-ti-ya*
42 ^{m}*Ké-li-ya* DUMU *Un-te-šup* ^{m}*En-šúk-rù* DUMU *Ta-a-a*
43 ^{m}LUGAL-^{d}XXX DUMU *Ar-šá-tu*$_{4}$*-ya* ^{m}*Ḫu-zi-ri* DUMU *Ša-at-tu*$_{4}$*-mar-ti*
44 ^{m}ŠEŠ-AMA*-šá* DUMU *Ti-eš*$_{15}$*-ši-mi-ka*$_{4}$
45 ^{m}*Ku-um-mi-ya* DUMU *Pu-ḫi* ^{m}*Tup-pí-iz-zi* DUMU *Ké-li-ya*
46 ^{m}*Eḫ-li-te-šup* DUMU *Ta-i-še-en-ni*
47 ^{m}*Na-ni-pu-kùr* DUMU *Ḫa-lu-ut-ta*
48 ^{m}*Ma-it-ta* DUMU ÌR-^{d}X
49 ^{m}*Pu-ú-ta* DUMU *Ú-ké*
50 ^{m}*Dá-a-a-ni* DUMU *Zi-ké*
51 28 $^{LÚ.MEŠ}$*a-li-ik il-ki*

---

52 ^{NA_4}KIŠIB ^{m}*A-kap-še-en-ni*
S.I.

HSS XIII, 6

(1–28) 1 homer of barley of/for the sons of Kurišni; 1 homer of barley of/for Ekeke son of Ḫampate; 1 homer of barley of/for Taya son of ditto; Šukri-tešup son of Ḫaip-šarri, Zilip-šerta son of Eḫli-tešup, Umpiya son of Ḫutiya, Tain-šuḫ son of Šekaru, Niḫriya son of Akap-tukke, Turari son of Paya, Šeḫel-tešup son of Kutukka, the sons of Ḫaiš-tešup, Nan-tešup son of Ar-teya, Purusa son of Niḫriya, Kulmiya son of Keliya, Šukri-tešup son of Aril-lumti, Urḫiya son of Ḫutiya, the sons of Teḫip-tilla son of Eḫli-tešup, Urḫiya son of Arrumpa, Ḫašip-tilla son of Iriri-tilla, Nai-tilla son of Teššuya, the sons of Teḫip-tilla son of Puḫi-šenni, Akap-tukke son of Kakki, Amur-rabī son of Ḫutiya, Utḫap-tae son of Zike, Akip-tilla son of Šurkip-šarri, Waqar-bêli son of Taya, Ak(ka)dingirra son of Sin-napšir. 27 "charioteers."

(29–51) Teḫip-apu son of Kelš-apu, Sin-rêmēnī son of Êrišu, Ḫašip-apu son of Akip-apu, Ḫuziri son of Arik-kaya, Taḫarišti son of Tarîbat-sin, Teḫiya son of Ḫamanna, Itḫ-eki son of Adatteya, Ar-šanta son of Šurkip-šarri, Niḫriya son of Tauka, Ḫupita son of Ḫamanna, Paya son of Ar-tešše, Eḫlip-apu son of Nupanaya, Ḫanaya son of Šešwe, Akip-šenni son of Kirriya, Kawinni son of Šummiya, Itḫ-apu son of Wantiya, Keliya son of Un-tešup, En-šukru son of Taya, Šarru-sin son of Ar-šatuya, Ḫuziri son of Šattu-marti, Aḫ-ummiša son of Tieš-šimika, Kummiya son of Puḫi, Tuppizzi son of Keliya, Eḫli-tešup son of Tai-šenni, Nanip-ukur son of Ḫalutta, Maitta son of Ward-ištar, Puta son of Uke, Dayyānu son of Zike. 28 "goers of the going."

---

(52) Seal impression of Akap-šenni[173] (*seal impression*)

96. HSS XIV, 568 (SMN 568)

Findspot: Unknown
Publication: Lacheman 1950:16–17[174]
Edition: None

Text #96 is a declaration made by joint vendors of an orchard. They affirm the sale, one made by means of real estate adoption, give details, and confirm that they received their "gift," that is, the sale price. Receipt of the "gift" may have been the occasion of this declaration.

The purchaser of this valuable real estate (urban orchard land) is a slave. Whether or not the slave acts as an agent for his master, here a powerful and wealthy prince, is not known. Nor, for our purposes, does it matter. It is the slave who is the principle. He has the right to obtain (and presumably to relinquish) title to real estate. Since the text states that the sellers will bear the *ilku*, this implies, at the very least, that the buyer, the slave, could have been responsible for the impost. Of course, I believe I have demonstrated that, regardless of what the text says, the buyer, the slave, eventually bears responsibility for the *ilku*.

Obverse
1 [EME]-*šu-nu*^{MEŠ} *ša* ^{m}*Ka*$_{4}$*-i-te-š*[*up š*]*a*
2 [^{m}]*-te-šup ù ša* ^{m}*Tar-m*[*i-y*]*a* DUMU.[MEŠ] *Ta*[*r-*][175]
3 [*i-na*] *pa-ni ši-bu-ti*^{MEŠ} *iq-ta-bu-ú*
4 [^{m}*K*] *a*$_{4}$*-i-til-la* ÌR **(5)**[176] *ša* ^{m}*Ši-il-wa-te-šup* DUMU LUGAL
5 *a-na ma-ru-ti ni-te-pu-uš* GIŠ.SAR.MEŠ
6 *i-na a-ṣé-e* KÁ.GAL *e-qí i-na le-et*
7 GIŠ.SAR *ša* ^{m}*Tar-mi-te-šup* 1 *ma-at* 40 *i-na am-ma-ti*
8 *li-wi-is-sú i-na ḫu-ub-bal-li ša* GIŠ.SAR
9 *a-na* ^{m}*Ka*$_{4}$*-i-til-la ni-it-ta-din ù ni-nu*
10 5 ANŠE ŠE *ki-ma* NÍG.BA.MEŠ*-ni a-šar* ^{m}*Ka*$_{4}$*-i-til-la*
11 *ni-il-te-qè il-ku ša* GIŠ.SAR *ni-nu-ma*
12 *na-ša-nu šum-ma* GIŠ.SAR *up-ta-aq-qa-*<*ar*>
13 *nu-za-ak-ka*$_{4}$*-ma a-na* ^{m}*Ka*$_{4}$*-i-til-la ni-na-an-din*
14 *ma-an-nu ša* KI.BAL.MEŠ$^{-tu}$ 1 MA.NA <KÙ.BABBAR>
Lower Edge
15 [1] MA.NA KÙ.SIG$_{17}$ *ú-ma-al-la*
16 *ṭup-pu* AŠ EGIR.MEŠ *šu-du-ut* É.GAL *i-na* URU-DINGIR.MEŠ
Reverse
17 *a-šar* KÁ.GAL *e-qí ša-ṭì-ir*
18 IGI *Tù-ra-ri* DUMU *Ta-e* IGI *Ḫa-ši-ya*
19 DUMU *Ar-nu-ur-ḫé* IGI *Ḫu-pí-ta* DUMU *Ip-šá-ḫa-lu*[177]
20 *an-nu-tù ša* GIŠ.SAR *mu-šal-wu-ú*
21 IGI *Ta-i-te-šup* DUMU *I-ri-ya*
22 IGI *A-ri-ip-a-bu-ul-li* DUMU *Ar-nu-ur-ḫé*
23 IGI *Na-i-še-en-ni* DUMU *Te-šup-a-tal*
24 IGI [*El*]*-hi-ip-til-la* DUB.SAR DUMU *Wu-ur-ru-ku-un-ni*
Upper Edge
25 NA$_{4}$ ^{m}*A-ri-ip-a-bu-ul-li*
26 NA$_{4}$ ^{m}*El-*[*ḫi*]*-ip-til-la* DUB.SAR$^{-rù}$
27 NA$_{4}$ ^{m}*Ta-i-te-*[*šup*]
28 NA$_{4}$ ^{m}[*Ḫ*]*u-pí-ta*
29 NA$_{4}$ ^{m}*Tù-ra-ri*
30 NA$_{4}$ ^{m}*Ḫa-ši-ya*

Left Edge

31 NA$_4$ ^{m}*Tar-mi-ya* NA$_4$ ^{m}[*Ka*$_4^{?}$-*i*$^{?}$]-*te-šup*

HSS XIV, 568

(1–2) Declaration of Kai-tešup, of ...-tešup, and of Tarmiya son[s] of Tar-.....

(3–9) [Before] witnesses, they averred: "We have adopted Kai-tilla, a slave of Šilwa-tešup son of the king. We have given to Kai-tilla an orchard at the exit of the *ēqu*(?)[178] town gate, adjacent to the orchard of Tarmi-tešup, the perimeter of the orchard along its fence being 1 hundred 40 cubits.

(9–11) "And we have taken 5 homers of barley from Kai-tilla as our gift.

(11–12) "Furthermore, we bear the *ilku* of the orchard.

(12–13) "Should the orchard be the object of a claim, we shall clear (it) and give (it) to Kai-tilla."

(14–15) He who abrogates (this contract) shall pay 1 mina <of silver> (and) [1] mina of gold.

(16–17) The tablet was written after the palace proclamation in Āl-ilāni, at the *ēqu*(?) town gate.

(18–24) Before Turari son of Tae; before Hašiya son of Arn-urḫe; before Ḫupita son of Ipša-ḫalu. These are the measurers of the orchard. Before Tai-tešup son of Iriya; before Arip-abulli son of Arn-urḫe; before Nai-šenni son of Tešup-atal, before Elḫip-tilla, scribe, son of Wurrukunni.

(25–31) Seal of Arip-abulli; seal of Elḫip-tilla, the scribe; seal of Tai-tešup; seal of Ḫupita; seal of Turari; seal of Ḫašiya; seal of Tarmiya; seal of [Kai?]-tešup.

Notes

Introduction

1. From Theodore J. Lewis's Series Editor's Foreword.

2. It is not that archaeology becomes superseded. It is essential in all periods. Certainly, the historian is vitally dependent on the archaeologist for documents. And documents are another type, albeit a very special type, of artifact. So archaeology must deal with documents as it deals with pots and stamp seals and paintings and fire pits. Cf. Stolper 1992: 255b.

3. That is why very good archaeologists often write what they think is history, but is, in reality, a description of the past. They fail to recognize that history is an intellectual discipline with its own methodologies.

4. Texts are even occasionally explicitly self-referential. They say things like, "when you hear this message…." Another type of self-reference is exemplified in CH Epilogue: "I [i.e., Hammurabi] have inscribed my precious pronouncements upon my stela [i.e., upon the very object on which the words appear] and set it up…." (Roth 1995: 133–34).

5. W. S. Gilbert, *The Pirates of Penzance*, Act I.

6. For a similar appreciation, but with a caveat regarding primary sources, see van de Mieroop 1997.

7. Of late, historians have neglected the importance of the literary task. Belle-lettristic history writing has, for the most part, languished for over a century.

8. Herodotus is an entrée but a troublesome one if we expect accuracy or transparency even for the events closest in time to the author. See the classic essay of T. Cuyler Young, Jr. (1980: esp. 237–39). Cf. Young 1988: 5–6.

9. A Herodotus-like military drama is not, or should not, be what the ancient historian is looking for. Besides, military drama is not lacking, even in seemingly dry reports (see text #13) and is enhanced by its understatement and its fundamental factuality. And, added to this tension and information from a single narrative is the possibility of combining this one text with other such to build a picture of a campaign and ultimately a war. For such an example, see ch. 1

10. See, e.g., the comments introducing text #89, below.

11. Some of the material presented here is adapted from Maidman 1995: 931–34.

12. Another town, called Gasur, existed on the same site in earlier periods and has also yielded documents.

13. The temple text collection lacks conceptual coherence as far as I can tell.

14. Most of the administrative texts cluster to the last decade or so of the town's existence. This is a common pattern for ancient Near Eastern archives. The tablets on which the texts were written were, for the most part, periodically disposed of in one way or another (tablets take up needed space). Most of the surviving tablets would have been written after the last disposal and

before the destruction or abandonment of the settlement in which they were found.

15. However, the texts are weighted toward the last years of the town.

16. However it is not exhaustive as a survey of text genres. Testamentary wills, e.g., though well attested at Nuzi, are conspicuous by their absence from this volume.

17. Presentation of texts by archaeological findspot is a crucial aid in understanding the contents of our texts, supplying vital context for the words, context in terms of topographical positioning of the tablet in antiquity, and context in terms of other documents and artifacts with which the tablet is associated. That should be the way texts receive their first publications and editions. See further below, as an appendix to this introduction, for a chart of findspots in Nuzi represented in this collection of texts.

18. Indeed, focus on the archive *qua* archive is itself an historical dimension worth recognizing and developing. This would justify studying *all* texts of a given archive, regardless of their coherence at any other level. Archival collocation by itself merits the consideration and attention of the historian.

19. Though not ecclesiastical, in these cases.

20. All relevant or crucial texts have been treated in each case.

21. The best introduction to these texts remains Gadd 1926.

22. The Kirkuk texts *are* useful in demonstrating Arrapḫa City's participation in the Assyrian War. See von Dassow 2009.

23. We may assert, at the least, that such accounts have not survived.

24. The stories, as told in these texts, constitute the only entrée into the course of Nuzi's political history writ large: Arrapḫa, as the Nuzi texts testify, is joined by Mittanni in opposition to Assyria's thrust eastwards. Note that the narrative mostly emerges from administrative texts. No Herodotus here!

25. *All* texts are historical. The term "historical" is often applied just to narrative accounts commissioned by the palace. These latter may include royal annals, chronicles, and other genres.

26. For an earlier evaluation of the mayor at Nuzi, see Cassin 1982. Cf. Wilhelm 1992a: 116, note to §6.

27. This quality and characteristic of these texts, dubbed the "Kušši-ḫarpe dossier," is adumbrated by Cassin (1982: 113) and Zaccagnini (2003: 569, par. 2.1.2.2).

28. But the mine is hardly exhausted by this one "treasure." The following is a partial list of data revealed *en passant*. The corvée (Akk. *ilku*) is under the mayor's authority or jurisdiction (text #32—he exempts; text #37—he uses it for his own private benefit); the corvée is organized district by district (text #37); the mayor *may* legally be able to alienate municipal real estate (text #31; N.B.: more fundamentally, there may be such a thing as municipal real estate); the local government is responsible for bridge maintenance (text #49; the government is probably responsible for bridge construction as well); there exists a municipal officer in charge of sheep collection, at the least for supplying the *eššešu*-festival (the Kipiya texts); Nuzi stands in a position of superiority, perhaps authority, over other towns in the vicinity (text #35); the task force (Sum. $ERIN_2$) exists as an institution, a legal fiction, possibly represented by its leader and ultimately under the authority of the mayor (text #48); more broadly, the task force, the "palace," and the mayoralty all exist and are attested as organizational entities.

29. See already Lion 2000: 158–59.

30. Further information on predators and prey alike are forthcoming from their appearance in government records and other documentation bearing little or no direct relevance to private economic activity.

31. This is "appeal to authority," also known as the "[historical] fallacy of argument *ad*

verecundiam" (Fischer 1970: 283).

32. Thus the authoritative *Reallexikon der Assyriologie* misunderstands the *ilku* (Kienast 1976: 58a, asserting that the *ilku* is not bound to the land but to the land's original owner).

33. Cf. Foster and Foster 2009: 100; and Byrne 2007: 13, n. 52. Byrne (2007: 12, n. 52) also implies incorrectly that land sale is only once described as being sold for a "price." But see, simply, *CAD* Š/III, 25b, for multiple (but not exhaustive) examples.

34. On this enterprise and its failure, see Eichler 1989.

35. Arrapḫa was also a client-state of Mittanni. Assyria's attack on Arrapḫa was thus also an attack on Mittanni, as well as a move to simply control the territory on its eastern border.

36. I shall detail this elsewhere.

37. It is known that all the texts come from Nuzi and were excavated during organized excavations between 1925 and 1931. In some cases, the exact findspots of the artifacts were either not recorded or recorded in an ambiguous fashion or have been lost.

38. These data are mostly derived and extracted from Starr 1939: passim; Lacheman 1958: v–viii; Lacheman 1974: 360–68; and Pedersén 1998: 17–28. More details on these findspots are to be found in those sources. Site plans are to be found in Starr 1937: passim and Pedersén 1998: 18–29.

39. Or P 465. The room straddles squares K and P.

40. What was once called room C2 was subsequently called L2 and M2. It is impossible to determine which room is meant in any given case (Lacheman 1958: vii).

41. This extended archive begins with Teḫip-tilla's parents and extends to his great-grandson.

Chapter 1

1. See Fadhil 1983: 197–201 for an earlier treatment of the topic. Cf. Zaccagnini 1979b: 20–25.

2. Starr 1939: 87, 89, 108, 167, 344, 347, and *passim*.

3. The term "empire" is used with caution. Its use implies that one government dominates another in its external and, at least in part, its internal affairs. But IsraelEphʿal (personal communication) defines empire as that state of affairs where one government encounters resistence to its hegemony over another such entity. If Ephʿal's definition of empire be accepted, then we do not know if Mittanni's control of Arrapḫa was imperial or not.

4. Since Assyrian violence signaled the end of Nuzi, attestations of peaceful relations must, therefore, be earlier, even if the documents are not dated.

5. The texts presented below are often exemplary of their kind, not exhaustive.

6. Females from Assyria appear to have arrived at Nuzi according to *JEN* V, 499; and Lacheman 1967: 13–14 (his text #5), but it is unclear whether, in the former case, they are Assyrian escapees/refugees or Arrapḫans ransomed from Assyria. In the latter case, the female is certainly a local Nuzian.

7. *JEN* V, 459 also involves an Assyrian *ḫapiru* and is very close to text #8. The name of the Assyrian translates to something like "Native-of-the-Tigris."

8. These observations may be vitiated, at least in part and potentially, if we recognize, with Israel Ephʿal (personal communication), that the presence of isolated ethnic minorities or foreigners in a polity with an ethnic majority has no necessary connection with the political re-

lations existing between two adjacent states dominated by those different ethnicities. In the present case, Assyrians could peacefully live in Nuzi, though hostility might obtain between Assyria and Arrapḫa. But even were this so, and it seems eminently reasonable, the evidence at our disposal, considered collectively (texts ##1–7), might point to peaceful relations. Note that all this evidence comes from earlier generations (where it can be identified at all). None comes from the last generation. This might be suggestive of the position I am advocating, but it is certainly not dispositive.

9. For a general and impressionistic observation to this effect, see Fincke 2000: 149.

An observation is in order regarding the government administrative texts relating to military preparations. There are grounds for supposing that such documents focus chronologically and geographically on the central and eastern campaigns. No such text clearly points to any western activity. I develop a possible implication of this phenomenon in a forthcoming article.

10. For details on this chronological observation, see Maidman 2008: 207–8, n. 37. It should further be noted that Nuzi generated no siege documents; there are no obvious indications of dire economic straits owing to military events. Cf., for such documents, Ephʿal 2009: 135–43, where the city of Emar *does* have such documents, these from roughly the same period as the Nuzi texts. This shows that the phenomenon of siege documents already existed then. Cf., for a later period, Oppenheim 1955.

11. And yet, no such directive addressed to Nuzi's mayor has been discovered. And Nuzi, where the text was found, would have been a "border" town after a successful Assyrian attack on the Turša region. If this is correct, then the directive cannot have preceded that attack.

12. It must be emphasized here and throughout these remarks that discussion of these texts in the context of the historical narrative presented here is not to be construed as implying strict chronological ordering. To be sure, text #8 must have been written toward the start of the suggested process, followed (eventually) by text #13. And texts ##21 and 23 must be assigned to a later period. Yet these documents are not dated. The reader (and especially the writer!) must be wary of the following. The order of the texts presented here appear to make logical narrative and causative sense. But such sense does not prove that the order of events as presented is correct. Logic is no adequate substitute for evidence. *Caveat lector*. See, however, below, on an attested claim of Tiglath-Pileser I as constituting analogical evidence.

13. Indeed, many texts testify to the mustering of troops, including chariotry, and to the disposition of various types of military equipment. The texts presented here are a mere sampling.

14. On the heavy involvement of Ḫanigalbat / Mittanni on behalf of Arrapḫa, see below; Zaccagnini 1979b: 20–25; and Lion 2008: 72–73, 75.

15. Less likely: did not go *into* battle. Chariotry lost seems a newer, more crucial, and useful datum worthy of being recorded. See further below, introduction to text #12.

16. Lewy 1959: 22; Zaccagnini 1979b: 14, 18, 19, 20; Jankowska 1982: 142; Fadhil 1983: 121, 162. A most extreme such depiction appears in Wilhelm 1989: 35.

17. Assyria was the destroyer: Harrak 1987: 52–55; Pedersén 1998: 17 ("probable").

18. Fadhil 1983:162b attempts to link directly text #18 with text # 26, placing Taribatu (text #18) and Ṣilliya (text #26) in northwest Arrapḫa, subject to Assyrian attack and Našbat (text #18) in the south near Lubdi (text # 26) subject to Babylonian attack. Fadhil's attempt fails because the two texts are united only superficially, by a common genre and quartermaster official. Otherwise, text # 26 is too laconic and text #18 too obscure to support these deductions. (Assyrian battles near Lubti are plausible and, in a different period, actually did occur. See below, for the example of Tiglath-Pileser I.)

19. See below, introductory comments to text #18, for details.

20. The improbability of Babylonian aggression against territory bordering on Assyria increases greatly when considering the larger international political picture. Babylonia whines to Egypt that Assyria no longer recognizes its inferior and dependent position vis-à-vis Babylonia in precisely the period of our texts. Shortly thereafter, an Assyrian-Babylonian dynastic marriage places an Assyrian royal grandson on the Babylonian throne. When that grandson is assassinated, an Assyrian attack on Babylon ensues. The rebellious element is eliminated and a second grandson is installed.

21. By "border," I mean territory where authority begins to be claimed by another state, not a specific line that can be surveyed. Such modern borders did not, for the most part, exist in the ancient Near East. Israel Eph'al (personal communication) defines such territorial authority as the state's ability to collect taxes from a territory's inhabitants.

22. Text #13, the fullest description of the consequences of the struggle at Turša, was clearly written a considerable time before the end of Nuzi. See Maidman 2008: 207–8, n. 37 for the evidence for this claim.

23. It is part of the borderland of which HSS XV, 1 speaks.

24. Yorghan Tepe (the site of ancient Nuzi) is located 16 kilometers southwest of Kirkuk (the site of ancient Arrapḫa). The towns of Zizza and Apena must be located near Nuzi since both places loom large in the local Nuzi landscape. Both are locations of major land holdings of Nuzians.

25. Does "Arman" reflect the earlier Arwa, located in central Arrapḫan territory and a town where anti-Assyrian chariotry was stationed?

26. Grayson 1991: 53 (Tiglath-Pileser I; A.0.87.10, lines 36–38).

27. As early as the late Old Assyrian period, almost half a millennium before these events, the city of Arrapḫa was already important to Assyria. Around 1830 the city was captured by Assyria (Glassner 2004: 162–63 [the earliest of the Assyrian eponym chronicles]). After the Nuzi period and especially beginning with the late Middle Assyrian period, Arrapḫa assumes importance as a major city within the Assyrian state, though occasionally the city fell into Babylonian and Elamite hands. First-millennium governors of Arrapḫa are repeatedly attested as important Assyrian eponym officials (i.e., years are named after them). Arrapḫa's fall to Babylonian forces in 616 marks the beginning of the destruction of the Assyrian state (Glassner 2004: 218–19 [part of the Neo-Babylonian chronicle series]).

28. Texts pertaining to this stage of the hostilities are noted in Dosch 1993: 12–13.

29 Note that another text, HSS XIV, 14, links these two towns: horses (as, before, men) are to be dispatched to both places. However, although soldiers, horses, and (potential) urban violence are described, it is far from clear that enemy action is involved. Deller and Fadhil, 1972: 211, offer a sober description of this text as possibly indicating enemy presence in Zizza. Cf. Lewy 1968: 158b. This suggestive but somewhat obscure text is therefore omitted from this volume.

30. Zizza too may have been defended by Mittannians. Singers from Ḫanigalbat are identified as being in Zizza (Zaccagnini 1979b: 12–14). These women may have been attached to the Mittanni army. Incidentally, if this is correct, it would identify this text as chronologically anterior to the fall of Zizza, obvious in any case.

31. For a succinct description of the equipment and paraphernalia attaching to the chariotry of Nuzi's army, see Drews 1988: 87–88, 229.

32. See Fincke 1993: 30.

33. Texts pertaining to this stage of the hostilities are, once again, noted in Dosch 1993: 12–13.

34. See Fadhil 1983: 340 on the battle at Ṣilliya.

35. Fadhil 1983: 162b interprets this text as demonstrating that Arrapḫa (and Ḫanigalbat) were fighting a two-front war: against the Babylonians at Lubti in the south and against Assyria at Ṣilliya in the northwest. This explanation violates Ockham's Razor, coming, as it does, with the weighty baggage of many assumptions and virtually no supporting evidence. For further details, see Fadhil 1983: 121b (an Arrapḫan victory!), 162a–b.

36. HSS, XV, 82 may be relevant in this context but is frustratingly laconic. It is, therefore, not included among the text treated in this chapter. The document is a list of chariots under the command of familiar individuals. These chariots are numbered together with associated armor for *some* of them and with whole chariots in one case. It is tempting to interpret the enumerated armor and chariots as lost or damaged paraphernalia. And such damage would most naturally be associated with military action. Moreover, the text was written probably in the town of Ṣilliya (the first part of the GN is broken away). This might imply that the losses were incurred during fighting at Lubti and that the battle for Ṣilliya took place after Lubti fell.

However, neither damage nor conflict nor victory nor defeat nor an enemy is explicitly mentioned in this text. And so, no matter how suggestive HSS XV, 82 may be, excessive speculation is required to make this text communicate its message. It is noted here in lieu of further development.

37. Cf., with the foregoing reconstruction, that of Freu 2003: 140–44.

38. For brief descriptions of the findspots of the tablets in this volume, see above, Introduction, pp. 13–14. For an overview of the assorted findspots of the Nuzi texts, see Pedersén 1998: 15–29.

39. Published in transliteration only.

40. A useful discussion appears in Zaccagnini 1979b: 18, n. 76.

41. A somewhat detailed but highly flawed discussion of this text appears in Jankowska 1982: 145.

42. The barley itself was meant to serve the needs of a few days up to two months, depending on the recipient and individual circumstances. Thus, strictly speaking, this is not an account of monthly expenditures.

43. For example, HSS XIV, 46, 47, 50 (= text #3).

44. The ration is two seahs per youth per month, thus conforming to the typical ration for Wilhelm's young males – group I (Wilhelm 1980: 22). The metrology for Nuzi dry measures is as follows (the figures follow Wilhelm 1980: 27):

1 homer = 10 seahs

1 (PI) = 6 seahs

1 seah = 8 *qa*s

One seah is approximately 6.7 liters.

Since the (PI) represents a number of seahs fewer than what add up to a homer, the translation, for the sake of simplicity, employs "homers," "seahs," and "*qa*s" only.

45. Those rations, 2 seahs per woman per month, also conform to Wilhelm's calculations for mature female slaves (Wilhelm 1980: 22).

46. So already Deller and Fadhil 1972: 200.

47. Lewy 1959: 13, n. 1, e.g., accepts this interpretation and considers these to be a royal body guard. See also *CAD* Š/II, 303b ("the king's own horses" [*sic*]).

48. Compare the clear Nuzi GÌR-signs at HSS IX, 24:16 and HSS XIX, 5:37.

49. See HSS XIV, 46:2; 50:2; 52:2; and other texts.

50. "Envoy" translates *ubāru*, who is not merely a "foreigner" as maintained by Jankowska

(1982: 143). If that were the case, then the word should appear, at least some of the time, without further qualification. It seems not to have so appeared. And why does it appear at all when individuals are designated according to the lands from which they come? *ubāru* in those contexts would be tautological and superfluous. An *ubāru* at Nuzi is designated as coming from particular countries: Mari (HSS XV, 84:7), Akkad (i.e., Babylonia; HSS XIV, 136:21), especially Ḫanigalbat (i.e., the kingdom of Mittanni, overlord of Arrapḫa, the petty state of which Nuzi was part; see Fincke 1993: 89 for the many references), and, of course, Assyria (our texts ##2 and 3). Cf. HSS XIV, 56:19, a broken context. Perhaps significantly, no *ubāru* is said to have come from Kassite-Land or the land of the Lullubians, entities with no attested state structures. *ubāru*s are, as in the present case, at least partially sustained by the host government. Thus they are "envoys" (perhaps sometimes even "ambassadors," though direct evidence is lacking). As such, the term is understood by Pfeiffer and Speiser 1936: 124; Lewy 1959: 14; and, most recently, Zaccagnini 1979b: 15 (and further bibliography at n. 61).

51. That this is a scribal omission is demonstrated by closely parallel texts such as HSS XIV, 46:4 and 49:4. The connection of the present text and its PNs to those texts and *theirs* and to others still, has been observed by Zaccagnini 1974: 28–29 with n. 26; 1979b: 14; and Jankowska 1982: 144–46. Cf. Lewy 1959: 14.

52. Cf. HSS XIV, 47:16; 49:18; 52:30, all texts highly similar to this one.

53. Waterers or some other occupation involving water must be meant. Cf. *CAD* M/II, 156b.

54. This is the title of a high court or bureaucratic official.

55. A brief, idiosyncratic, discussion of this text appears in Lewy 1959: 13, n. 1. Cf. also Zaccagnini 1979b: 18, n. 77.

56. For this restoration, cf. 2:25.

57. Cf. 2:27, 29. This PN may be a conflation of the two PNs mentioned in that related document.

58. The catalog number for *EN* 9/3, 284 actually appears as SMN 3157. This is probably wrong. SMN 3505 is the number assigned to it when it was published as HSS XVI, 326. This is probably right. See note 59.

59. This room number is associated with the artifact when it is identified as SMN 3505 and published as HSS XVI, 326. As *EN* 9/3, 284, its findspot is given as room C36. But no mention is made of tablets having been found at this locus. See Starr 1939: 235.

60. So *EN* 9/3, 284. HSS XVI, 326 has, incorrectly, *bá*. See Lion 2005: 200.

61. So *EN* 9/3, 284. HSS XVI, 326 has, incorrectly, UDU.SAL.MEŠ. See Lion 2005: 200.

62. For partial editions, see the entries to this text in Maidman 2005: 246.

63. Cf. *JEN* V, 456:9.

64. The reconstruction follows *NPN*, p. 11a and is based on this individual's appearance in other contemporary texts.

65. So *NPN*, p. 37a, based on this person's reappearance once elsewhere in the same time frame.

66. The mina at Nuzi weighs about 500 grams, a little more than a pound (Powell 1989–1990: 514b).

67. The son's name belongs to the Kassite language, the father's to the Hurrian. Similar instances are not rare in the Nuzi texts. Thus, ethno-linguistic affiliation at Nuzi may not, with certainty, be determined by means of the language of personal names alone.

68. For partial editions, see the entries to this text in Maidman 2005: 237a.

69. Or the like.

70. The term is superfluous here, even inappropriate, since the subject of this clause is ex-

plicitly named.

71. "A substitute slave" or the like is contained in the lacuna (i.e., the gap).

72. For partial editions, see the entries to this text in Maidman 2005: 238a. Bottéro 1954: 43 is especially helpful.

73. Note, however, that a *ḫapiru* can be a scribe (*EN* 9/3, 55:22).

74. Collated. The sign does not appear in Chiera 1934b: pl. 187.

75. The witnesses in this list are mostly common ones in the corpus of texts from the archives of Teḫip-tilla son of Puḫi-šenni. Therefore, the missing patronymics here can often be reconstructed with some confidence. In some cases, the reconstructed spellings (*not* the names themselves) are approximate.

76. The last two sign fragments do not appear in Chiera 1934b: pl. 187. See *NPN*, p. 34a; but cf. p. 23a.

77. This publication is the basis of the present study.

78. For a different evaluation of this GN, see Cassin 1982: 116, n. 7.

79. The meaning of *pāṭu* (ZAG) is a crux in this text. Zaccagnini 1979c: 19 with n. 21, in rendering the term "territory," obscures the essential feature of the lexeme and of the document as a whole. It is borderland that is the object of special attention. The clause contained in lines 15–19 all but demands this interpretation.

80. These restorations may be slightly excessive given the size of the gap. By deleting [*a-n*]*a* (with the remaining [*n*]*a* representing the last part of the first word), a slightly different meaning results. See below, note 83.

81. For this restoration, cf. line 48, identifying a known king of Arrapḫa.

82. *ša*!(= KI) ⌜*i*⌝+*na*!(= LA). These signs yield little sense to me. *ki-i*(-)*la*, the likelier reading, is no improvement.

83. A slightly shorter restoration of the text's opening gap yields something like the following translation: "[Thus] the mayor of Tašuḫḫe: '[The king] has issued a directive. . . .'" However, that would raise a new problem: why would the king have sealed this particular document? The sense of the text as a whole is unaffected by this alternate reading. See above, note 80.

84. Probably, but not necessarily, a tower in this case rather than an entire district.

85. This appears to be an expansion of lines 5–7. There hinterland is specified, here borderland.

86. Who? The mayor? The governor? Other *dimtu* owners? See also lines 45–47.

87. Cf. lines 9–10.

88. If the restoration is correct, then the royal palace may be meant here.

89. This publication is the better copy and is the basis for the present study.

90. Cf. the treatments of Lewy 1959: 16 with n. 3; and Zaccagnini 1979b: 4–6.

91. See already Lewy 1959: 16.

92. See already Zaccagnini 1979b: 5; and Kendall 1981: 210.

93. Cf. Lewy 1959: 16.

94. See Zaccagnini 1979b: 21; and Kendall 1981: 209 ("chariot squadron").

95. The arithmetic for this section is difficult since there are gaps where numbers once appeared, since there are unexpected disagreements between these lines (ll. 15–18) and lines 10–13, and since the scribe may have committed an error in his calculations. See Zaccagnini 1979b: 4 for possible text reconstructions, and cf. Kendall 1981: 210.

96. This individual has special connections to the Arrapḫan chariotry. See, e.g., *JEN* VI, 612:2 and HSS XV, 114:8.

97. Published in transliteration only.

98. Less likely: "missing." Cf. Lion 2008:74, citing HSS XV, 3, where further battle losses are enumerated.

99. Cf. *CAD* P, 517a.

100. Or: "1 set of reins, (and) in it. . . ."

101. The latter copy is employed here for convenience.

102. See also Dosch 1993: ch. 1, esp. pp. 17–20.

103. For further on this and similar texts, see comments to text #19.

104. My observation in Maidman 2008: 209, that neither text was sealed, is thus wrong.

105. For speculations on this point, see Maidman 2008: 207–9.

106. Chiera and Speiser 1927: 56 read *ú-tũ* (*sic*), but "B" has a clear E at this point.

107. This reading is confirmed by *JEN* VI, 670:30′.

108. The expected sign is also absent in *JEN* VI, 670:37′.

109. Cf. line 51.

110. Cf. line 58. So already Fincke 1993: 71.

111. "B" locates the destination as [the town of] Tazzu. Thus this *dimtu* may well be located in the jurisdiction of the town of Tazzu.

112. "B": "western *dimtu* of Ḫaiš-tešup."

113. The expected word is also absent in "B."

114. There were two distinct *dimtu*s of Teḫip-tilla, one in Turša (this one) and one farther east, in Zizza. However, since text #13 deals with events in the Turša region, "eastern" here must refer to an area in the eastern part of this *dimtu* or to an easterly *dimtu*-tower (as opposed to another one, farther west) in this Turša *dimtu*-district of Teḫip-tilla.

115. Cf. lines 31–33.

116. Cf. lines 22–24.

117. This house, according to "B" (line 39′) is located in the town of . . .-x-abraššemi, a GN probably to be reconstructed: Ilabra(t)-šemī. See Fadhil 1983: 198; and Fincke 1993: 114.

118. "B" adds here: "from the *dimtu* of Unap-tae they took [Tanu]."

119. "B" adds here: "a palace slave."

120. This suggests that this is a list of losses, perhaps to establish grounds for recovery or compensation.

121. There is, in fact, no seal impression before or after this line. The tablet is well preserved at this point. Therefore, this text is probably a draft copy or an archival copy of a document that was meant to be despatched.

122. Published in transliteration only.

123. Cf. Fadhil 1983: 199a.

124. These emendations and the resulting interpretation follow Fadhil 1983: 199a.

125. Meaning unknown.

126. Published in transliteration only.

127. Cf. Fadhil 1983: 199.

128. This correction is adopted from Fadhil 1983: 199a; and Fincke 1993: 132. It yields the name of a well-attested town. On the other hand, a town called "Kana" is nowhere else attested in the Nuzi texts.

129. The reading of this GN, doubtless correct, is adopted from Fadhil 1983: 198a; and Fincke 1993: 114.

130. This reconstruction is adopted from Fadhil 1983: 199b; and Fincke 1993: 136.

131. This assertion suggests that, in at least one case (and probably more), the removal of slaves from their Arrapḫan masters was a matter of liberation and not acquisition of spoils.

132. In text #13, this class of good is mentioned only at the very end (line 72).

133. Published in transliteration only.

134. Cf. Jankowska 1969: 279–81.

135. It appears that there is a linguistic as well as a political divide separating Assyria from Arrapḫa.

136. So already Lewy 1959: 24.

137. For the restoration of this PN, see Fadhil 1983: 198b.

138. These names are Kassite. (Elements of these names are even found among Kassite residents of Nuzi.) This strongly suggests that Kassites may have been as settled and as much at home in Assyria as we know they were in Arrapḫa. See ch. 3, note 39 on p. 251; and Maidman 1984. Note that "Kassite" is not synonymous here with "Babylonian." (Babylonians are called "Akkadians" in the Nuzi texts.) These Kassites have their core settlements in the Zagros Mountains, east of Arrapḫa.

139. Fincke 1998b: 377 restores tentatively: "These are [the Assyrians]. . . ." It is an attractive suggestion.

140. Pfeiffer and Lacheman 1942: ix, identify the room as C76, a designation no longer employed.

141. Published in transliteration only.

142. This should be a harvest month, a time when military activity tends *not* to take place.

143. Such "day-dates" are not confined to Nuzi texts. They are found in documents from third-millennium Uri-sagrig (David Owen, personal communication) and Ebla (Maria Giovanna Biga, personal communication).

144. The Babylonians are fighting in an unknown country (indeed, even the name of the place, though the tablet is preserved at this point, is ambiguous) and *one* person is supplied with *one* outfit—not much of a military reaction! In fact, the disjunction between the items noted in this document and the import of the date formulas is notable.

145. For the reading here and in line 15, see Fadhil 1983: 162a; and Fincke 1993: 276.

146. This is the preferred interpretation of Mayer 1978: 68; Zaccagnini 1979b: 19; and Fadhil 1983: 162a.

147. Meaning unclear. But cf. Mayer 1976: 213–14; and Fadhil 1983: 162b-63a.

148. The present study is based on the second of Lacheman's two publications of this text, Lacheman 1955: pl. 28. In Lacheman 1955: viii, this text is cataloged as #28. It appears in Lacheman 1955: pl. 28 as #29.

149. The same findspot presumably applies to both artifacts.

150. For these texts and others related to this trio of documents (including text #12), see Zaccagnini 1979b: 21.

151. This was also recognized by Zaccagnini 1979b: 21.

152. This precludes the interpretation of Zaccagnini 1979b: 21.

153. That is, they are decuria. On the identity of these individuals as charioteers, see Zaccagnini 1979b: 21–22.

154. *malû* here means fully equipped ("fully harnessed") according to Dosch 1993: 23; and *CAD* M/1, 173b. Dosch and Wilhelm apud Dosch 2009: 154 both suggest that the term means "at full (strength [or complement])."

155. This denotes either men whose horses were *not* "full" (i.e., fully equipped), or, far more likely, men who were horseless to begin with. *šukituḫlu*-men seem never to be associated with horses. *CAD* Š/3, 218b reasonably hazards "foot soldier(?)." Perhaps *šukituḫlu* is the Hurrian semantic equivalent of *ša* ANŠE.KUR.RA.MEŠ *la i-šu-ú*, "who are horseless" of text #20:58; or

of GÌR, "foot (soldier)," suggested by some in texts ## 2:2 and 3:2. Wilhelm apud Dosch 2009: 154 proposes that a *šukituḫlu* is a person with one horse or with a one-horse wagon. Cf. Dosch 1993: 23. For still another interpretation, see Mayer 1976: 212–13.

156. Cf. HSS XV, 28, a listing of the same categories of soldier (and more) from the right (wing) who did not come back.

157. The horse may appear there rather than in the first section because it belonged to a "*malû*-man" (who was also lost?). Tablets enumerating extensive horse losses appear elsewhere. See, e.g., HSS XV, 114.

158. Despite the seeming erasure of the first sign of this PN, the name is to be interpreted, "Turar-tešup." Cf. text #20:16.

159. Cf. text #12 for the further woes of this and other commanders mentioned in this text.

160. The latter publication is employed here for convenience.

161. K. Deller apud Dosch 2009: 151, note to line 58, argues that, because they did not have horses, these men did not go *to* the battle (reading lines 57–58: … *a-na* [*ta-ḫa-zi*] …). But the verb, as most clearly implied in text #21, is used to indicate return *from* battle.

162. A PN on line 32 was erased after line 34 was written.

163. Dosch 2009: 149 interprets this line as follows: [*ša*] AN[ŠE.KUR].RA! *ul* TUK [(BI)]

164. By haplography.

165. The last part of this line is also written by Lacheman, 1955: pl. 36, upside down between lines 6 and 7. Dosch 2009: 150 with n. 14, places that "orphan" on the reverse at the end of line 47 or 48.

166. Dosch 2009: 150 restores these lines to read: "Tablet of the men of [the left (wing)] each of whom did not have a horse," in agreement with lines 58–59. However, such a heading seems nowhere else attested.

167. As noted already above, this figure seems higher than warranted by either the total of the names listed or by the totals given within the text.

168. Lacheman (1976: 312) suggests "blanket."

169. These numbers exclude, of course, numbers effaced in the text. The structure and characteristics of text #21 closely resemble those of HSS XV, 16 which lists similar equipment for the right (wing).

170. "Hundred" is in the singular. Hence the reconstruction "[1]" is assured.

171. Cf. text ##19:21; 20:17.

172. Cf. text #20:56.

173. Cf. text #20:31.

174. Cf. text #20:46.

175. Cf. text #19:33 and, possibly, text #20:42.

176. A type of equipment.

177. Cf. text ##19:21; 20:17.

178. Cf. text #20:56.

179. Cf. text #20:26.

180. Cf. text #20:31.

181. Cf. text #20:46.

182. Cf. text #19:33 and, possibly, text #20:42.

183. This latter publication is employed here; it is the better copy.

184. However, see Lewy 1968: 158a, for lines 11–18.

185. Lit. "one who walks on the plain." Such a "plainsman" in the Nuzi texts is a type of soldier, perhaps one who treks the land, i.e., a type of infantryman. Cf. Maidman 1993a: 35.

186. "Physician" or another kind of craftsman. Both are attested with this spelling in the Nuzi texts. "Qîšt-amurri the physician(?)" appears in the right margin of line 2 and is clearly a scribal afterthought. His presence here, after the PN Ḫašip-tilla (whose name was not erased), makes no contextual sense. The scribe may have compounded one error (the wrong PN initially) with a second (failure to erase the first error after adding the correct PN).

187. The scribe used the wrong word.

188. The distribution of grain described here is not to be construed as a response to the event described in the date formula.

189. So Lewy 1968: 158a.

190. A further ambiguity results if one considers the date formula as extending to line 13 instead of line 12. The enemy would, in that case, have occupied (lit. "dwelled in") Zizza and taken (grain?) from stores. But that would be a peculiar formula. I interpret lines 12b–13 as referring to the taking of grain (from Nuzi?; or at least from the place the writer resides) to be given to the Nuzi queen.

191. Lit. "queen of the town of Āl-ilāni." The literal translation would imply that this town had a queen, i.e., a female ruler or wife of the local king. This would be misleading. The king of Arrapḫa had queens in different towns: Āl-ilāni, Nuzi (cf. line 8), and so on.

192. For these measures, see p. 234, n. 44.

193. Lit. "queen of the town of Nuzi."

194. This month probably corresponds to May–June.

195. For this comestible, see briefly, *CAD* B, 97a.

196. I.e., the package of items just listed.

197. Lit. "queen of the town of Anzukalli(?)."

198. Ḫiari probably corresponds to April–May.

199. These soldiers probably form a standard company-sized unit. The size, sixty, represents, at least in Mesopotamia, a round number.

200. The exact meaning of *atuḫlu*, the title of the officer, is not yet known.

201. Even if one or even several of these names are shifted from one category to another, the overall picture remains unaffected.

202. This observation already appears, in passing, in Lewy 1959: 17 with n. 3; and Deller 1987: #53.

203. Cf. *NPN*'s contribution to our appreciation of Nuzi's ethno-linguistic makeup based on the aggregate of Nuzi's personal names.

204. Cf. the interpretation of Deller 1987: #53.

205. "Utti" or "Utamti."

206. Cf. Dosch 1993: 13.

207. But see Zaccagnini 1979b: 20–21.

208. Cf. HSS XIV, 80 = HSS XV, 280 (the better copy), for what appears to be a text of the same sort. The Ḫanigalbatian chariotry is mentioned, but no notice of its deployment.

209. This copy is the basis of the present study.

210. That is, the event is not a mere unrelated date formula.

211. Though Nuzi is located in Arrapḫa's north-central sector and thus could supply east and west with more or less equal logistical ease (presuming similar topography), it is simpler to assume that this text, enumerating a few minor disbursements, refers to people and activities in a single region.

212. For a similar document with some of the same disbursing officials, see text #29.

213. This space is partially occupied by text runover from the obverse, line 10.

214. HSS XIII, 464, a record of disbursement of barley to charioteers in Ṣilliya may reflect the same events.

215. This month probably corresponds to December–January, an unexpected time for battle.

216. This latter publication is the basis of the present study.

217. See the discussion in Fincke 1993: 291.

218. This reading follows Fincke 1993: 292.

219. Since the remaining quantity of barley amounts to only about two liters, a substantial amount must have been represented in the text's gap.

220. If I have read the Akkadian correctly at this point, the original wording is as awkward as the English is.

221. If this peculiarly spelled word represents the local month of Sabûtu, then the time of year is likely September–October.

222. For the phrase, "on campaign," *ana ḫurādi(mma)* (and the like), at home in Middle Assyrian texts (close in time and geography to the Nuzi texts), see Freydank 1976: 111–12; and Freydank apud Heltzer 1979: 246. Cf. Machinist 1982: 26. In the Nuzi texts, the phrase is anomalous (a phrase containing *tāḫazu* would be an approximation expected here). One wonders whether the peculiar "it was said" (line 5; such a locution is, to my knowledge, nowhere else found in *šundu* [i.e., "when"]-clauses) is a way of introducing the Assyrianism, *ana ḫurādimma*. The sense would be something like: "when the enemy came into GN, as they say, 'on campaign'." It is to be noted that this speculation grows out of my contention that the enemy is Assyrian. It is *not* in itself evidence in support of that contention..

It is an irony that *ḫurādu*, used commonly in the Assyrian dialect of Akkadian, may have been a borrowing from Hurrian (the dominant language, as it happens, of Nuzi). See Stieglitz 1981: 371–72. The most complete recent discussion of *ḫurādu*, including references and earlier scholarly studies, appears in Jakob 2003: 202–8.

In the scholarly references noted above and in those appearing in Jakob, this interesting Nuzi example for *ḫurādu* has escaped notice.

223. The form of the verb "to come" here is peculiar.

224. This copy is the basis of the present study.

225. Cf., e.g., text #26. Both mention similar garments and names of distributors: Tirwin-atal (ll.7, 32; 26:10), Ḫeltip-apu (l. 14; 26:24), Kulpen-atal (ll. 28, 38; 26:13).

As in text #26, so too here items of realia are often left untranslated owing to lack of sufficient context.

226. For further connections between these two towns, see Fincke 1993: 289.

227. After this last sign appears an erased AŠ-sign.

228. In Lacheman 1950: 45, *nu* is followed by: *lu-bu-u*]*l-tù*.MEŠ. This is not reflected in Lacheman's cuneiform copies.

229. Lacheman, 1950: 45, reads *š*[*a*].

230. Lacheman, 1950: 45, reads the PN ^{m}*Ḫa-ši-ri-ru*.

231. Lacheman1939b: 209; 1950: pl. 102 inadvertently repeats this line as both the last line of the reverse and the first line of the upper edge.

232. The restoration of this first word of the line represents a tentative adoption of Lacheman's idea (Lacheman 1950: 46; text # 643 there is a transliteration of HSS XIV, 238).

233. Meaning unknown.

234. This is the title of a functionary, probably having a connection to the chariotry.

235. This month is probably equivalent to October-November.

236. This Tilla is not to be identified with Old Babylonian Tillā, for which see Groneberg

1980: 236–37.

237. It appears that Ḫut-tešup was both quartermaster and recipient.

238. *ziyanātu* may well denote "felt." See Schneider-Ludorff 1998. Note, however, that *ziyanātu* is qualified as a leather object, below, text #64:13.

239. Cf. the similar lines 15–19 and the note thereto.

240. This month is probably equivalent to November–December.

241. Or "deposited" or—more likely than either—none of the above.

242. The translation of this last segment is doubtful. The sense is unclear and, further, note that, in line 28 and in text #26:13, it is Kulpen-atal who withdraws the items.

243. Published in transliteration only.

244. HSS XV, 82, far more directly pertinent to Nuzi's military history than is text #30, has been omitted because of its ambiguity, and because excessive speculation is required to ensure its conformity to the criteria of relevance I employ for this chapter. Yet, the present text uniquely contributes to our understanding of Arrapḫa–Assyria geographical connections. Its great utility, therefore, justifies its presence among the texts treated in this chapter.

245. The wives are identified by their homelands.

246. Fincke, 1993: 173 and 247, goes so far as to say that the other two towns, Šarnitaki (line 7) and Marta-... (line 10) from which the women have disappeared, must, like Aššur, have been located in Assyria.

247. Contrast HSS XVI, 390, a very similar text, but one difficult to associate with known military activity and, therefore, irrelevant for our purposes.

248. For a reconstruction of the missing town name, see Dosch and Deller 1981: 105–6.

249. That is, a wife from the *land*, not city, of Arrapḫa.

250. "These" were probably the three men. One is explicitly dubbed a slave and all, lacking patronymics in this document, may have been slaves answerable to Wantiya.

Chapter 2

1. For most of these documents, only transliterations have been published. The precision of good hand copies is therefore lacking, and more than minimal interpretation is necessary to establish meaning in these texts. Jeanette Fincke, who has examined many of the original artifacts, confirms (personal communication) that (a) Pfeiffer's and Speiser's Latin transliterations from the cuneiform are sometimes not particularly reliable; and (b) additional fragments, unavailable to Pfeiffer and Speiser (and hence to me), have now been attached to some of the tablets of this dossier. My thanks go to Fincke for sharing her evaluations with me.

2. He is never named "mayor" (Akk. *ḫazannu*) in these texts. However, a man bearing this unusual PN is occasionally named in the Nuzi texts as part of a document's date formula (see Cassin 1982: 110–11). That the one-time mayor is here the main defendant stands to reason from (a) the rarity of his name; and (b) the nature of the legal circumstances of these cases. He is accused of various offences arising from access to, and inappropriate exploitation of, government property and personnel.

3. If the Kušši-ḫarpe named here is the mayor of the same name, then either Kušši-ḫarpe was an official but not yet mayor at the time of these texts or that he was no longer mayor. The former is strained, but possible (though cynical: his promotion would have followed these proceedings), the latter likely. Cf. Mayer 1978: 128, n. 3.

4. One brief narrative account of these events was unavailable to me: Koschaker 1941. Cf. Gordon 1941.

5. I.e., all texts that can be *directly* connected only. So, e.g., *P-S* 11 may be part of the dossier. Distraint does seem to be involved. But no telltale PNs or other connections are apparent. Therefore, despite the inclusion of this text by Pfeiffer and Speiser (1936: 19; cf. p. 75), it is omitted here. So too *EN* 10/1, 62, where nocturnal theft takes place.

6. The texts are not dated, so a firm chronology is, in any case, precluded.

7. Pfeiffer and Speiser (1936: 64) contend that no verdicts are recorded for these cases. In this instance, at least, an impending verdict seems to have been in the offing.

8. Chapter 5 deals with the *ilku* in detail.

9. His status is established in text #37, described below.

10. An underling of a toady of Kušši-ḫarpe. See text #37.

11. Kušši-ḫarpe had other agents as well, including Šimi-tilla (text #53) and Arim-matka (text #49).

12. He is once identified as the son of Abeya: text #35:43.

13. Cf. also text #46:3.

14. The overwhelming number of lawsuits among the Nuzi texts involves confession by the accused. The Kušši-ḫarpe dossier is exceptional in this regard.

15. See above for an indication of Kušši-ḫarpe's betrayal of Zilip-tilla.

16. Other cases in this text involve Kušši-ḫarpe, Zilip-tilla, and other subordinates of Kušši-ḫarpe. It is difficult to identify Mayor Ḫašip-apu (l. 12) with the Ḫašip-apu discussed here. Ḫašip-apu is a fairly common PN in the Nuzi texts.

17. This assumes that Birk-ilišu's loyalty is not an illusion, one based on the failure to discover a text recording his defection.

18. The mayor was subject to—if not appointed by—the king. See text #8. The mayor's case might well have been appealed to the monarch.

19. Cf. the comments on this dossier in Dosch 1993: 146.

20. An unpublished edition appears in Hayden 1962: 176–77. According to the transliteration presented there, the Lacheman, Owen, and Morrison et al. 1987 publication may have inadvertently omitted and misplaced some signs. The affected lines as read by Hayden are as follows:

(16) ^{m}*Za-pá-ki a-na-ku a-na*

(17) ^{m}*Qí-iš-te-ya* *ka*$_{4}$*-du* NUMUN-*šú*

(18) *ú-še-él-mu-ma šum-ma*

21. Lines 1–2 are restored following (with slight modification) Fadhil 1981: 370, a convincing reconstruction.

22. For the meaning of *irana*, see Fadhil 1981: 369–70 and Zaccagnini 1984a: 93, n. 20, on the one hand, and Wilhelm 1992b: 503–6, on the other. Cf., below, p. 194.

23. This seems to be a unique syllabic spelling of *zēru*, a word appearing elsewhere at Nuzi as NUMUN.

24. "Price" follows Fadhil and Zaccagnini; "gift" follows Wilhelm. See above, n. 22.

25. Reading here with Hayden 1962: 176, who reads the last word of line 16 as if it belonged to the end of line 17.

26. Published in transliteration only. The authors state that the reverse is "partially lost and partially uninscribed." It seems, therefore, that some signs remain which are not rendered in the transliteration.

27. A plausible context would be that Akap-tae gave a bribe to Kušši-ḫarpe to obtain an

exemption from the *ilku*. For the *ilku*-tax, a corvée, see ch. 5.

28. Cf. Wilhelm 1995b: 152. I have collated this text. Readings below reflect this collation.

29. One sign fragment remains.

30. A DIŠ was erased at this point.

31. IŠ TE is also possible.

32. [*u*]*l* is also possible.

33. BU-*ta* is possible.

34. It is just possible that "we go the going" is here expressed, that is, "we are performing the *ilku*-obligation." For details on this tax and those who pay it, see below, ch. five.

35. Cf. Wilhelm 1995b: 152.

36. For SMN 1173, see Wilhelm 1995b: 152.

27. Published in transliteration only.

38. Following *CAD* R, 312b.

39. This has nothing to do with the word appearing at the end of text #46:3.

40. *mardatu* denotes colorful, specially worked fabric. See *CAD* M/I, 277a–78a; and Mayer 1977 (he opts for "Teppich," i.e., tapestry).

41. *pūru* is a term only vaguely understood. See *CAD* P, 528a. The homonym meaning "lot" is to be dissociated from the present word. For the homonym, see, e.g., Postgate 1989: 144. The Nuzi texts occasionally mention ŠE *ša pūri*. It is possible that *ša pūri* relates to the legal history of the land on which such grain was grown.

42. Ellipsis seems to have occurred here. Perhaps what is meant is the following. He demanded one sheep from Ḫaniu. (It was paid, and, in addition,) he took a pig (from Ḫaniu, effecting) the release of Ḫaniu's brother.

43. *ziblu* is an obscure term. Pfeiffer and Speiser (1936: 67) suggest "manure." *CAD* Z, 103b, associates this term with a verb sometimes applicable to taxation. Both suggestions suffer from a lack of supporting analogues from elsewhere in the Nuzi corpus.

44. That is: "They ordered worse for you than this. Don't complain!"

45. Possible, but less likely: "He beat Kipiya son of Abeya, my shepherd."

46. For dry measures at Nuzi, see p. 234, n. 44.

47. Cf. Wilhelm 1995b: 152. I have collated this tablet. Readings below reflect this collation.

48. Although the copy has a clear *ra*, the sign looks more like *ša*.

49. The copy has *nu*, but *ti* seems clear.

50. The copy has *i*, but DUMU is clear.

51. The copy has *lu*, but *ku* is clear.

52. The copy has *mi* where I read *ul*.

53. This join (adding text to lines 39-41; the additions are in bold face) was brought to my attention by Jeanette Fincke (personal communication). She further communicates that this and other tablets from this dossier have benefited from assorted joins. For her generosity in informing me of these joins, fruits of her labor, I warmly thank Dr. Fincke.

54. Published in transliteration only.

55. A form of the verb, *leqû*, "to take," seems appropriate here.

56. Or the like.

57. Or the like.

58. The gap must contain a form of the verb *epēšu*, of which only the phonetic complement survives.

59. A form of the verb, *epēšu*, likely appeared at this point. So too Pfeiffer and Speiser 1936: 13. Possibly a form of *šakānu*, "to place," was written. See Lion 2000: 159 (text #15).

60. Surely, this is a typographical error for *ù*.

61. This is probably a typographical error for *lì*. Cf. line 5.

62. The rendering of the latter part of this line follows *CAD* Š/II, 55a, contra Pfeiffer and Speiser 1936: 13–14, 67.

63. For this definition, see Wilhelm 1992a: 49–50; and Fincke 1995: 19. Cf. *CAD* A/II, 77b–78a.

64. For details pertaining to this social class, see ch. 5.

65. The general sense of lines 27–39 (dealing with a single "case") seems clear enough. Kušši-ḫarpe stands accused of, and denies, directing an underling, Šaḫlu-tešup, to obtain government-owned oil for finishing goods and to produce those goods for Kušši-ḫarpe's private use. The underling passes on this order to an underling of his, Ḫašip-apu, who accomplishes both the collection and the production.

(The last three lines, where Kušši-ḫarpe denies that he ordered Šaḫlu-tešup to obtain oil demands that the first lines not be interpreted as Kušši-ḫarpe's demand to Ḫašip-apu. Thus line 29's *umma šuma*, "thus he," must refer to Šaḫlu-tešup, although the syntactic fit is not as comfortable as it would be if the referent were Ḫašip-apu: line 31 echoes lines 29–30, and line 31 was certainly spoken by Ḫašip-apu.)

However, the quotations, and quotations within quotations, and further quotations within the sub-quotations make the sense of the words of these lines difficult to unravel. Cuneiform fails to indicate systematically congeries of quotations. As best as I can understand (and other interpretations are theoretically possible: cf. Peiffer and Speiser 1936: 65 [patently wrong]; Lion 2000: 160 [somewhat plausibly]), the structure of these thirteen lines is as follows.

(27–32) Ḫašip-apu speaks
    (29–30) Ḫašip-apu quotes Šaḫlu-tešup
        (29b) Šaḫlu-tešup quotes Kušši-ḫarpe

(33–36) Šaḫlu-tešup speaks
    (33–34) testifying
    (35–36) directly accusing Kušši-ḫarpe
        (parts of 35–36) quotes Kušši-ḫarpe

(37–39) Kušši-ḫarpe speaks
    (38–39) quoting what he himself was alleged to have said previ ously

66. Lit.: "gave into my hand."

67. Probably military apparel, perhaps attached to the helmet. See de Moor 1970: 308, 311.

68. The following lines (ending with line 39) and the earlier ones (starting with line 33) seem to make best sense if the implicit referent of this message ("you yourself") is Kušši-ḫarpe. Perhaps we are to envision that, at this moment, Šaḫlu-tešup turns to face Kušši-ḫarpe in court. See also note 65 above.

69. The meaning of the clearly-preserved verb, *mašāru*, in this context remains unclear.

70. Published in transliteration only. Restorations are those of Pfeiffer and Lacheman 1942: 90. The statements "Top destroyed" and "(Rest destroyed)" likewise derive from this source.

71. Published in transliteration only.

72. Cf. Wilhelm 1995b: 152.

73. Or *te*? (collated).

74. The sign looks more like *qè* than *sí* (collated).

75. Published in transliteration only.

76. The spelling of this PN follows *NPN*, p. 115a, correcting Pfeiffer and Speiser 1936: 19.

77. This line, omitted in Pfeiffer and Speiser 1936: 19, follows *NPN*, p. 115a.

78. Lines 13-16 as numbered here are plausible corrections to Pfeiffer and Speiser 1936: 19, which is in error.

79. Pfeiffer and Speiser 1936: 19 has -*pi*, which is not a Nuzi spelling.

80. The spelling of this PN follows *NPN*, p. 115a, correcting Pfeiffer and Speiser 1936: 19.

81. In the cuneiform corpus, this term appears only here and in the last sentence, below. Its specific meaning is therefore unknown. See *CAD* K, 289.

82. Published in transliteration only.

83. Was Unaya, then, an official responsible for some aspect of the ḫarem?

84. Published in transliteration only.

85. The reconstruction (including the question mark) is that of Pfeiffer and Speiser 1936: 18. It is a very attractive suggestion.

86. The reconstruction is that of Pfeiffer and Speiser 1936: 18.

87. Cf. line 52. If the last word of that line is related to this word, then the latter is a semi-metathetical spelling.

88. The two parenthetical elements seem required but may not appear where expected in Pfeiffer and Speiser 1936: 18.

89. Namely, as a guide.

90. This man was identified earlier as hailing from Arrapḫa, and so Āl-ilāni is to be identified with the town of Arrapḫa. But, despite this and the assertion of Fincke (1993: 13, 37) (amongst others) the two toponyms are probably not strictly interchangeable. Āl-ilāni ("City-of-the-Gods") likely was a precinct of Arrapḫa containing both ecclesiastical and private holdings. See Maidman 1976a: 414–15, n. 754.

91. Itḫišta seems to be asserting that Birk-ilišu is ultimately responsible for the ransom paid by Itḫišta since Birk-ilišu (unjustly) arrested the brother. It seems counterintuitive that the one who hired the guide is responsible for his welfare rather than the other way around.

92. Guichard 1994: 30–31 argues that the wood and the chariot box made of this wood here represent, by synecdoche, the chariot as a whole. A resulting translation would be: "and 2 (*ḫalmadru*) chariot yoke crosspieces," or the like. Cf. Schneider-Ludorff 1995: 64–65, who describes the objects as *ḫalmadru*-chariot wheels. Two, i.e., a pair, would supply a single chariot.

93. For this example of bribery, see Kümmel 1982: 57–58.

94. This is eerily reminiscent of the Metsad Ḥashavyahu ostracon and of the laws of Exod 22:25 and Deut 24:12–13 that the ostracon recalls.

95. This equals .8 homer, almost 54 liters. For Nuzi dry measures, see p. 234.

96. The meaning is unclear to me. Is the issue the arrest of a free man not judged guilty of a crime?

97. Something is wrong here. Either Pfeiffer and Speiser misread the signs or the ancient scribe wrote the wrong signs. Apart from the dubious logic of such a large amount, such a large quantity would be written as 3 homers, 1 *pān*, 1 *sūt*, not as it appears here. It would be akin to writing 3,007 milliliters instead of 3.007 liters—not impossible, but very unlikely.

98. Published in transliteration only.

99. The readings of Lacheman and Owen 1995: 311 supersede those of Pfeiffer and Speiser 1936: 20. Where Pfeiffer and Speiser read signs no longer visible in the Lacheman and Owen copy, these are indicated below, in the notes.

100. Pfeiffer and Speiser 1936: 20 have LUGAL preserved.

101. Pfeiffer and Speiser 1936: 20 mistakenly put this word at the end of line 9.

102. Pfeiffer and Speiser 1936: 20 read here: *il-te-*[*qè*]

103. Pfeiffer and Speiser 1936: 20 have: *ù ya-*[ ].

104. Pfeiffer and Speiser 1936: 20 render this PN: ᵐ*Pé-*[*eš*]*-ki-il-li-šu.*

105. Pfeiffer and Speiser 1936: 20 read LUGAL as preserved.

106. Pfeiffer and Speiser 1936: 20 read the complete word here: *id-dì-na*.

107. Dosch 1993: 86 reads: *aš-š*[*a*?*-b*]*á-ku-mi*, "I am an *aššābu* (i.e., a tenant)." This yields no better sense.

108. Pfeiffer and Speiser 1936: 20 have, instead of ⸢*i*⸣, *ú-*[ ].

109. Pfeiffer and Speiser 1936: 20 read: *it-ti*.

110. Pfeiffer and Speiser 1936: 20: "(2 or 3 lines destroyed)."

111. Published in transliteration only.

112. KU-*ri* must equal *lu-ba-ri* (l. 61). *CAD* L, 229b, suggests two alternatives to achieve this equation.

113. Pfeieffer and Speiser 1936: 17 read this sign as a clear *ù*.

114. In the publication of this text (transliteration only), Pfeiffer and Speiser read "4" in the transliteration (1936: 16) but "5" in the translation (1936: 70). Appeals to the numbers in lines 24 and 27 (the latter with lines 29–30) do not settle the issue.

115. As a *quid pro quo* for the sheep received?

116. The verb here may be used to indicate transfer of the commodities to the palace.

117. It appears that Arim-matka here backs up Kipiya's claim.

118. I do not understand the import of these words. Is this a criticism and reason for keeping two of the four sheep? This is the position of Pfeiffer and Speiser (1936: 64). Or is this an apophthegm?

119. For the substitution of sheep for carts, see already text #48.

120. Again, Arim-matka supports Kipiya.

121. Kipiya's?

122. Pfeiffer and Speiser 1936: 71: "On the afore-mentioned day." The word appears to contrast with "that month," indicating a unit of time. *ūmišu*, "his/that day" seems to bear out this surmise. See *CAD* Ṭ, 128b.

123. The present version, some restorations included, owes much to Fincke's insights, as well as to the observations of Pfeiffer and Lacheman 1942: 62.

124. This spelling for the festival is, admittedly, peculiar. Cf. the more strained solution of Fincke 2002b: 30. Her "ANŠE! ŠE *ša bi-la-am*" makes neither grammatical nor contextual sense.

125. This line is restored after Fincke 2002b: 306, who reads the line in light of lines 6–7.

126 The meaning is perhaps as follows. Kipiya demands something of Ataya. As a result, Ataya sells land and delivers (part of?) the purchase price to Kipiya. Nevertheless, despite this payment, Ataya was seized (for alleged insufficient payment?).

127. Kipiya took one sheep for one homer of barley. The sheep later became ill and presumably died. Kipiya took back the price and another sheep besides. Cf., vaguely, CH, par. 278. If the same principle applies here, the price alone, not the second sheep, should have been returned.

128. If I understand the verb correctly, then I do not understand the significance of this act.

129. Published in transliteration only. All restorations presented here derive from this publication.

130. Pfeiffer and Speiser: 20 record no signs for this "line." Their line numbering has been retained for convenience.

131. So too *CAD* Š/II, 372a. *CAD* E, 172a restores: *ša-at*-[*ti*]. The meaning is the same in either case.

132. Pfeiffer and Speiser 1936: 20 merely have "Sin."

133. Restoring [*an-ni*].

134. Published in transliteration only.

135. For an interpretation different from the one presented in this volume, see Lion 2000: 161 (#118). Pfeiffer and Speiser 1936: 69–70 make little sense of this text.

136. Whether Kušši-ḫarpe is himself responsible for returning the overpayment or illegally diverts the funds from Kipiya is unknown.

137. Pfeiffer and Speiser 1936: 15 render [*ni*]-*il-te-qè-ma*. However, the singular "I" (rather than the plural ["We"]) is probably called for.

138. Cf. line 9.

139. This is an error for "90". On line 7, the scribe again wrote "92," but, this time, he corrected himself, erasing the "2," leaving "90". Cf. also line 25.

140. On the nuances of the term, *kazzaurnu*, see *CAD* K, 311b and Wilhelm 1988: 62.

141. For another instance of substituting sheep for carts, see text #45.

142. That is, in excess of the 60 sheep needed for the festival.

143. That is, if they give more than 150 sheep, say 160, they get back 100, leaving 60 for the festival.

144. That is, if they give fewer than 150 sheep, say 130 or 120, they get back 70 or 60, leaving 60 for the festival.

145. This interpretation assumes that the scribe "misspelled" or "mispronounced" the verb—perhaps a dubious assumption. *innabbû* is expected.

146. That is, Kipiya claims that all sheep exceeding sixty are taken by Kušši-ḫarpe for himself. He, Kipiya, does not sell those sheep.

147. Published in transliteration only.

148. *En passant*, the text establishes that bridges were owned by the government which most likely built them. They would have been built employing labor owed by the citizenry through the corvée, the *ilku*-tax.

149. From whom, we do not know.

150. From a different perspective, the work pays off the initial debt to the government.

151. This is why I assume Arim-matka acts on Kušši-ḫarpe's behalf.

152. This assumes that ailing livestock are the responsibility of their nurse. They die; he pays. Cf., distantly, CH, par. 225.

153. The nature of this office is unknown, the meaning of the term obscure.

154. This may be an elliptical way of claiming that Kušši-ḫarpe failed to investigate the matter or to offer relief.

155. He (Eḫlip-apu) gave them (to "my brother") *or* he ("my brother") gave them (to me). The latter seems probable.

156. An antichretic loan is a loan whereby the lender of a commodity secures the loan by obtaining from the borrower real estate or mobilia. The interest on the loan is the use to which the security is put during the lifetime of the loan. The profit-producing security is returned when the loan (capital only) is repaid. See Eichler 1973: 40–41, and below, text #92.

157. Perhaps a loan gone bad because unrepaid.

158. Published in transliteration only. All restorations are those of Pfeiffer and Lacheman 1942: 83. The statements "Top destroyed," "(destroyed)," and "(Rest destroyed)" likewise derive from this source.

159. Pfeiffer and Lacheman 1942: 83 erroneously numbered this line: 6 (i.e., a second line 6). Thus, this line and all subsequent lines are to be renumbered accordingly.

160. Why this reconstruction was preferred eludes me. Line 27's *at-ta-*[*din*] would not be a sufficient justification.

161. Pfeiffer and Lacheman 1942: 83 interpret, here: *-šu-<nu>-ma.*

162. Cf. texts ##39:13; 46:66; etc.

163. See Schneider-Ludorff 1998.

164. Cf. Wilhelm 1995b: 152.

165. Published in transliteration only. Lines denoted "destroyed" are those so indicated in Pfeiffer and Lacheman 1942: 49.

166. The word is virtually completely restored here, significantly restored in line 23, and totally restored in line 31. Therefore, its validity is dubious. Even more curious, what does this word mean? Why have Pfeiffer and Lacheman restored it?

167. *Sic.* Pfeiffer and Lacheman (1942: 48) may have made a typographical error here.

168. Pfeiffer and Lacheman's (1942: 49) *a* for *na* is surely a typographical error. Cf. the correct restoration in line 16.

169. [*šu*]-*ši*-[*ib*] would be a plausible reconstruction here. This is also suggested by *CAD* M/I, 341b.

170. Pfeiffer and Lacheman's (1942: 49) restoration, [*e-ri-iš*] makes no sense to me.

171 Pfeiffer and Lacheman's (1942: 49) *ma* for *na* here is a typographical error.

172. This restoration is to be preferred to Pfeiffer and Lacheman's (1942: 49) *ù*.

173. This restoration of Pfeiffer and Lacheman (1942: 49) does not yield particularly good sense.

174. Pfeiffer and Lacheman's (1942: 49) *lil* is a typographical error for *lik.*

175. "LÚ" represents Pfeiffer and Lacheman's (1942: 49) "*amêlu*" which is mistyped as "*anêlu.*"

176. The words of line 4 seem fairly clear but no coherent meaning results: "someone you did not give." The context immediately preceding and succeeding these words is missing.
146

177. This speculative and very dubious assumption is based on the desire to somehow assign an agent to the following imperative, "Say!".

178. Where this quotation within a quotation ends, I cannot tell.

179. If Pfeiffer and Lacheman (1942: 49) have accurately read and transliterated these signs, then this looks like a PN, though the expected masculine determinative does not precede it and though this PN is nowhere else attested in the Nuzi texts.

180. Published in transliteration only.

181. Cf. HSS V, 49:22.

182. *su,* not *šu. NPN,* p. 112a corrects Pfeiffer and Speiser 1936: 15.

183. Released (or unbound) from what? If service, what kind and under what circumstances? What were the circumstances of the release?

184. The term for "word" can also denote "(law) case." Thus, this segment has been translated "(There is) no case" or the like. However, in the Nuzi texts, a different word usually serves for "case."

185. And who is *this* woman? Is her "shed" special?

186. Cf. Wilhelm 1995b: 152. I have collated this text, and the readings below reflect this collation. 148

187. This trace does not appear in Fincke 1996: 459.

188. Possibly a D perfect of *muššuru*, "to release." Cf. text #53:3 for the same idea using a different verb—or a garbled version of the same verb.

189. This word is to be expected. Cf. text #53:6.

190. Collated.

Chapter 3

1. An extended if somewhat idiosyncratic treatment of the events covered in this series of texts appears in H. Lewy 1942: 326–34. Cf. Dosch 1993: 35–36.

2. But why, one wonders, does a penalty clause appear in this declaration?

3. At least some members of this large class were members of the same clan. See above, p. xxv for the family tree of the Kizzuk clan.

4. One of the senders, Ar-tirwi, bears the same name as one of the judges in text #56.

5. That Ḫutiya son of Kuššiya is the same person as Ḫutiya father of Kel-tešup is all but proven by the juxtaposition of *JEN* VI, 666:1, 11 and *JEN* VIII, 969.

6. That is, an affidavit of sorts, introduced by the telltale formula: *umma* PN, "Thus so-and-so."

7. See text #61:8–9.

8. These seven include the four mentioned in text #58.

9. These are the opponents-at-law in the second generation of the Ḫutiya/Kel-tešup Family, as Bêlšunu and Šatu-kewi had been in the first. Wantari's father, Ukuya (text #61:2), must be the man named in text #56:26, in an unclear but clearly relevant context. Cf. also possibly text #58:14 with note.

10. If there were such a trial, it probably took place at a stage prior to that represented by texts ## 60 and 61.

Text #61, the definitive climax to the second episode of the Kizzuk saga, is better understood thanks to (a) text #59, alluding to a royal order actually mentioned in text #61; and (b) text #60, a declaration directly mentioned and quoted (if not precisely) in text #61.

11. Ṭâb-ukur must either have been the ancestor of these litigants or better, the ancestor of the vendor of the land to Bêlšunu and Šatu-kewi.

12. Of course, this does not mean that title to land named after an "ancestor" necessarily remained in the family. Descendants, indeed the "ancestor" himself, could alienate land through sale or any other accepted device.

13. Is acceptance of this obligation, then, just a ruse (albeit a costly one) to buttress the claim of ownership?

14. Presumably the adversaries of the Ḫutiya/Kel-tešup Family remained on the land as tenants.

15. The vexing question, "why was this tactic not made explicit?," remains unanswered. Legal tactics were, in general, not spelled out in such tablets. However, there is some evidence of this strategy having been employed elsewhere. See, tentatively, Maidman 1989: 380. And this would successfully parry the question. We may not know why it was not made explicit, but the tactic itself cannot thereby be called into question.

16. The rendering of this line follows Dosch 1993: 147.

17. Dosch and Deller, 1981: 110, would read here ⸢*ma*⸣ and, in line 27, *ma*! (= ŠU). *JEN* VIII, 967:19 could be read [*m*]*a* or [*š*]*u* and so is no help. However, *JEN* III, 310:37 has ⸢*š*⸣*u*, and *NPN*,

p. 119b asserts that the ŠU-sign is "distinct."

18. He is a brother of Ḫutiya son of Kuššiya.

19. For further connections of these five with the family of Ḫutiya son of Kuššiya, see Dosch 1993: 148.

20. A *dimtu* can be a tower or a district in which such a tower is located. Context can, as in this case, determine which is meant. See, in greater detail, above, p. 17.

21. The last two signs of this line follow H. Lewy 1942: 341 with n. 4.

22. Or -[*qa-am-ma*] or the like.

23. H. Lewy, 1942: 341, restores [^{m}*Ḫu-ti-pu-kùr*] based on text #57 which, she avers, represents the same PN.

24. Following H. Lewy 1942: 341.

25. H. Lewy, 1942: 341, restores AŠ [URU]-DINGIR, i.e., "in the City-of-the-Gods."

26. H. Lewy, 1942: 341, reads: *um-ma*.

27. H. Lewy, 1942: 341, restores: [*Ḫu-ti-pu-kùr*].

28. The context seems to be that the land was sold to them by means of real-estate adoption, for which purpose they were adoptees (and hence immediate "heirs").

29. The plural imperative at line 36 implies that there is more than one recipient of this letter.

30. The restorations in lines 2 and 3 are based on the likelihood that (a) text #57 is a letter (not a trial record); and (b) that the sealers of the document, identified in lines 37 and 38, are the senders of the letter. Cf., already, H. Lewy 1942: 339.

31. Or the like for this PN.

32. This restoration is based on text #55:7. Dosch and Deller, 1981: 95, are to be corrected accordingly.

33. Following Dosch and Deller 1981: 95.

34. The obscure *ammatu* must mean something like "ancestor" (see already H. Lewy 1942: 327, 340; Dosch and Deller 1981: 95; and Dosch 1993: 68) rather than "grandfather" (Hayden 1962: 127; and Dosch 1993: 35), since Kizzuk is the great-great-grandfather, at the nearest, of the speaker, Ḫutiya son of Kuššiya son of Ariḫ-ḫamanna son of Turi-kintar son? of? Kizzuk. See the chart on p. xxv above.

35. The verb is erroneously in the singular.

36. The verb has a singular form, unexpected here.

37. That is, the grandfather of Ḫutiya.

38. That is, we were the adoptees in a real-estate adoption contract and, accordingly, received title to the land as an immediate inheritance share. (This practice was ubiquitous and well attested in Nuzi.)

39. "Household" (Akk. *bītu*) is the self-designation given to the large-scale Kassite social unit at the level of the clan or tribe. The extended family of Ḫutiya, as reconstructed on p. xxv, is, by the linguistic affiliation of many of its personal names, of Kassite ethnicity. On the Kassite minority among the Hurrian ethnic majority at Nuzi in general and this Kizzuk Kassite clan in particular, see Maidman 1984. Cf. also ch. 1, note 138.

40. Cf. the locutions of text #57:16–20.

41. H. Lewy, 1942: 344, reads *Ù*. If correct, the consequent PN, Ukaya, possibly recalls Ukuya father of Wantari (text #61:2; cf. text #56:26). Wantari was Kel-tešup's adversary and claimant of the ancestral *dimtu*. See already H. Lewy 1942: 333.

42. Lines 15 and 16 are damaged and well illustrate Nixon's Law: "The size or location of a lacuna (i.e., a gap in a text) stands in direct proportion and corresponds to the importance of the missing context." Sense—and unsatisfactory sense at that—can be achieved only at the price of

very tentative reconstructions:

15 ⌜A$^{?}$.ŠÀ$^{?}$⌝ *ša* ^{m}*Ki-*⌜*iz*$^{!}$*-zu*$^{!}$*-uk*⌝$^{!}$*-we*

16 ⌜*ù*⌝ URU *la*$^{!}$ *n*[*i*]$^{!}$*-de*$_{4}$^{MEŠ}

There are two questionable signs ("?"), five dubious interpretations of signs ("!"), and an anomalously placed plural marker (MEŠ). Cf. H. Lewy 1942: 344, whose rendering (not to mention her translation) is more problematic still.

43. For the restorations, Cf. text #61:9.

44. For the restorations, Cf., again, text #61:9.

45. Cf. Finke 1993: 315.

46. That is, the royal court. Cf. text #61:8–9.

47. Unexpectedly, the verb is in the singular.

48. This is an example of merism, representing the totality of the area of the *dimtu*. Were actual directions meant, the cardinal points would have been mentioned. Cf. text #61:51–55.

49. All the other tablets in this series were found in room 12, except one—text #55 from the related room 10; and so a findspot of room "13" is most probably an erroneous notation by the archaeologist.

50. For this term, see Dosch 1993: 68. Cf. Maidman 1976a: 179 for a closely related term.

51. For this reading of the syllable, cf. HSS XIV, 149:7.

52. For the reading of this PN, see *NPN*, p. 27b *sub* ARIL-LUMTI 9), as against Chiera 1934a: pl. CCCII.

53. Following Fincke 1998a: 67.

54. That reply is actually alluded to in the earlier (failed?) survey affidavit, text #59 (ll. 1–6).

55. Text #60 is that very tablet.

56. I.e., "ancestral." For this sense, see Maidman 1976a: 179; and, in essence, Dosch 1993: 68. Cf. Hayden 1962: 122, based, it seems, on Speiser 1941: 50–51, n. 2 ("near," or "nearby (land)"); and H. Lewy 1942: 346 ("yours").

57. Cf. H. Lewy 1942: 347. For a different understanding of the rare term, *palaḫḫu*, i.e., as "service," "labor," or the like, see, e.g., Koschaker 1944: 177, n. 27; and Lion 2000: 158. Such a meaning would make little sense in this context.

Chapter 4

1. The single most serious flaw of the Nuzi texts (serious, that is, to the historian) is the lack of a developed and regular system of date formulas by which events described in documents can be ordered relative to other events. Such ordering almost always depends on internal criteria. Sometimes this is easy (e.g., one document mentions that A sells land to B, another notes that the A's grandson has failed to vacate that land and that B's grandson has taken him to court), sometimes not. One must always be cautious in ordering these texts, lest the ordering reflect *a priori* assumptions by the student as to what "should" have happened serially. This warning applies to the first four chapters of this volume, where the order of events is important. This does not apply to ch. 5.

2. Data always trump logic. A small, new datum can collapse an elegant construction erected on a foundation of logic.

Another description of the Ḫišmeya Family and a slightly different ordering of the texts is to be found in Fadhil 1983: 185a–89a.

Overlap of witnesses among many of these documents suggests that these texts were written in close chronological (and, of course, geographical: the town of Turša is specifically named) proximity to each other. Substantial differences in the witness lists suggest that the proximity was not immediate.

3. This group of texts does not include HSS XIII, 403 or HSS XVI, 127. HSS XIII, 403 mentions one Uššen-naya (line 10) as recipient, together with other women, of barley rations from the palace. She reappears in a similar context, HSS XVI, 127:8, together with other women named in HSS XIII, 403. Here they are defined as concubines of / from the town of Zizza, in the Nuzi region. In theory, this Uššen-naya could be Ḫišmeya's mother. However, Carlo Zaccagnini (1979b: 13) has demonstrated that this group, members of which appear in still other texts, are likely singers imported to the palace from the land of Ḫanigalbat. Therefore, "our" Uššen-naya is most likely not attested in HSS XIII, 403 or in HSS XVI, 127.

4. Adoption-contract forms were adapted to facilitate transfer of real estate title. Details of this phenomenon are described in the introductory remarks in ch. 5.

5. Cf. Maidman 1976a: 250–52, 505–6.

6. Perhaps she is involved since she is known elsewhere to have engaged in economic activity in this region. Therefore, she would have distributed mobilia here, in a place where she already had economic interests. Here too she may have received Ḫišmeya's texts, documenting contracts with her husband.

7. Šarra-šadûni is the only principal sealing the document. Neither Enna-mati nor Šarra-šadûni's brothers appear as sealers. All the other sealers are mere witnesses.

8. The first surviving seal legend is that of a well-known scribe, the second the ceder of land.

9. Published in transliteration only.

10. The initial element of the name ending line 8 corresponds to that of the witness named on lines 29 and 40. Equation is possible.

11. A sporadic symbolic act performed by the one paying for a commodity as an indication that his obligation has been discharged. Whatever the exact nature of the act is, it is not, as commonly supposed, the impression of fabric onto the clay of the tablet. See Wilhelm 1992a: 135–36.

12. Zaccagnini 1979a: 850–53 (esp. 851–52) has established that (a) the Nuzi homer measures 100 × 80 "feet" (i.e., *purīdu*) and that (b) this datum, describing a single homer, appears in Nuzi texts relating to fields of *any* size. See e.g., below, texts ##68:5–7; 70:5–7.

13. No physical join has been made between these two artifacts. See Maidman 2005: 65, 113. However, the "fit" is a good one in terms of the resulting content of lines 1–7—with one exception. Line 2, as reconstructed, represents a unique spelling of the PN, Šarra-šadûni, and, with a double "š," a difficult spelling at that. It is possible, of course, that I have misread this line of JENu 1041f or that the posited join is illusory.

Yet another join is possible. JENu 1041g is a small piece containing the ends of six or seven lines. Since line 4 seems to represent [URU *Te-en*]*-te-we* and line 5 [^{f}*Uš-še-en*]*-na-a-a*, and since the similarly-numbered JENu 1041f is certainly part of the Ḫišmeya dossier, it appears likely that JENu 1041g derives also from a "Ḫišmeya" tablet. It may even be the case that lines 1–6 (interpreting the last signs as part of one line, not two) represent the end of text #66:15–19, 21. Thus a revised reading of these lines could yield:

15 … *ša-aš-*[*šu aš-l*]*u*! (= K[I]?)
16 … *š*[*a* ^{m}]*-ku-šu-*[ ]
17 …^{m}*El-ḫi-*⸢*ip*⸣*-*[*til*?*-l*]*a*? (=MA)
18 …A.GÀR *š*[*a*? URU *Te-en*]*-te-we*

19 .... [f]*Uš-še-en-na-a-a*

21 .... *dú-uḫ̮-nu*?

14. If the signs interpreted as a broken rendering of "field" be reinterpreted as a broken (i.e., partial) rendering of "6," then 5.6 + 3.5 + .9 homers (the areas of the three plots) would add up to the total of 10 homers asserted at the end of this clause. However, imprecise addition is known to occur in these texts, and the present context may be an example of this kind of imprecision.

15. *NPN*, pp. 52b *sub* HANAI̯A 25); and 119b *sub* PURUHLEI̯A 1) read here: *Pu-ru-uh-le-e-a*.

16. This is based on texts ##64:27; 67:30; 68:29.

17. This is based on texts ##67:31; 68:25–26.

18. "City gate" was written twice, in two different ways, KÁ.GAL and *a-bu-ul-li* (traces of which remain unerased). The repetitive word was then effaced, though not thoroughly.

19. Or: "it surrounds the land of Ḫ̮ulukka."

20. The description of the chariot wheels, given in line 19, is totally obscure. Cf. e.g., *CAD* M/II, 170a; Š/II, 292b; Fadhil 1983: 185b. Technical terms (e.g., components, colors, species of plants and animals, types of stones) often lack sufficient context to determine close definition.

21. This witness is a brother of Ḫ̮išmeya and is himself a principal party in another text in this dossier, text #70. Cf. also text #71, especially line 10.

22. That is, the silver equivalent of the goods.

23. Something is obviously wrong here. The second part of line 6 appears to read as I have rendered it in transliteration. But "30" cannot be the length since 80 is the width. Given the standard area of 100 × 80 *purīdu* for the homer (see Zaccagnini 1979a: 850–53; and Powell 1989, 1990: 487–88), "100" is called for but cannot be restored here in any of its forms. See further, Maidman 1998: 101 with note 8.

24. Published in transliteration only.

25. No convincing interpretation of these wedges has been forthcoming.

26. Here too, a convincing interpretation is lacking.

27. "2" is the standard number of minas appropriate to clauses such as this. The number signs, however, read "1/3" in both cases here. If this amount were meant, "20 sheqels" (= ⅓ mina) would have been written.

28. The member of the family most frequently involved with Enna-mati and with his wife, Uzna, is here a witness to the proceedings—a penultimate loose end? (The next document, text #71, was likely the very last loose end.)

29. The tin is not mentioned. Was its value paid out in sheep and/or goats?

30. As a term qualifying land, the meaning of this word is unknown.

31. Or: "suburbs."

32. The principal party. This is unusual and may indicate that a particular gravity attached to this, his undertaking.

Chapter 5

1. See especially Lewy 1942.
2. See especially Jankowska 1969.
3. See Maidman 1976a: 92–123.
4. Or representative texts showing key data where more than one text could be summoned.

5. Texts characterized by ambiguous, unclear, or vague data are not presented. N.B. This does not mean that I would avoid texts containing clear data that fail to support my position.

6. The most seriously developed of the different alternate perspectives on the *ilku* is elucidated in Dosch 1993: 70. See also Wilhelm 1978: 208.

7. von Soden 1969: 58 (§55C a).

8. See, further Dosch 1993: 74–76 and von Dassow 2009: 609: 612–13.

9. The fullest, most nuanced treatment of the subject is the masterful Dosch 1993. Much that is noted here has been confronted by Dosch in that work. (We often reach different conclusions.) See also Maidman 1993a; 1995: 941–42; and von Dassow 2009: 612–15.

10. Especially the *rākib narkabti.*

11. See Zaccagnini 1984a: 90; 1984b: 715.

12. See also Dosch 1993: 83.

13. In this case, release from such labor is noted.

14. All these may amount to the same thing.

15. See also Zaccagnini 1984b:716; and Dosch 1993: 71.

16. See also Zaccagnini 1984b: 718.

17. If it is not, then the question of the mobility of the *ilku* outside an "original" family is a non-issue.

18. This makes sense. The economic basis of the tax is the capacity of the land to produce wealth. No land, no wealth, and, therefore, no ability to bear the tax.

19. See also the very explicit *JEN* 789, treated in Maidman 1999: 362–72.

20. Translation adapted from Roth 1995: 88 and correction sheet. Paragraph 40 states this, the general proposition. Paragraph 38 states an anticipatory exception.

21. These are best called "real estate adoptions" to distinguish them from genuine adoptions.

22. This is certainly logical, and it makes economic sense. Evidence of immediate transfer appears sporadically. One very clear instance is described in HSS IX, 20. That text, a real estate adoption, involves a prior antichretic loan (*tidennūtu*). In that transaction the loan is secured by real estate. (The real estate, while acting as security, also represents the loan's interest; hence it is an "antichretic" loan. For this type of loan, see Eichler 1973; and see already ch. 2, text #49).

The document describes the following. A adopts B and bequeaths to him land. B makes a gift to A of barley. A then notes that C currently holds that very land as security for a loan. B is to pay off that loan and then "take" that land.

Thus the real estate is transferred once the obligation is discharged, not after the death of the "father." Extrapolating, bequeathal of real estate in real estate adoption contracts has nothing to do with the seller's death.

See also text #74 and, in general, clear-title clauses in real estate contracts for further evidence of immediate transfer.

23. In genuine adoptions, support, burial, and mourning are among a son's obligations. See text #85 for an abbreviated description of such obligations.

24. So too Zaccagnini 1984a: 80–83, a well-argued presentation of this position. But cf. Zaccagnini 1984a: 90–91.

25. Dosch 1993: 127–28, hazards a guess.

26. This is disputed in Dosch 1987: 228–29; and 1993: 123–28, 143–44, and passim—unconvincingly.

27. Cf. *JEN* VI, 600.

28. I ignore here those telling instances where the son (= buyer) bears it and those instances where there is no *ilku* clause at all. They pose no problem, as already indicated above.

29. See, for possible support of this position, below, p. 257, n. 75.

30. According to my surmise, the shift takes place in the first full tax year.

31. So too Zaccagnini 1984a: 85; 1984b: 719.

32. See already Zaccagnini 1984a: 85.

33. See also *JEN* 722 (treated by Maidman 1994: 177–80), and 31 (treated by Gordon 1935: 117–18; and Cassin 1938: 83–85).

34. Cf. Zaccagnini 1984a: 87; 1984b: 719.

35. She is actually said not to bear it when receiving land. But (a) the text thereby implies that she *could* have borne it; and (b) by my interpretation, eventually she *did* bear it.

36. See also Fincke 1998a: 235 *ad* #170 (= our text #75) and the reference there noted.

37. See also Dosch 1993: 162 on Nuzi slaves of relatively high status.

38. For a general survey of the *ilku* throughout the second and first millennia, see Kienast 1976: 52–59.

39. Postgate 1982: 304 and 312, n. 4, the latter citing texts ##73, 74.

40. Published in transliteration only.

41. The meaning of "*di-a-ni*" eludes me.

42. On the possible range of activities of this man, see Jankowska 1981: 199; and Fadhil 1983: 339.

43. This interpretation follows Zaccagnini 1984: 715, n. 3, although he interprets *ilku* as military labor, contrary to the position adopted in this chapter.

44. There is a certain garbling of patronymics between these two texts. However, the similarities between them are so extensive and crucial that their relationship should not be doubted. Details of the relationship and seeming contradictions in the two documents are elucidated in Maidman 2002: 74–75.

45. The land is part of a *piršanni dimtu*. That designation appears with Zizza real estate and Zizza real estate only.

46. For a possible close parallel from nearby Assyria in the not-so-nearby year of 709 B.C., see SAA VI, 31, especially rev. line 30 (Kwasman and Parpola 1991: 29–32).

47. There is an erasure after *it*. It appears to have been the start of *ti*. The scribe appears confused here, making three erasures on a single line. He may exhibit confusion elsewhere in regard to the issue, not of spelling, but of patronymics. See above, note 44. See also an inappropriate pronominal suffix in line 7.

48. The judges (and the scribe) seal the tablet (lines 30–35). Note that the first of the judges is the brother of Teḫip-tilla, recipient of the land upon which the trial focuses.

49. *dimtu* here denotes a district, not a tower. *piršanni* is a descriptive term (meaning unknown) applied to *dimtu*-districts near the town of Zizza, as noted above. The fullest discussion of this term remains Maidman 1976a: 180–83.

50. I have collated ERL 49.

51. See Wilhelm apud Fincke 1998a: 235 *sub* 170. It is there noted that, despite a label suggesting that this tablet comes from room A23, the content points to room A34.

The personal names of this text find echoes in other tablets from room A34. (For those tablets, see Dosch 2009: 73–117 (##1–34).) Especially striking is the similarity of the present text, lines 10 and 11, with HSS XIII, 416:9–10, the latter text stemming from room A34.

52. A lower horizontal wedge precedes the trace as drawn.

53. This room is in the temple area of the main mound.

54. Cf. *CAD* A/2, 374b: "whosoever removes a man in the king's city from his feudal [*sic*] service." There are at least two problems with this understanding. First there is no attested

"king's city" elsewhere in the Nuzi texts. Nor does the concept of a royal city appear in the corpus. Second, the lines following this segment make no logical sense if this rendering is adopted.

55. See the preliminary edition of Paradise 1972: 49–52.

56. Incest is *not* an issue. The adoption and subsequent marriage do not relate directly to each other in terms of family relationship. They are two discrete legal devices.

57. This may be a scribal error for *Ḫu*-(*ti*)-*ip*-LUGAL.

58. A ritual gesture.

59. Probably "after the proclamation" is lost in the gap along with "this tablet."

60. The line numbering in the publication is incorrect.

61. Or room P 465. Room 465 straddles areas K and P.

62. The term is *paiḫu*, denoting a building plot, most usually urban. For its meaning and range in the Nuzi texts, see Maidman 1976a: 376–78 n.480; and Deller 1981: 53–54.

63. This is a unit of weight applied to wool. See Zaccagnini 1990 for details and previous literature.

64. This room is part of the house of Šilwa-tešup son of the king.

65. This sort of description is not rare in texts where real property changes hands.

66. This also explains the findspot of the tablet: an archive room in the prince's house.

67. See *NPN*, p. 30a, *sub Ar-ki-te-šup*.

68. As noted above, this is very unusual. Typically, the one ceding real estate clears that property of claims and claimants.

69. This would have been a royal proclamation having to do with the status of, or transactions in, real estate.

70. No actual seal impressions are indicated in the publication.

71. This edition must be used with caution.

72. The phraseology is idiosyncratic, *if* I have understood the phrases correctly. See especially lines, 17, 19, 35–39.

73. On the upper edge?

74. This is a sheer guess deriving from *ziqpu* "sapling."

75. For the Nuzi calendar, see Wilhelm 1980: 28. This is a rare, if not unique, instance where we know *when* a transaction took place. It seems late in the year, well after the harvest but perhaps before the new tax year. If so, this would buttress my suggestion that the seller of real estate typically retains the *ilku* for the real estate for the year of sale if his ownership ceased late in the year, i.e., after the harvest but before the *ilku* was discharged. However, this is but a single text, and too much weight ought not to be imposed on it.

76. The following chronology seems to obtain: new proclamation (affecting real estate ownership); king's command (November / December; probably also affecting real estate [and mitigating some of the effects of the proclamation?]); current transaction (January / February; under the conditions of the month-old royal command?).

77.. It is "silver" in the sense of goods constituting the purchase price of the real estate.

78. This word is quite unexpected here. A tower with interior space is at stake here. "Land" would not be the primary way of designating this complex. ("Structure" might.) Perhaps "land" should here represent "real estate" at large.

79. This seal impression must have been accompanied, somewhere, by a legend: "seal of PN."

80. B, identified in *JEN* IV, 400 and *JEN* V, 521, represents largely, but not completely, overlapping parties. Various sons of Milki-tešup constitute the core of B.

81. These are probably *JEN* IV, 400 and text #82 (both of which clearly remained in C's

family for at least two generations). The PNs of *JEN* V, 521 allow us to identify the co-contractors in the present text as two brothers and their nephew. It also allows us to fully restore all their names.

82. For this line, present neither in the publication nor in the edition, see *NPN*, p. 77a *sub* ITḪI-ZIZZA 1).

83. The first two are brothers. The third is their nephew, Šamḫari son of En-šaku. The third brother, En-šaku, was likely dead by the time of this transaction. Indeed, this document, concluding a prior transaction, may have been necessitated by the death of En-šaku shortly after the original document was drawn up. His son and heir, therefore, may here be "signing on" to his late father's contract. All three current parties are called "brothers" because of their common status as adopters of Teḫip-tilla.

84. The only certainty regarding this term is that it denotes some sort of structure. See Maidman 2008: 217 n. 65 for the literature.

85. I.e., the inheritance share established in a previous contract and document. For some reason, not all (albeit most of) the real estate purchased in the original transaction found its way to Teḫip-tilla. See the second previous note for a possible reason. The present document concludes that previous transaction.

86. Or some similar containers.

87. This is, of course, a scribal error.

88. That is, even more than the stereotypically large amounts of two minas of gold or of two minas of silver and two minas of gold usually found in these clauses.

89. The seal impressions themselves are not noted in the publication.

90. Published in transliteration only.

91. The start of line 6 is not noted in the publication.

92. Direct discourse is an unusual feature in tablets of adoption.

93. "The tablet ... of." This translation is taken from *CAD* Š/III, 32a.

94. No seal impressions are noted in the publication.

95. On the one hand, the publication's restoration here makes sense: Šamaḫul is the only witness name beginning with "Ša-". On the other hand, "Šamaḫul" clearly appears later, as the last of the sealers. Perhaps the sealer is Ta-... (l. 38). The signs ŠA and TA may sometimes be confused.

96. This restoration is all but assured by the survival of the initial divine determinative. The same appears in line 42 above, for "Sin-abu."

97. But see a valuable partial preliminary edition and study in Purves 1945: 82–84.

98. See Purves 1945: 83, where Purves notes this position but rejects it—unconvincingly, in my view. See also below, where Wilhelm's counter-proposal is noted and rejected.

99. Fadhil 1981: 369–70; and Zaccagnini 1984a: 93 n. 20 opt for "price." Wilhelm 1992b: 503–6 argues for "gift." See already above chapter two, text #31.

100. The price, one sheqel of gold for one hundred homers of land (including valuable orchard land) is very low. Scholars have debated the reason for this low price. However, in the present context, the price itself and the reason for it are irrelevant.

101. See, e.g., *EN* 9/1, 1 and 2.

102. For the reading of these partially effaced signs, mostly absent in the publication, see Purves 1945: 82a.

103. For the spelling of this PN, see Purves 1940: 182 with n. 101.

104. Winnirke was Puḫi-šenni's wife and a real estate power in her own right.

105. Lines 27–30, containing the sealers' legends, are omitted.

106. The Akkadian verb subsumes, in contexts such as this, the ideas of caring for, venerating, and serving as a son.

107. "He" is emphasized in the Akkadian.

108. I have collated this text; the transliteration reflects this.

109. This would be a temporary obligation, one, according to my interpretation, to be borne for the current tax year only.

110. The restorations follow Wilhelm 1995a: 72 n. 4.

111. The restorations follow Wilhelm 1995a: 72 n. 4.

112. Or the like.

113. Not *Qa*, as in the publication. The corrected reading appears in *NPN*, p. 79a *sub Qa-na-aq-qa*.

114. The scribal rendering of the Akkadian for "south" is here quite anomalous.

115. The fraternity of these men rests in their common position in this contract. They were all adopted as sons.

116. This is the term for a generic body of water used in the water ordeal.

117. This rendering follows the translation of Wilhelm 1995a: 72 n. 4.

118. This restoration is assured by the verb typically associated with the *ilku*, "to bear." The wording of these lines is itself typical of *ilku*-clauses.

119. The seal impressions themselves are not noted in the publication.

120. The transliteration presented below is slightly different and more precise than that of the edition. Only one substantive change results, at line 14.

121. If only one had the time!

122. "Our fathers," says the Akkadian, seemingly clearly at this point. But this is a troubling datum. How can their fathers have transferred that real estate to Teḫip-tilla, when it was they themselves—not their fathers—who acquired the land in the first place (see text #86, which records the anterior transaction to that described in text #87 [see immediately below for this connection])? It is possible that the scribe erred here in asserting this element of the background. Yet such a claim of error is special pleading; it is an appeal to an *ad hoc* solution. It may be true, but it does not inspire much confidence.

Only slightly less shaky would be my second suggestion that, despite appearances, the somewhat broken line 9 does not mention "our fathers" but asserts that the ceders themselves formerly adopted Teḫip-tilla and, in that way, ceded the land to him. This would have the added benefit (N.B., benefit is not evidence) of establishing the means by which the transfer took place. Neither adoption nor any other device is currently mentioned in the text. However, this solution can only be achieved by means of a radical rereading and revision of lines 8, 9, and 16 and by possibly assuming scribal omission. This would be an ugly solution indeed.

A solution must be sought, though, for it remains clear that, despite the simple sense of the signs that are preserved, the recipients of real estate in text #86 are the ceders of text #87.

123. Perhaps he was no longer an owner and so did not participate in this alienation. Was he bought out?

124. The relationship of these names in the two texts is complex but not wholly obscure. *JEN* V, 508 is crucial in this regard. For the moment, see the relevant personal names in the personal names index of this volume.

125. This revises ⸢*x*⸣-*ú-ri-ni* in the edition. For this alternative, cf. text #86:11.

126. A claim, or threat of a claim might have been raised, or perhaps illegal occupancy took place. Otherwise this document would not have been necessary.

127. I have collated this tablet.

128. The purchase price is probably detailed in lines 8–10, no longer decipherable.

129. The transliteration below refines that of this edition.

130. The number is restored on the basis of text #90:25, describing the same land.

131. The name is restored from text #90:6, describing the same land.

132. I overlooked this line in the transliteration in Maidman 1999: 337; I included the line in the translation of the text on the same page.

133. Only the first line is missing. It will have read "Tablet of adoption of Turariya son of PN" or the like.

134. Different modern sources ascribe the text to room "13?," "15," and "no room no." See Maidman 2005:20. Room T13 is plausibly correct. That chamber contained the archive of Tarmi-tilla son of Šurki-tilla (and grandson of Teḫip-tilla son of Puḫi-šenni), the purchaser of the land transferred in this document.

135. Text #89:4–8 // text #90:5–9.

136. Despite the occasional appearance of this term in the Nuzi texts (see *CAD* K, 290b; the list there is not exhaustive), its meaning remains obscure. All attempts to translate the term are guesses. Cf. text #93:22.

137. The syntax is peculiar. It is possible that this is a defective writing for "market place of the palace (lit. big [or great] house)."

138. Lines 26–30, containing the sealers' legends, are omitted in this edition.

139. Were it a debt connected to the property being transferred, it would have been covered by a variation of the standard clear-title clause. Instead, there is an idiosyncratic formulation.

140. The seal impressions themselves are not noted in the publication.

141. There are enough substantive peculiarities and apparent scribal errors in this text to warrant a new collation and republication .

142. See, however, Eichler 1973: 130–31 for a substantial translation and commentary.

143. Slaves too receive mobilia: food, clothing, housing.

144. This is a reasonable surmise, but a surmise nonetheless. The principal parties of this contract are nowhere else attested in the Nuzi corpus of texts.

145. Note that real estate is never a component of the contract itself. It seems an utter irrelevancy to the borrower.

146. The sign is partially erased. Then an erasure follows.

147. Lit. "11 sheep." In Akkadian, the last word can, and here is, used for both.

148. Lit. "silver," that is, silver as a standard of value, here of livestock and metal.

149. The words of this verbal phrase are completely preserved—and totally obscure. This is especially to be regretted since it potentially sheds light on the matter of the *ilku*.

150. Who is he?

151. Eichler 1973: 130, translates: "… then Nula-zaḫi and Wur-te shall clear Utḫab-tae… ."

152. The signs are clear; the reading of the signs is a mere guess.

153. This study follows the cuneiform copy.

154. It is here irrelevant that I consider that she would have borne the *ilku* anyway eventually. Even if she would not have, the implication of the clause—that she *could* have been expected to bear it—remains.

155. The sign was written, then erased.

156. This is not the ubiquitous Teḫip-tilla son of Puḫi-šenni.

157. This amounts to 3.5 homers.

158. For this term, cf. text #90:22.

159. Published in transliteration only.

160. See Maidman 1976b: 131–32. Why this should be the case I do not know. But that it *is* the case is a phenomenon I have noticed after reading and studying thousands of Nuzi texts. The exceptions are clear only when the names are noted in texts of widely separated generations.

161. See the treatment of text #95 in Dosch 1993: 5, 7, 8, 9, 81–83.

162. Dosch links the descriptions of these two groups to wartime disruption, but this is unlikely. The persons named in text #94 lived about two generations prior to the outbreak of hostilities with Assyria. And that conflict is the only one involving Nuzi of which we have knowledge.

163. Dosch's reading requires two troubling assumptions: the scribe miswrote one sign (though it makes sense as is) and a second sign is totally effaced. Pfeiffer and Lacheman assume that the scribe did not err; as for the damaged sign, they contend that a trace or traces remain (and does/do not support Dosch's hypothetical reconstruction). Thus Pfeiffer and Lacheman deserve serious consideration.

164. Pfeiffer and Lacheman 1942: 33 read, in effect: *Ké*-[*wi-ta-e*]. Dosch 2009:109, reads: *Ze*!-[*en-ni*].

165. Dosch 2009: 109, reads: [^{m}*A-ri-il-lu*].

166. Pfeiffer and Lacheman 1942: 33; and Dosch 2009: 109, all read: *Ké*-[*wi-ta-e*].

167. Published in transliteration only.

168. It appears most likely that Dosch's edition (posthumous, sadly) is based on collation of the tablet. Her readings are fuller than and improve on the original publication in several places. The present study is based on her edition except at line 34 where she accidentally omitted an entry. That entry is included here, on the basis of the Pfeiffer-Lacheman publication.

169. See Dosch 2009: 108, note to line 28. In the present work, there seem to be close prosopographical connections between texts ##95, 85, 86; and between texts ## 95 and 94.

170. See Wilhelm 1981: 342; and Morrison 1987: 196.

171. But this is an *ad hoc* explanation.

172. Dosch 2009: 106, reads the last sign as *ni*! with a resulting well-attested name. However, the immediately preceding sign would then be anomalous. The Pfeiffer-Lacheman reading is therefore retained. The resulting "Nupanaya" would be a hypocoristicon of "Nupanani."

173. Dosch 2009: 108, note to lines 29–50, notes that this individual is elsewhere attested as a military officer.

174. The publication consists of transliteration only, no copy. Seal impressions are not noted though their identifying legends are.

175. The publication has: "*Ta*[*r-mi-ya*]". However, this is most unlikely: I know of no certain case at Nuzi where father and son bear the same name. In his unpublished notes, Lacheman has: "*Tar*-[ ]".

176. The publication erroneously identifies two(?) lines as line 5. This is the first of the two. I ignore it in the subsequent line numbering.

177. The last two signs do not appear in the publication. They are (no doubt, correctly) included in unpublished notes of Lacheman.

178. The exact meaning of this term is unknown. It somehow qualifies an Āl-ilāni town gate. Cf. *ēqu*, in *CAD* E, 253b, a term having to do with the cult.

Text Concordance

WAW #	PUBLICATION
1	*P-S* 84
2	HSS XIV, 48
3	HSS XIV, 50
4	*EN* 9/3, 284
5	*JEN* VI, 613
6	*JEN* V, 446
7	*JEN* V, 458
8	HSS XV, 1
9	HSS XV, 22
10	HSS XV, 5
11	HSS XIII, 195
12	HSS XV, 99
13	*JEN* V, 525
14	HSS XIII, 383
15	HSS XVI, 393
16	*EN* 9/3, 472
17	HSS XVI, 328
18	HSS XIII, 63
19	HSS XV, 29
20	HSS XV, 40
21	HSS XV, 14 + *EN* 10/3, 194
22	HSS XV, 43
23	HSS XIV, 131
24	HSS XV, 32
25	HSS XIV, 171
26	HSS XIV, 249
27	HSS XIV, 174
28	HSS XIV, 238
29	HSS XIV, 248
30	HSS XVI, 391
31	*EN* 9/1, 470
32	*P-S* 13
33	*EN* 10/1, 59
34	*EN* 10/1, 61
35	*P-S* 3 + *EN* 10/1, 10
36	*EN* 10/1, 60
37	*P-S* 1 + *EN* 10/2, 70
38	HSS XIII, 466
39	*P-S* 2
40	*EN* 10/1, 63
41	*P-S* 9
42	*P-S* 10
43	*P-S* 8
44	*EN* 9/3, 471 = *P-S* 14
45	*P-S* 6
46	*EN* 10/3, 175+
47	*P-S* 12
48	*P-S* 5
49	*P-S* 7
50	HSS XIII, 430
51	*EN* 10/2, 117
52	HSS XIII, 286
53	*P-S* 4
54	*EN* 10/1, 58
55	*JEN* VI, 644
56	*JEN* IV, 388
57	*JEN* IV, 325
58	*JEN* V, 512
59	*JEN* II, 135
60	*JEN* II, 184
61	*JEN* IV, 321
62	*JEN* III, 280
63	HSS XIII, 62
64	*JEN* I, 68
65	*JEN* VI, 597+
66	*JEN* VI, 603+(?)
67	*JEN* II, 212
68	*JEN* VII, 776+

69	HSS XIII, 232	84	*JEN* V, 552
70	*JEN* IV, 415	85	HSS V, 57
71	*JEN* II, 101	86	*JEN* V, 467
72	HSS XIII, 369	87	*JEN* VII, 699
73	*JEN* V, 498	88	*JEN* VII, 707
74	*JEN* IV, 327	89	*JEN* VII, 782
75	*EN* 10/2, 170	90	*JEN* VI, 599
76	HSS XIV, 9	91	HSS V, 58
77	HSS XIX, 51	92	*EN* 9/1, 165
78	*EN* 9/3, 482	93	HSS XIV, 110 =
79	*EN* 9/1, 7		HSS XIV, 604
80	HSS IX, 35	94	HSS XIII, 212
81	*EN* 9/1, 4	95	HSS XIII, 6
82	*JEN* II, 206	96	HSS XIV, 568
83	HSS XIII, 143		

PUBLICATION	**WAW #**
EN 9/1	
4	81
7	79
165	92
470	31
EN 9/3	
284	4
471 (= *P-S* 14)	44
472	16
482	78
EN 10/1	
10 + *P-S* 3	35
58	54
59	33
60	36
61	34
63	40
EN 10/2	
70 + *P-S* 1	37
117	51
136 + HSS XVI, 328	17
170	75
EN 10/3	
175 +	46
194 + HSS XV, 14	21
HSS V	
57	85
58	91
HSS IX	
35	80
HSS XIII	
6	95
62	63
63	18
143	83
195	11
212	94
232	69
286	52
369	72
383	14
430	50
466	38
HSS XIV	
9	76
48	2
50	3

Bibliography

Bottéro, Jean. 1954. *Le Problème des Ḫabiru à la 4e Rencontre Assyriologique Internationale*. Cahiers de la Societé Asiatique 12. Paris: Imprimerie Nationale.

Byrne, Ryan. 2007. "The Refuge of Scribalism in Iron I Palestine." *BASOR* 345: 1–31.

Cassin, E.-M. 1938. *L'Adoption à Nuzi*. Paris: Maisonneuve.

———. 1982. "Heur et malheur du *ḪAZANNU* (Nuzi)." Pages 98–117 in *Les Pouvoirs locaux en Mésopotamie et dans les régions adjacentes*. Brussels: Institute des hautes études de Belgique.

Chiera, Edward. 1927. *Inheritance Texts*. Vol. 1 of *Joint Expedition [of the American School of Oriental Research in Baghdad] with the Iraq Museum at Nuzi*. Paris: Geuthner.

———. 1929. *Texts of Varied Contents*. HSS 5. Cambridge, Mass.: Harvard University Press.

———. 1930. *Declarations in Court*. Vol. 2 of *Joint Expedition [of the American School of Oriental Research in Baghdad] with the Iraq Museum at Nuzi*. Paris: Geuthner.

———. 1931. *Exchange and Security Documents*. Vol. 3 of *Joint Expedition [of the American School of Oriental Research in Baghdad] with the Iraq Museum at Nuzi*. Paris: Geuthner.

———. 1934a. *Proceedings in Court*. Vol. 4 of *Joint Expedition [of the American School of Oriental Research in Baghdad] with the Iraq Museum at Nuzi*. Philadelphia: American Schools of Oriental Research.

———. 1934b. *Mixed Texts*. Vol. 5 of *Joint Expedition [of the American School of Oriental Research in Baghdad] with the Iraq Museum at Nuzi*. Philadelphia: American Schools of Oriental Research.

Chiera, Edward and Ephraim A. Speiser. 1927. "Selected 'Kirkuk' Documents." *JAOS* 47: 36–60.

Cole, Steven W. and Peter Machinist. 1998. *Letters from Priests to the Kings Esarhaddon and Assurbanipal*. SAA 13. Helsinki: Helsinki University Press.

Dassow, Eva von. 2009. "Sealed Troop Rosters from the City of Arrapḫe." Pages 605–36 in *General Studies and Excavations at Nuzi 11/2 in Honor of David I. Owen*. SCCNH 18. Edited by Gernot Wilhelm. Bethesda, Md.: CDL.

Deller, Karlheinz. 1981. "Die Hausgötter der Familie Šukrija S. Huja." Pages 47–76 in *Studies on the Civilization and Culture of Nuzi and the Hurrians in Honor of Ernest R. Lacheman*. SCCNH 1. Edited by M.A. Morrison et al. Winona Lake, Ind.: Eisenbrauns.

———. 1984. Akkadische Lexikographie *CAD* M: II Nuzi." *Orientalia* 53: 94–107.

———. 1987. "Ḫanigalbatäische Personennamen." *N.A.B.U.* 1987/2: #53.

Deller, Karlheinz and Abdulillah Fadhil. 1972. "NIN.DINGIR.RA / *entu* in Texten aus Nuzi und Kurruḫanni." *Mesopotamia* 7: 193–213.

Dosch, Gudrun. 1987. "Non-Slave Labor in Nuzi." Pages 223–35 in *Labor in the Ancient Near East*. AOS 68. Edited by Marvin A. Powell. New Haven: American Oriental Society.

———. 1993. *Zur Struktur der Gesellschaft des Königreichs Arrapḫe*. HSAO 5. Heidelberg: Heidelberger Orientverlag.

———. 2009. "Zur Struktur der Gesellschaft des Königreichs Arrapḫe: Texte über die Streitwagenfahrer (*rākib narkabti*)." Pages 71–228 in *General Studies and Excavations at Nuzi 11/2 in Honor of David I. Owen*. SCCNH 18. Edited by Gernot Wilhelm. Bethesda, Md.: CDL.

Dosch, Gudrun and Karlheinz Deller. 1981. "Die Familie Kizzuk: Sieben Generationen in Temtena und Šuriniwe." Pages 91–113 in *Studies on the Civilization and Culture of Nuzi and the Hurrians in Honor of Ernest R. Lacheman*. SCCNH 1. Edited by M. A. Morrison et al. Winona Lake, Ind.: Eisenbrauns.

Drews, Robert. 1988. *The Coming of the Greeks: Indo-European Conquests in the Aegean and the Near East*. Princeton: Princeton University Press.

Eichler, Barry L. 1973. *Indenture at Nuzi: The Personal* tidennūtu *Contract and its Mesopotamian Analogues*. YNER 5. New Haven: Yale University Press.

———. 1989. "Nuzi and the Bible: A Retrospective." Pages 107–19 in *DUMU-E$_2$-DUB-BA-A: Studies in Honor of Åke W. Sjöberg*. Occasional Publications of the Samuel Noah Kramer Fund 11. Edited by H. Behrens et al. Philadelphia: Occasional Publications of the Samuel Noah Kramer Fund.

Ephʿal, Israel. 2009. *The City Besieged: Siege and Its Manifestations in the Ancient Near East*. CHANE 36. Leiden: Brill / Magnes.

Fadhil, Abdulillah. 1981. "Ein frühes *ṭuppi mārūti* aus Tell al-Faḫḫār / Kurruḫanni." Pages 363–76 in *Studies on the Civilization and Culture of Nuzi and the Hurrians in Honor of Ernest R. Lacheman*. SCCNH 1. Edited by M. A. Morrison et al. Winona Lake, Ind.: Eisenbrauns.

———. 1983. *Studien zur Topographie und Prosopographie der Provinzstädte des Königreichs Arrapḫe: Fünfzig ausgewählte URU-Toponyme*. Baghdader Forschungen 6. Mainz: von Zabern.

Fales, F. M. and J. N. Postgate. 1992. *Imperial Administrative Records*, Part I: *Palace and Temple Administration*. SAA 7. Helsinki: Helsinki University Press.

———. 1995. *Imperial Administrative Records*, Part II: *Provincial and Military Administration*. SAA 11. Helsinki: Helsinki University Press.

Fincke, Jeanette. 1993. *Die Orts- und Gewässernamen der Nuzi-Texte*. RGTC 10. Wiesbaden: Reichert.

———. 1995. "Beiträge zum Lexikon des Hurritischen von Nuzi." Pages 5–21 in *Edith Porada Memorial Volume*. SCCNH 7. Edited by David I. Owen et al. Bethesda, Md.: CDL.

———. 1996. "Excavations at Nuzi 10/1, 1–65." Pages 379–468 in *Richard F.S. Starr Memorial Volume*. SCCNH 8. Edited by David I. Owen and Gernot Wilhelm. Bethesda, Md.: CDL.

———. 1998a. "Excavations at Nuzi 10/2, 66–174." Pages 219–373 in *General Studies an Excavations at Nuzi* 10/2. SCCNH 9. Edited by David I. Owen and Gernot Wilhelm. Bethesda, Md.: CDL.

———. 1998b. "Appendix to EN 10/2: Transliterations of Selected EN 10/2 Texts Joined to Previously Published Texts." Pages 375–84 in *General Studies and Excavations at Nuzi* 10/2. SCCNH 9. Edited by David I. Owen and Gernot Wilhelm. Bethesda, Md.: CDL.

———. 2000. "Transport of Agricultural Produce in Arrapḫe." Pages 147–70 in *Rainfall and Agriculture in Northern Mesopotamia: Proceedings of the Third MOS Symposium.* PIHANS 88. Edited by R. M. Jas. Leiden: Nederlands Instituut voor het Nabije Oosten.

———. 2002a. "Excavations at Nuzi 10/3, 175–300." Pages 169–304 in *General Studies and Excavations at Nuzi* 10/3. SCCNH 12. Edited by David I. Owen and Gernot Wilhelm. Bethesda, Md.: CDL.

———. 2002b. "Appendix to EN 10/3: Transliterations of EN 10/3 Texts Joined to Previously Published Texts." Pages 305–20 in *General Studies and Excavations at Nuzi* 10/3. SCCNH 12. Edited by David I. Owen and Gernot Wilhelm. Bethesda, Md.: CDL.

Fischer, David Hackett. 1970. *Historians' Fallacies: Toward a Logic of Historical Thought.* New York: Harper & Row.

Foster, Benjamin R. and Karen Polinger Foster. 2009. *Civilizations of Ancient Iraq*. Princeton: Princeton University Press.

Freu, Jacques. 2003. *Histoire du Mitanni*. Paris: Association KUBABA.

Freydank, Helmut. 1976. "Untersuchungen zur sozialen Struktur in mittelassyrischer Zeit." *AoF* 4: 111–30.

Fuchs, Andreas and Simo Parpola. 2001. *Letters from Babylonia and the Eastern Provinces.* Part 3 of *The Corrspondence of Sargon II.* SAA 15. Helsinki: Helsinki University Press.

Gadd, C. J. 1926. "Tablets from Kirkuk." *RA*, 23: 49–161.

Gelb, Ignace J., Pierre M Purves, and Allan A. MacRae. 1943 *Nuzi Personal Names*. OIP 57. Chicago: University of Chicago Press.

Glassner, Jean-Jacques. 2004. *Mesopotamian Chronicles*. WAW 19. Edited by Benjamin R. Foster. Atlanta: Society of Biblical Literature.

Gordon, Cyrus H.. 1935 "Fifteen Nuzi Tablets Relating to Women." *Le Muséon*, 48: 113–32.

———. 1936. "An Akkadian Parallel to Deuternomy 21:1ff." *RA* 33: 1–6.

———. 1941. "The People Versus the Mayor." *Smith Alumnae Quarterly* 33: 227.

Grayson, A. Kirk. 1991. *Assyrian Rulers of the Early first Millennium BC, I (1114–859 BC).* RIMA 2. Toronto: University of Toronto Press.

Groneberg, Brigitte. 1980. *Die Orts- und Gewässernamen der altbabylonischen Zeit.* RGTC 3. Wiesbaden: Reichert.

Guichard, Michaël. 1994. "Les Chars et leurs carrosserie." *N.A.B.U.* 1994/2: #31.

Harrak, Amir. 1987. *Assyria and Hanigalbat: A Historical Reconstruction of Bilateral Relations from the Middle of the Fourteenth to the End of the Twelfth Centuries BC.* TSO 4. New York: Georg Olms Verlag.

Hayden, Roy Edmund. 1962. "Court Procedure at Nuzu." Ph.D. dissertation, Brandeis University.

Heltzer, Michael. 1979. "Some Problems of the Military Organization of Ugarit (Ugaritic *ḫrd* and Middle-Assyrian *ḫurādu*)." *OA* 18: 245–53.

Hunger, Hermann. 1992. *Astrological Reports to Assyrian Kings*. SAA 8. Helsinki: Helsinki University Press.

Jakob, Stefan. 2003. *Mittelassyrische Verwaltung und Sozialstruktur: Untersuchungen*. CM 29. Boston: Brill/Styx.

Jankowska, N. B. 1962. "Zur Geschichte der hurritischen Gesellschaft (auf Grund von Rechtsurkunden aus Arrapḫa und Alalaḫ." Pages 226–32 in *Proceedings of the Twenty-fifth Congress of Orientalists*, vol. 1. Moscow: Oriental Literature Publishing House.

———. 1969. "Communal Self-Government and the King of the State of Arrapḫa." *JESHO* 12: 233–82.

———. 1981. "Life of the Military Élite in Arrapḫe." Pages 195–200 in *Studies on the Civilization and Culture of Nuzi and the Hurrians in Honor of Ernest R. Lacheman*. SCCNH 1. Edited by M. A. Morrison and D. I. Owen. Winona Lake, Ind.: Eisenbrauns.

———. 1982. The Mitannian Šattiwasa in Arrapḫe." Pages 138–49 in *Societies and Languages of the Ancient Near East: Studies in Honour of I. M. Diakonoff*. Warminster: Aris & Phillips.

Kataja, L. and R. Whiting. 1995. *Grants, Decrees and Gifts of the Neo-Assyrian Period*. SAA 12. Helsinki: Helsinki University Press.

Kendall, Timothy. 1981. "*gurpisu ša awēli*: The Helmets of the Warriors at Nuzi." Pages 201–31 in *Studies on the Civilization and Culture of Nuzi and the Hurrians in Honor of Ernest R. Lacheman*. SCCNH 1. Edited by M. A. Morrison and D. I. Owen. Winona Lake, Ind.: Eisenbrauns.

Kienast, B. 1976. Ilku. Pages 52b–59a in *RlA* V.1/2. Edited by D. O. Edzard. Berlin: de Gruyter.

Koliński, Rafał. 2001. *Mesopotamian* dimātu *of the Second Millennium BC*. BAR International Series 1004. Oxford: Archaeopress.

Koschaker, P. 1941. "Ein politischer Propogandaprozess in Nuzi aus dem 15. Jahrhundert v. Chr." *Jahrbuch der preussischen Akademie der Wissenschaften* 1940, 1941: 85–86.

———. 1944. "Drei Rechtsurkunden aus Arrapḫa." *ZA* 48: 161–221.

Kümmel, Hans Martin. 1982. "Bestechung im Alten Orient." Pages 55–64 in *Korruption im Altertum: Konstanzer Symposium, Oktober 1979*. Edited by Wolfgang Schuller. Munich: Oldenbourg.

Kuntz, Tom. 1998. "At Harvard, A Political Sex Scandal That's Not News, But Ancient History." Section 4. The Week in Review, p. 7, col. 1 of *The New York Times*, Sunday, 18 October, 1998.

Kwasman, Theodore and Simo Parpola. 1991. *Tiglath-Pileser III through Esarhaddon*. Part 1 of *Legal Transactions of the Royal Court of Nineveh*. SAA 6. Helsinki: Helsinki University Press.

Lacheman, Ernest R. 1939a. *Miscellaneous Texts*. Vol. 6 of *Joint Expedition [of the American School of Oriental Research in Baghdad] with the Iraq Museum at Nuzi*. New Haven: American Schools of Oriental Research.

———. 1939b. "Nuziana II." *RA* 36: 113–219.

———. 1950. *Miscellaneous Texts from Nuzi,* Part II. Vol. 5 of *Excavations at Nuzi.* HSS 14. Cambridge, Mass.: Harvard University Press.

———. 1955. *The Administrative Archives.* Vol. 6 of *Excavations at Nuzi.* HSS 15. Cambridge, Mass.: Harvard University Press.

———. 1958. *Economic and Social Documents.* Vol. 7 of *Excavations at Nuzi.* HSS 16. Cambridge, Mass.: Harvard University Press.

———. 1962. *Family Laws.* Vol. 8 of *Excavations at Nuzi.* HSS 19. Cambridge, Mass.: Harvard University Press.

———. 1967. "Les Tablettes de Kerkouk au Musée d'Art et d'Histoire de Genève." *Genava,* 15: 5–23.

———. 1974. "Le Palais et la royauté de la ville de Nuzi: Les Rapports entre les données archéologiques et les données épigraphiques." Pages 359–71 in *Le Palais et la royauté (archéologie et civilization).* Edited by Paul Garelli. CRRAI 19. Paris: Geuthner.

———. 1976. "Nuzi Miscellanea." Pages 311–12 in *Kramer Anniversary Volume: Cuneiform Studies in Honor of Samuel Noah Kramer.* Edited by Barry L. Eichler. AOAT 25. Kevelaer: Butzon & Bercker.

Lacheman, Ernest R. and Maynard P. Maidman. 1989. *Joint Expedition with the Iraq Museum at Nuzi 7: Miscellaneous Texts.* SCCNH 3. Winona Lake, Ind.: Eisenbrauns.

Lacheman, Ernest R. and D. I. Owen. 1995. "Excavations at Nuzi 9/3." Pages 85–357 in *General Studies and Excavations at Nuzi 9/3.* Edited by Ernest R. Lacheman and D. I. Owen. SCCNH 5. Winona Lake, Ind.: Eisenbrauns.

Lacheman, Ernest R., D. I. Owen, and M. A. Morrison *et al.* 1987. "Excavations at Nuzi 9/1." Pages 355–702 in *General Studies and Excavations at Nuzi 9/1.* Edited by D. I. Owen and M. A. Morrison. SCCNH 2. Winona Lake, Ind.: Eisenbrauns.

Lewy, Hildegard. 1942. "The Nuzian Feudal System." *OrNS* 11: 1–40, 209–50, 297–349.

———. 1959. "Miscellanea Nuziana." *OrNS* 28: 1–25.

———. 1968. "A Contribution to the Historical Geography of the Nuzi Texts." *JAOS* 88 [/1 = E.A. Speiser Memorial Volume]: 150–62.

Lion, Brigitte. 2000. "Les Textes judiciaires du royaume d'Arrapha." Pages 141–62, 251–52 in *Rendre la justice en Mésopotamie: Archives judiciaires du Proche-Orient ancien (IIIe–Ier millénaires avant J.-C.).* Edited by Francis Joannès. Saint-Denis: Presses Universitaires de Vincennes.

———. 2005. "69. HSS 16 326 (= SMN 3505) = EN 9/3 284 (= SMN 3157)." P. 200 in *General Studies and Excavations at Nuzi 11/1.* Edited by David I. Owen and Gernot Wilhelm. SCCNH 11. Bethesda, Md.: CDL.

———. 2008. "L'Armée d'après la documentation de Nuzi." Pages 71–81 in *Les Armées du Proche-Orient ancient (IIIe–Ier mill. av. J.-C.): Actes du colloque international organisé à Lyons les 1er et 2 décembre 2006, Maison de l'Orient et de la Méditerranée.* Edited by Philippe Abrahami and Laura Battini. BAR International Series. Oxford: Hedges.

Liverani, Mario. 2005. *Israel's History and the History of Israel.* Trans. Chiara Peri and Philip R. Davies. London: Equinox.

Machinist, Peter. 1982. "Provincial Governance in Middle Assyria and Some New Texts from Yale." *Assur* 3/2: 1–37 + 4 pls. (=*Assur* 3: 65–101 + 4 pls.).

Maidman, Maynard Paul. 1976a. "A Socio-Economic Analysis of a Nuzi Family Archive." Ph.D. dissertation, University of Pennsylvania.

———. 1976b. "The Teḫip-tilla Family of Nuzi: A Genealogical Reconstruction." *JCS* 28: 127–55; 29:64 [1977].

———. 1984. "Kassites Among the Hurrians: A Case Study from Nuzi." *BSMS* 8: 15– 21.

———. 1987. "*JEN* 812: An Unusual Peronnel Text from Nuzi." Pages 157–66 in *General Studies and Excavations at Nuzi 9/1*. SCCNH 2. Edited by D. I. Owen and M. A. Morrison. Winona Lake, Ind.: Eisenbrauns.

———. 1989. "A Revised Publication of a Unique Nuzi Text." Pages 371–81 in *DUMU-E_2-DUB-BA-A: Studies in Honor of Åke W. Sjöberg*. Occasional Publications of the Samuel Noah Kramer Fund 11. Edited by H. Behrens *et al.* Philadelphia: Occasional Publications of the Samuel Noah Kramer Fund.

———. 1993a. "Le Classi Sociali di Nuzi." Pages 29–49 in *Seminari anno 1992*. Consiglio nazionale delle ricerche, istituto per gli studi micenei ed egeo-anatolici.

———. 1993b. "Some Late Bronze Age Legal Tablets from the British Museum: Problems of Context and Meaning." Pages 42–89 in *Law, Politics and Society in the Ancient Mediterranean World*. Edited by Baruch Halpern and Deborah W. Hobson. Sheffield: Sheffield Academic Press.

———. 1994. *Two Hundred Nuzi Texts from the Oriental Institute of the University of Chicago*, Part I. SCCNH 6. Bethesda, Md.: CDL.

———. 1995. "Nuzi: Portrait of an Ancient Mesopotamian Provincial Town." Pages 931–47 in *Civilizations of the Ancient Near East*, vol. 2. Edited by Jack M. Sasson. New York: Scribner's Sons.

———. 1998. "JEN 775–780: The Text Editions." Pages 95–123 in *General Studies and Excavations at Nuzi* 10/2. SCCNH 9. Edited by D. I. Owen *et al.* Bethesda, Md.: CDL.

———. 1999. "JEN 781–789: The Text Editions." Pages 329–73 in *Nuzi at Seventy-Five*. SCCNH 10. Edited by David I. Owen and Gernot Wilhelm. Bethesda, Md.: CDL.

———. 2002. "JEN 790–798: The Text Editions." Pages 41–79 in *General Studies and Excavations at Nuzi* 10/3. Edited by David I. Owen and Gernot Wilhelm. Bethesda, Md.: CDL.

———. 2003. *Joint Expedition with the Iraq Museum at Nuzi 8: The Remaining Major Texts in the Oriental Institute of the University of Chicago*. SCCNH 14. Bethesda, Md.: CDL.

———. 2005. *The Nuzi Texts of the Oriental Institute: A Catalogue Raisonné*. SCCNH 16. Edited by D.I. Owen et al. Bethesda, Md.: CDL.

———. 2008. "Peace and War at Nuzi: A Prosopographical Foray." Pages 199–220 in *Treasures on Camels' Humps: Historical and Literary Studies from the Ancient Near East Presented to Israel Eph'al*. Edited by Mordechai Cogan and Dan'el Kahn. Jerusalem: The Hebrew University Magnes Press.

Mayer, Walter. 1976. "Beiträge zum Ḫurro-Akkadischen Lexikon I." *UF* 8: 209–14.

———. 1977. "*Mardatu* 'Teppich.'" *UF* 9: 173–89.

———. 1978. *Nuzi Studien I: Die Archive des Palastes und die Prosopographie der Berufe*. AOAT 205/1. Neukirchen-Vluyn: Verlag Butzon & Bercker Kevelaer.

Mieroop, Marc van de. 1997. "Why Did They Write on Clay?" *Klio*, 79: 7–18.

———. 2007. *A History of the Ancient Near East, ca. 3000–323 B.C.* 2nd ed. Malden, Mass.: Blackwell.

Moor, Johannes de. 1970. "Studies in the New Alphabetic Texts from Ras Shamra, II." *UF* 2: 303–27.

Morrison, Martha A. 1987. "The Southwest Archives at Nuzi." Pages 167–201 in *General Studies and Excavations at Nuzi 9/1*. SCCNH 2. Edited by D. I. Owen and M. A. Morrison. Winona Lake, Ind.: Eisenbrauns.

Oppenheim, A. Leo. 1955. "Siege Documents from Nippur." *Iraq* 17: 69–89.

———. 1956–. *The Assyrian Dictionary of the Oriental Institute of the University of Chicago*. Chicago: The Oriental Institute of the University of Chicago.

———. 1977. *Ancient Mesopotamia: Portrait of a Dead Civilization*. Rev. edition. Chicago: University of Chicago Press.

Paradise, Jonathan Solomon. 1972. "Nuzi Inheritance Practices." Ph.D. dissertation, University of Pennsylvania.

Parpola, Simo. 1980. "The Murderer of Sennacherib." Pages 171–82 in *Death in Mesopotamia: Papers Read at the XXVIe Rencontre assyriologique internationale*. Edited by Bendt Alster. Mesopotamia 8. Copenhagen: Akademisk Forlag.

———. 1987. *Letters from Assyria and the West*. Part 1 of *The Correspondence of Sargon II*. SAA 1. Helsinki: Helsinki University Press.

———. 1993. *Letters from Assyrian and Babylonian Scholars*. SAA 10. Helsinki: Helsinki University Press.

Pedersén, Olof. 1998. *Archives and Libraries in the Ancient Near East, 1500–300B.C.* Bethesda, Md.: CDL.

Pfeiffer, Robert H. 1932. *The Archives of Shilwateshub Son of the King*. Vol. 2 of *Excavations at Nuzi*. HSS 9. Cambridge, Mass.: Harvard University Press.

Pfeiffer, Robert H. and Ernest R. Lacheman. 1942. *Miscellaneous Texts from Nuzi, Part I*. Vol. 4 of *Excavations at Nuzi*. HSS 13. Cambridge, Mass.: Harvard University Press.

Pfeiffer, Robert H. and E. A. Speiser. 1936. *One Hundred New Selected Nuzi Texts*. AASOR 16. New Haven: American Schools of Oriental Research.

Postgate, J. N. 1982. "*ilku* and Land Tenure in the Middle Assyrian Kingdom, A Second Attempt." Pages 304–13 in *Societies and Languages of the Ancient Near East: Studies in Honour of I.M. Diakonoff*. Warminster: Aris & Phillips.

———. 1989. "The Ownership and Exploitation of Land in Assyria in the 1st Millennium B.C." Pages 141–52 in *Reflets des deux fleuves: Volume de mélanges offerts à André Finet*. Akkadica, Supplementum 6. Edited by Marc Lebeau and Philippe Talon. Leuven: Peeters.

Powell, M. A. 1989–1990. "Masse und Gewichte." Pages 457–517 in *RlA* 7.5/6, 7/8. Edited by D. O. Edzard. Berlin: de Gruyter.

Purves, Pierre M. 1940 "The Early Scribes of Nuzi." *AJSL*, 57: 162–87.

———. 1945. "Commentary on Nuzi Real Property in the Light of Recent Studies." *JNES* 4: 68–86.

Roth, Martha T. 1995. *Law Collections from Mesopotamia and Asia Minor*. With a contribution by Harry A. Hoffner, Jr. Edited by Piotr Michalowski. WAW 6. Atlanta: Scholars Press.

Saarisalo, Aapeli. 1934. "New Kirkuk Documents Relating to Slaves." *Studia Orientalia*,5/3: I–VIII, 1–101.

Schneider-Ludorff, Helga. 1995. "Die Streitwagen und ihre Räder (Bemerkungen zu M. Guichard, « Les Chars et leur carrosserie » in *N.A.B.U.*, 1994/31)." *N.A.B.U.* 1995/3: 64–65.

———. 1998. "Filz in Nuzi?" Pages 163–68 in *General Studies and Excavations at Nuzi 10/2*. SCCNH 9. Edited by D. I. Owen *et al.* Bethesda, Md.: CDL.

Soden, Wolfram von. 1969. *Grundriss der akkadischen Grammatik*. AnOr 33/47. Rome: Pontificium Institutum Biblicum.

Speiser, Ephraim A. 1930. "New Kirkuk Documents Relating to Family Laws." AASOR 10 [for 1928–1929]: 1–73.

———. 1941. *Introduction to Hurrian*. AASOR 20. New Haven: American Schools of Oriental Research.

———. 1951. "Ancient Mesopotamia: A Light That Did Not Fail." *The National Geographic Magazine* 99/1: 41–105.

Starr, Richard F. S. 1937. *Nuzi: Report on the Excavations at Yorgan Tepa near Kirkuk .... 1927–1936*. vol. 2: *Plates and Plans*. Cambridge, Mass.: Harvard University Press.

———. 1939. *Nuzi: Report on the Excavations at Yorgan Tepa near Kirkuk .... 1927–1936*. vol. 1: *Text*. Cambridge, Mass.: Harvard University Press.

Stieglitz, Robert R. 1981. "Ugaritic *ḫrd* 'Warrior': A Hurrian Loanword." *JAOS* 101: 371–372.

Stolper, Matthew W. 1992. "The Written Record." Pages 253–60 in *The Royal City of Susa: Ancient Near Eastern Treasures in the Louvre*. New York: Metropolitan Museum of Art.

Wilhelm, Gernot. 1978. "Zur Rolle des Grossgrundbesitzes in der hurritischen Gesellschaft." *RHA* 36: 205–13.

———. 1980. *Das Archiv des Šilwa-teššup*, vol. 2: *Rationenlisten I*. Wiesbaden: Harrassowitz.

———. 1981. "Zusammenschlüsse von Nuzi-Texten." Pages 341–347 in *Studies on the Civilization and Culture of Nuzi and the Hurrians in Honor of Ernest R. Lacheman*. SCCNH 1. Edited by M. A. Morrison et al. Winona Lake, Ind.: Eisenbrauns.

———. 1988. "Gedanken zur Frühgeschichte der Hurriter und zum hurritisch- urartäischen Sprachvergleich." Pages 43–67 in *Hurriter und Hurritisch*. Konstanzer Altorientalische Symposien 2. Xenia 21. Edited by Volkert Haas. n.p.: Universitätsverlag Konstanz GMBH.

———. 1989. *The Hurrians*. Trans. Jennifer Barnes. Warminster: Aris & Phillips.

———. 1992a. *Das Archiv des Šilwa-teššup, vol. 4: Darlehensurkunden und verwandte Texte*. Wiesbaden: Harrassowitz.

———. 1992b. "Hurritisch *e/irana/i* 'Geschenk'." Pages 501–6 in *Hittite and Other Anatolian and Near Eastern Studies in Honour of Sedat Alp*. Anadolu Medeniyetlerini Araştırma Ve Tanıtma Vakkfı Yayınları 1. Edited by Heinrich Otten *et al.* Ankara: Türk Tarih Kurumu Basımevi.

———. 1995a. "Ein neuer Text zum Ordal in Nuzi (*JEN* 659+SMN 1651)." Pages 71–74 in *General Studies and Excavations at Nuzi 9/3*. SCCNH 5. Edited by Ernest R. Lacheman and D. I. Owen. Winona Lake, Ind.: Eisenbrauns.

———. 1995b. "Identifikationen von ERL-Nummern." Pages 151–55 in *Edith Porada Memorial Volume*. SCCNH 7. Edited by David I. Owen et al. Bethesda, Md.: CDL.

Young, T. Cuyler, Jr. 1980. "480/479 B.C.—A Personal Perspective." *Iranica Antiqua* 15: 214–39.

———. 1988. "The Early History of the Medes and the Persians and the Achaemenid Empire to the Death of Cambyses." Pages 1–52 in *The Cambridge Ancient History*, 2nd ed., vol. 4: *Persia, Greece and the Western Mediterranean c. 525 to 479 B.C.* Edited by John Boardman *et al.* Cambridge: Cambridge University Press.

Zaccagnini, Carlo. 1974. "Šattiwaz(z)a." *OA* 13: 25–34.

———. 1979a. "Notes on the Nuzi Surface Measures." *UF* 11: 849–56.

———. 1979b. "Les Rapports entre Nuzi et Ḫanigalbat." *Assur* 2/1: 1–27.

———. 1979c. *The Rural Landscape of the Land of Arrapḫe*. QGS 1. Rome: University of Rome.

———. 1984a. "Land Tenure and Transfer of Land at Nuzi (XV–XIV Century B.C.)." Pages 79–94 in *Land Tenure and Social Transformation in the Middle East*. Edited by Tarif Khalidi. Beirut: American University of Beirut.

———. 1984b. "Proprieta' fondiaria e dipendenza rurale nella Mesopotamia settentrionale (XV–XIV secolo a.C.)." *Studi Storici* 3: 697–723.

———. 1990. "The Nuzi Wool Measures Once Again." *OrNS* 59: 312–19.

———. 2003. "Mesopotamia: Nuzi." Pages 565–617 in A *History of Ancient Near Eastern Law,* Vol. 1. Handbook of Oriental Studies, Sec. 1: The Near and Middle East, 72/1. Edited by Raymond Westbrook. Leiden: Brill.

INDICES

PERSONAL NAMES

Mâšartānu f. Alpuya 94:30
Mâšartānu f. Zilip-šerta 94:29
Mat-tešup s. Paziya 86:51, 54
Mat-tešup s. Pur-nanzi 92:39, 44
Mat-tešup f. Ulmi-tilla 77:29
Mat-teya s. Naya 81:49, 51
Mat-teya 20:48
Mele-ḫarpa f. Paliya 94:25
Meleya f. Ḫutiya 86:10; 87:13
Milk-apu s. A-... 5:27
Milkaya (f. Adad-šarri?) 44:5
Milki-tešup f. Alkiya 82:2; 88:2
Milki-tešup f. Ziliya 82:[1]
Milkuya f. Ar-zizza 88:21
Milkuya f. Ḫaš-ḫarpa 87:38
Minaš-šuk s. Zaziya 86:2, 12, 16, 27, 31, 35; 87:10
Miššа s. Teḫip-tilla 81:48
Mukaru s. Unap-tae 66:42; 70:31a, 44
Muš-tešup s. Ḫašiya 7:11, 23
Muš-tešup s. Nai-tešup 80:31
Muš-tešup f. Šaḫini 94:10
Muš-tešup f. Urḫiya 80:34
Muš-teya s. Pilmašše 61:72
Muš-teya f. Akkuya 83:40
Muš-teya f. Utḫap-tae 89:2, 10; 90:2
Muš-teya [(king)] 8:48
Mušuya s. Aša-tuni 5:26
Mutta-kil(?) 19:9
Na-... f. Akap-šenni 79:24
Naḫi-ašu f. Wantiya 86:44
Naḫiš-šalmu f. Erwi-šarri 91:2, 7
Naḫiš-šalmu f. Niḫriya 70:42; 71:30
Naḫiš-šalmu 9:12
Naipa 24:14
Nai-šenni s. Tešup-atal 96:23
Naiš-kelpe f. Piru 7:12, [25]
Nai-tešup f. Muš-tešup 80:32
Nai-tešup f. Pai-tilla, g.f. Arim-matka 77:1
Nai-tilla s. Teššuya 95:20
Naltukka f. Ḫanaya 87:41
Naltukka f. Kikkiya 70:41
Namḫeya s. Ar-zipni 93:36, 48
Nanip-ukur s. Ḫalutta 95:47
Naniya f. Eteš-šenni, g.f. Pal-tešup 85:2
Naniya f. Teḫup-šenni 91:19
Naniya br. Itḫip-atal 43:21
Nan-tešup s. Ar-teya 95:12
Nan-tešup f. Ḫanikuzzi 83:44
Nan-tešup f. Šiname-tilla 92:34
Nan(?)-te?-šup f. ...-ma? 75:8
Nan-tešup 20:56; 21:30; 46:24
Nan-teya 20:24
Nanuperra 13:52
Nartu[1] f. Uluti 93:40?
Našwi s. Kalūli 86:42
Našwi f. Enna-mati 94:31
Naya f. Mat-teya 81:49
Niḫri-tešup s. Pui-tae 61:60
Niḫri-tešup 12:13
Niḫri-tilla s. Arrum-... 86: 37, 54
Niḫriya s. Akap-tukke 95:8
Niḫriya s. [Ennaya?] 7:17
Niḫriya s. Ḫuziri 83:[2], 10, 15, 23, 25, 30
Niḫriya s. Kalūli 86:47
Niḫriya s. Naḫiš-šalmu 70:42; 71:30, 32
Niḫriya s. Tauka 95:36
Niḫriya f. Purusa 95:13
Niḫriya f. Teḫip-šarri 94:34
Niḫriya 45:21; 56:31; 58:8, 21
Nik-AN-... 16:24
Nikriya s. Šurkip-šarri 80:35
Nikriya f. Tae 64:26
Nimkiya, palace slave 13:17
Nin-... 20:44
Ninki-tešup 10:4
Nin-teya 46:17
Ninu-atal f. Taya 86:46
Ninu-atal 9:4; 35:19; 39:6
Nirpi-tešup, *šukituḫlu* 19:36
Nui-šeri f. Wardiya(?) 84:15?
Nula-zuḫi 92:27
Nullu s. Ḫanatu 83:46, 51
Numi-kutu 9:14
Nupanaya f. Eḫlip-apu 95:39
Paikku 20:17
Pai-šarri s. Kel-tešup 81:41, 51
Pai-tilla s. Keliya 5:20, 31

1. *nârtu* may be the name of a profession, not a patronymic.

2. Cf. the interpretation of Deller (1987: #53).

3. Or, less likely, simply "Punniya."
4. Or, more likely, "Punniya f. …."
5. For this name, cf. *JEN* 967:19.
6. "Physician" or other craftsman.

Šaḫlu-tešup 37:22, 28, 33, 37
Šakarakti s. Ar-tirwi 5:21, 29
Šalim-pāliḫ-adad f. Ar-teya 7:21
Šama-… s. … 90:39
Šamaḫul s. Itḫip-šarri 83:41, 52??, 55
Šamaḫul f. Puḫi-šenni 71:23
Šamaḫul f. Šukri-tešup 13:55
Šamaš-damiq s. Itḫ-apiḫe, scribe 55:32, 39
Šamaš-RI s. Silakku-abi 64:29, 40; 67:28, 45
Šamaš-RI 64:8?
Šamḫari s. En-[šaku] 82:3, 19, 23, 28, 31
Šantiteya 24:25
Šarra-šadûni s. Itḫišta 66:2?; br. Ḫišmeya and Akiya, 71:1, 10–11, 20, 32
Šarriya f. Ḫerriya 83:45
Šarru-sin s. Ar-šatuya 95:43
Šarru-sin s. Takkaraya 86:52
Šar-tešup s. Unap-tae 92:38, 43
Šar-tešup s. Utḫap-tae 61:70
Šar-tešup 12:3; 19:24; 20:20; 28:1
Šar-tilla s. Iluya, scribe 80:37
Šaten-šuḫ 2:19; 6:13
Šati-kintar f. Kai-tešup 81:40
Šatta-u̯azza 2:17
Šattu-marti f. Ḫuziri 95:43
Šatu-kewi 56:3, 13, 19, 25; 57:4, 26
Še-… 9:2
Šeḫal-te 9:12
Šeḫel-tešup s. Kutukka 95:10
Šeḫli-… 20:10
Šeḫliya s. Akaya 86:3; 87:1
Šeḫurni f. Arik-kani 80:32
Šekan s. …-ki-tilla, br. Sin-abu 83:42, 51
Šekar-tilla 12:6; 20:51
Šekaru s. Eḫ[liya?] 7:15
Šekaru s. Ili-aḫi 87:40
Šekaru s. Šelwin-atal 82:39
Šekaru f. Ḫanakka 7:14; 86:48; 87:[33]
Šekaru f. Tain-šuḫ 95:7
Šekaru f. Urḫiya 87:43
Šekaya 20:40
Šêlebu f. Ḫitimpa 79:29
Šellapai s. Šukriya 13:49
Šellapai f. Šimika-atal 77:24
Šellapai f. Tae 91:17
Šelwin-atal f. Šekaru 82:39
Šelwin-atal f. Wantiš-še 82:40
Šenna-tati 19:4
Šennaya s. Ḫašip-apu 74:1, 8, 10, 17, 20, 28
Šennaya 94:17
Šeršiya f. Utḫap-tae 93:42
Šeršiya 73:3, 9
Šešwe f. Ḫanaya 95:40
Ši-… 9:1
Šien-zaḫ f. Watwa 79:28
Šilaḫi s. Šurkip-šarri 94:3
Šilaḫi s. …-šarri 89:30
Šilwa-tešup, son of the king 80:5, 15, 18, 20, 25, 27; 96:4
Šilwaya s. Pur-marutta[7] 55:27, 33
Šimi-…. *See* Šimika-atal s. Teḫip-tilla.
Šimika-atal s. Šellapai 77:24, 35
Šimika-atal s. Teḫip-tilla 90:36, 41? (or: Šimi-…)
Šimika-atal f. Kikkiya 87:45
Šimika-atal 9:5
Šimi-tilla 53:4; 54:11, 14
Šiname-tilla s. Nan-tešup 92:34, 41
Šinamu 24:3
Šipiš-šarri s. Utḫap-tae 80:35
Šipki-tešup[8] s. Šukriya 80:33
Šu-…-ta 24:13
Šukr-apu s. Arip-apu 79:26, 36
Šukr-apu 19:6
Šukrip-a<pu?> 13:57
Šukri-tešup s. Aril-lumti 94:13; 95:15
Šukri-tešup s. Ḫaip-šarri 95:4
Šukri-tešup s. Kip-talili 82:38
Šukri-tešup s. Šamaḫul 13:55
Šukri-tešup s. Turari, scribe 93:43, 50
Šukri-tešup, *šukituḫlu* 19:12
Šukri-tešup 20:40; 35:37; 43:60
Šukriya s. Kurišni 5:19, 30; 6:12
Šukriya s. Maliya 86:7; 87:5

7. For this name, cf. *JEN* 967:19.

8. The name was incorrectly copied and consequently yielded: "Arki-tešup."

Tarmiya 12:11; 19:11; 31:7; 44:16; 89:8; 90:9; 93:11
Tatip-tešup 2:27
Tatip-tilla 3:15; 27:3
^{f}Tatuni d. Kelip-ukur, g.d. Ḫanatu 77:4, 16
Tauka s. A-... 7:19
Tauka s. Zikura 66:41; 68:27, 36; 70:33
Tauka f. Niḫriya 95:36
Tauka f. ...-BE? 75:5
Tauka 9:11
Taula 20:38
Tawaren-tilla f. Umpiya 18:4
Taya s. Apil-sin, scribe 7:22, 26
Taya s. Araya 42:6
Taya s. Arip-šarri 70:35, 44
Taya s. Ḫampate, br. Ekeke 95:3
Taya s. Ninu-atal 86:46
Taya f. Enna-mati 55:29, 38
Taya f. En-šukru 95:42
Taya f. Itḫ-apiḫe 82:45
Taya f. Puḫi-šenni 13:12
Taya f. Šumu-libšī 86:53
Taya f. Tupkiya 94:21
Taya f. Waqar-bêli 95:26
Taya 13:57; 94:16
Te-... f. Ḫutip-šarri 87:36
Teḫip-apu s. Kelš-apu[9] 94:11; 95:29
Teḫip-apu s. ...-ki?-ya 81:1, 15, 21, 23, 26, 32, 50
Teḫip-apu f. Arip-apu 61:59
Teḫip-apu 2:45; 20:24
Teḫip-šarri s. Niḫriya 94:34
Teḫip-šarri 15:16; 53:23
Teḫip-tilla s. Eḫli-tešup 95:17
Teḫip-tilla s. Ḫašiya, NUN.ZA-*tu*$_4$ 82:35, 50
Teḫip-tilla s. Ḫašuar 61:64
Teḫip-tilla s. Puḫi-šenni 5:3, 5, [7], 9, 12; 6:4, 8, 11; 7:4, 8, 10; 74:8, 24; 82:4, 9, 11, 16 (twice), 18, 24, 32; 87:15,19, 24, 25, 27; 95:21

9. He is once a "charioteer" and once a "goer of the going"!

Teḫip-tilla s. Teššuya 94:32
Teḫip-tilla f. Enna-mati 62:[3]; 64:4; 65:5; 66:[6]; 67:2; 68:3; 70:3; 71:12
Teḫip-tilla f. Miššа 81:48
Teḫip-tilla f. Šimika-atal 90:36
Teḫip-tilla f. ^{f}Tarmen-naya 93:4
Teḫip-tilla 2:29; 19:31; 20:37; 49:48; 58:4, 17
Teḫiya s. Ar-šali 93:37, 49
Teḫiya s. Ḫamanna 95:34
Teḫiya s. Ḫašip-apu 74:3, 10, 14, 16, 27
Teḫiya f. Ariya 94:27
Teḫiya 50:1; 66:23
Teḫpiru, scribe 5:28
Teḫup-šenni s. Naniya 91:19
Teḫup-šenni 37:45, 53
Teššuya s. Ziliya 94:28
Teššuya s. ... 88:[1], 7, 12, 15, 16
Teššuya f. Nai-tilla 95:20
Teššuya f. Teḫip-tilla 94:32
Teššuya 19:32; 20:27
Tešup-atal f. Nai-šenni 96:23
Tieš-šimika f. Aḫ-ummiša 95:44
Tieš-urḫe 19:19; 20:15; 27:6
Tiltaš-šura, *sukkallu* 61:58
Tiltaš-šura 2:9; 3:13
^{f}Tilun-naya 53:13, 19
Tirwin-atal 2:34; 18:22; 26:10; 27:4; 29:7, 32
Tuḫaya 58:5, 19
Tuḫmi-tešup f. Šullum-adad 92:3
Tuḫmiya 60:16
TuḫmukaRI 24:17
Tukki 24:24
Tulip-apu 20:26; 21:34
Tulpi-šarri 17:1
Tultukka 45:65, 67
Tumšimana s. Turi-kintar 55:5
Tupki-tilla s. Bêlaya 94:12
Tupki-tilla 12:14; 19:34; 20:36
Tupkiya s. Taya 94:21
Tupkiya f. Kerar-tešup 81:43
Tupkiya f. Ziliya 86:39
Tupkizza s. Ar-zizza 82:43, 48
Tuppizzi s. Keliya 95:45
Tura-... 20:54
Turari s. Aš?-... 7:20

10. Possibly another Urḫiya here.
11. Or: Urḫiya son of Šekaru.

12. This is possibly not a personal name, but the designation of a palace slave.

13. For another, Assyrian, interpretation of this name, see Fadhil 1983:199b.

14. Or "Punniya" is a simple personal name, not a patronymic.

15. Total lacunae (believe it or not) are not represented.

Geographical Names

Countries (KUR)

Akkad (=Babylonia) 18:5
Arrapḫa 8:15?; 10:21
Assyria 1:8; 2:13; 3:12; 4:4; 6:2; 7:2; 18:14
Ḫanigalbat 10:20; 24:27; 25:3, 10; 26:19; 43:63; 45:60
Kuššuḫḫu 2:39
NašBAT 18:7

Gentilics

Arrapḫāyu 17:16; 30:5
Aššurāyu 5:2; 13:2; 16:2, 5, 8, 13
Kuššuḫāyu 30:6, 9
Nullāyu 2:40; 62:13

Towns / Cities (URU)

Āl-ilāni[16] 23:3; 29:34, 37; 43:13, 15; 80:3, 29; 81:37; 96:16
Anzukalli 23:20?; 30:4; 36:13; 37:16, 22
Apa(we) 75:11
Apena 4:9; 22:17; 24:29; 74:12
Arn-apu 25:11
Arrapḫa[17] 43:9
Ar-šalipe 89:26
Arwa 25:12
Aššur 15:14, 17; 30:2
Ašuri 60:4; 61:30
Atakkal 36:12; 93:7, 33
Būr-adad(we) 67: 7
Dūr-ubla 92:46
Eteš-šenni 58:6; 59:8; 60:3; 61:29, 53
Ezira 58:11; 59:7; 60:1; 61:26, 54
Ḫabūba 13:3, 48; 17:3
Ḫašluniya 58:7; 59:7; 60:6; 61:32
Ḫaššiku(we) 43:3, 10
Ḫurāṣina-rabû 89:6?; 90:[7]?
Ḫurāṣina-ṣeḫru 79:5
Ilabra(t)-šemī 15:19; 16:14; 17:12
Ila-nīšu 35:6
Inta-ru/aš 16:6
Irēm-adad 59:11
Irḫaḫḫe 28:13; 29:26
Karāna 15:13; 16:2, 5, 8
Katiri 15:20
Kip-arrapḫe 13:27, 30, 33, 41, 56, 62, 65; 14:5, 9; 15:4, 9; 17:11
Kizzuk 57:16–17
Kuluttu 58:3; 59:9; 60:7; 61:27
Kumri 60:8; 61:24
Lubti 26:21; 27:8; 30:1
Marta-... 30:10
Natmane 15:16, 24; 64:7; 66:9; 70:8; 84:11
Nuzi 23:8; 26:29; 28:11; 37:24; 48:1, 11, 12, 17; 81:38; 83:9, 22, 36; 85:18; 90:32; 93:10
Parpara 13:14, 16, 18, 40; 17:9
Ṣilliya 26:9
Šarnitaki 30:7
Šimerunni 60:2; 61:28
Taku 13:50
Tarībatu(e) 18:12, 15
Tarkulli 86:11; 87:14
Tarmiya 16:3
Tašenni 3:3 (cf. l. 17)
Tašuḫḫe 8:1
Tazzu 13:6, 21, 43; 14:12?; 17:4
Teliperra 28:14; 29:22
Temtena 28:7
Tente(we) 64:10; 66:13, [18?], 49; 67:5; 70:12; 71:6, 9
Tilla 29:13
Tilu-ša-kakki? 59:10; 60:5; 61:31
Turša 13:2, 16, 17, 29, 32, 37, 43, 45, 48, 64, 67, 68, 70?; 15:3, 8; 42:19; 55:25; 64:41–42; 66:59; 67:27; 68:40; 70:48; 71:34
Turtaniya 43:22
Ṭâb-ukur 57:19

16. Āl-ilāni is probably a precinct of the city of Arrapḫa. See p. 246, n. 90.

17. See note 16.

Uak-k?-a 59:9
Wultukuriya 60:9; 61:25
Zamite 85:10
Zimḫalše 94:17
Zizza 19:41; 20:58; 21:59; 22:15, 18; 23:11
…-ni 3:17 (cf. URU Tašenni at l. 3)

dimtu-DISTRICTS (AN.ZA.KÀR)

Akku-… 75:10?
Belu(e) 13:8
Damqaya son of Waši 58:14
Ḫaiš-tešup 13:13
Irimu 13:71
Kāri 49:13
Kizzuk 55:8–9; 59:14; 60:12; 61:10–14, 34
Mulḫani 13:46, 51; 17:13
Nanuperra 13:52
Pie 13:5
Purnamiz-zaḫ 13:9, 24, 54, 60; 17:7
ša É.GAL 13:58, <70>
Šilaḫi(š) 43:8
Tamkar(ra) 35:14
Tarmiya s. Unap-šenni 13:22
Teḫip-tilla (in Turša) 13:20–21
Ṭâb-ukur 59:18, 20
Ulluya 61:55
Unap-tae 81:10[18]

CANALS (*atappu*)

Killi 82:12; 88:[6]
Nirašše 86:9; 87:11

RIVER (ÍD)

“ḫuršan” 86:25, [28]

GATE (KÁ.GAL)

ēqu 96:6, 17

OTHER / UNCLEAR

Nultaḫḫe 80:8

18. Here, the name of a *dimtu*-tower, not, as elsewhere in this list, a *dimtu*-district.

OCCUPATIONS[19]

archer (LÚ *ša* GIŠPAN) 9:2, [4], 7, [10], 13, 14, 15, 16, 17
assistant to the second-in-command (*šinaḫiluḫlu*) 2:43
atuḫlu-officer 26:17
Uru 24:28
boatman (*malāḫu*)
Tarîbatu 84:23
bookkeeper (*sassukku*)
Apuška s. Itḫip-šarri 66:35
carpenter (NAGAR)
Ḫamanna 35:26
Ḫutiya 37:14, 21
envoy (*ubāru*) 2:13; 3:12
foot (soldier) (GÌR) 2:2?; 3:2?
gardener (LÚ.NU.GIŠ.SAR) 35:28
gatekeeper (*maṣṣar* KÁ.GAL(*-lì*) / *abultannu*)
Itḫip-tilla s. Qîsteya 71:28–29
Kunnuya 85:22
Puḫi-šenni s. Aitiya 83:48–49, 50
harem servant (*taluḫlu*) 42:8
high priestess (NIN.DINGIR.RA) 4:7
infantryman(?) (*ālik* EDIN.NA) 22:1, 3, 5, 7, 9, 12
king (LUGAL)
Muš-teya 8:[2], [48?]
(land) foreman (*ikkaru*)
Ḫutiya 45:42?
kiziḫḫuru[20]
Akip-tašenni 29:4
mayor (*ḫazann*(*ūtu*)) 2:30?; 8:3, 7, 14, 19, 23; 33:5, 19; 36:17; 49:6
of Tašuḫḫe 8:1
Artašenni, most likely, of Nuzi 35:45
Bêlu-qarrād, of Kip-arrapḫe 17:10–11
Ḫašip-apu, most likely, of Nuzi 49:12
Ša-aššur-damqa, of Parpara 17:8
messenger (DUMU *šipri*)
Akap-šenni, messenger of the palace 49:1–2
musician (female) / songstress (*nârtu*[21]) 93:40
NUN.ZA-tu_4 (?)
Teḫip-tilla s. Ḫašiya 82:35, 50
palace slave (ÌR É.GAL)[22]
Ar-šimika 13:47
Ipša-ḫalu 30:3
Qîpu 13:66
physician or other craftsman (*a*-ZU)
Qîšt-amurri 22:2
prince (DUMU LUGAL). *See* "son of the king"
queen (SAL.LUGAL) 2:3; 3:4; 27:2
of Āl-ilāni 23:2–3
of Anzukalli(?) 23:20
of Nuzi 23:8
fTarmen-naya d. Teḫip-tilla 93:3–4, 13, 14, 20, 27
regional governor (*šakin māti*; GAR KUR) 8:25
Ḫutip-apu 59:1, 21; 61:9, 12, 22, 43, 47
runner (*lāsimu*)
Enna-mati 26:12
scribe (DUB.SAR(*-rù* / *-ri*) / ŠU)
Ak(ka)dingirra 53:25
Akkul-enni 76:17
Alki-tešup s. Waqar-bêli 91:25, 30
Amurru-šarr-ilī 84:12
Aril-lumti 61:68
Attilammu s. A-... 5:1, 10

19. This list excludes class designations such as *rākib narkabti*, lit. "charioteer," and *ālik ilki*, lit. "performers / goers of the *ilku* (impost)," both of which could be construed as designating occupations.

20. Possibly a chariotry functionary.

21. But possibly a patronymic or patronymic substitute.

22. See also ÌR É-*ti* at text #84:13. This is either a personal name or a designation for a palace slave. If the latter, then text #84:13 notes Anupirra son of a palace slave.

Balṭu-kašid 31:25
Ḫurpi-tešup 92:40
Ḫ<u(t)?>ip-šarri 77:31
Ḫutiya s. Uta-mansi 74:34
Ḫutiya 45:69
Iriya s. Kiannipu 87:52–53
Itḫ-apiḫe s. Taya 82:45, 52
Kinniya s. Ar-tešše 67:41–42, 44
Šamaš-damiq s. Itḫ-apiḫe 55:32, 39
Šar-tilla s. Iluya 80:37–38
Šukri-tešup s. Turari 93:43–44, 50
Šukriya s. Sin-napšir 85:26, 30
Šumu-libšī s. Taya 86:53, 56
Taya s. Apil-sin 7:22, 26
Teḫpiru 5:28
Turar-tešup s. Kel-tešup 83:47
Urḫi-tešup 61:case, 57, 73
Urḫi-tilla 26:7
Zunzu s. Intiya 64:36; 70:38; 71:21, 33
Zunzu 68:31, 41
shepherd (SIPA)
Ḫuziri, *ša ekalli* 13:34
Kipaya 45:7; and *mur'u* l. 16[23]
Kipiya s. Abeya 35:43
of Pakla-piti s. Enna-mati 13:19
of Wirziyae 13:1
slave (ÌR)[24] 13:31; 62:13
Arrumpa 15:2
Elḫip-tilla 62:8
Ipša-ḫalu 15:15
Kai-tilla 96:4, 9, 10,13
Pai-tilla 15:23
Ṣilli-kûbi 15:12
Tampup-šenni 62:[5]
Unap-tarni 43:41–42
Zizza 15:7
...-ri-... 15:19
soldier (*ḫurādu*) 28:6
son of the king (DUMU LUGAL) 2:2?; 3:2?
Ḫut-tešup 26:2; 29:18
Šilwa-tešup 80:5, 15, 18, 20, 25, 27; 96:4
son of the palace (DUMU É.GAL)
Ipša-ḫalu 84:24
sukkallu (SUKKAL)
Akiya 2:11; 59:2; 61:58; 76:16
Tiltaš-šura 61:58
šuanatḫu
Ulluya 49:9
šukituḫlu[25]
Eḫli-tešup 19:25–26
Ḫutip-šarri 19:20
Kipali 19:14
Nirpi-tešup 19:36
Purniḫu 19:25–26
Šukri-tešup 19:12
Šumulliya 19:20
Urḫi-tešup 19:25–26
...-tešup 19:12
temple administrator (SANGA)
Arn-urḫe s. Artašenni 84:14

23. Clearly *rê'û* = *mur'u*, resolving the doubt expressed in *CAD* M/II, 229a. But see Deller 1984: 106.

24. This heading is included as an occupation, not just a class.

25. Just possibly a foot soldier.

Text Genres[26]

contracts of antichretic loan, personal (*ṭuppi tidennūti*) 92
contracts of genuine adoption (*ṭuppi mārūti*) 77, 85
contracts of real estate adoption (i.e., sale) (*ṭuppi mārūti*) 64, 65, 66, 67, 68, 70, 79, 81, 82, 83, 88, 89, 90, 91, 93
contract of real estate exchange (*ṭuppi šupe''ulti*) 78
contract of real estate sale (no superscription) 84
contracts of self-sale into slavery 5, 6, 7
contract of slave exchange (*ṭuppi šupe''ulti*) 62
declaration (lit. "his / their tongue") 87 (regarding real estate), 96 (regarding real estate)
depositions attesting to property (of individuals) lost in battle 13, 14, 15, 16
directives, royal 8, 76
inventories of foodstuffs distributed to groups 25, 27 (probably)
inventory of animals distributed to individuals 4
inventories of foodstuffs distributed to individuals 2, 3, 23, 72, 95 ("goers of the going" and "charioteers")
inventory of scales distributed for the construction of armor 10
legal records (misc.) 71 (promise not to sue), 80 (statement that a real estate donation is taking place; clauses; sealers)
letter[27] 73
lists of armaments and other paraphernalia distributed, possessed, missing, expended in battle, etc. 1, 11, 12, 18, 21, 26, 29
lists of "charioteers" 75 (who bear the *ilku* in an atypical manner), 94 (with respect to agricultural responsibilities)
list of indeterminate function 17[28]
list of people missing 30
lists of troops of different sorts, listed by their officers, by their fate in battle (usually stressing battle losses), etc. 9, 19, 20, 22, 24
loan 63 (of barley; a memorandum, not a contract)
narrative 28[29]
receipt 69 (partial payment for land sold)
tablet of agreement (*ṭuppi tamgurti*) 86 (regarding disposition of real estate)
trial depositions 31, 32, 33?, 34?, 35, 36?, 37, 38, 39, 40?, 41, 42, 43, 44, 45, 46, 47, 48, 49, 50, 51?, 52, 53, 54, 58, 60
trial records 56 (called "memorandum" [l. 33]), 61, 74
trial texts other than depositions or records 55, 57 (letter relating a trial record), 59

26. The categories or genres are given in English. This reflects the fact that not all these genres reflect native designations, despite my efforts to adhere to the texts' self-designations. The taxonomy, in other words, is, at least in part, my own judgment. I choose not to justify those choices in this forum, since this would take us too far afield from the function of Writings from the Ancient World.

27. See also "trial texts other than depositions or records."

28. This is a broken text. It is clearly a list of notables of places to which the Assyrians took Arrapḫan property. The function of the list is unclear.

29. Barley is ordered distributed because of certain events. It was distributed.

CPSIA information can be obtained at www.ICGtesting.com
Printed in the USA
LVOW13s1705221213

366342LV00001B/12/P

9 781589 832138